PENGUIN CLASSICS

THE IMPORTANCE OF BEING EARNEST
AND OTHER PLAYS

OSCAR FINGAL O'FLAHERTIE WILLS WILDE was born in Dublin in 1854, the son of an eminent eye-surgeon and a nationalist poetess who wrote under the pseudonym of 'Speranza'. He went to Trinity College, Dublin and then to Magdalen College, Oxford, where he began to propagandize the new Aesthetic (or 'Art for Art's Sake') Movement. Despite winning a first and the Newdigate Prize for Poetry, Wilde failed to obtain an Oxford scholarship, and was forced to earn a living by lecturing and writing for periodicals. He published a largely unsuccessful volume of poems in 1881 and in the next year undertook a lecture tour of the United States in order to promote the D'Oyly Carte production of Gilbert and Sullivan's comic opera *Patience*. After his marriage to Constance Lloyd in 1884, he tried to establish himself as a writer, but with little initial success. However, his three volumes of short fiction, *The Happy Prince* (1888), *Lord Arthur Savile's Crime* (1891) and *A House of Pomegranates* (1891), together with his only novel, *The Picture of Dorian Gray* (1891), gradually won him a reputation confirmed and enhanced by the phenomenal success of his society comedies – *Lady Windermere's Fan*, *A Woman of No Importance*, *An Ideal Husband* and *The Importance of Being Earnest*, all performed on the West End stage between 1892 and 1895.

Success, however, was short-lived. In 1891 Wilde had met and fallen extravagantly in love with Lord Alfred Douglas. In 1895, when his success as a dramatist was at its height, Wilde brought an unsuccessful libel action against Douglas's father, the Marquess of Queensberry. Wilde lost the case and two trials later was sentenced to two years' imprisonment for acts of gross indecency. As a result of this experience he wrote *The Ballad of Reading Gaol*. He was released from prison in 1897 and went into an immediate self-imposed exile on the Continent. He died in Paris in ignominy in 1900.

RICHARD ALLEN CAVE is Professor of Drama and Theatre Arts at Royal Holloway in the University of London. He was born in Leicestershire and educated at St Catharine's College, Cambridge. His many publications include works on Renaissance and Modern theatre and on the relation between dance and drama. Anglo-Irish theatre has been his special interest for many years, both as critic and as director. He has also edited W. B. Yeats's *Selected Plays* for Penguin and is currently editing a volume of Yeats's *Writings on Theatre*, also for Penguin.

OSCAR WILDE

The Importance of Being Earnest
and Other Plays

Edited with Introduction, Commentaries and Notes by
RICHARD ALLEN CAVE

PENGUIN BOOKS

PENGUIN BOOKS

Published by the Penguin Group
Penguin Books Ltd, 80 Strand, London WC2R 0RL, England
Penguin Putnam Inc., 375 Hudson Street, New York, New York 10014, USA
Penguin Books Australia Ltd, 250 Camberwell Road, Camberwell, Victoria 3124, Australia
Penguin Books Canada Ltd, 10 Alcorn Avenue, Toronto, Ontario, Canada M4V 3B2
Penguin Books India (P) Ltd, 11 Community Centre, Panchsheel Park, New Delhi – 110 017, India
Penguin Books (NZ) Ltd, Cnr Rosedale and Airborne Roads, Albany, Auckland, New Zealand
Penguin Books (South Africa) (Pty) Ltd, 24 Sturdee Avenue, Rosebank 2196, South Africa

Penguin Books Ltd, Registered Offices: 80 Strand, London WC2R 0RL, England

www.penguin.com

Published in Penguin Books 2000
19

Editorial material copyright © Richard Allen Cave 2000

'Gribsby' scene from Act II of the four-act version of *The Importance of
Being Earnest* © Merlin Holland (published by Vanguard Press, 1987)
Wilde's sketch for *Salomé*: Reproduced by permission of the
Rosenbach Museum and Library, Philadelphia
Ricketts's sketch for *Salomé*: By courtesy of the Witt Library of the
Courtauld Institute of Art in the University of London

Set in 10/12.5 pt PostScript Monotype Baskerville
Typeset by Rowland Phototypesetting Ltd, Bury St Edmunds, Suffolk
Printed in England by Clays Ltd, St Ives plc

ISBN-13: 978-0-140-43606-8
ISBN-10: 0-140-43606-5

CONTENTS

INTRODUCTION

There are two popular images of Wilde: first there is the glittering wordsmith, shaper of scintillating epigrams that litter his published works as liberally as they sprang from his lips to entertain upper-class circles and dinner parties. Then there is the picture of that abject homosexual, jeered at by other passengers while waiting on Clapham Station in convict uniform and surrounded by policemen, who was destined to serve a two-year sentence in Reading Gaol for daring to pursue an intimate relationship with the son of a peer of the realm, when he was a mere Irishman and a commoner. The two images do not easily elide to create one distinct personality, and yet, taken together, they do help to define the quite distinctive quality and tenor of his work for the theatre. Wilde understood the nature of masks that allow one to play out numerous identities: he appreciated the social pressures that made the wearing of masks in late Victorian society a necessity because he was himself the victim and product of such pressures, being at once both colonized Irishman *and* socialite; husband in a seemingly traditional family household *and* frequenter of male brothels with his male aristocratic lover; successful dramatist who cultivated for his audience the smartest of good society *and* socialist who made no secret of the degree to which he considered the very audiences he courted merited criticism. His finest epigrams play with the rhetorical device of paradox, while his preferred mode of being was to inhabit paradox, to live out its contradictions as a studied philosophy. In his own life as in his creations for the stage, Wilde's game centred on masks, a game he relished again both in all seriousness and with delight in its manifest absurdities. His life and his art were a constant challenge to Victorian earnestness, which he exposed relentlessly as laughably pretentious at its best and viciously hypocritical at its worst. Being Irish by birth and being (by the moral and sexual codes of the period) 'deviant' were the making of him as a dramatist; he *seemed* socially acceptable because his charismatic manner disarmed judgement and he was admitted to 'good' society as a kind of allowed jester. However, history reveals how court fools and jesters were generally incisive and exacting critics of their audiences. Wilde was no exception and, like his predecessors, he did not finally escape whipping for his presumption. But even as that pathetic figure on Clapham Station, he was a living criticism of the society that had seen fit to place him there. From fool to martyr might appear a remarkable transition, but the change of masks from comic to tragic did not signify a change of theme and intention. The need to wear masks of any kind was continually the object of his most penetrating critique of himself (in his superb apology for his life, *De Profundis*) and of society (in his essays and his plays).

To return to the image of the golden wordsmith. For many this is the enduring appeal of the plays, the seemingly effortless fount of wit which led W. H. Auden to describe *The Importance of Being Earnest* as the 'purest example in English literature' of a 'verbal opera'.[1] Countless productions of the plays have focused on that element of their artistry to the exclusion of their other dramatic excellences; and this is to do Wilde a disservice. The plays are undoubtedly witty; there is no denying that strength. But Wilde was the consummate dramatist, possessing a profound insight into the range of the arts that together constitute theatre in performance. This particular collection comprises his finest achievements in the genre but, from the first, plays such as *Vera or The Nihilists* (published 1880, staged 1883) and *The Duchess of Padua* (1908, staged 1891), show him preoccupied with more than characterization and plotting: Wilde is clearly reaching out for a concept of total theatre, where colour and design, the spatial relations of actors within the playing space, music and movement, all contribute to shaping the thematic life of the drama. Act I of *Vera*, for example, which is set in Moscow, presents the audience with a powerful stage picture: in a garret lit 'by oil lamps hung from ceiling', which will cast giant shadows over the walls, tense figures, cloaked and masked in black, stand silent and apart; one sporting a scarlet mask writes at a table, while another dressed in yellow, acting as sentinel, his sword at the ready, guards the door. They are joined by other masked and cloaked figures, and the whole group on forming a semi-circle begin a ritual in which they assert their confederacy and repeat their oath of allegiance to the cause of political freedom. This is not a fussily detailed setting defining an attempt at historical accuracy such as was currently the popular style of stage design; instead an audience's perceptions are being influenced by colour-symbolism (shades of red and black will recur emblematically throughout the ensuing action), lighting, shadow play and an emotionally taut tableau that gives place to ritualized action in which the characters seek to find some degree of self-possession through affirming a unity of purpose. Immediately any preconceptions an audience might have on the subject of nihilists and anarchists is challenged by this presentation of a social group with its own ethical code of behaviour. There is suspense here, but not of the factitious kind that permeates much contemporaneous melodrama which takes political unrest and betrayal as its theme, such as Vitorien Sardou's *Fedora* (1882): the visual and vocal appeal of Wilde's invention challenges the conventional theatrical treatment of such subject-matter, inviting an audience to consider issues of political unrest from a wholly fresh perspective. *The Duchess of Padua* is set in a Renaissance world that is rendered fantastic and dreamlike (there is more than a hint of Webster about Wilde's conception and dialogue) by being pictured in patterns of black, white and vermilion. These effects might seem overly schematic from a written account, but when experienced in the theatre such symbolist design, if judiciously handled, can intimate to an audience exactly how they should *read* the performance they are watching. What Wilde was effectively doing here was teaching audiences new ways of interpreting their perceptions of performance. If such schemes with colour symbolism seem familiar enough to us today, that is the measure of how far-reaching Wilde's innovations were: he created the conditions whereby a new form of design-practice might come into being.

We can gain some insight into Wilde's principles of design from what has been recorded of his discussions with two designer-friends: Charles Ricketts and Graham Robertson. Interestingly these focus on his plans for the staging of the one-act *Salomé*. Shortly after the composition of the play in 1892, a production had gone into preparation for Sarah Bernhardt before the Lord Chamberlain stepped in and banned public performances. Robertson had been chosen to design only the setting (the costumes were to be selected from among those designed for Bernhardt's production of Sardou's *Cléopâtre*). However, Wilde was clearly concerned about their precise selection, since (as Robertson recounts) he wished to have 'every costume of some shade of yellow from clearest lemon to deep orange, with here and there just a hint of black . . . all upon a great empty sky of deepest violet'.[2] At some later point (the exact date is not known), Wilde also talked with Ricketts in detail about a potential scheme for the play, and each man sketched his ideas in an attempt to clarify and communicate his intentions. Wilde drew a floor-plan; Ricketts a quick view of how their shared setting would look from the audience's viewpoint; both sketches have survived (they are reproduced in the Notes to this play). Wilde's is preoccupied with the precise spatial relationship between the staircase, the cistern and an open space which will in time become Salomé's dance-floor; Ricketts's shows an impression of these ideas as a realized setting; this was to have comprised a black stage floor, surrounded by a skyscape coloured pale turquoise, while above it hung a kind of 'aerial tent' made by 'the perpendicular fall of strips of gilt matting'. Ricketts recalled that in talking together their thinking took wing to a point where he subsequently became unsure who was responsible for which particular suggestion concerning the finished look of the design. But it was decided that there should be a 'division of the actors into masses of colour', so that, for example, the Jews were in yellow, the Romans in purple and John in white.[3] What this would define with some clarity is the conflicting political groupings against which Herod and Salomé's private drama is played out. Equally apparent from the setting is Wilde's concern that the playing space admit only such effects (the staircase at the foot of which Herod's throne will be placed and the cistern which is Jokanaan's prison) as are absolutely essential to the development of the dramatic action. All else is a blank, seemingly characterless space. This is the world of Herod's rule, which Salomé at first subverts when she succeeds, despite the Tetrarch's orders, in liberating Jokanaan from the well. She then steadily invades that space to make it increasingly her own; and as she comes into complete control of it, so she will exert her will to bring throne and cistern into a terrible conjunction, despite all Herod's efforts to prevent her. This is minimalist design at its best and wholly modern in feeling and execution, drawing attention not to its own picturesque qualities (though aesthetically it is very pleasing in its calculated simplicity) but to the power games, the battle of wills that determine the development of the tragedy.

All actors are alert to the power lines within a given playing space, where they can command most attention. What is fascinating about Wilde's drama is the degree to which he conceived its staging in terms of the spatial relations between the actors at given points within the performance. How actors are placed and move within the playing space is often calculated to define the shifting power structures that are controlling the characters' responses. Wilde had an acute sense of the stage as a three-dimensional space and knew how to deploy actors within it to create subtexts which reveal the characters' inner selves in terms of their power or weakness relative to each other. This creative mastery of space is evident from his first major play, *Lady Windermere's Fan* (1892). Act II is set in Lady Windermere's drawing-room during her ball and supper to celebrate her birthday, and she waits by the door to greet her guests as they are announced and make their entrances. There are doors leading to a room where there is music and dancing and to an illuminated terrace overlooking St James's Park. A sense of ceremony and good form prevails and there is a relaxed ease among these upper-class visitors. Lady Windermere, however, is conspicuously tense, because (as we know) she intends, should Mrs Erlynne make an appearance, to hit the woman in the face with the fan she now holds tightly in her grasp. It is a moment of great tension for the audience. Mrs Erlynne arrives; Lady Windermere falters and cannot find the nerve and will-power to stage the scene she has planned; and Mrs Erlynne, unchecked, sails into the space that social decorum has defined as possessed by Lady Windermere. That space is surrounded by groups of women and men, mostly seated, who are all hostile to Mrs Erlynne. They are like an ill-favoured audience, alert to every nuance of her performance. But Mrs Erlynne, coolly taking the situation under control, makes a complete circuit of the space on Lord Windermere's arm and in the process contrives by a few well-judged words to cultivate everyone's good opinion of her. By the time she quits the stage she is being showered with invitations to future gatherings.

Mrs Erlynne has staged a remarkable comeback into high society by a brilliant display of will-power, wit and charismatic charm. Significantly, she has done so by upstaging Lady Windermere within her own private space; she has invaded and taken possession of that space purposefully to further her own ends, in a blatant act of defiance and courage. The movement of the characters within the playing space creates a psychological subtext, which prepares an audience for the ways that the play will develop during Act III, when Mrs Erlynne warns the eloping Lady Windermere that she does not have the strength, daring and iron self-possession to get herself back into society, if she were once to take a step that would make her an outsider. As audience we know precisely what is meant by this, since we have *experienced* Mrs Erlynne's attempted return in the previous act, and can appreciate its cost in terms of a willed determination, in which we have simultaneously seen Lady Windermere decidedly lacking. Movement throughout Act II is both naturalistic and symbolic, and on the symbolic level it has a precise function within the dramatic structure of the play. Equally significant in terms of the shifting power relations within the play is Wilde's insistence that George Alexander, the first director of *Lady Windermere's Fan*, should stage the last act in such a way that Mrs Erlynne is a constantly seated figure, while Lord and Lady Windermere and Lord Augustus are required to move on and off stage repeatedly at her bidding. Though in the eyes of the two men she appears morally culpable, she is again totally self-possessed, a still presence whose control over the other three characters is absolute as she consciously manipulates them towards as happy an ending as circumstances allow. In her stillness she emerges as the moral centre of the play's world, just as in Act II in her movements she was defined as the play's most vital creation. It is through such sensitively judged theatrical means that Wilde is endorsing his description of Mrs Erlynne in his subtitle as 'a good woman'.

An analogous use of stage space can be found in the final act of *A Woman of No Importance* (1893), when Lord Illingworth unscrupulously invades the privacy of Mrs Arbuthnot's drawing-room, even though he has expressly been refused admission. That he enters is a vivid expression of the rights he feels that he suddenly can assert over her and her decisions. By the standards of conventional etiquette it is a gross breach of good form. And, when he finds he is not getting his way, he is quite prepared to insult Mrs Arbuthnot, since there is no representative of the 'good' society he generally frequents to overhear him. His hypocrisy and his questionable moral standing are forcefully exposed by the very fact of his intrusive entrance, and it requires a full assertion of Mrs Arbuthnot's will-power finally to expel his overbearing presence from her space. And she does this by a gesture (striking him in the face with his own glove) which proves he is no gentleman for all his social pretensions. The debonair persona he vaunts throughout the earlier scenes is here found to be a mask overlaying a decided brute, whom she has every right to refuse to marry. Again the movement of characters within the stage space endorses the play's challenging moral stance.

Wilde could also use the idea of invasion for comic effect. In Act III of *An Ideal Husband* (1895) all Lord Goring's attempts to relish the quiet privacy of his home of an evening are disrupted by the arrival of persons from the world of public affairs whom he least wishes to see: his father (Lord Caversham), his best friend (Chiltern) and his friend's worst enemy (Mrs Cheveley). Since he appreciates that they must on no account see each other, he has to resort to secreting them in different rooms, which has the effect of bringing the action closer and closer to farce, as each new arrival insists on being admitted to his house. For all their power-games and rhetorical self-pity when they fail, Chiltern and Mrs Cheveley are rendered slightly absurd by the farcical tendencies of the theatrical treatment. The one character to emerge with dignity from this act is Lord Goring. Wilde, by means of this unexpected dramatic method and tone, is establishing him as possessing an astute political and moral sensibility and as the one character with sufficient insight to guide the Chilterns into reappraising their fraught marital relationship. Even more amusing are Lady Bracknell's sudden disruptions of other people's privacy in the interests of decorum throughout *The Importance of Being Earnest* (1895). She has set herself up as a guardian of public morals and twice in the play swoops in unexpectedly to determine whether the behaviour of others is in any way compromising her own or her daughter's reputations. But as with the farcical episodes in *An Ideal Husband*, the comedy has a bitter satirical edge to it: Wilde's plays repeatedly show how women themselves have been set up within this male-dominated society to be the ones who police the conduct of their gender. Lady Bracknell's zeal carries a concern with policing others to a ridiculous extreme, but the social critique underpinning the caricature is exact.

One of the most subtly nuanced symbolic deployments of stage space occurs in the one-act drama *A Florentine Tragedy* (1894). Simone enters to find his wife, Bianca, entertaining an aristocrat, Guido, who seems to be dominating both the space that is Simone's home and Bianca. Simone is unsure whether this is just an expression of Guido's sense of aristocratic privilege or whether the entertainment has extended to adultery. Patiently he bides his time, hesitantly searching through the dialogue with Guido for some proof of his suppositions. He continually frames his conversation so that it hovers on the edge of accusation, to bring the other two to a pitch of tense expectancy, but then deflects the crisis in ways that leave the others in a state of total uncertainty. Simone contrives to sell all his merchandise to the Duke's son at an outrageous profit, then intimates it is time Guido departed. As the aristocrat reaches for his sword, the merchant jokingly suggests measuring lengths with him to test their respective blades and skill (throughout the sexual innuendo is precisely intended). In the ensuing duel which suddenly fills the entire stage with violent action, Simone traps, disarms and kills Guido. During the opening half of the drama the language is replete with imagery about luxury and cost, later it intimates masculine desire and sexual display. The men contest for ownership of the stage space (one by right of marriage; the other by right of aristocratic presence and command). Bianca sides always with Guido, proving where her affections lie even as she voices her disgust with Simone's relentless and insistent materialism. Ownership of the space becomes synonymous with possession of Bianca, and what the action defines as crucially tragic is the absolute commodification of her as a woman. As in all these instances, movement within the confines of the stage space is invested steadily with a symbolic potential that takes one to the heart of the play's moral and social argument. This is theatrical craftsmanship of the highest order, where the dimensions of the playing space during a performance are made to take on a powerful psychological dynamic over and above what that space is required to represent in terms of social place and time. Space in Wilde's plays in terms of theatrical semiotics is arguably the most informative of signifiers.

The most celebrated of sustained patterns of movement within a precise space is Salomé's dance, which has a near-mythical cultural status. Yet, as Joseph Donohue notes,[4] this climactic moment in Wilde's play is contained within a stage direction that is nothing short of laconic in its brevity: 'SALOMÉ *dances the dance of the seven veils.*' We are offered no scenario; Wilde trusts wholly to the invention of the performer. (It is clear from his correspondence with actor–managers that he saw rehearsal as a collaborative venture, demanding respect for the artistic skills and creativity of everyone involved. Much in respect of this danced sequence will depend on the performer's personal style and range of movement, technical accomplishment, stamina and ability to define a psychological subtext through the use of the body as a medium of expression.) That Wilde recognized the power of movement to convey an intense, if enigmatic significance within a carefully structured narrative is evident from his placing of the dance within *Salomé* as emblematic of the mesmeric obsession which grips each of the central characters: the princess, the Tetrarch and the prophet. But the dance is the point where private obsession takes on public display, and so provokes social and political consequences.

Clearly Wilde had thought through the implications of the dance (he was never to see the play realized in performance) and begun to appreciate the power of movement as a system of signification. Argu-ably this may explain why in his next play, *A Woman of No Importance*, the conclusion to the third act is played out wholly in silence so that mime and not speech conveys a complexity of meanings. Initially Wilde had conceived the close of the act (when Mrs Arbuthnot stops Gerald at the moment he is about to attack Lord Illingworth by informing him that they are father and son) as a conventional melo-dramatic tableau. But the episode underwent a series of revisions which began to introduce movement and a more creative use of body-language. Four characters are on stage when Mrs Arbuthnot reveals the truth; her outburst is witnessed by the American heiress, Hester, whom Illingworth has just physically insulted and so provoked Gerald's attack. By staging a static tableau, Wilde merely provided a resounding, if overly sensational conclusion. What the discussion above of *Lady Windermere's Fan* has shown is the extent to which Wilde possessed what one might term an architectural perception of dramatic structure in the way that elements of the stage action in Act II (Mrs Erlynne's acquisition of total command of the space) prepare an audience in subtle ways for aspects of the argument which are developed in Act III (about Lady Windermere's lack of the necessary strength of will to effect a comeback in society, were she to fall foul of its moral code). At the close of Act III of *A Woman of No Importance*, and perhaps influenced by his experiment with dance in *Salomé*, Wilde played down the impact of Mrs Arbuthnot's actual revelation by extending the action considerably beyond it. First he devised a means of getting three of the characters off stage, leaving Mrs Arbuthnot alone in a state of misery and shame. Dissatisfied with this solution, however, he revised what had begun to grow into a mime so that Gerald is now required to move to his mother, seize her hands and search her face so intently that she sinks prostrate. Hester meanwhile 'steals' out, while Lord Illingworth struggles to contain his temper. Gerald raises his mother up, supports her in his arms and 'leads her from the room', leaving Illingworth isolated at the fall of the curtain. This now does much more than resolve the action; it intimates potential for growth, foreshadowing without precisely defining developments that the final act will explore. Mime here embodies a narrative without prescribing a specific interpretation of its content. In concluding one movement of the play, Wilde focuses an audience's imaginative engagement on the psychology of the characters. To take but one example: Hester's withdrawal from the room in a manner which should convey to the audience the impression that her motivation is *stealth*. What motivates that body-language? Maybe it expresses a coy, puritanical disgust at Mrs Arbuthnot's revelation, or perhaps embarrassment for Gerald at having to assimilate such a reshaping of his whole sense of identity, or it may be tact, which requires her to leave the 'family' to recover from their loss of face in private together. Or is her response more personal, encompassing a sense of shock at the extent to which her moral zeal has recently led her, albeit unconsciously, to injure the sensibility of another woman and one she had tried to make her friend on the grounds of a seeming compatibility? By restricting the expression of Hester's motive to mime, Wilde provokes the audience's critical and interpretative faculties to consider the range of possibilities and that requires them to enter sensitively into the moral issues that the play is examining.

The most surprising deployment of a style of movement that approximates to dance is to be found in *The Importance of Being Earnest*, where it increasingly becomes the means of sustaining the farcical tone. Quite whether Wilde was responsible for creating this effect in discussion with Alexander who also first directed this play or whether Alexander himself can claim the credit is not clear; but certainly original audiences watched the action becoming increasingly dance-like in performance. Wilde did not originally intend that Alexander should stage the play but a set of chance circumstances led to his taking it on. Wilde also apparently over a friendly dinner confidentially informed both Alexander, who played Jack Worthing, and Allen Aynesworth, the first Algernon, that neither would have been his ideal choice for their respective roles. Alexander certainly never played a role remotely like it; and in many ways it was wholly alien to the stage persona he was creating in parts where he generally could indulge a penchant for either lyrical romanticism (he made a hit with *The Prisoner of Zenda*) or for stern moral probity (his other major successes in the 1890s were Lord Windermere and Aubrey Tanqueray). The role of Jack Worthing demanded that he have the courage to send up the popular image of himself, since Jack invariably is at his most ridiculous and absurd when he is being either romantic or intensely 'earnest'; and Alexander seems to have delighted in doing so, entering into self-parody with an engaging zest and wit.

Alexander obviously relished the superb opportunities offered him by Jack's entrance in Act II, dressed in full mourning, since he moved the actors playing Chasuble and Prism slowly down stage at this point in such a way as to delay their catching sight of him so that the audience had sufficient time fully to appreciate the significance of his costume and laugh out long and loud. That he enjoyed being the butt of laughter is evident from how, as director, he replaced conventional planned movement later in that act with a form of staging that approximates to choreography. Once the women have battled for their heroes over cake and tea, and the cover has been blown on their men whose experiments in the art of Bunburying are by now totally exposed, the play moves deeper and deeper into artificiality as the two couples face identical crises. Language becomes increasingly patterned, as the dialogue for each couple exactly mirrors the responses of the other pair to the point where both men and the women begin speaking together in unison. To bring this off, the characters discuss who should beat time to establish a proper rhythm; and yet rhythm of an internal kind must have been shared by the four actors if they were to carry off deftly the synchronized and symmetrical patterns of movement with which Alexander accompanied the patterned speech. On making their entrance in Act III, for example, the two men nonchalantly approached a sofa in tandem, sat, crossed their legs in identical style, attended to the creases in their trousers, then simultaneously looked across at the two women. This is stylizing everyday movement till it becomes virtually dance: as it requires expert timing if it is to be carried off convincingly, the performers must sustain throughout a shared inner rhythm exactly like dancers.

What this sustained stylization suggested in theatrical terms was the degree to which mannerism afflicted all the representatives of the upper classes, of the Church and of education in the play, reducing them to puppet-like mechanisms. Propriety, etiquette and 'good form' are here being ridiculed as well-rehearsed absurdities. The theatricality exposes the emptiness of the social codes as so much posturing.

Movement carries in these moments a pronounced satirical impetus and so becomes the means of effecting a precise social critique. Whether Wilde influenced Alexander's style of direction here (he was holidaying in Algiers for much of the time the play was in rehearsal), or whether Alexander was simply responding creatively to the intimations of Wilde's style of dialogue is less important than the fact that *The Importance of Being Earnest* invited in performance a mode of physicalization in its latter half that closely approximated to dance-routines. Even the manipulation of salvers of muffins and tea-cake in the final sequence of Act II (while the men are competing for an appropriate decorum through which to recover lost 'face') requires a choreographic precision if it is to generate and sustain a rising crescendo of laughter. Words alone are not enough to carry the comedy; the movement parodies and subverts the measured dignity deemed fitting for rituals of the tea-table, and it is movement in consequence which controls the social satire. There is more than Wilde the wordsmith at work here.

Vera and *The Duchess of Padua* are of interest in revealing more than Wilde's engagement from the time of his earliest dramatic writing with the arts of performance: both demonstrate a particular technique that Wilde was to make crucially his own in his better-known plays. Melodramas about espionage, political insurrection and duplicitous intriguing were legion on European stages at the time that Wilde devised *Vera or The Nihilists*. Similarly his tragedy in blank verse, creating an imagined Renaissance world, is part of a long tradition of nineteenth-century tragic dramas ambitious to emulate the works of Shakespeare and his contemporaries. In both plays there is at once a sense of the familiar balanced with a perception of acute difference: *Vera* is less preoccupied with sensationalism than with exploration of what constitutes psychologically the rebellious sensibility and its particular codes of values; and while *The Duchess of Padua* seems overly caught up with echoing *Macbeth*, it also embraces a searching enquiry not into the nature of ambition but into the emotional desiccation that afflicts the adulterous sensibility. Indeed it is as if the familiar is there precisely to accentuate what is different from the norm of the genres of drama that Wilde is imitating. To read the reviews that greeted Wilde's plays when they were first produced is to become aware of a recurring theme: a constant need on the part of the critics to hint that Wilde was shamelessly borrowing material from currently or recently successful plays. What they tend to focus on is the similarities; but, if one reads these now long-forgotten works, what impresses one is more the nature of Wilde's ability to take conventional, at times even hackneyed, material and transform it into drama that is challenging, fresh and socially or emotionally subversive. It is as if Wilde set out to seduce his audiences with what appeared at first quite conventional situations and character-types, so that they would relax their defences and thus be more exposed to his steady manipulation of the material to present a moral and social agenda wholly the reverse of the prototype.

Lady Windermere's Fan begins with the lady in question being approached first by a silver-tongued aristocrat who tempts her with an adulterous liaison and secondly by a titled gossip-monger warning her that her husband is himself known to be conducting an affair with a woman with a shameful past. There are the makings here for complex plotting involving amorous intrigues and exposures and for characters who can easily be *placed* morally by the audience in the manner of Haddon Chambers's play *The Idler* (1891). It had but recently played at the very same theatre in which Wilde's play opened and with virtually the same cast, and critics were quick to draw parallels between it and *Lady Windermere's Fan*, even going so far as to accuse Wilde of plagiarism. Wilde would doubtless have claimed that the influences on his creativity went back in time even further and that the climactic moments of his third act drew quite heavily on the famous screen-scene from Sheridan's *The School for Scandal*. But Wilde's characters defeat expectation: the woman with the past proves to be the moral centre of the play in possessing both a shrewd intelligence and great resources of compassion; the husband is not errant but so hidebound by conventional morality that he is potentially a dangerous bigot; and the wife, who succumbs to temptation in a fit of pique, grows into an awareness of her own naivety and begins to resist her husband's authority on social and moral grounds rather than out of a need simply to express her emotional independence. By the end an alert audience has been required to reappraise what passes in society for conventional ethics *and* the dramatic stereotypes of character and situation through which those conventions are culturally enshrined. *Lady Windermere's Fan* is an enacted critique of contemporary culture.

Most of Wilde's plays pursue this same strategy of what today would be called intertextuality. *A Woman of No Importance* was written for Beerbohm Tree, who hoped through it to repeat something of the success he had sustained in Henry Arthur Jones's *The Dancing Girl* (1891), in which he was still performing some months before Wilde commenced work. But, whereas in Jones's play (as in countless plays of the period about fallen women) the seduced Quaker heroine dies as a morally fitting close while her aristocratic seducer, the Duke of Guisebury (Tree's role), survives, in *A Woman of No Importance*, Mrs Arbuthnot lives to rebuke her former seducer and disgrace him in his own eyes. *An Ideal Husband* draws on countless melodramas about political chicanery that followed in the wake of Sardou's *Dora* of 1877 (known in England under the title of *Diplomacy*), but Wilde most unusually weds such material with an Ibsen-inspired investigation of how the discovery of a past misdemeanour in the world of public affairs can affect the private intimacies of a marital relationship in the present and in the likely future, particularly when the culprit reveals a developed taste for wielding power over others. *The Importance of Being Earnest* also has its dramatic forebears in plays dealing with lost parents, such as *The Foundling* (1894) by William Lestocq and E. M. Robson, and much of its tone, its treatment of the two contrasting heroines and even its most memorable visual *coup de théâtre* (Jack's appearance in mourning) can be traced to W. S. Gilbert's blackest of farces, *Engaged* (1877). But where Gilbert's target is a lower middle class in the grip of mercenary instincts, Wilde's characters are from the 'best' society, whose attempts at polite behaviour and debonair self-possession are ceaselessly frustrated by their amatory instincts so that his farce springs from the conflict in individuals between their innate nature and their acquired culture. In all these instances, Wilde's text deploys the familiar as a basis from which to challenge accepted thinking and codes of behaviour. Or to express this in different terms: Wilde plays witty games with popular examples of contemporary culture to expose their underlying ideological structures, thereby bringing an audience to question the degree to which their theatre-going covertly shapes their private value judgements. Taste (as throughout Wilde's critical essays) is an issue of principle.

Significantly Wilde sought the most fashionable of theatres and actor–managers to present his work. While on the one hand he needed to make money to offset the costs of Bosie's and his own extravagance and frankly pursued celebrity and success, he also needed a theatrically aware audience of a very particular kind for his dramatic strategies to have their maximum effect. And the selected venues all attracted a decidedly upper-class clientele.[5] The play where Wilde sets out to seduce his audience with a most flattering image of themselves is *A Woman of No Importance*, which begins with a whole act in which (to Wilde's satisfaction) nothing whatever happens. We are invited to a weekend house-party at a country mansion, where titled matrons and dowagers, globe-trotting heiresses, stalwart members of parliament, dandies, languorous widows and young men with no brains, no money, no position and an infinite wealth of time on their hands congregate to talk idly before tea in a delightfully cultivated garden. It is a heightened, generalized representation: relaxed, intimate, witty and slightly naughty (though always in the most tactfully calculated way). By the second act one of the group, the American heiress, has begun to voice a degree of criticism of the society in which she finds herself, but she is quickly put in her place by the rest and laughingly dismissed as a 'Puritan' of dubious origins involving the manufacturing trades, who cannot be expected to appreciate the manners or culture of a true élite. In the process that élite begins to appear less than glittering, as snobbery and smugness are revealed. Next Wilde introduces to them an outsider, Mrs Arbuthnot, who is painfully aware of her marginalized status and of the patronage being shown herself and her son. How the group responds to her and she to them extends and enriches Wilde's critique of his upper-class worthies, until in the final moments the man who seemed initially the most brilliant representative of that circle, Lord Illingworth, finds himself dismissed from the stage by Mrs Arbuthnot on the grounds that he is morally despicable and no gentleman. Wilde's audience have cunningly and

effectively been led into participating imaginatively in a satirical decon-
struction of their own culture and moral sensibility. Similarly the
glittering diplomatic gathering staged within the opening act of *An
Ideal Husband* in time stands revealed as a masquerade behind which
a select few close ranks around one particularly prominent member
of the Establishment and effect a convenient cover-up of a shady
episode from his past.

From the moment in the opening scene of *The Importance of Being
Earnest* when the otherwise tight-lipped, impassive Lane lets slip that
he has 'only been married once' and that 'in consequence of a misunderstanding' between himself and 'a young person', all the characters
quickly expose themselves as leading double lives: even Lady Bracknell,
who has set herself up as society's guardian, scenting out improprieties
as if she were the only reliable arbiter of probity and taste, is found
out to be a parvenue and not to the aristocratic manner born, when
she also inadvertently lets slip that, when she married, she 'had no
fortune of any kind', but that she 'never dreamed for a moment of
allowing that to stand in [her] way'. The farce strips the characters of
all their high-flown and high-born pretensions, and we laugh uproari-
ously at their futile efforts to avoid admitting to themselves that they
are total hypocrites.

Wilde's Irish background and allegiances are relevant here. He was
born in Dublin on 16 October 1854. His father, Sir William, was
an eminent surgeon; his mother (best known by her pseudonym,
'Speranza'), who sustained the more profound influence over the
young Wilde, was a poet and collector of Irish folklore and legend, all
in the interests of promoting a fervent nationalism, which she imparted
to her son. The 1890s were to see the defeat in the Lords of the second
Home Rule Bill for Ireland in the wake of Charles Stewart Parnell's
public disgrace and death (significantly Parnell's magnificent political
career was forcibly ended after he was cited in divorce proceedings).
With the politicians having seemingly failed the Irish cause, the Dublin
intelligentsia took upon themselves the task of interrogating colonial
rule by addressing England's subtle hold over cultural expression. The
Irish National Literary Society (1892), the Gaelic League (1893), the

Irish Agricultural Organization Society (1894), the Irish Trades Union Congress (1894) and the Irish Literary Theatre Society, which within six years had evolved into the Irish National Theatre (1898), were founded in an unprecedented burst of nationalist activity. Cultural historians tend generally not to include Wilde within this movement to establish Irish letters as having a distinctive voice independent of English culture. Theorists, such as Edward Said, investigating the nature of colonial power in its varying manifestations, have demonstrated how the colonizing force, once firmly based in possession of the land which has been invaded, sets itself up as an absolute cultural authority, insisting upon the application of its own value-systems to all aspects of existence by the colonized people.[6] This is a subtler psychological invasion, permeating through to the roots of cultural experience and expression on which a private identity for individuals is founded. Most of Wilde's plays take as their focus the English ruling class who comprise the Establishment, the honoured arbiters and legislators of taste, of personal morals and of social conduct. His primary impulse is satirical, as if he is questioning the grounds on which such pillars of society claim their élitism, ascendency and right to rule or to colonize. These staunch upholders of the British Empire are mostly found wanting in charity, self-knowledge, independence of mind, wit, energy, insight; their cultural values are based on material acquisition; their capacity for ordering their own lives is easily disrupted; their moral sense is constructed in the interests of good form; and hypocrisy renders them either dangerous or absurd. Wilde with his own conscious delight in masks, surfaces and disguises was skilled at detecting unacknowledged pretensions in others; such pretension is the bedrock of the social world of his plays and so its poise is for ever vitiated by anxieties and insecurity. And Wilde had the temerity to take these critiques into theatres which were in the heartland of that society's public gatherings. The entertainment-value of these plays for their first audiences was a mask behind which Wilde endeavoured to define the need in his spectators for a more developed social conscience. His was a radical drama, wholly at one with the nationalist-inspired cultural revolution being attempted in Dublin. But whereas that Irish campaign was waged chiefly on the periphery, Wilde's criticism was directed at the metropolis. It was a dangerous game and, as so often in English politics, disgrace in his private life led to a rapid demolition of his public status and achievement. Where his Irish contemporaries set about staging a renaissance of Irish cultural values, Wilde more damagingly deconstructed Englishness to the point where he proved its authoritarian stance to be utterly preposterous. He made the English laugh at their earnestness, tight discipline and sense of purpose.

Wilde's preferred modes of staging were innovatory. His interrogation of what was currently fashionable in the way of dramatic conventions was deeply subversive. His manipulation of the traditional generic and stylistic boundaries between high comedy, melodrama and farce to destabilize audience expectation was for original spectators highly disconcerting. The effortless brio with which he exploited theatricality as a means to define a searching social criticism was the mark of a most sophisticated satirist with a clear political and moral agenda. His depiction of games with masks as being a necessary tactic for survival for his characters was in line with advanced contemporary thinking (Herbert Spencer, William James, Walter Pater) that was challenging concepts of 'fixed' identity. At every level Wilde's plays were revolutionary in the theatre of their time. In now designating those plays *modern classics* we must never lose sight of that crucial fact. When reviving those plays in the theatre today, whether with professional or amateur casts, we must allow the darker resonances that permeate Wilde's representations of moneyed leisure their full expression.[7] Actors and directors must find ways of acknowledging in production the social, intellectual and political contexts which influenced the conception and writing of the plays and which give them their precise, unique and challenging qualities. There is far more to Wilde's practice of theatre than a brilliant way with words.

NOTES

1. W. H. Auden, *Secondary Worlds* (London: Faber, 1968), p. 92.
2. Graham Robertson, *Time Was* (London: Hamish Hamilton, 1931), pp. 126–7.

3. Charles Ricketts, *Pages on Art* (London: Constable, 1913), pp. 243–4. The passage is quoted in full in the Notes to *Salomé* below.

4. Joseph Donohue, 'Distance, Death and Desire in *Salomé*', in Peter Raby (ed.), *The Cambridge Companion to Oscar Wilde* (Cambridge: Cambridge University Press, 1997), p. 131.

5. Wilde's attitude to the aristocracy and the English upper classes is too complex to define with any degree of precision. He was infatuated with the son of a marquis, but that proximity steadily inspired in him a sharp vein of criticism, as *De Profundis* and his letters reveal. Bosie's own view of his class, shaped by antagonisms and personal biases, may well have influenced Wilde's. Several of the plays are dedicated to aristocrats, statesmen or society beauties, and there is nothing in the phrasing to suggest anything but friendship and admiration for the specific dedicatees. Yet the dramatic action that in each case follows is undeniably a vehicle for the sharpest social satire. The plays tended to be written at times when Wilde's relations with Bosie were strained, usually because of financial crises brought about by the latter's extravagant life-style. It is not surprising that the earliest version of *The Importance of Being Earnest* is littered with references (most were subsequently deleted) to debts, solicitors and bailiffs. From Wilde's Oxford days, friendships with titled individuals featured in his life, though significantly most lapsed after his imprisonment. Attraction (from a variety of motives) and detached criticism, therefore, can be sensed as existing in a state of uneasy tension, much as they did in respect of George Bernard Shaw.

6. See Edward W. Said, *Culture and Imperialism* (London: Chatto and Windus, 1993), especially the chapter 'Resistance and Opposition' (pp. 230–340), in which he comments on the situation in Ireland.

7. Joel Kaplan (in his essay 'Wilde on the Stage' in *The Cambridge Companion to Oscar Wilde*, which reviews the history of the plays in performance) observes that it is only since Lindsay Kemp's staging of *Salomé* in the 1970s that Wilde has been rediscovered as a playwright for our time. Since then, as he demonstrates, the focus has shifted from opulent settings and costuming in the manner of Rex Whistler or Cecil Beaton to all-but-bare stages where attention is directed exclusively at the subtleties of the actors' playing. Plotting has in consequence become less important than psychological motivation, although the mannered acting and delivery have not entirely been displaced. Kaplan also notes that '*The Importance of Being Earnest* has, thus far, eluded the kind of wholesale rediscovery that has characterised recent stagings of *Salomé* and the Society dramas. In part the play has remained hostage to the success of its Gielgud revivals, and the expectations shaped by Asquith's 1952 film' (p. 270). Kaplan and Sheila Stowell discuss this further in *Wilde on Stage: A Cultural and Performance History* (Cambridge: Cambridge University Press, 1997).

A NOTE ON THE TEXTS

In preparing this edition, I have used as my base text for most of the plays the Penguin edition entitled: *Oscar Wilde: 'The Importance of Being Earnest' and Other Plays* (Harmondsworth, 1954; reprinted 1986). This anonymously edited volume seems to have been set from the playtexts included in Robert Ross's *Collected Edition of the Works of Oscar Wilde* (1908). I have corrected the Penguin playtexts in respect of *Lady Windermere's Fan*, *A Woman of No Importance*, *An Ideal Husband* and *The Importance of Being Earnest* by collating them against the texts published in the New Mermaids Series, edited by Ian Small and Russell Jackson, which are the only modern editions to offer substantial information about, and readings from, the extant manuscripts, typescripts and promptcopies. These editions are: *Lady Windermere's Fan*, ed. Ian Small (Ernest Benn and Norton and Co.: London and New York, 1980); *The Importance of Being Earnest*, ed. Russell Jackson (Ernest Benn and Norton and Co.: London and New York, 1980); and *Two Society Comedies: 'A Woman of No Importance' and 'An Ideal Husband'*, ed. (respectively) by Ian Small and Russell Jackson (Ernest Benn and Norton and Co.: London and New York, 1983).

There is to date no edition of *Salomé* with detailed critical apparatus. (Only the publication of the intended *Collected Edition of the Works of Oscar Wilde* by Oxford University Press will remedy that situation.) The original Penguin text of *Salomé* has been collated with and corrected against the first edition of the English version published by Mathews and Lane in 1894; and *A Florentine Tragedy* has been reproduced and edited from the text published by Ross in '*Salomé' and 'A Florentine Tragedy'* (1908).

For material on the four-act version of *The Importance of Being Earnest* I am indebted to Ruth Berggren's magnificent edition, which was published by the Vanguard Press of New York in 1987. In editing that particular comedy I also had recourse to the edition published by Methuen in 1910, which George Alexander presented as a souvenir of his twenty years in management at the St James's Theatre.

Most substantive corrections to the 1954 Penguin edition made here in consequence of the collating described above have been commented upon in the notes to the various plays. Often those notes describe the evolution of certain passages and effects, showing how particular readings came into being through various drafts. Emendations relating to the stylistic layout especially of the stage directions and punctuation, which have generally been made to achieve consistency (no comma before a conjunction in a series, for example, or the use of three points in all ellipses), have not been annotated. The correcting of typographical errors has also been made silently.

Unlike the 1954 Penguin edition, this volume deliberately presents the works in order of composition, which gives a clearer sense of the extraordinary range of Wilde's invention, especially during the years 1894–5; and I have chosen to place details about the casts of first productions in the commentaries, where they seem more appropriately to belong in discussions about the plays' theatrical history (rather than as conventionally situated immediately between the title page and the first act).

SELECT BIBLIOGRAPHY

There is now a huge body of critical publications about Wilde and his works. What is recorded here are volumes, chiefly dealing with Wilde as playwright, which have had a direct bearing on the shaping of this edition and the writing of the introduction, commentaries and notes. Many contain extensive bibliographies which will direct the interested reader to further titles.

Neil Bartlett, *Who Was That Man? A Present for Mr Oscar Wilde* (London: Serpent's Tail, 1988).

Max Beerbohm, *Last Theatres* (London: Rupert Hart-Davis, 1970).

Richard Allen Cave, *Charles Ricketts' Stage Designs* (Cambridge: Chadwyck-Healey Ltd, 1987).

—, 'Staging the Irishman', in J. S. Bratton *et al.*, *Acts of Supremacy: The British Empire and the Stage, 1790–1930* (Manchester and New York: Manchester University Press, 1991), pp. 62–128.

—, *Terence Gray and the Cambridge Festival Theatre* (Cambridge: Chadwyck-Healey Ltd, 1980).

Joseph Donohue with Ruth Berggren (eds.), *Oscar Wilde's 'The Importance of Being Earnest': The First Production* (Gerrards Cross: Colin Smythe, 1995).

Richard Ellmann, *Oscar Wilde* (London: Hamish Hamilton, 1987).

Rupert Hart-Davis (ed.), *The Letters of Oscar Wilde* (London and New York: Rupert Hart-Davis Ltd and Harcourt Brace & World Inc., 1962).

—, *More Letters of Oscar Wilde* (London: John Murray, 1985).

Joel Kaplan (ed.), *Modern Drama: Special Issue – Oscar Wilde*, 37:1 (Spring 1994).

Joel Kaplan and Sheila Stowell, *Theatre and Fashion: Oscar Wilde to the Suffragettes* (Cambridge: Cambridge University Press, 1994).

Frank McGuinness, 'The Spirit of Play in Oscar Wilde's *De Profundis*', in Chris Morash (ed.), *Creativity and Its Contexts* (Dublin: Lilliput Press, 1995), pp. 49–59.

Kerry Powell, *Oscar Wilde and the Theatre of the 1890s* (Cambridge: Cambridge University Press, 1990).

Peter Raby (ed.), *The Cambridge Companion to Oscar Wilde* (Cambridge: Cambridge University Press, 1997).

Charles Ricketts, *Pages on Art* (London: Constable, 1913).

C. George Sandulescu (ed.), *Rediscovering Oscar Wilde* (Gerrards Cross: Colin Smythe, 1994).

Alan Sinfield, *The Wilde Century* (London and New York: Cassell, 1994).

Ian Small, *Oscar Wilde Revalued: An Essay on New Materials and Methods of Research* (Greensboro, NC: ELT Press, 1993).

Katharine J. Worth, *The Irish Drama of Europe from Yeats to Beckett* (London: Athlone Press, 1978).

—, *Oscar Wilde* (London and Basingstoke: Macmillan, 1983).

Lady Windermere's Fan

A PLAY
ABOUT A GOOD WOMAN

TO
THE DEAR MEMORY
OF
ROBERT EARL OF LYTTON[1]
IN AFFECTION
AND
ADMIRATION

The Persons of the Play

LORD WINDERMERE

LORD DARLINGTON

LORD AUGUSTUS LORTON

MR DUMBY

MR CECIL GRAHAM

MR HOPPER

PARKER, *Butler*

LADY WINDERMERE

THE DUCHESS OF BERWICK

LADY AGATHA CARLISLE

LADY PLYMDALE

LADY STUTFIELD

LADY JEDBURGH

MRS COWPER-COWPER

MRS ERLYNNE

ROSALIE, *Maid*

TIME

The Present

PLACE

London

The action of the play takes place within twenty-four hours, beginning on a Tuesday afternoon at five o'clock, and ending the next day at 1.30 p.m.

FIRST ACT

SCENE

Morning-room of Lord Windermere's house in Carlton House Terrace.[1]

Doors C. and R. Bureau with books and papers R. Sofa with small tea-table L. Window opening on to terrace L. Table R.]

[LADY WINDERMERE *is at table R., arranging roses in a blue bowl.]*

[*Enter* PARKER.]

PARKER: Is your ladyship at home[2] this afternoon?
LADY WINDERMERE: Yes – who has called?
PARKER: Lord Darlington, my lady.
LADY WINDERMERE [*hesitates for a moment*]: Show him up – and I'm at home to anyone who calls.
PARKER: Yes, my lady.

[*Exit C.*]

LADY WINDERMERE: It's best for me to see him before tonight. I'm glad he's come.

[*Enter* PARKER *C.*]

PARKER: Lord Darlington.

[*Enter* LORD DARLINGTON *C.*]

[*Exit* PARKER.]

LORD DARLINGTON: How do you do, Lady Windermere?
LADY WINDERMERE: How do you do, Lord Darlington? No, I can't shake hands with you. My hands are all wet with these roses. Aren't they lovely? They came up from Selby this morning.
LORD DARLINGTON: They are quite perfect. [*Sees a fan lying on the table.*] And what a wonderful fan! May I look at it?

5

LADY WINDERMERE: Do. Pretty, isn't it! It's got my name on it, and everything. I have only just seen it myself. It's my husband's birthday present to me. You know today is my birthday?

LORD DARLINGTON: No? Is it really?

LADY WINDERMERE: Yes, I'm of age[3] today. Quite an important day in my life, isn't it? That is why I am giving this party tonight. Do sit down. [*Still arranging flowers.*]

LORD DARLINGTON [*sitting down*]: I wish I had known it was your birthday, Lady Windermere. I would have covered the whole street in front of your house with flowers for you to walk on. They are made for you.

[*A short pause.*]

LADY WINDERMERE: Lord Darlington, you annoyed me last night at the Foreign Office. I am afraid you are going to annoy me again.

LORD DARLINGTON: I, Lady Windermere?

[*Enter* PARKER *and Footman C., with tray and tea things.*]

LADY WINDERMERE: Put it there, Parker. That will do. [*Wipes her hands with her pocket-handkerchief, goes to tea-table L. and sits down.*] Won't you come over, Lord Darlington?

[*Exit* PARKER *C.*]

LORD DARLINGTON [*takes chair and goes across L. C.*]: I am quite miserable, Lady Windermere. You must tell me what I did. [*Sits down at table L.*]

LADY WINDERMERE: Well, you kept paying me elaborate compliments the whole evening.

LORD DARLINGTON [*smiling*]: Ah, nowadays we are all of us so hard up, that the only pleasant things to pay *are* compliments. They're the only things we *can* pay.

LADY WINDERMERE [*shaking her head*]: No, I am talking very seriously. You mustn't laugh, I am quite serious. I don't like compliments, and I don't see why a man should think he is pleasing a woman enormously when he says to her a whole heap of things that he doesn't mean.

LORD DARLINGTON: Ah, but I did mean them. [*Takes tea which she offers him.*]

LADY WINDERMERE [*gravely*]: I hope not. I should be sorry to have to quarrel with you, Lord Darlington. I like you very much, you know that. But I shouldn't like you at all if I thought you were what most other men are. Believe me, you are better than most other men, and I sometimes think you pretend to be worse.

LORD DARLINGTON: We all have our little vanities, Lady Windermere.

LADY WINDERMERE: Why do you make that your special one? [*Still seated at table L.*]

LORD DARLINGTON [*still seated L. C.*]: Oh, nowadays so many conceited people go about Society pretending to be good, that I think it shows rather a sweet and modest disposition to pretend to be bad. Besides, there is this to be said. If you pretend to be good, the world takes you very seriously. If you pretend to be bad, it doesn't. Such is the astounding stupidity of optimism.

LADY WINDERMERE: Don't you *want* the world to take you seriously, then, Lord Darlington?

LORD DARLINGTON: No, not the world. Who are the people the world takes seriously? All the dull people one can think of, from the Bishops down to the bores. I should like *you* to take me very seriously, Lady Windermere, *you* more than anyone else in life.

LADY WINDERMERE: Why – why me?

LORD DARLINGTON [*after a slight hesitation*]: Because I think we might be great friends. Let us be great friends. You may want a friend some day.

LADY WINDERMERE: Why do you say that?

LORD DARLINGTON: Oh! – we all want friends at times.

LADY WINDERMERE: I think we're very good friends already, Lord Darlington. We can always remain so as long as you don't –

LORD DARLINGTON: Don't what?

LADY WINDERMERE: Don't spoil it by saying extravagant silly things to me. You think I am a Puritan, I suppose? Well, I have something of the Puritan in me. I was brought up like that. I am glad of it. My mother died when I was a mere child. I lived always with Lady

Julia, my father's elder sister, you know. She was stern to me, but she taught me what the world is forgetting, the difference that there is between what is right and what is wrong. *She* allowed of no compromise. *I* allow of none.

LORD DARLINGTON: My dear Lady Windermere!

LADY WINDERMERE [*leaning back on the sofa*]: You look on me as being behind the age.[4] – Well, I am! I should be sorry to be on the same level as an age like this.

LORD DARLINGTON: You think the age very bad?

LADY WINDERMERE: Yes. Nowadays people seem to look on life as a speculation.[5] It is not a speculation. It is a sacrament. Its ideal is Love. Its purification is sacrifice.

LORD DARLINGTON [*smiling*]: Oh, anything is better than being sacrificed!

LADY WINDERMERE [*leaning forward*]: Don't say that.

LORD DARLINGTON: I do say it. I feel it – I know it.

[*Enter* PARKER *C.*]

PARKER: The men want to know if they are to put the carpets on the terrace for tonight, my lady?

LADY WINDERMERE: You don't think it will rain, Lord Darlington, do you?

LORD DARLINGTON: I won't hear of its raining on your birthday.

LADY WINDERMERE: Tell them to do it at once, Parker.

[*Exit* PARKER *C.*]

LORD DARLINGTON [*still seated*]: Do you think then – of course I am only putting an imaginary instance – do you think that in the case of a young married couple, say about two years married, if the husband suddenly becomes the intimate friend of a woman of – well, more than doubtful character – is always calling upon her, lunching with her and probably paying her bills – do you think that the wife should not console herself?

LADY WINDERMERE [*frowning*]: Console herself?

LORD DARLINGTON: Yes, I think she should – I think she has the right.

LADY WINDERMERE: Because the husband is vile – should the wife be vile also?[26]

LORD DARLINGTON: Vileness is a terrible word, Lady Windermere.

LADY WINDERMERE: It is a terrible thing, Lord Darlington.

LORD DARLINGTON: Do you know I am afraid that good people do a great deal of harm in this world. Certainly the greatest harm they do is that they make badness of such extraordinary importance. It is absurd to divide people into good and bad. People are either charming or tedious. I take the side of the charming, and you, Lady Windermere, can't help belonging to them.

LADY WINDERMERE: Now, Lord Darlington. [*Rising and crossing R., front of him.*] Don't stir, I am merely going to finish my flowers. [*Goes to table R. C.*]

LORD DARLINGTON [*rising and moving chair*]: And I must say I think you are very hard on modern life, Lady Windermere. Of course there is much against it, I admit. Most women, for instance, nowadays, are rather mercenary.

LADY WINDERMERE: Don't talk about such people.

LORD DARLINGTON: Well, then, setting aside mercenary people, who, of course, are dreadful, do you think seriously that women who have committed what the world calls a fault should never be forgiven?

LADY WINDERMERE [*standing at table*]: I think they should never be forgiven.

LORD DARLINGTON: And men? Do you think that there should be the same laws for men as there are for women?

LADY WINDERMERE: Certainly!

LORD DARLINGTON: I think life too complex a thing to be settled by these hard and fast rules.[7]

LADY WINDERMERE: If we had 'these hard and fast rules', we should find life much more simple.

LORD DARLINGTON: You allow of no exceptions?

LADY WINDERMERE: None!

LORD DARLINGTON: Ah, what a fascinating Puritan you are, Lady Windermere!

LADY WINDERMERE: The adjective was unnecessary, Lord Darlington.

LORD DARLINGTON: I couldn't help it. I can resist everything except temptation.

LADY WINDERMERE: You have the modern affectation of weakness.

LORD DARLINGTON [*looking at her*]: It's only an affectation, Lady Windermere.

[*Enter* PARKER *C.*]

PARKER: The Duchess of Berwick and Lady Agatha Carlisle.

[*Enter the* DUCHESS OF BERWICK *and* LADY AGATHA CARLISLE *C. Exit* PARKER *C.*]

DUCHESS OF BERWICK [*coming down C., and shaking hands*]: Dear Margaret, I am so pleased to see you. You remember Agatha, don't you? [*Crossing L. C.*] How do you do, Lord Darlington? I won't let you know my daughter, you are far too wicked.

LORD DARLINGTON: Don't say that, Duchess. As a wicked man I am a complete failure. Why, there are lots of people who say I have never really done anything wrong in the whole course of my life. Of course they only say it behind my back.

DUCHESS OF BERWICK: Isn't he dreadful? Agatha, this is Lord Darlington. Mind you don't believe a word he says. [LORD DARLINGTON *crosses R. C.*] No, no tea, thank you, dear. [*Crosses and sits on sofa.*] We have just had tea at Lady Markby's. Such bad tea, too. It was quite undrinkable. I wasn't at all surprised. Her own son-in-law supplies it. Agatha is looking forward so much to your ball tonight, dear Margaret.

LADY WINDERMERE [*seated L. C.*]: Oh, you mustn't think it is going to be a ball, Duchess. It is only a dance in honour of my birthday. A small and early.[8]

LORD DARLINGTON [*standing L. C.*]: Very small, very early and very select, Duchess.

DUCHESS OF BERWICK [*on sofa L.*]: Of course it's going to be select. But we know *that*, dear Margaret, about *your* house. It is really one of the few houses in London where I can take Agatha, and where I feel perfectly secure about dear Berwick. I don't know what society is coming to. The most dreadful people seem to go everywhere.

They certainly come to my parties – the men get quite furious if one doesn't ask them. Really, someone should make a stand against it.

LADY WINDERMERE: *I* will, Duchess. I will have no one in my house about whom there is any scandal.

LORD DARLINGTON [*R. C.*]: Oh, don't say that, Lady Windermere. I should never be admitted! [*Sitting.*]

DUCHESS OF BERWICK: Oh, men don't matter. With women it is different. We're good. Some of us are, at least. But we are positively getting elbowed into the corner. Our husbands would really forget our existence if we didn't nag at them from time to time, just to remind them that we have a perfect legal right to do so.

LORD DARLINGTON: It's a curious thing, Duchess, about the game of marriage – a game, by the way, that is going out of fashion – the wives hold all the honours, and invariably lose the odd trick.[9]

DUCHESS OF BERWICK: The odd trick? Is that the husband, Lord Darlington?

LORD DARLINGTON: It would be rather a good name for the modern husband.

DUCHESS OF BERWICK: Dear Lord Darlington, how thoroughly depraved you are!

LADY WINDERMERE: Lord Darlington is trivial.

LORD DARLINGTON: Ah, don't say that, Lady Windermere.

LADY WINDERMERE: Why do you *talk* so trivially about life, then?

LORD DARLINGTON: Because I think that life is far too important a thing ever to talk seriously about it. [*Moves up C.*]

DUCHESS OF BERWICK: What does he mean? Do, as a concession to my poor wits, Lord Darlington, just explain to me what you really mean.

LORD DARLINGTON [*coming down back of table*]: I think I had better not, Duchess. Nowadays to be intelligible is to be found out. Good-bye! [*Shakes hands with* DUCHESS.] And now – [*goes up stage*] – Lady Windermere, good-bye. I may come tonight, mayn't I? Do let me come.

LADY WINDERMERE [*standing up stage with* LORD DARLINGTON]: Yes, certainly. But you are not to say foolish, insincere things to people.

LORD DARLINGTON [*smiling*]: Ah! you are beginning to reform me. It is a dangerous thing to reform anyone, Lady Windermere. [*Bows, and exit C.*]

DUCHESS OF BERWICK [*who has risen, goes C.*]: What a charming wicked creature! I like him so much. I'm quite delighted he's gone! How sweet you're looking! Where *do* you get your gowns? And now I must tell you how sorry I am for you, dear Margaret. [*Crosses to sofa and sits with* LADY WINDERMERE.] Agatha, darling!

LADY AGATHA: Yes, mamma. [*Rises.*]

DUCHESS OF BERWICK: Will you go and look over the photograph album that I see there?

LADY AGATHA: Yes, mamma. [*Goes to table up L.*]

DUCHESS OF BERWICK: Dear girl! She is so fond of photographs of Switzerland. Such a pure taste, I think. But I really am so sorry for you, Margaret.

LADY WINDERMERE [*smiling*]: Why, Duchess?

DUCHESS OF BERWICK: Oh, on account of that horrid woman. She dresses so well, too, which makes it much worse, sets such a dreadful example. Augustus – you know my disreputable brother – such a trial to us all – well, Augustus is completely infatuated about her. It is quite scandalous, for she is absolutely inadmissible into society. Many a woman has a past, but I am told that she has at least a dozen, and that they all fit.[10]

LADY WINDERMERE: Whom are you talking about, Duchess?

DUCHESS OF BERWICK: About Mrs Erlynne.

LADY WINDERMERE: Mrs Erlynne? I never heard of her, Duchess. And what *has* she to do with me?

DUCHESS OF BERWICK: My poor child! Agatha, darling!

LADY AGATHA: Yes, mamma.

DUCHESS OF BERWICK: Will you go out on the terrace and look at the sunset?

LADY AGATHA: Yes, mamma. [*Exit through window L.*]

DUCHESS OF BERWICK: Sweet girl! So devoted to sunsets! Shows such refinement of feeling, does it not? After all, there is nothing like Nature, is there?

LADY WINDERMERE: But what is it, Duchess? Why do you talk to me about this person?

DUCHESS OF BERWICK: Don't you really know? I assure you we're all so distressed about it. Only last night at dear Lady Jansen's everyone was saying how extraordinary it was that, of all men in London, Windermere should behave in such a way.

LADY WINDERMERE: My husband – what has *he* got to do with any woman of that kind?

DUCHESS OF BERWICK: Ah, what indeed, dear? That is the point. He goes to see her continually, and stops for hours at a time, and while he is there she is not at home to any one. Not that many ladies call on her, dear, but she has a great many disreputable men friends – my own brother particularly, as I told you – and that is what makes it so dreadful about Windermere. We looked upon *him* as being such a model husband, but I am afraid there is no doubt about it. My dear nieces – you know the Saville girls, don't you? – such nice domestic creatures – plain, dreadfully plain, but so good – well, they're always at the window doing fancy work, and making ugly things for the poor, which I think so useful of them in these dreadful socialistic days, and this terrible woman has taken a house in Curzon Street, right opposite them – such a respectable street, too! I don't know what we're coming to! And they tell me that Windermere goes there four and five times a week – they *see* him. They can't help it – and although they never talk scandal, they – well, of course – they remark on it to every one. And the worst of it all is that I have been told that this woman has got a great deal of money out of somebody, for it seems that she came to London six months ago without anything at all to speak of, and now she has this charming house in Mayfair, drives her ponies in the Park[11] every afternoon and all – well, all – since she has known poor dear Windermere.

LADY WINDERMERE: Oh, I can't believe it!

DUCHESS OF BERWICK: But it's quite true, my dear. The whole of London knows it. That is why I felt it was better to come and talk to you, and advise you to take Windermere away at once to Homburg or to Aix,[12] where he'll have something to amuse him, and where you can watch him all day long. I assure you, my dear, that on several occasions after I was first married, I had to pretend to be very ill, and was obliged to drink the most unpleasant mineral waters, merely to get Berwick out of town. He was so extremely susceptible. Though I am bound to say he never gave away any large sums of money to anybody. He is far too high-principled for that!

LADY WINDERMERE [*interrupting*]: Duchess, Duchess, it's impossible! [*Rising and crossing stage to C.*] We are only married two years. Our child is but six months old. [*Sits in chair R. of L. table.*]

DUCHESS OF BERWICK: Ah, the dear pretty baby! How is the little darling? Is it a boy or a girl? I hope a girl – Ah, no, I remember it's a boy! I'm so sorry. Boys are so wicked. My boy is excessively immoral. You wouldn't believe at what hours he comes home. And he's only left Oxford a few months[13] – I really don't know what they teach them there.

LADY WINDERMERE: Are *all* men bad?

DUCHESS OF BERWICK: Oh, all of them, my dear, all of them, without any exception. And they never grow any better. Men become old, but they never become good.

LADY WINDERMERE: Windermere and I married for love.

DUCHESS OF BERWICK: Yes, we begin like that. It was only Berwick's brutal and incessant threats of suicide that made me accept him at all, and before the year was out, he was running after all kinds of petticoats, every colour, every shape, every material. In fact, before the honeymoon was over, I caught him winking at my maid, a most pretty, respectable girl. I dismissed her at once without a character.[14] – No, I remember I passed her on to my sister; poor dear Sir George is so short-sighted, I thought it wouldn't matter. But it did, though – it was most unfortunate. [*Rises.*] And now, my dear child, I must go, as we are dining out. And mind you don't take this little aberration of Windermere's too much to heart. Just take him abroad, and he'll come back to you all right.

LADY WINDERMERE: Come back to me? [*C.*]

DUCHESS OF BERWICK [*L. C.*]: Yes, dear, these wicked women get our husbands away from us, but they always come back, slightly damaged, of course. And don't make scenes, men hate them!

LADY WINDERMERE: It is very kind of you, Duchess, to come and tell me all this. But I can't believe that my husband is untrue to me.

DUCHESS OF BERWICK: Pretty child! I was like that once. Now I know that all men are monsters. [LADY WINDERMERE *rings bell.*] The only thing to do is to feed the wretches well. A good cook does wonders, and that I know you have. My dear Margaret, you are not going to cry?

LADY WINDERMERE: You needn't be afraid, Duchess, I never cry.

DUCHESS OF BERWICK: That's quite right, dear. Crying is the refuge of plain women, but the ruin of pretty ones. Agatha, darling!

LADY AGATHA [*entering L.*]: Yes, mamma. [*Stands back of table L. C.*]

DUCHESS OF BERWICK: Come and bid good-bye to Lady Windermere, and thank her for your charming visit. [*Coming down again.*] And by the way, I must thank you for sending a card[15] to Mr Hopper – he's that rich young Australian people are taking such notice of just at present. His father made a great fortune by selling some kind of food in circular tins – most palatable, I believe – I fancy it is the thing the servants always refuse to eat. But the son is quite interesting. I think he's attracted by dear Agatha's clever talk. Of course, we should be very sorry to lose her, but I think that a mother who doesn't part with a daughter every season has no real affection. We're coming tonight, dear. [PARKER *opens C. doors.*] And remember my advice, take the poor fellow out of town at once, it is the only thing to do. Good-bye, once more; come, Agatha.

[*Exeunt* DUCHESS *and* LADY AGATHA *C.*]

LADY WINDERMERE: How horrible! I understand now what Lord Darlington meant by the imaginary instance of the couple not two years married. Oh! it can't be true – she spoke of enormous sums of money paid to this woman. I know where Arthur keeps his bank book – in one of the drawers of that desk. I might find out by that. I *will* find out. [*Opens drawer.*] No, it is some hideous mistake. [*Rises and goes C.*] Some silly scandal! He loves *me*! he loves *me*! But why should I not look? I am his wife, I have a right to look! [*Returns to bureau, takes out book and examines it page by page, smiles and gives a sigh of relief.*] I knew it! there is not a word of truth in this stupid story. [*Puts book back in drawer. As she does so, starts and takes out another book.*] A second book – private – locked! [*Tries to open it, but fails. Sees paper knife on bureau, and with it cuts cover from book. Begins to start at the first page.*] 'Mrs Erlynne – £600 – Mrs Erlynne – £700 – Mrs Erlynne – £400.' Oh! it is true! It is true! How horrible. [*Throws book on floor.*]

[*Enter* LORD WINDERMERE *C.*]

LORD WINDERMERE: Well, dear, has the fan been sent home yet? [*Going R. C. Sees book.*] Margaret, you have cut open my bank book. You have no right to do such a thing!

LADY WINDERMERE: You think it wrong that you are found out, don't you?

LORD WINDERMERE: I think it wrong that a wife should spy on her husband.

LADY WINDERMERE: I did not spy on you. I never knew of this woman's existence till half an hour ago. Someone who pitied me was kind enough to tell me what everyone in London knows already – your daily visits to Curzon Street, your mad infatuation, the monstrous sums of money you squander on this infamous woman! [*Crossing L.*]

LORD WINDERMERE: Margaret! don't talk like that of Mrs Erlynne, you don't know how unjust it is!

LADY WINDERMERE [*turning to him*]: You are very jealous of Mrs Erlynne's honour. I wish you had been as jealous of mine.

LORD WINDERMERE: Your honour is untouched, Margaret. You don't think for a moment that – [*Puts book back into desk.*]

LADY WINDERMERE: I think that you spend your money strangely. That is all. Oh, don't imagine I mind about the money. As far as I am concerned, you may squander everything we have. But what I *do* mind is that you who have loved me, you who have taught me to love you, should pass from the love that is given to the love that is bought. Oh, it's horrible! [*Sits on sofa.*] And it is I who feel degraded! *you* don't feel anything. I feel stained, utterly stained. You can't realize how hideous the last six months seem to me now – every kiss you have given me is tainted in my memory.

LORD WINDERMERE [*crossing to her*]: Don't say that, Margaret. I never loved any one in the whole world but you.

LADY WINDERMERE [*rises*]: Who is this woman, then? Why do you take a house for her?

LORD WINDERMERE: I did not take a house for her.

LADY WINDERMERE: You gave her the money to do it, which is the same thing.

LORD WINDERMERE: Margaret, as far as I have known Mrs Erlynne –

LADY WINDERMERE: Is there a Mr Erlynne – or is he a myth?

LORD WINDERMERE: Her husband died many years ago. She is alone in the world.

LADY WINDERMERE: No relations? [*A pause.*]

LORD WINDERMERE: None.

LADY WINDERMERE: Rather curious, isn't it? [*L.*]

LORD WINDERMERE: [*L. C.*]: Margaret, I was saying to you – and I beg you to listen to me – that as far as I have known Mrs Erlynne, she has conducted herself well. If years ago –

LADY WINDERMERE: Oh! [*Crossing R. C.*] I don't want details about her life!

LORD WINDERMERE [*C.*]: I am not going to give you any details about her life. I tell you simply this – Mrs Erlynne was once honoured, loved, respected. She was well born, she had position – she lost everything – threw it away, if you like. That makes it all the more bitter. Misfortunes one can endure – they come from outside, they are accidents. But to suffer for one's own faults – ah! – there is the sting of life. It was twenty years ago, too. She was little more than a girl then. She had been a wife for even less time than you have.

LADY WINDERMERE: I am not interested in her – and – you should not mention this woman and me in the same breath. It is an error of taste. [*Sitting R. at desk.*]

LORD WINDERMERE: Margaret, you could save this woman. She wants to get back into society, and she wants you to help her. [*Crossing to her.*]

LADY WINDERMERE: Me!

LORD WINDERMERE: Yes, you.

LADY WINDERMERE: How impertinent of her! [*A pause.*]

LORD WINDERMERE: Margaret, I came to ask you a great favour, and I still ask it of you, though you have discovered what I had intended you should never have known, that I have given Mrs Erlynne a large sum of money. I want you to send her an invitation for our party tonight. [*Standing L. of her.*]

LADY WINDERMERE: You are mad! [*Rises.*]

LORD WINDERMERE: I entreat you. People may chatter about her, do chatter about her, of course, but they don't know anything definite against her. She has been to several houses – not to houses where you would go, I admit, but still to houses where women who are in what is called Society nowadays do go. That does not content her. She wants you to receive her once.

LADY WINDERMERE: As a triumph for her, I suppose?

LORD WINDERMERE: No; but because she knows that you are a good woman – and that if she comes here once she will have a chance of a happier, a surer life than she has had. She will make no further effort to know you. Won't you help a woman who is trying to get back?

LADY WINDERMERE: No! If a woman really repents, she never wishes to return to the society that has made or seen her ruin.

LORD WINDERMERE: I beg of you.

LADY WINDERMERE [*crossing to door R.*]: I am going to dress for dinner, and don't mention the subject again this evening. Arthur [*going to him C.*], you fancy because I have no father or mother that I am alone in the world, and that you can treat me as you choose. You are wrong, I have friends, many friends.

LORD WINDERMERE [*R. C.*]: Margaret, you are talking foolishly, recklessly. I won't argue with you, but I insist upon your asking Mrs Erlynne tonight.

LADY WINDERMERE [*R. C.*]: I shall do nothing of the kind. [*Crossing L. C.*]

LORD WINDERMERE: You refuse? [*C.*]

LADY WINDERMERE: Absolutely!

LORD WINDERMERE: Ah, Margaret, do this for my sake; it is her last chance.

LADY WINDERMERE: What has that to do with me?

LORD WINDERMERE: How hard good women are!

LADY WINDERMERE: How weak bad men are!

LORD WINDERMERE: Margaret, none of us men may be good enough for the women we marry – that is quite true – but you don't imagine I would ever – oh, the suggestion is monstrous!

LADY WINDERMERE: Why should *you* be different from other men? I am told that there is hardly a husband in London who does not waste his life over *some* shameful passion.

LORD WINDERMERE: I am not one of them.

LADY WINDERMERE: I am not sure of that!

LORD WINDERMERE: You are sure in your heart. But don't make chasm after chasm between us. God knows the last few minutes have thrust us wide enough apart. Sit down and write the card.

LADY WINDERMERE: Nothing in the whole world would induce me.

LORD WINDERMERE [*crossing to bureau*]: Then I will! [*Rings electric bell, sits and writes card.*]

LADY WINDERMERE: You are going to invite this woman? [*Crossing to him.*]

LORD WINDERMERE: Yes.

[*Pause. Enter* PARKER.]

Parker!

PARKER: Yes, my lord. [*Comes down L. C.*]

LORD WINDERMERE: Have this note sent to Mrs Erlynne at No. 84A Curzon Street. [*Crossing to L. C. and giving note to* PARKER.] There is no answer!

[*Exit* PARKER *C.*]

LADY WINDERMERE: Arthur, if that woman comes here, I shall insult her.

LORD WINDERMERE: Margaret, don't say that.

LADY WINDERMERE: I mean it.

LORD WINDERMERE: Child, if you did such a thing, there's not a woman in London who wouldn't pity you.

LADY WINDERMERE: There is not a *good* woman in London who would not applaud me. We have been too lax. We must make an example, I propose to begin tonight. [*Picking up fan.*] Yes, you gave me this fan today; it was your birthday present. If that woman crosses my threshold, I shall strike her across the face with it.

LORD WINDERMERE: Margaret, you couldn't do such a thing.

LADY WINDERMERE: You don't know me! [*Moves R.*]

[*Enter* PARKER.]

Parker!

PARKER: Yes, my lady.

LADY WINDERMERE: I shall dine in my own room. I don't want dinner, in fact. See that everything is ready by half past ten. And, Parker, be sure you pronounce the names of the guests very distinctly tonight. Sometimes you speak so fast that I miss them. I am particularly anxious to hear the names quite clearly, so as to make no mistake. You understand, Parker?

PARKER: Yes, my lady.

LADY WINDERMERE: That will do!

[*Exit* PARKER C.]

[*Speaking to* LORD WINDERMERE] Arthur, if that woman comes here – I warn you –

LORD WINDERMERE: Margaret, you'll ruin us!

LADY WINDERMERE: Us! From this moment my life is separate from yours. But if you wish to avoid a public scandal, write at once to this woman, and tell her that I forbid her to come here!

LORD WINDERMERE: I will not – I cannot – she must come!

LADY WINDERMERE: Then I shall do exactly as I have said. [*Goes R.*] You leave me no choice. [*Exit R.*]

LORD WINDERMERE [*calling after her*]: Margaret! Margaret! [*A pause.*] My God! What shall I do? I dare not tell her who this woman really is. The shame would kill her.[16] [*Sinks down into a chair and buries his face in his hands.*]

ACT DROP

SECOND ACT

SCENE
Drawing-room in Lord Windermere's house.

[*Door R. U. opening into ball-room, where band is playing. Door L. through which guests are entering. Door L. U. opens on to illuminated terrace. Palms, flowers and brilliant lights. Room crowded with guests.*[1] LADY WINDERMERE *is receiving them.*]

DUCHESS OF BERWICK [*up C.*]: So strange Lord Windermere isn't here. Mr Hopper is very late, too. You have kept those five dances for him, Agatha? [*Comes down.*]

LADY AGATHA: Yes, mamma.

DUCHESS OF BERWICK [*sitting on sofa*]: Just let me see your card.[2] I'm so glad Lady Windermere has revived cards. – They're a mother's only safeguard. You dear simple little thing! [*Scratches out two names.*] No nice girl should ever waltz with such particularly younger sons! It looks so fast! The last two dances you might pass on the terrace with Mr Hopper.

[*Enter* MR DUMBY *and* LADY PLYMDALE *from the ball-room.*]

LADY AGATHA: Yes, mamma.

DUCHESS OF BERWICK [*fanning herself*]: The air is so pleasant there.

PARKER: Mrs Cowper-Cowper. Lady Stutfield. Sir James Royston. Mr Guy Berkeley.

[*These people enter as announced.*]

DUMBY: Good evening, Lady Stutfield. I suppose this will be the last ball of the season?

LADY STUTFIELD: I suppose so, Mr Dumby. It's been a delightful season, hasn't it?

DUMBY: Quite delightful! Good evening, Duchess. I suppose this will be the last ball of the season?

DUCHESS OF BERWICK: I suppose so, Mr Dumby. It has been a very dull season, hasn't it?

DUMBY: Dreadfully dull! Dreadfully dull!

MRS COWPER-COWPER: Good evening, Mr Dumby. I suppose this will be the last ball of the season?

DUMBY: Oh, I think not. There'll probably be two more. [*Wanders back to* LADY PLYMDALE.]

PARKER: Mr Rufford. Lady Jedburgh and Miss Graham. Mr Hopper.

[*These people enter as announced.*]

HOPPER: How do you do, Lady Windermere? How do you do, Duchess? [*Bows to* LADY AGATHA.]

DUCHESS OF BERWICK: Dear Mr Hopper, how nice of you to come so early. We all know how you are run after in London.

HOPPER: Capital place, London! They are not nearly so exclusive in London as they are in Sydney.

DUCHESS OF BERWICK: Ah! we know your value, Mr Hopper. We wish there were more like you. It would make life so much easier. Do you know, Mr Hopper, dear Agatha and I are so much interested in Australia. It must be so pretty with all the dear little kangaroos flying about. Agatha has found it on the map. What a curious shape it is! Just like a large packing case. However, it is a very young country, isn't it?

HOPPER: Wasn't it made at the same time as the others, Duchess?

DUCHESS OF BERWICK: How clever you are, Mr Hopper. You have a cleverness quite of your own. Now I mustn't keep you.

HOPPER: But I should like to dance with Lady Agatha, Duchess.

DUCHESS OF BERWICK: Well, I *hope* she has a dance left. Have you a dance left, Agatha?

LADY AGATHA: Yes, mamma.

DUCHESS OF BERWICK: The next one?

LADY AGATHA: Yes, mamma.

HOPPER: May I have the pleasure? [LADY AGATHA *bows.*]

DUCHESS OF BERWICK: Mind you take great care of my little chatterbox, Mr Hopper.

[LADY AGATHA *and* MR HOPPER *pass into ball-room.*]

[*Enter* LORD WINDERMERE *L.*]

LORD WINDERMERE: Margaret, I want to speak to you.

LADY WINDERMERE: In a moment. [*The music stops.*]

PARKER: Lord Augustus Lorton.

[*Enter* LORD AUGUSTUS.]

LORD AUGUSTUS: Good evening, Lady Windermere.

DUCHESS OF BERWICK: Sir James, will you take me into the ball-room? Augustus has been dining with us tonight. I really have had quite enough of dear Augustus for the moment.

[SIR JAMES ROYSTON *gives the* DUCHESS *his arm and escorts her into the ball-room.*]

PARKER: Mr and Mrs Arthur Bowden. Lord and Lady Paisley. Lord Darlington.

[*These people enter as announced.*]

LORD AUGUSTUS [*coming up to* LORD WINDERMERE]: Want to speak to you particularly, dear boy. I'm worn to a shadow. Know I don't look it. None of us men do look what we really are. Demmed good thing, too. What I want to know is this. Who is she? Where does she come from? Why hasn't she got any demmed relations? Demmed nuisance, relations! But they make one so demmed respectable.

LORD WINDERMERE: You are talking of Mrs Erlynne, I suppose? I only met her six months ago. Till then, I never knew of her existence.

LORD AUGUSTUS: You have seen a good deal of her since then.

LORD WINDERMERE [*coldly*]: Yes, I have seen a good deal of her since then. I have just seen her.

LORD AUGUSTUS: Egad! the women are very down on her. I have been dining with Arabella this evening! By Jove! you should have heard

what she said about Mrs Erlynne. She didn't leave a rag on her
. . . [*Aside.*] Berwick and I told her that didn't matter much, as the
lady in question must have an extremely fine figure. You should
have seen Arabella's expression! . . . But, look here, dear boy. I
don't know what to do about Mrs Erlynne. Egad! I might be
married to her; she treats me with such demmed indifference. She's
deuced clever, too! She explains everything. Egad! She explains
you. She has got any amount of explanations for you – and all of
them different.

LORD WINDERMERE: No explanations are necessary about my friendship with Mrs Erlynne.

LORD AUGUSTUS: Hem! Well, look here, dear old fellow. Do you think
she will ever get into this demmed thing called Society? Would you
introduce her to your wife? No use beating about the confounded
bush. Would you do that?

LORD WINDERMERE: Mrs Erlynne is coming here tonight.

LORD AUGUSTUS: Your wife has sent her a card?

LORD WINDERMERE: Mrs Erlynne has received a card.

LORD AUGUSTUS: Then she's all right, dear boy. But why didn't you
tell me that before? It would have saved me a heap of worry and
demmed misunderstandings!

[LADY AGATHA *and* MR HOPPER *cross and exit on terrace L.U.E.*]

PARKER: Mr Cecil Graham!

[*Enter* MR CECIL GRAHAM.]

CECIL GRAHAM (*bows to* LADY WINDERMERE, *passes over and shakes hands
with* LORD WINDERMERE]: Good evening, Arthur. Why don't you
ask me how I am? I like people to ask me how I am. It shows a
widespread interest in my health. Now, tonight I am not at all well.
Been dining with my people. Wonder why it is one's people are
always so tedious? My father would talk morality after dinner. I
told him he was old enough to know better. But my experience is
that as soon as people are old enough to know better, they don't
know anything at all. Hullo, Tuppy! Hear you're going to be
married again; thought you were tired of that game.

LORD AUGUSTUS: You're excessively trivial, my dear boy, excessively trivial!

CECIL GRAHAM: By the way, Tuppy, which is it? Have you been twice married and once divorced, or twice divorced and once married? I say you've been twice divorced and once married. It sounds so much more probable.

LORD AUGUSTUS: I have a very bad memory. I really don't remember which. [*Moves away R.*]

LADY PLYMDALE: Lord Windermere, I've something most particular to ask you.

LORD WINDERMERE: I am afraid – if you will excuse me – I must join my wife.

LADY PLYMDALE: Oh, you mustn't dream of such a thing. It's most dangerous nowadays for a husband to pay any attention to his wife in public. It always makes people think that he beats her when they're alone. The world has grown so suspicious of anything that looks like a happy married life. But I'll tell you what it is at supper. [*Moves towards door of ball-room.*]

LORD WINDERMERE [*C.*]: Margaret! I *must* speak to you.

LADY WINDERMERE: Will you hold my fan for me, Lord Darlington? Thanks. [*Comes down to him.*]

LORD WINDERMERE [*crossing to her*]: Margaret, what you said before dinner was, of course, impossible?

LADY WINDERMERE: That woman is not coming here tonight.

LORD WINDERMERE [*R. C.*]: Mrs Erlynne is coming here, and if you in any way annoy her or wound her, you will bring shame and sorrow on us both. Remember that! Ah, Margaret! only trust me! A wife should trust her husband!

LADY WINDERMERE [*C.*]: London is full of women who trust their husbands. One can always recognize them. They look so thoroughly unhappy. I am not going to be one of them. [*Moves up.*] Lord Darlington, will you give me back my fan, please? Thanks ... A useful thing a fan, isn't it? ... I want a friend tonight, Lord Darlington: I didn't know I would want one so soon.

LORD DARLINGTON: Lady Windermere! I knew the time would come some day; but why tonight?

LORD WINDERMERE: I *will* tell her. I must. It would be terrible if there were any scene. Margaret . . .

PARKER: Mrs Erlynne!

[LORD WINDERMERE *starts.* MRS ERLYNNE *enters, very beautifully dressed and very dignified.*[3] LADY WINDERMERE *clutches at her fan, then lets it drop on the floor. She bows coldly to* MRS ERLYNNE, *who bows to her sweetly in turn, and sails into the room.*]

LORD DARLINGTON: You have dropped your fan, Lady Windermere.

[*Picks it up and hands it to her.*]

MRS ERLYNNE [*C.*]: How do you do, again, Lord Windermere? How charming your sweet wife looks! Quite a picture!

LORD WINDERMERE [*in a low voice*]: It was terribly rash of you to come!

MRS ERLYNNE [*smiling*]: The wisest thing I ever did in my life. And, by the way, you must pay me a good deal of attention this evening. I am afraid of the women. You must introduce me to some of them. The men I can always manage. How do you do, Lord Augustus? You have quite neglected me lately. I have not seen you since yesterday. I am afraid you're faithless. Everyone told me so.

LORD AUGUSTUS [*R.*]: Now really, Mrs Erlynne, allow me to explain.

MRS ERLYNNE [*R. C.*]: No, dear Lord Augustus, you can't explain anything. It is your chief charm.

LORD AUGUSTUS: Ah! if you find charms in me, Mrs Erlynne –

[*They converse together.* LORD WINDERMERE *moves uneasily about the room watching* MRS ERLYNNE.]

LORD DARLINGTON [*to* LADY WINDERMERE]: How pale you are!

LADY WINDERMERE: Cowards are always pale!

LORD DARLINGTON: You look faint. Come out on the terrace.

LADY WINDERMERE: Yes. [*To* PARKER.] Parker, send my cloak out.

MRS ERLYNNE [*crossing to her*]: Lady Windermere, how beautifully your terrace is illuminated. Reminds me of Prince Doria's at Rome.

[LADY WINDERMERE *bows coldly, and goes off with* LORD DARLINGTON.]

Oh, how do you do, Mr Graham? Isn't that your aunt, Lady Jedburgh? I should so much like to know her.

CECIL GRAHAM [*after a moment's hesitation*[4] *and embarrassment*]: Oh, certainly, if you wish it. Aunt Caroline, allow me to introduce Mrs Erlynne.

MRS ERLYNNE: So pleased to meet you, Lady Jedburgh. [*Sits beside her on the sofa.*] Your nephew and I are great friends. I am so much interested in his political career. I think he's sure to be a wonderful success. He thinks like a Tory, and talks like a Radical, and that's so important nowadays. He's such a brilliant talker, too. But we all know from whom he inherits that. Lord Allendale was saying to me only yesterday, in the Park, that Mr Graham talks almost as well as his aunt.

LADY JEDBURGH [*R.*]: Most kind of you to say these charming things to me! [MRS ERLYNNE *smiles, and continues conversation.*]

DUMBY [*to* CECIL GRAHAM]: Did you introduce Mrs Erlynne to Lady Jedburgh?

CECIL GRAHAM: Had to, my dear fellow. Couldn't help it! That woman can make one do anything she wants. How, I don't know.

DUMBY: Hope to goodness she won't speak to me! [*Saunters towards* LADY PLYMDALE.]

MRS ERLYNNE [*C. To* LADY JEDBURGH]: On Thursday? With great pleasure. [*Rises, and speaks to* LORD WINDERMERE, *laughing.*] What a bore it is to have to be civil to these old dowagers! But they always insist on it!

LADY PLYMDALE [*to* MR DUMBY]: Who is that well-dressed woman talking to Windermere?

DUMBY: Haven't got the slightest idea! Looks like an *édition de luxe* of a wicked French novel,[5] meant specially for the English market.

MRS ERLYNNE: So that is poor Dumby with Lady Plymdale? I hear she is frightfully jealous of him. He doesn't seem anxious to speak to me tonight. I suppose he is afraid of her. Those straw-coloured women have dreadful tempers. Do you know, I think I'll dance with you first, Windermere. [LORD WINDERMERE *bites his lip and frowns.*] It will make Lord Augustus so jealous! Lord Augustus! [LORD AUGUSTUS *comes down.*] Lord Windermere insists on my dancing with him first, and, as it's his own house, I can't well refuse. You know I would much sooner dance with you.

LORD AUGUSTUS [*with a low bow*]: I wish I could think so, Mrs Erlynne.

MRS ERLYNNE: You know it far too well. I can fancy a person dancing through life with you and finding it charming.

LORD AUGUSTUS [*placing his hand on his white waistcoat*]: Oh, thank you, thank you. You are the most adorable of all ladies!

MRS ERLYNNE: What a nice speech! So simple and so sincere! Just the sort of speech I like. Well, you shall hold my bouquet. [*Goes towards ball-room on* LORD WINDERMERE'S *arm.*] Ah, Mr Dumby, how are you? I am so sorry I have been out the last three times you have called. Come and lunch on Friday.

DUMBY [*with perfect nonchalance*]: Delighted!

[LADY PLYMDALE *glares with indignation at* MR DUMBY. LORD AUGUSTUS *follows* MRS ERLYNNE *and* LORD WINDERMERE *into the ball-room holding bouquet.*]

LADY PLYMDALE [*to* MR DUMBY]: What an absolute brute you are! I never can believe a word you say! Why did you tell me you didn't know her? What do you mean by calling on her three times running? You are not to go to lunch there; of course you understand that?

DUMBY: My dear Laura,[6] I wouldn't dream of going!

LADY PLYMDALE: You haven't told me her name yet! Who is she?

DUMBY [*coughs slightly and smoothes his hair*]: She's a Mrs Erlynne.

LADY PLYMDALE: That woman!

DUMBY: Yes; that is what everyone calls her.

LADY PLYMDALE: How very interesting! How intensely interesting! I really must have a good stare at her. [*Goes to door of ball-room and looks in.*] I have heard the most shocking things about her. They say she is ruining poor Windermere. And Lady Windermere, who goes in for being so proper, invites her! How extremely amusing! It takes a thoroughly good woman to do a thoroughly stupid thing. You are to lunch there on Friday!

DUMBY: Why?

LADY PLYMDALE: Because I want you to take my husband with you. He has been so attentive lately, that he has become a perfect nuisance. Now, this woman is just the thing for him. He'll dance attendance upon her as long as she lets him, and won't bother me. I assure you, women of that kind are most useful. They form the basis of other people's marriages.

DUMBY: What a mystery you are!

LADY PLYMDALE [*looking at him*]: I wish *you* were!

DUMBY: I am – to myself. I am the only person in the world I should like to know thoroughly; but I don't see any chance of it just at present.[7]

[*They pass into the ball-room, and* LADY WINDERMERE *and* LORD DAR-LINGTON *enter from the terrace.*]

LADY WINDERMERE: Yes. Her coming here is monstrous, unbearable. I know now what you meant today at tea-time. Why didn't you tell me right out? You should have!

LORD DARLINGTON: I couldn't! A man can't tell these things about another man! But if I had known he was going to make you ask her here tonight, I think I would have told you. That insult, at any rate, you would have been spared.

LADY WINDERMERE: I did not ask her. He insisted on her coming – against my entreaties – against my commands. Oh! the house is tainted for me! I feel that every woman here sneers at me as she dances by with my husband. What have I done to deserve this? I gave him all my life. He took it – used it – spoiled it! I am degraded in my own eyes; and I lack courage – I am a coward! [*Sits down on sofa.*]

LORD DARLINGTON: If I know you at all, I know that you can't live with a man who treats you like this! What sort of a life would you have with him? You would feel that he was lying to you every moment of the day. You would feel that the look in his eyes was false, his voice false, his touch false, his passion false. He would come to you when he was weary of others; you would have to comfort him. He would come to you when he was devoted to others; you would have to charm him. You would have to be to him the mask of his real life, the cloak to hide his secret.[8]

LADY WINDERMERE: You are right – you are terribly right. But where am I to turn? You said you would be my friend, Lord Darlington. – Tell me, what am I to do? Be my friend now.

LORD DARLINGTON: Between men and women there is no friendship possible. There is passion, enmity, worship, love, but no friendship. I love you –

LADY WINDERMERE: No, no! [*Rises.*]

LORD DARLINGTON: Yes, I love you! You are more to me than anything in the whole world. What does your husband give you? Nothing. Whatever is in him he gives to this wretched woman, whom he has thrust into your society, into your home, to shame you before everyone. I offer you my life –

LADY WINDERMERE: Lord Darlington!

LORD DARLINGTON: My life – my whole life. Take it, and do with it what you will . . . I love you – love you as I have never loved any living thing. From the moment I met you I loved you, loved you blindly, adoringly, madly! You did not know it then – you know it now! Leave this house tonight. I won't tell you that the world matters nothing, or the world's voice, or the voice of society. They matter a great deal. They matter far too much. But there are moments when one has to choose between living one's own life, fully, entirely, completely – or dragging out some false, shallow, degrading existence that the world in its hypocrisy demands. You have that moment now. Choose! Oh, my love, choose.[9]

LADY WINDERMERE [*moving slowly away from him, and looking at him with startled eyes*]: I have not the courage.

LORD DARLINGTON [*following her*]: Yes; you have the courage. There may be six months of pain, of disgrace even, but when you no longer bear his name, when you bear mine, all will be well. Margaret, my love, my wife that shall be some day – yes, my wife! You know it! What are you now? This woman has the place that belongs by right to you. Oh! go – go out of this house, with head erect, with a smile upon your lips, with courage in your eyes. All London will know why you did it; and who will blame you? No one. If they did,

what matter? Wrong? What is wrong? It's wrong for a man to
abandon his wife for a shameless woman. It is wrong for a wife to
remain with a man who so dishonours her. You said once you
would make no compromise with things. Make none now. Be brave!
Be yourself!

LADY WINDERMERE: I am afraid of being myself. Let me think. Let
me wait! My husband may return to me. [*Sits down on sofa.*]

LORD DARLINGTON: And you would take him back! You are not what
I thought you were. You are just the same as every other woman.
You would stand anything rather than face the censure of a world,
whose praise you would despise. In a week you will be driving with
this woman in the Park. She will be your constant guest – your
dearest friend. You would endure anything rather than break with
one blow this monstrous tie. You are right. You have no courage;
none!

LADY WINDERMERE: Ah, give me time to think. I cannot answer you
now. [*Passes her hand nervously over her brow.*]

LORD DARLINGTON: It must be now or not at all.

LADY WINDERMERE [*rising from the sofa*]: Then, not at all! [*A pause.*]

LORD DARLINGTON: You break my heart!

LADY WINDERMERE: Mine is already broken. [*A pause.*]

LORD DARLINGTON: Tomorrow I leave England. This is the last time
I shall ever look on you. You will never see me again. For one
moment our lives met – our souls touched. They must never meet
or touch again. Good-bye, Margaret. [*Exit.*]

LADY WINDERMERE: How alone I am in life! How terribly alone!

[*The music stops.*[10] *Enter the* DUCHESS OF BERWICK *and* LORD PAISLEY
laughing and talking. Other guests come in from the ball-room.]

DUCHESS OF BERWICK: Dear Margaret, I've just been having such a
delightful chat with Mrs Erlynne. I am so sorry for what I said to
you this afternoon about her. Of course, she must be all right if *you*
invite her. A most attractive woman, and has such sensible views
on life. Told me she entirely disapproved of people marrying more
than once, so I feel quite safe about poor Augustus. Can't imagine
why people speak against her. It's those horrid nieces of mine –

the Saville girls – they're always talking scandal. Still, I should go to Homburg, dear, I really should. She is just a little too attractive. But where is Agatha? Oh, there she is. [LADY AGATHA *and* MR HOPPER *enter from terrace L.U.E.*] Mr Hopper, I am very, very angry with you. You have taken Agatha out on the terrace, and she is so delicate.

HOPPER [*L. C.*]: Awfully sorry, Duchess. We went out for a moment and then got chatting together.

DUCHESS OF BERWICK [*C.*]: Ah, about dear Australia, I suppose?

HOPPER: Yes!

DUCHESS OF BERWICK: Agatha, darling! [*Beckons her over.*]

LADY AGATHA: Yes, mamma!

DUCHESS OF BERWICK [*aside*]: Did Mr Hopper definitely –

LADY AGATHA: Yes, mamma.

DUCHESS OF BERWICK: And what answer did you give him, dear child?

LADY AGATHA: Yes, mamma.

DUCHESS OF BERWICK [*affectionately*]: My dear one! You always say the right thing. Mr Hopper! James! Agatha has told me everything. How cleverly you have both kept your secret.

HOPPER: You don't mind my taking Agatha off to Australia, then, Duchess?

DUCHESS OF BERWICK [*indignantly*]: To Australia? Oh, don't mention that dreadful vulgar place.

HOPPER: But she said she'd like to come with me.

DUCHESS OF BERWICK [*severely*]: Did you say that, Agatha?

LADY AGATHA: Yes, mamma.

DUCHESS OF BERWICK: Agatha, you say the most silly things possible. I think on the whole that Grosvenor Square would be a more healthy place to reside in. There are lots of vulgar people live in Grosvenor Square, but at any rate there are no horrid kangaroos crawling about. But we'll talk about that tomorrow. James, you can take Agatha down. You'll come to lunch, of course, James. At half-past one, instead of two. The Duke will wish to say a few words to you, I am sure.

HOPPER: I should like to have a chat with the Duke, Duchess. He has not said a single word to me yet.

DUCHESS OF BERWICK: I think you'll find he will have a great deal to say to you tomorrow. [*Exit* LADY AGATHA *with* MR HOPPER.] And now good night, Margaret. I'm afraid it's the old, old story, dear. Love – well, not love at first sight, but love at the end of the season, which is so much more satisfactory.

LADY WINDERMERE: Good night, Duchess.

[*Exit the* DUCHESS OF BERWICK *on* LORD PAISLEY'S *arm.*]

LADY PLYMDALE: My dear Margaret, what a handsome woman your husband has been dancing with! I should be quite jealous if I were you! Is she a great friend of yours?

LADY WINDERMERE: No!

LADY PLYMDALE: Really? Good night, dear. [*Looks at* MR DUMBY *and exit.*]

DUMBY: Awful manners young Hopper has!

CECIL GRAHAM: Ah! Hopper is one of Nature's gentlemen, the worst type of gentleman I know.

DUMBY: Sensible woman, Lady Windermere. Lots of wives would have objected to Mrs Erlynne coming. But Lady Windermere has that uncommon thing called common sense.

CECIL GRAHAM: And Windermere knows that nothing looks so like innocence as an indiscretion.

DUMBY: Yes, dear Windermere is becoming almost modern. Never thought he would. [*Bows to* LADY WINDERMERE *and exit.*]

LADY JEDBURGH: Good night, Lady Windermere. What a fascinating woman Mrs Erlynne is! She is coming to lunch on Thursday; won't you come too? I expect the Bishop and dear Lady Merton.

LADY WINDERMERE: I am afraid I am engaged, Lady Jedburgh.

LADY JEDBURGH: So sorry. Come, dear. [*Exeunt* LADY JEDBURGH *and* MISS GRAHAM.]

[*Enter* MRS ERLYNNE *and* LORD WINDERMERE.]

MRS ERLYNNE: Charming ball it has been! Quite reminds me of old days. [*Sits on sofa.*] And I see that there are just as many fools in society as there used to be. So pleased to find that nothing has altered! Except Margaret. She's grown quite pretty. The last time

I saw her – twenty years ago, she was a fright in flannel. Positive fright, I assure you.[11] The dear Duchess! and that sweet Lady Agatha! Just the type of girl I like! Well, really, Windermere, if I am to be the Duchess's sister-in-law –

LORD WINDERMERE [*sitting L. of her*]: But are you – ?

[*Exit* MR CECIL GRAHAM *with rest of guests.* LADY WINDERMERE *watches, with a look of scorn and pain,* MRS ERLYNNE *and her husband. They are unconscious of her presence.*]

MRS ERLYNNE: Oh, yes. He's to call tomorrow at twelve o'clock! He wanted to propose tonight. In fact he did. He kept on proposing. Poor Augustus, you know how he repeats himself. Such a bad habit! But I told him I wouldn't give him an answer till tomorrow. Of course I am going to take him. And I dare say I'll make him an admirable wife, as wives go. And there is a great deal of good in Lord Augustus. Fortunately it is all on the surface. Just where good qualities should be. Of course you must help me in this matter.

LORD WINDERMERE: I am not called on to encourage Lord Augustus, I suppose?

MRS ERLYNNE: Oh, no! I do the encouraging. But you will make me a handsome settlement, Windermere, won't you?

LORD WINDERMERE [*frowning*]: Is that what you want to talk to me about tonight?

MRS ERLYNNE: Yes.

LORD WINDERMERE [*with a gesture of impatience*]: I will not talk of it here.

MRS ERLYNNE [*laughing*]: Then we will talk of it on the terrace. Even business should have a picturesque background. Should it not, Windermere? With a proper background women can do anything.

LORD WINDERMERE: Won't tomorrow do as well?

MRS ERLYNNE: No; you see, tomorrow I am going to accept him. And I think it would be a good thing if I was able to tell him that I had – well, what shall I say? – £2,000 a year left me by a third cousin – or a second husband – or some distant relative of that kind. It would be an additional attraction, wouldn't it? You have a delightful opportunity of paying me a compliment, Windermere. But you are not very clever at paying compliments. I am afraid Margaret doesn't encourage you in that excellent habit. It's a great mistake on her part. When men give up saying what is charming, they give up thinking what is charming. But seriously, what do you say to £2,000? £2,500, I think. In modern life margin is everything. Windermere, don't you think the world an intensely amusing place? I do!

[*Exit on terrace with* LORD WINDERMERE. *Music strikes up in ball-room.*]

LADY WINDERMERE: To stay in this house any longer is impossible. Tonight a man who loves me offered me his whole life. I refused it. It was foolish of me. I will offer him mine now. I will give him mine. I will go to him! [*Puts on cloak and goes to the door, then turns back. Sits down at table and writes a letter, puts it into an envelope, and leaves it on table.*] Arthur has never understood me. When he reads this, he will. He may do as he chooses now with his life. I have done with mine as I think best, as I think right. It is he who has broken the bond of marriage – not I! I only break its bondage.

[*Exit.*]

[PARKER *enters L. and crosses towards the ball-room R. Enter* MRS ERLYNNE.]

MRS ERLYNNE: Is Lady Windermere in the ball-room?
PARKER: Her ladyship has just gone out.
MRS ERLYNNE: Gone out? She's not on the terrace?
PARKER: No, madam. Her ladyship has just gone out of the house.
MRS ERLYNNE [*starts, and looks at the servant with a puzzled expression on her face*]: Out of the house?
PARKER: Yes, madam – her ladyship told me she had left a letter for his lordship on the table.
MRS ERLYNNE: A letter for Lord Windermere?
PARKER: Yes, madam!
MRS ERLYNNE: Thank you.

[*Exit* PARKER. *The music in the ball-room stops.*] Gone out of her house! A letter addressed to her husband! [*Goes over to bureau and looks at letter. Takes it up and lays it down again with a shudder of fear.*] No, no!

It would be impossible! Life doesn't repeat its tragedies like that! Oh, why does this horrible fancy come across me? Why do I remember now the one moment of my life I most wish to forget? Does life repeat its tragedies? [*Tears letter open and reads it, then sinks down into a chair with a gesture of anguish.*] Oh, how terrible! The same words that twenty years ago I wrote to her father![12] and how bitterly I have been punished for it! No; my punishment, my real punishment is tonight, is now! [*Still seated R.*]

[*Enter* LORD WINDERMERE *L.U.E.*]

LORD WINDERMERE: Have you said good night to my wife? [*Comes C.*]
MRS ERLYNNE [*crushing letter in hand*]: Yes.
LORD WINDERMERE: Where is she?
MRS ERLYNNE: She is very tired. She has gone to bed. She said she had a headache.
LORD WINDERMERE: I must go to her. You'll excuse me?
MRS ERLYNNE [*rising hurriedly*]: Oh, no! It's nothing serious. She's only very tired, that is all. Besides, there are people still in the supper-room. She wants you to make her apologies to them. She said she didn't wish to be disturbed. [*Drops letter.*] She asked me to tell you!
LORD WINDERMERE [*picks up letter*]: You have dropped something.
MRS ERLYNNE: Oh, yes, thank you, that is mine. [*Puts out her hand to take it.*]
LORD WINDERMERE [*still looking at letter*]: But it's my wife's handwriting, isn't it?
MRS ERLYNNE [*takes the letter quickly*]: Yes, it's – an address. Will you ask them to call my carriage, please?[13]
LORD WINDERMERE: Certainly.

[*Goes L. and exit.*]

MRS ERLYNNE: Thanks! What can I do? What can I do? I feel a passion awakening within me that I never felt before. What can it mean? The daughter must not be like the mother – that would be terrible. How can I save her? How can I save my child? A moment may ruin a life. Who knows that better than I? Windermere must be got out of the house; that is absolutely necessary. [*Goes L.*] But how shall I do it? It must be done somehow. Ah!

[*Enter* LORD AUGUSTUS *R.U.E. carrying bouquet.*]

LORD AUGUSTUS: Dear lady, I am in such suspense! May I not have an answer to my request?

MRS ERLYNNE: Lord Augustus, listen to me. You are to take Lord Windermere down to your club at once, and keep him there as long as possible. You understand?

LORD AUGUSTUS: But you said you wished me to keep early hours!

MRS ERLYNNE [*nervously*]: Do what I tell you. Do what I tell you.

LORD AUGUSTUS: And my reward?

MRS ERLYNNE: Your reward? Your reward? Oh, ask me that tomorrow. But don't let Windermere out of your sight tonight. If you do I will never forgive you. I will never speak to you again. I'll have nothing to do with you. Remember you are to keep Windermere at your club, and don't let him come back tonight.

[*Exit L.*]

LORD AUGUSTUS: Well, really, I might be her husband already. Positively I might. [*Follows her in a bewildered manner.*]

ACT DROP

THIRD ACT

Lord Darlington's rooms.

[*A large sofa is in front of fireplace R. At the back of the stage a curtain is drawn across the window. Doors L. and R. Table R. with writing materials. Table C. with syphons, glasses and Tantalus frame. Table L. with cigar and cigarette-box. Lamps lit.*][1]

LADY WINDERMERE [*standing by the fireplace*]: Why doesn't he come? This waiting is horrible. He should be here. Why is he not here, to wake by passionate words some fire within me? I am cold – cold as a loveless thing.[2] Arthur must have read my letter by this time. If he cared for me he would have come after me, would have taken me back by force. But he doesn't care. He's entrammelled by this woman – fascinated by her – dominated by her. If a woman wants to hold a man, she has merely to appeal to what is worst in him. We make gods of men and they leave us. Others make brutes of them and they fawn and are faithful. How hideous life is! . . . Oh! it was mad of me to come here, horribly mad.[3] And yet, which is the worst, I wonder, to be at the mercy of a man who loves one, or the wife of a man who in one's own house dishonours one? What woman knows? What woman in the whole world? But will he love me always, this man to whom I am giving my life? What do I bring him? Lips that have lost the note of joy, eyes that are blinded by tears, chill hands and icy heart. I bring him nothing. I must go back – no; I can't go back, my letter has put me in their power – Arthur would not take me back! That fatal letter! No! Lord Darlington leaves England tomorrow. I will go with him – I have no choice. [*Sits down for a few moments. Then starts up and puts on her cloak.*] No, no! I will go back, let Arthur do with me what he pleases. I can't

38

wait here. It has been madness my coming. I must go at once. As for Lord Darlington – Oh, here he is! What shall I do? What can I say to him? Will he let me go away at all? I have heard that men are brutal, horrible . . . Oh! [*Hides her face in her hands.*]

[*Enter* MRS ERLYNNE *L.*]

MRS ERLYNNE: Lady Windermere! [LADY WINDERMERE *starts and looks up. Then recoils in contempt.*] Thank Heaven I am in time. You must go back to your husband's house immediately.

LADY WINDERMERE: Must?

MRS ERLYNNE [*authoritatively*]: Yes, you must! There is not a second to be lost. Lord Darlington may return at any moment.

LADY WINDERMERE: Don't come near me!

MRS ERLYNNE: Oh! You are on the brink of ruin, you are on the brink of a hideous precipice. You must leave this place at once, my carriage is waiting at the corner of the street. You must come with me and drive straight home.

[LADY WINDERMERE *throws off her cloak and flings it on the sofa.*][4]

MRS ERLYNNE: What are you doing?

LADY WINDERMERE: Mrs Erlynne – if you had not come here, I would have gone back. But now that I see you, I feel nothing in the whole world would induce me to live under the same roof as Lord Windermere. You fill me with horror. There is something about you that stirs the wildest – rage within me. And I know why you are here. My husband sent you to lure me back that I might serve as a blind to whatever relations exist between you and him.

MRS ERLYNNE: Oh! You don't think that – you can't.

LADY WINDERMERE: Go back to my husband, Mrs Erlynne. He belongs to you and not to me. I suppose he is afraid of a scandal. Men are such cowards. They outrage every law in the world, and are afraid of the world's tongue. But he had better prepare himself. He shall have a scandal. He shall have the worst scandal there has been in London for years. He shall see his name in every vile paper, mine on every hideous placard.

MRS ERLYNNE: No – no –

LADY WINDERMERE: Yes! he shall. Had he come himself, I admit I would have gone back to the life of degradation you and he had prepared for me – I was going back – but to stay himself at home, and to send you as his messenger – oh! it was infamous – infamous.

MRS ERLYNNE [*C.*]: Lady Windermere, you wrong me horribly – you wrong your husband horribly. He doesn't know you are here – he thinks you are safe in your own house. He thinks you are asleep in your own room. He never read the mad letter you wrote to him!

LADY WINDERMERE [*R.*]: Never read it!

MRS ERLYNNE: No – he knows nothing about it.

LADY WINDERMERE: How simple you think me! [*Going to her.*] You are lying to me!

MRS ERLYNNE [*restraining herself*]: I am not. I am telling you the truth.

LADY WINDERMERE: If my husband didn't read my letter, how is it that you are here? Who told you I had left the house you were shameless enough to enter? Who told you where I had gone to? My husband told you, and sent you to decoy me back. [*Crosses L.*]

MRS ERLYNNE [*R. C.*]: Your husband has never seen the letter. I – saw it, I opened it. I – read it.

LADY WINDERMERE [*turning to her*]: You opened a letter of mine to my husband? You wouldn't dare!

MRS ERLYNNE: Dare! Oh! to save you from the abyss into which you are falling, there is nothing in the world I would not dare, nothing in the whole world. Here is the letter. Your husband has never read it. He never shall read it. [*Going to fireplace.*] It should never have been written. [*Tears it and throws it into the fire.*]

LADY WINDERMERE [*with infinite contempt in her voice and look*]: How do I know that that was my letter after all? You seem to think the commonest device can take me in!

MRS ERLYNNE: Oh! why do you disbelieve everything I tell you? What object do you think I have in coming here, except to save you from utter ruin, to save you from the consequence of a hideous mistake? That letter that is burnt now *was* your letter. I swear it to you!

LADY WINDERMERE [*slowly*]: You took good care to burn it before I had examined it. I cannot trust you. You, whose whole life is a lie, how could you speak the truth about anything? [*Sits down.*]

MRS ERLYNNE [*hurriedly*]: Think as you like about me – say what you choose against me, but go back, go back to the husband you love.

LADY WINDERMERE [*sullenly*]: I do *not* love him!

MRS ERLYNNE: You do, and you know that he loves you.

LADY WINDERMERE: He does not understand what love is. He understands it as little as you do – but I see what you want. It would be a great advantage for you to get me back. Dear Heaven! what a life I would have then! Living at the mercy of a woman who has neither mercy nor pity in her, a woman whom it is an infamy to meet, a degradation to know, a vile woman, a woman who comes between husband and wife!

MRS ERLYNNE [*with a gesture of despair*]: Lady Windermere, Lady Windermere, don't say such terrible things. You don't know how terrible they are, how terrible and how unjust.[5] Listen, you must listen! Only go back to your husband, and I promise you never to communicate with him again on any pretext – never to see him – never to have anything to do with his life or yours. The money that he gave me, he gave me not through love, but through hatred, not in worship, but in contempt. The hold I have over him –

LADY WINDERMERE [*rising*]: Ah! you admit you have a hold!

MRS ERLYNNE: Yes, and I will tell you what it is. It is his love for you, Lady Windermere.

LADY WINDERMERE: You expect me to believe that?

MRS ERLYNNE: You must believe it! It is true. It is his love for you that has made him submit to – oh! call it what you like, tyranny, threats, anything you choose. But it is his love for you. His desire to spare you – shame, yes, shame and disgrace.

LADY WINDERMERE: What do you mean? You are insolent! What have I to do with you?

MRS ERLYNNE [*humbly*]: Nothing.[6] I know it – but I tell you that your husband loves you – that you may never meet with such love again in your whole life – that such love you will never meet – and that if you throw it away, the day may come when you will starve for love and it will not be given to you, beg for love and it will be denied you – Oh! Arthur loves you!

LADY WINDERMERE: Arthur? And you tell me there is nothing between you?[7]

MRS ERLYNNE: Lady Windermere, before Heaven your husband is guiltless of all offence towards you! And I – I tell you that had it ever occurred to me that such a monstrous suspicion would have entered your mind I would have died rather than have crossed your life or his – oh! died, gladly died! [*Moves away to sofa R.*]

LADY WINDERMERE: You talk as if you had a heart. Women like you have no hearts. Heart is not in you. You are bought and sold. [*Sits L. C.*]

MRS ERLYNNE [*Starts, with a gesture of pain. Then restrains herself, and comes over to where* LADY WINDERMERE *is sitting. As she speaks, she stretches out her hands towards her, but does not dare to touch her*]:[8] Believe what you choose about me. I am not worth a moment's sorrow. But don't spoil your beautiful young life on my account! You don't know what may be in store for you, unless you leave this house at once. You don't know what it is to fall into the pit, to be despised, mocked, abandoned, sneered at – to be an outcast! to find the door shut against one, to have to creep in by hideous byways, afraid every moment lest the mask should be stripped from one's face, and all the while to hear the laughter, the horrible laughter of the world, a thing more tragic than all the tears the world has ever shed. You don't know what it is. One pays for one's sin, and then one pays again, and all one's life one pays. You must never know that. – As for me, if suffering be an expiation, then at this moment I have expiated all my faults, whatever they have been; for tonight you have made a heart in one who had it not, made it and broken it. – But let that pass.[9] I may have wrecked my own life, but I will not let you wreck yours. You – why, you are a mere girl, you would be lost. You haven't got the kind of brains that enables a woman to get back. You have neither the wit nor the courage. You couldn't stand dishonour! No! Go back, Lady Windermere, to the husband who loves you, whom you love. You have a child, Lady Windermere. Go back to that child who even now, in pain or in joy, may be calling to you. [LADY WINDERMERE *rises.*] God gave you that child. He will require from you that you make his life fine, that you watch over him. What answer will you make to God if his life is ruined through you? Back to your house, Lady Windermere – your husband loves you! He has never swerved for a moment from the love he bears you. But even if he had a thousand loves, you must stay with your child. If he was harsh to you, you must stay with your child. If he ill-treated you, you must stay with your child. If he abandoned you, your place is with your child.[10]

[LADY WINDERMERE *bursts into tears and buries her face in her hands.*]

[*Rushing to her.*] Lady Windermere!

LADY WINDERMERE [*holding out her hands to her, helplessly, as a child might do*]: Take me home. Take me home.[11]

MRS ERLYNNE [*is about to embrace her. Then restrains herself. There is a look of wonderful joy in her face*]: Come! Where is your cloak? [*Getting it from sofa.*] Here. Put it on. Come at once!

[*They go to the door.*]

LADY WINDERMERE: Stop! Don't you hear voices?

MRS ERLYNNE: No, no! There is no one!

LADY WINDERMERE: Yes, there is! Listen! oh! that is my husband's voice![12] He is coming in! Save me! Oh, it's some plot! You have sent for him.

[*Voices outside.*]

MRS ERLYNNE: Silence! I'm here to save you, if I can. But I fear it is too late! There! [*Points to the curtain across the window.*] The first chance you have, slip out, if you ever get a chance!

LADY WINDERMERE: But you?

MRS ERLYNNE: Oh! never mind me. I'll face them.

[LADY WINDERMERE *hides herself behind the curtain.*]

LORD AUGUSTUS [*outside*]: Nonsense, dear Windermere, you must not leave me!

MRS ERLYNNE: Lord Augustus! Then it is I who am lost! [*Hesitates for a moment, then looks round and sees door R., and exit through it.*]

[*Enter* LORD DARLINGTON, MR DUMBY, LORD WINDERMERE, LORD AUGUSTUS LORTON *and* MR CECIL GRAHAM.]

DUMBY: What a nuisance their turning us out of the club at this hour! It's only two o'clock. [*Sinks into a chair.*] The lively part of the evening is only just beginning. [*Yawns and closes his eyes.*]

LORD WINDERMERE: It is very good of you, Lord Darlington, allowing Augustus to force our company on you, but I'm afraid I can't stay long.

LORD DARLINGTON: Really! I am so sorry! You'll take a cigar, won't you?

LORD WINDERMERE: Thanks! [*Sits down.*]

LORD AUGUSTUS [*to* LORD WINDERMERE]: My dear boy, you must not dream of going. I have a great deal to talk to you about, of demmed importance, too. [*Sits down with him at L. table.*]

CECIL GRAHAM: Oh! We all know what that is! Tuppy can't talk about anything but Mrs Erlynne.

LORD WINDERMERE: Well, that is no business of yours, is it, Cecil?

CECIL GRAHAM: None! That is why it interests me. My own business always bores me to death. I prefer other people's.

LORD DARLINGTON: Have something to drink, you fellows. Cecil, you'll have a whisky and soda?

CECIL GRAHAM: Thanks. [*Goes to table with* LORD DARLINGTON.] Mrs Erlynne looked very handsome tonight, didn't she?

LORD DARLINGTON: I am not one of her admirers.

CECIL GRAHAM: I usen't to be, but I am now. Why! she actually made me introduce her to poor dear Aunt Caroline. I believe she is going to lunch there.

LORD DARLINGTON [*in surprise*]: No?

CECIL GRAHAM: She is, really.

LORD DARLINGTON: Excuse me, you fellows. I'm going away tomorrow. And I have to write a few letters. [*Goes to writing-table and sits down.*]

DUMBY: Clever woman, Mrs Erlynne.

CECIL GRAHAM: Hallo, Dumby! I thought you were asleep.

DUMBY: I am, I usually am!

LORD AUGUSTUS: A very clever woman. Knows perfectly well what a demmed fool I am – knows it as well as I do myself.

[CECIL GRAHAM *comes towards him laughing.*]

Ah, you may laugh, my boy, but it is a great thing to come across a woman who thoroughly understands one.

DUMBY: It is an awfully dangerous thing. They always end by marrying one.

CECIL GRAHAM: But I thought, Tuppy, you were never going to see her again! Yes! you told me so yesterday evening at the club. You said you'd heard –

[*Whispering to him.*]

LORD AUGUSTUS: Oh, she's explained that.

CECIL GRAHAM: And the Wiesbaden affair?

LORD AUGUSTUS: She's explained that too.

DUMBY: And her income, Tuppy? Has she explained that?

LORD AUGUSTUS [*in a very serious voice*]: She's going to explain that tomorrow.

[CECIL GRAHAM *goes back to C. table.*]

DUMBY: Awfully commercial, women nowadays. Our grandmothers threw their caps over the mills, of course, but, by Jove, their granddaughters only throw their caps over mills that can raise the wind for them.

LORD AUGUSTUS: You want to make her out a wicked woman. She is not!

CECIL GRAHAM: Oh! Wicked women bother one. Good women bore one. That is the only difference between them.

LORD AUGUSTUS [*puffing a cigar*]: Mrs Erlynne has a future before her.

DUMBY: Mrs Erlynne has a past before her.

LORD AUGUSTUS: I prefer women with a past. They're always so demmed amusing to talk to.

CECIL GRAHAM: Well, you'll have lots of topics of conversation with *her*, Tuppy.[13] [*Rising and going to him.*]

LORD AUGUSTUS: You're getting annoying, dear boy; you're getting demmed annoying.

CECIL GRAHAM [*puts his hands on his shoulders*]: Now, Tuppy, you've lost your figure and you've lost your character. Don't lose your temper; you have only got one.

LORD AUGUSTUS: My dear boy, if I wasn't the most good-natured man in London –

CECIL GRAHAM: We'd treat you with more respect, wouldn't we, Tuppy? [*Strolls away.*]

DUMBY: The youth of the present day are quite monstrous. They have absolutely no respect for dyed hair. [LORD AUGUSTUS *looks round angrily.*]

CECIL GRAHAM: Mrs Erlynne has a very great respect for dear Tuppy.

DUMBY: Then Mrs Erlynne sets an admirable example to the rest of her sex. It is perfectly brutal the way most women nowadays behave to men who are not their husbands.

LORD WINDERMERE: Dumby, you are ridiculous, and Cecil, you let your tongue run away with you. You must leave Mrs Erlynne alone. You don't really know anything about her, and you're always talking scandal against her.

CECIL GRAHAM [*coming towards him L. C.*]: My dear Arthur, I never talk scandal. *I* only talk gossip.

LORD WINDERMERE: What is the difference between scandal and gossip?

CECIL GRAHAM: Oh! gossip is charming! History is merely gossip. But scandal is gossip made tedious by morality. Now, I never moralize. A man who moralizes is usually a hypocrite, and a woman who moralizes is invariably plain. There is nothing in the whole world so unbecoming to a woman as a Nonconformist conscience. And most women know it, I'm glad to say.

LORD AUGUSTUS: Just my sentiments, dear boy, just my sentiments.

CECIL GRAHAM: Sorry to hear it, Tuppy; whenever people agree with me, I always feel I must be wrong.

LORD AUGUSTUS: My dear boy, when I was your age –

CECIL GRAHAM: But you never were, Tuppy, and you never will be. [*Goes up C.*] I say, Darlington, let us have some cards. You'll play, Arthur, won't you?

LORD WINDERMERE: No, thanks, Cecil.

DUMBY [*with a sigh*]: Good heavens! how marriage ruins a man! It's as demoralizing as cigarettes, and far more expensive.

CECIL GRAHAM: You'll play, of course, Tuppy?

LORD AUGUSTUS [*pouring himself out a brandy and soda at table*]: Can't, dear boy. Promised Mrs Erlynne never to play or drink again.

CECIL GRAHAM: Now, my dear Tuppy, don't be led astray into the paths of virtue. Reformed, you would be perfectly tedious. That is the worst of women. They always want one to be good. And if we are good, when they meet us, they don't love us at all. They like to find us quite irretrievably bad, and to leave us quite unattractively good.

LORD DARLINGTON [*rising from R. table, where he has been writing letters*]: They always do find us bad!

DUMBY: I don't think we are bad. I think we are all good, except Tuppy.

LORD DARLINGTON: No, we are all in the gutter, but some of us are looking at the stars. [*Sits down at C. table.*]

DUMBY: We are all in the gutter, but some of us are looking at the stars? Upon my word, you are very romantic tonight, Darlington.

CECIL GRAHAM: Too romantic! You must be in love. Who is the girl?

LORD DARLINGTON: The woman I love is not free, or thinks she isn't.

[*Glances instinctively at* LORD WINDERMERE *while he speaks.*]

CECIL GRAHAM: A married woman, then! Well, there's nothing in the world like the devotion of a married woman. It's a thing no married man knows anything about.

LORD DARLINGTON: Oh! She doesn't love me. She is a good woman. She is the only good woman I have ever met in my life.

CECIL GRAHAM: The only good woman you have ever met in your life?

LORD DARLINGTON: Yes!

CECIL GRAHAM [*lighting a cigarette*]: Well, you are a lucky fellow! Why, I have met hundreds of good women. I never seem to meet any but good women. The world is perfectly packed with good women. To know them is a middle-class education.

LORD DARLINGTON: This woman has purity and innocence.[14] She has everything we men have lost.

CECIL GRAHAM: My dear fellow, what on earth should we men do going about with purity and innocence? A carefully thought-out buttonhole is much more effective.

DUMBY: She doesn't really love you then?

LORD DARLINGTON: No, she does not!

DUMBY: I congratulate you, my dear fellow. In this world there are only two tragedies. One is not getting what one wants, and the other is getting it. The last is much the worst; the last is a real tragedy! But I am interested to hear she does not love you. How long could you love a woman who didn't love you, Cecil?

CECIL GRAHAM: A woman who didn't love me? Oh, all my life!

DUMBY: So could I. But it's so difficult to meet one.

LORD DARLINGTON: How can you be so conceited, Dumby?

DUMBY: I didn't say it as a matter of conceit. I said it as a matter of regret. I have been wildly, madly adored. I am sorry I have. It has been an immense nuisance. I should like to be allowed a little time to myself now and then.

LORD AUGUSTUS [*looking round*]: Time to educate yourself, I suppose.

DUMBY: No, time to forget all I have learned. That is much more important, dear Tuppy. [LORD AUGUSTUS *moves uneasily in his chair*.]

LORD DARLINGTON: What cynics you fellows are!

CECIL GRAHAM: What is a cynic? [*Sitting on the back of the sofa*.]

LORD DARLINGTON: A man who knows the price of everything and the value of nothing.

CECIL GRAHAM: And a sentimentalist, my dear Darlington, is a man who sees an absurd value in everything, and doesn't know the market price of any single thing.

LORD DARLINGTON: You always amuse me, Cecil. You talk as if you were a man of experience.

CECIL GRAHAM: I am. [*Moves up to front of fireplace*.]

LORD DARLINGTON: You are far too young!

CECIL GRAHAM: That is a great error. Experience is a question of instinct about life. I have got it. Tuppy hasn't. Experience is the name Tuppy gives to his mistakes. That is all. [LORD AUGUSTUS *looks round indignantly*.]

DUMBY: Experience is the name everyone gives to their mistakes.

CECIL GRAHAM [*standing with his back to the fireplace*]: One shouldn't commit any. [*Sees* LADY WINDERMERE'S *fan on sofa.*]

DUMBY: Life would be very dull without them.

CECIL GRAHAM: Of course you are quite faithful to this woman you are in love with, Darlington, to this good woman?

LORD DARLINGTON: Cecil, if one really loves a woman, all other women in the world become absolutely meaningless to one. Love changes one – *I* am changed.

CECIL GRAHAM: Dear me! How very interesting! Tuppy, I want to talk to you. [LORD AUGUSTUS *takes no notice.*]

DUMBY: It's no use talking to Tuppy. You might just as well talk to a brick wall.

CECIL GRAHAM: But I like talking to a brick wall – it's the only thing in the world that never contradicts me! Tuppy!

LORD AUGUSTUS: Well, what is it? What is it? [*Rising and going over to* CECIL GRAHAM.]

CECIL GRAHAM: Come over here. I want you particularly. [*Aside.*] Darlington has been moralizing and talking about the purity of love, and that sort of thing, and he has got some woman in his rooms all the time.

LORD AUGUSTUS: No, really! really!

CECIL GRAHAM [*in a low voice*]: Yes, here is her fan. [*Points to the fan.*]

LORD AUGUSTUS [*chuckling*]: By Jove! By Jove!

LORD WINDERMERE [*up by the door*]: I am really off now, Lord Darlington. I am sorry you are leaving England so soon. Pray call on us when you come back! My wife and I will be charmed to see you!

LORD DARLINGTON [*up stage with* LORD WINDERMERE]: I am afraid I shall be away for many years. Good night!

CECIL GRAHAM: Arthur!

LORD WINDERMERE: What?

CECIL GRAHAM: I want to speak to you for a moment. No, do come!

LORD WINDERMERE [*putting on his coat*]: I can't – I'm off!

CECIL GRAHAM: It is something very particular. It will interest you enormously.

LORD WINDERMERE [*smiling*]: It is some of your nonsense, Cecil.

CECIL GRAHAM: It isn't! It isn't really.

LORD AUGUSTUS [*going to him*]: My dear fellow, you mustn't go yet. I have a lot to talk to you about. And Cecil has something to show you.

LORD WINDERMERE [*walking over*]: Well, what is it?

CECIL GRAHAM: Darlington has got a woman here in his rooms. Here is her fan. Amusing, isn't it? [*A pause.*]

LORD WINDERMERE: Good God! [*Seizes the fan* – DUMBY *rises.*]

CECIL GRAHAM: What is the matter?

LORD WINDERMERE: Lord Darlington!

LORD DARLINGTON [*turning round*]: Yes!

LORD WINDERMERE: What is my wife's fan doing here in your rooms? Hands off, Cecil. Don't touch me.

LORD DARLINGTON: Your wife's fan?

LORD WINDERMERE: Yes, here it is!

LORD DARLINGTON [*walking towards him*]: I don't know!

LORD WINDERMERE: You must know. I demand an explanation. [*To* CECIL GRAHAM.] Don't hold me, you fool.

LORD DARLINGTON [*aside*]: She is here after all!

LORD WINDERMERE: Speak, sir! Why is my wife's fan here? Answer me! By God! I'll search your rooms, and if my wife's here, I'll – [*Moves.*]

LORD DARLINGTON: You shall not search my rooms. You have no right to do so. I forbid you!

LORD WINDERMERE: You scoundrel! I'll not leave your room till I have searched every corner of it! What moves behind that curtain? [*Rushes towards the curtain C.*]

MRS ERLYNNE [*enters behind R.*]: Lord Windermere!

LORD WINDERMERE: Mrs Erlynne!

[*Everyone starts and turns round.* LADY WINDERMERE *slips out from behind the curtain and glides from the room L.*]

MRS ERLYNNE: I am afraid I took your wife's fan in mistake for my own, when I was leaving your house tonight. I am so sorry. [*Takes fan from him.* LORD WINDERMERE *looks at her in contempt.* LORD DARLINGTON *in mingled astonishment and anger.* LORD AUGUSTUS *turns away. The other men smile at each other.*][15]

ACT DROP

FOURTH ACT

LADY WINDERMERE [*lying on sofa*]: How can I tell him? I can't tell him. It would kill me. I wonder what happened after I escaped from that horrible room. Perhaps she told them the true reason of her being there, and the real meaning of that – fatal fan of mine. Oh, if he knows – how can I look him in the face again? He would never forgive me. [*Touches bell.*] How securely one thinks one lives – out of reach of temptation, sin, folly. And then suddenly – Oh! Life is terrible. It rules us, we do not rule it.[1]

[*Enter* ROSALIE *R.*]

ROSALIE: Did your ladyship ring for me?

LADY WINDERMERE: Yes. Have you found out at what time Lord Windermere came in last night?

ROSALIE: His lordship did not come in till five o'clock.

LADY WINDERMERE: Five o'clock. He knocked at my door this morning, didn't he?

ROSALIE: Yes, my lady – at half-past nine. I told him your ladyship was not awake yet.

LADY WINDERMERE: Did he say anything?

ROSALIE: Something about your ladyship's fan. I didn't quite catch what his lordship said. Has the fan been lost, my lady? I can't find it, and Parker says it was not left in any of the rooms. He has looked in all of them and on the terrace as well.

LADY WINDERMERE: It doesn't matter. Tell Parker not to trouble. That will do. [*Exit* ROSALIE.]

LADY WINDERMERE [*rising*]: She is sure to tell him. I can fancy a person doing a wonderful act of self-sacrifice, doing it spontaneously, recklessly, nobly – and afterwards finding out that it costs too much. Why should she hesitate between her ruin and mine? . . . How strange! I would have publicly disgraced her in my own house. She accepts public disgrace in the house of another to save me . . . There is a bitter irony in things, a bitter irony in the way we talk of good and bad women . . . Oh, what a lesson! and what a pity that in life we only get our lessons when they are of no use to us! For even if she doesn't tell, I must. Oh, the shame of it, the shame of it. To tell it is to live through it all again. Actions are the first tragedy in life, words are the second. Words are perhaps the worst. Words are merciless . . . Oh! [*starts as* LORD WINDERMERE *enters.*]

LORD WINDERMERE [*kisses her*]: Margaret – how pale you look!

LADY WINDERMERE: I slept very badly.

LORD WINDERMERE [*sitting on sofa with her*]: I am so sorry. I came in dreadfully late, and didn't like to wake you. You are crying, dear.

LADY WINDERMERE: Yes, I am crying, for I have something to tell you, Arthur.

LORD WINDERMERE: My dear child,[2] you are not well. You've been doing too much. Let us go away to the country. You'll be all right at Selby. The season is almost over. There is no use staying on. Poor darling! We'll go away today, if you like. [*Rises.*] We can easily catch the 3.40. I'll send a wire to Fannen. [*Crosses and sits down at table to write a telegram.*]

LADY WINDERMERE: Yes; let us go away today. No; I can't go today, Arthur. There is some one I must see before I leave town – some one who has been kind to me.

LORD WINDERMERE [*rising and leaning over sofa*]: Kind to you?

LADY WINDERMERE: Far more than that. [*Rises and goes to him.*] I will tell you, Arthur, but only love me, love me as you used to love me.

LORD WINDERMERE: Used to? You are not thinking of that wretched woman who came here last night? [*Coming round and sitting R. of her.*] You don't still imagine – no, you couldn't.

LADY WINDERMERE: I don't. I know now I was wrong and foolish.

LORD WINDERMERE: It was very good of you to receive her last night – but you are never to see her again.

LADY WINDERMERE: Why do you say that? [*A pause.*]

LORD WINDERMERE [*holding her hand*]: Margaret, I thought Mrs Erlynne was a woman more sinned against than sinning, as the phrase goes. I thought she wanted to be good, to get back into a place that she had lost by a moment's folly, to lead again a decent life. I believed what she told me – I was mistaken in her. She is bad – as bad as a woman can be.

LADY WINDERMERE: Arthur, Arthur, don't talk so bitterly about any woman. I don't think now that people can be divided into the good and the bad as though they were two separate races or creations. What are called good women may have terrible things in them, mad moods of recklessness, assertion, jealousy, sin. Bad women, as they are termed, may have in them sorrow, repentance, pity, sacrifice. And I don't think Mrs Erlynne a bad woman – I know she's not.

LORD WINDERMERE: My dear child, the woman's impossible. No matter what harm she tries to do us, you must never see her again. She is inadmissible anywhere.

LADY WINDERMERE: But I want to see her. I want her to come here.

LORD WINDERMERE: Never!

LADY WINDERMERE: She came here once as *your* guest. She must come now as *mine*. That is but fair.

LORD WINDERMERE: She should never have come here.

LADY WINDERMERE [*rising*]: It is too late, Arthur, to say that now. [*Moves away.*]

LORD WINDERMERE [*rising*]: Margaret, if you knew where Mrs Erlynne went last night, after she left this house, you would not sit in the same room with her. It was absolutely shameless, the whole thing.

LADY WINDERMERE: Arthur, I can't bear it any longer. I must tell you. Last night –

[*Enter* PARKER *with a tray on which lie* LADY WINDERMERE'S *fan and a card.*]

PARKER: Mrs Erlynne has called to return your ladyship's fan which she took away by mistake last night. Mrs Erlynne has written a message on the card.

LADY WINDERMERE: Oh, ask Mrs Erlynne to be kind enough to come up. [*Reads card.*] Say I shall be very glad to see her. [*Exit* PARKER.] She wants to see me, Arthur.

LORD WINDERMERE [*takes card and looks at it*]: Margaret, I *beg* you not to. Let me see her first, at any rate. She's a very dangerous woman. She is the most dangerous woman I know. You don't realize what you're doing.

LADY WINDERMERE: It is right that I should see her.

LORD WINDERMERE: My child, you may be on the brink of a great sorrow. Don't go to meet it. It is absolutely necessary that I should see her before you do.

LADY WINDERMERE: Why should it be necessary?

[*Enter* PARKER.]

PARKER: Mrs Erlynne.

[*Enter* MRS ERLYNNE.]

[*Exit* PARKER.]

MRS ERLYNNE: How do you do, Lady Windermere? [*To* LORD WINDERMERE.] How do you do? Do you know, Lady Windermere, I am so sorry about your fan. I can't imagine how I made such a silly mistake. Most stupid of me. And as I was driving in your direction, I thought I would take the opportunity of returning your property in person with many apologies for my carelessness, and of bidding you good-bye.

LADY WINDERMERE: Good-bye? [*Moves towards sofa with* MRS ERLYNNE[3] *and sits down beside her.*] Are you going away, then, Mrs Erlynne?

MRS ERLYNNE: Yes; I am going to live abroad again. The English climate doesn't suit me. My – heart is affected here, and that I don't like. I prefer living in the south. London is too full of fogs and – serious people,[4] Lord Windermere. Whether the fogs produce the serious people or whether the serious people produce the fogs, I don't know, but the whole thing rather gets on my nerves, and so I'm leaving this afternoon by the Club Train.[5]

LADY WINDERMERE: This afternoon? But I wanted so much to come and see you.

MRS ERLYNNE: How kind of you! But I am afraid I have to go.

LADY WINDERMERE: Shall I never see you again, Mrs Erlynne?

MRS ERLYNNE: I am afraid not. Our lives lie too far apart. But there is a little thing I would like you to do for me. I want a photograph of you, Lady Windermere – would you give me one? You don't know how gratified I should be.

LADY WINDERMERE: Oh, with pleasure. There is one on that table. I'll show it to you. [*Goes across to the table.*]

LORD WINDERMERE [*coming up to* MRS ERLYNNE *and speaking in a low voice*]: It is monstrous your intruding yourself here after your conduct last night.

MRS ERLYNNE [*with an amused smile*]: My dear Windermere, manners before morals!⁶

LADY WINDERMERE [*returning*]: I'm afraid it is very flattering – I am not so pretty as that. [*Showing photograph.*]

MRS ERLYNNE: You are much prettier. But haven't you got one of yourself with your little boy?

LADY WINDERMERE: I have. Would you prefer one of those?

MRS ERLYNNE: Yes.

LADY WINDERMERE: I'll go and get it for you, if you'll excuse me for a moment. I have one upstairs.

MRS ERLYNNE: So sorry, Lady Windermere, to give you so much trouble.

LADY WINDERMERE [*moves to door R.*]: No trouble at all, Mrs Erlynne.

MRS ERLYNNE: Thanks so much.

[*Exit* LADY WINDERMERE *R.*]

You seem rather out of temper this morning, Windermere. Why should you be? Margaret and I get on charmingly together.

LORD WINDERMERE: I can't bear to see you with her. Besides, you have not told me the truth, Mrs Erlynne.

MRS ERLYNNE: I have not told her the truth, you mean.

LORD WINDERMERE [*standing C.*]: I sometimes wish you had. I should have been spared then the misery, the anxiety, the annoyance of the last six months. But rather than my wife should know – that the mother whom she was taught to consider as dead, the mother whom she has mourned as dead, is living[7] – a divorced woman, going about under an assumed name, a bad woman preying upon life, as I know you now to be – rather than that, I was ready to supply you with money to pay bill after bill, extravagance after extravagance, to risk what occurred yesterday, the first quarrel I have ever had with my wife. You don't understand what that means to me. How could you? But I tell you that the only bitter words that ever came from those sweet lips of hers were on your account, and I hate to see you next her. You sully the innocence that is in her. [*Moves L. C.*] And then I used to think that with all your faults you were frank and honest. You are not.

MRS ERLYNNE: Why do you say that?

LORD WINDERMERE: You made me get you an invitation to my wife's ball.

MRS ERLYNNE: For my daughter's ball – yes.

LORD WINDERMERE: You came, and within an hour of your leaving the house you are found in a man's rooms – you are disgraced before everyone. [*Goes up stage C.*]

MRS ERLYNNE: Yes.

LORD WINDERMERE [*turning round on her*]: Therefore I have a right to look upon you as what you are – a worthless, vicious woman. I have the right to tell you never to enter this house again, never to attempt to come near my wife –

MRS ERLYNNE [*coldly*]: My daughter, you mean.

LORD WINDERMERE: You have no right to claim her as your daughter. You left her, abandoned her when she was but a child in the cradle, abandoned her for your lover, who abandoned you in turn.

MRS ERLYNNE [*rising*]: Do you count that to his credit, Lord Windermere – or to mine?

LORD WINDERMERE: To his, now that I know you.

MRS ERLYNNE: Take care – you had better be careful.

LORD WINDERMERE: Oh, I am not going to mince words for you. I know you thoroughly.

MRS ERLYNNE [*looking steadily at him*]:[8] I question that.

LORD WINDERMERE: I *do* know you. For twenty years of your life you lived without your child, without a thought of your child. One day you read in the papers that she had married a rich man. You saw your hideous chance. You knew that to spare her the ignominy of learning that a woman like you was her mother, I would endure anything. You began your blackmailing.

MRS ERLYNNE [*shrugging her shoulders*]: Don't use ugly words, Windermere. They are vulgar. I saw my chance, it is true, and took it.

LORD WINDERMERE: Yes, you took it – and spoiled it all last night by being found out.

MRS ERLYNNE [*with a strange smile*]: You are quite right, I spoiled it all last night.

LORD WINDERMERE: And as for your blunder in taking my wife's fan from here and then leaving it about in Darlington's rooms, it is unpardonable. I can't bear the sight of it now. I shall never let my wife use it again. The thing is soiled for me. You should have kept it and not brought it back.

MRS ERLYNNE: I think I *shall* keep it. [*Goes up.*] It's extremely pretty. [*Takes up fan.*] I shall ask Margaret to give it to me.

LORD WINDERMERE: I hope my wife will give it to you.

MRS ERLYNNE: Oh, I'm sure she will have no objection.

LORD WINDERMERE: I wish that at the same time she would give you a miniature she kisses every night before she prays – It's a miniature of a young innocent-looking girl with beautiful *dark* hair.

MRS ERLYNNE: Ah, yes, I remember. How long ago that seems. [*Goes to a sofa and sits down.*] It was done before I was married. Dark hair and an innocent expression were the fashion then,[9] Windermere!

[*A pause.*]

LORD WINDERMERE: What do you mean by coming here this morning? What is your object? [*Crossing L. C. and sitting.*]

MRS ERLYNNE [*with a note of irony in her voice*]: To bid good-bye to my dear daughter, of course. [LORD WINDERMERE *bites his underlip in anger.* MRS ERLYNNE *looks at him, and her voice and manner become serious. In her accents as she talks there is a note of deep tragedy. For a moment she reveals herself.*] Oh, don't imagine I am going to have a pathetic scene with her, weep on her neck and tell her who I am, and all that kind of thing. I have no ambition to play the part of a mother. Only once in my life have I known a mother's feelings. That was last night. They were terrible – they made me suffer – they made me suffer too much. For twenty years, as you say, I have lived childless – I want to live childless still. [*Hiding her feelings with a trivial laugh.*] Besides, my dear Windermere, how on earth could I pose as a mother with a grown-up daughter? Margaret is twenty-one, and I have never admitted that I am more than twenty-nine, or thirty at the most. Twenty-nine when there are pink shades, thirty when there are not. So you see what difficulties it would involve. No, as far as I am concerned, let your wife cherish the memory of this dead, stainless mother. Why should I interfere with her illusions? I find it hard enough to keep my own. I lost one illusion last night. I thought I had no heart. I find I have, and a heart doesn't suit me, Windermere. Somehow it doesn't go with modern dress. It makes one look old. [*Takes up a hand-mirror from table and looks into it.*] And it spoils one's career at critical moments.

LORD WINDERMERE: You fill me with horror – with absolute horror.

MRS ERLYNNE [*rising*]: I suppose, Windermere, you would like me to retire into a convent, or become a hospital nurse, or something of that kind, as people do in silly modern novels.[10] That is stupid of you, Arthur; in real life we don't do such things – not so long as we have any good looks left, at any rate.[11] No – what consoles one nowadays is not repentance, but pleasure. Repentance is quite out of date. And besides, if a woman really repents, she has to go to a bad dressmaker, otherwise no one believes in her. And nothing in the world would induce me to do that. No; I am going to pass entirely out of your two lives. My coming into them has been a mistake – I discovered that last night.

LORD WINDERMERE: A fatal mistake.

MRS ERLYNNE [*smiling*]: Almost fatal.

LORD WINDERMERE: I am sorry now I did not tell my wife the whole thing at once.

MRS ERLYNNE: I regret my bad actions. You regret your good ones – that is the difference between us.

LORD WINDERMERE: I don't trust you. I *will* tell my wife. It's better for her to know, and from me. It will cause her infinite pain – it will humiliate her terribly, but it's right that she should know.

MRS ERLYNNE: You propose to tell her?

LORD WINDERMERE: I am going to tell her.

MRS ERLYNNE [*going up to him*]: If you do, I will make my name so infamous that it will mar every moment of her life. It will ruin her, and make her wretched. If you dare to tell her, there is no depth of degradation I will not sink to, no pit of shame I will not enter.[12] You shall not tell her – I forbid you.

LORD WINDERMERE: Why?

MRS ERLYNNE [*after a pause*]: If I said to you that I cared for her, perhaps loved her even – you would sneer at me, wouldn't you?

LORD WINDERMERE: I should feel it was not true. A mother's love means devotion, unselfishness, sacrifice. What could you know of such things?

MRS ERLYNNE: You are right. What could I know of such things? Don't let us talk any more about it – as for telling my daughter who I am, that I do not allow. It is my secret, it is not yours. If I make up my mind to tell her, and I think I will, I shall tell her before I leave the house – if not, I shall never tell her.

LORD WINDERMERE [*angrily*]: Then let me beg of you to leave our house at once. I will make your excuses to Margaret.

[*Enter* LADY WINDERMERE *R. She goes over to* MRS ERLYNNE *with the photograph in her hand.* LORD WINDERMERE *moves to back of sofa, and anxiously watches* MRS ERLYNNE *as the scene progresses.*]

LADY WINDERMERE: I am so sorry, Mrs Erlynne, to have kept you waiting. I couldn't find the photograph anywhere. At last I discovered it in my husband's dressing-room – he had stolen it.

MRS ERLYNNE [*takes the photograph from her and looks at it*]: I am not surprised – it is charming. [*Goes over to sofa with* LADY WINDERMERE, *and sits down beside her. Looks again at the photograph.*] And so that is your little boy! What is he called?

LADY WINDERMERE: Gerard, after my dear father.

MRS ERLYNNE [*laying the photograph down*]: Really?

LADY WINDERMERE: Yes. If it had been a girl, I would have called it after my mother. My mother had the same name as myself, Margaret.

MRS ERLYNNE: My name is Margaret too.

LADY WINDERMERE: Indeed!

MRS ERLYNNE: Yes. [*Pause.*] You are devoted to your mother's memory, Lady Windermere, your husband tells me.

LADY WINDERMERE: We all have ideals in life. At least we all should have. Mine is my mother.

MRS ERLYNNE: Ideals are dangerous things. Realities are better. They wound, but they're better.

LADY WINDERMERE [*shaking her head*]: If I lost my ideals, I should lose everything.[13]

MRS ERLYNNE: Everything?

LADY WINDERMERE: Yes. [*Pause.*]

MRS ERLYNNE: Did your father often speak to you of your mother?

LADY WINDERMERE: No, it gave him too much pain. He told me how my mother had died a few months after I was born. His eyes filled with tears as he spoke. Then he begged me never to mention her name to him again. It made him suffer even to hear it. My father – my father really died of a broken heart. His was the most ruined life I know.

MRS ERLYNNE [*rising*]: I am afraid I must go now, Lady Windermere.

LADY WINDERMERE [*rising*]: Oh no, don't.

MRS ERLYNNE: I think I had better. My carriage must have come back by this time. I sent it to Lady Jedburgh's with a note.

LADY WINDERMERE: Arthur, would you mind seeing if Mrs Erlynne's carriage has come back?

MRS ERLYNNE: Pray don't trouble, Lord Windermere.

LADY WINDERMERE: Yes, Arthur, do go, please.

[LORD WINDERMERE *hesitates for a moment and looks at* MRS ERLYNNE. *She remains quite impassive. He leaves the room.*][14]

[*To* MRS ERLYNNE]: Oh! What am I to say to you? You saved me last night. [*Goes towards her.*]

MRS ERLYNNE: Hush – don't speak of it.

LADY WINDERMERE: I must speak of it. I can't let you think that I am going to accept this sacrifice. I am not. It is too great. I am going to tell my husband everything. It is my duty.

MRS ERLYNNE: It is not your duty – at least you have duties to others besides him. You say you owe me something?

LADY WINDERMERE: I owe you everything.

MRS ERLYNNE: Then pay your debt by silence. That is the only way in which it can be paid. Don't spoil the one good thing I have done in my life by telling it to anyone. Promise me that what passed last night will remain a secret between us. You must not bring misery into your husband's life. Why spoil his love? You must not spoil it. Love is easily killed. Oh! how easily love is killed. Pledge me your word, Lady Windermere, that you will *never* tell him. I insist upon it.

LADY WINDERMERE [*with bowed head*]: It is your will, not mine.

MRS ERLYNNE: Yes, it is my will. And never forget your child – I like to think of you as a mother. I like you to think of yourself as one.

LADY WINDERMERE [*looking up*]: I always will now. Only once in my life I have forgotten my own mother – that was last night. Oh, if I had remembered her I should not have been so foolish, so wicked.

MRS ERLYNNE [*with a slight shudder*]: Hush, last night is quite over.

[*Enter* LORD WINDERMERE.]

LORD WINDERMERE: Your carriage has not come back yet, Mrs Erlynne.

MRS ERLYNNE: It makes no matter. I'll take a hansom. There is nothing in the world so respectable as a good Shrewsbury and Talbot.[15] And now, dear Lady Windermere, I am afraid it is really good-bye. [*Moves up C.*] Oh, I remember. You'll think me absurd, but do you know I've taken a great fancy to this fan that I was silly enough to run away with last night from your ball. Now, I wonder would you give it to me? Lord Windermere says you may. I know it is his present.

LADY WINDERMERE: Oh, certainly, if it will give you any pleasure. But it has my name on it. It has 'Margaret' on it.

MRS ERLYNNE: But we have the same Christian name.

LADY WINDERMERE: Oh, I forgot. Of course, do have it. What a wonderful chance our names being the same!

MRS ERLYNNE: Quite wonderful. Thanks – it will always remind me of you. [*Shakes hands with her.*]

[*Enter* PARKER.]

PARKER: Lord Augustus Lorton. Mrs Erlynne's carriage has come.

[*Enter* LORD AUGUSTUS.]

LORD AUGUSTUS: Good morning, dear boy. Good morning, Lady Windermere. [*Sees* MRS ERLYNNE.] Mrs Erlynne!

MRS ERLYNNE: How do you do, Lord Augustus? Are you quite well this morning?

LORD AUGUSTUS [*coldly*]: Quite well, thank you, Mrs Erlynne.

MRS ERLYNNE: You don't look at all well, Lord Augustus. You stop up too late – it is so bad for you. You really should take more care of yourself. Good-bye, Lord Windermere. [*Goes towards door with a bow to* LORD AUGUSTUS. *Suddenly smiles and looks back at him.*] Lord Augustus! Won't you see me to my carriage? You might carry the fan.

LORD WINDERMERE: Allow me!

MRS ERLYNNE: No; I want Lord Augustus. I have a special message for the dear Duchess. Won't you carry the fan, Lord Augustus?

LORD AUGUSTUS: If you really desire it, Mrs Erlynne.

MRS ERLYNNE [*laughing*]: Of course I do. You'll carry it so gracefully. You would carry off anything gracefully, dear Lord Augustus.

[*When she reaches the door she looks back for a moment at* LADY WINDERMERE. *Their eyes meet. Then she turns, and exit C. followed by* LORD AUGUSTUS.]

LADY WINDERMERE: You will never speak against Mrs Erlynne again, Arthur, will you?

LORD WINDERMERE [*gravely*]: She is better than one thought her.

LADY WINDERMERE: She is better than I am.

LORD WINDERMERE [*smiling as he strokes her hair*]: Child, you and she belong to different worlds. Into your world evil has never entered.

LADY WINDERMERE: Don't say that, Arthur. There is the same world for all of us, and good and evil, sin and innocence, go through it hand in hand. To shut one's eyes to half of life that one may live securely is as though one blinded oneself that one might walk with more safety in a land of pit and precipice.

LORD WINDERMERE [*moves down with her*]: Darling, why do you say that?

LADY WINDERMERE [*sits on sofa*]: Because I, who had shut my eyes to life, came to the brink. And one who had separated us –

LORD WINDERMERE: We were never separated.

LADY WINDERMERE: We never must be again. O Arthur, don't love me less, and I will trust you more. I will trust you absolutely. Let us go to Selby. In the Rose Garden at Selby the roses are white and red.

[*Enter* LORD AUGUSTUS[16] *C.*]

LORD AUGUSTUS: Arthur, she has explained everything. [LADY WINDERMERE *looks horribly frightened at this.* LORD WINDERMERE *starts.* LORD AUGUSTUS *takes* WINDERMERE *by the arm and brings him in front of stage. He talks rapidly and in a low voice.* LADY WINDERMERE *stands watching them in terror.*] My dear fellow, she has explained every demmed thing. We all wronged her immensely. It was entirely for my sake she went to Darlington's rooms. Called first at the Club – fact is, wanted to put me out of suspense – and being told I had gone on – followed – naturally frightened when she heard a lot of us coming in – retired to another room – I assure you, most gratifying to me, the whole thing. We all behaved brutally to her. She is just the woman for me. Suits me down to the ground. All the conditions she makes are that we live entirely out of England. A very good thing too. Demmed clubs, demmed climate, demmed cooks, demmed everything. Sick of it all!

LADY WINDERMERE [*frightened*]: Has Mrs Erlynne –?

LORD AUGUSTUS [*advancing towards her with a low bow*]: Yes, Lady Windermere – Mrs Erlynne has done me the honour of accepting my hand.

LORD WINDERMERE: Well, you are certainly marrying a very clever woman!

LADY WINDERMERE [*taking her husband's hand*]: Ah, you're marrying a very good woman![17]

CURTAIN

Salomé

A TRAGEDY IN ONE ACT

The Persons of the Play

HEROD ANTIPAS, *Tetrarch of Judaea*
JOKANAAN, *The Prophet*
THE YOUNG SYRIAN, *Captain of the Guard*
TIGELLINUS, *A Young Roman*
A CAPPADOCIAN
A NUBIAN
FIRST SOLDIER
SECOND SOLDIER
THE PAGE OF HERODIAS
JEWS, NAZARENES, ETC.
A SLAVE
NAAMAN, *The Executioner*
HERODIAS, *Wife of the Tetrarch*
SALOMÉ, *Daughter of Herodias*
THE SLAVES OF SALOMÉ

SCENE

A great terrace in the Palace of Herod, set above the banqueting-hall.
Some soldiers are leaning over the balcony. To the right there is a gigantic
staircase, to the left, at the back, an old cistern surrounded by a wall of
green bronze. Moonlight.[1]

THE YOUNG SYRIAN: How beautiful is the Princess Salomé tonight!

THE PAGE OF HERODIAS: Look at the moon![2] How strange the moon
  seems! She is like a woman rising from a tomb. She is like a dead
  woman. You would fancy she was looking for dead things.

THE YOUNG SYRIAN: She has a strange look. She is like a little princess
  who wears a yellow veil, and whose feet are of silver. She is like a
  princess who has little white doves for feet. You would fancy she
  was dancing.

THE PAGE OF HERODIAS: She is like a woman who is dead. She moves
  very slowly.

[*Noise in the banqueting-hall.*]

FIRST SOLDIER: What an uproar! Who are those wild beasts howling?

SECOND SOLDIER: The Jews. They are always like that. They are
  disputing about their religion.

FIRST SOLDIER: Why do they dispute about their religion?

SECOND SOLDIER: I cannot tell. They are always doing it. The Pharisees,
  for instance, say that there are angels, and the Sadducees declare
  that angels do not exist.

FIRST SOLDIER: I think it is ridiculous to dispute about such things.

THE YOUNG SYRIAN: How beautiful is the Princess Salomé tonight!

THE PAGE OF HERODIAS: You are always looking at her. You look at
  her too much.[3] It is dangerous to look at people in such fashion.
  Something terrible may happen.

THE YOUNG SYRIAN: She is very beautiful tonight.

FIRST SOLDIER: The Tetrarch[4] has a sombre look.

SECOND SOLDIER: Yes; he has a sombre look.

FIRST SOLDIER: He is looking at something.

SECOND SOLDIER: He is looking at someone.

FIRST SOLDIER: At whom is he looking?

SECOND SOLDIER: I cannot tell.

THE YOUNG SYRIAN: How pale the Princess is! Never have I seen her so pale. She is like the shadow of a white rose in a mirror of silver.

THE PAGE OF HERODIAS: You must not look at her. You look too much at her.

FIRST SOLDIER: Herodias has filled the cup of the Tetrarch.

THE CAPPADOCIAN: Is that the Queen Herodias, she who wears a black mitre sewn with pearls, and whose hair is powdered with blue dust?

FIRST SOLDIER: Yes, that is Herodias, the Tetrarch's wife.

SECOND SOLDIER: The Tetrarch is very fond of wine. He has wine[5] of three sorts. One which is brought from the island of Samothrace, and is purple like the cloak of Caesar.

THE CAPPADOCIAN: I have never seen Caesar.

SECOND SOLDIER: Another that comes from a town called Cyprus, and is yellow like gold.

THE CAPPADOCIAN: I love gold.

SECOND SOLDIER: And the third is a wine of Sicily. That wine is red like blood.

THE NUBIAN: The gods of my country[6] are very fond of blood. Twice in the year we sacrifice to them young men and maidens; fifty young men and a hundred maidens. But it seems we never give them quite enough, for they are very harsh to us.

THE CAPPADOCIAN: In my country[7] there are no gods left. The Romans have driven them out. There are some who say that they have hidden themselves in the mountains, but I do not believe it. Three nights I have been on the mountains seeking them everywhere. I did not find them. And at last I called them by their names, and they did not come. I think they are dead.

FIRST SOLDIER: The Jews worship a God that you cannot see.

THE CAPPADOCIAN: I cannot understand that.

FIRST SOLDIER: In fact, they only believe in things that you cannot see.

THE CAPPADOCIAN: That seems to me altogether ridiculous.

THE VOICE OF JOKANAAN: After me shall come another mightier than I. I am not worthy so much as to unloose the latchet[8] of his shoes. When he cometh, the solitary places shall be glad. They shall blossom like the lily. The eyes of the blind shall see the day, and the ears of the deaf shall be opened. The new-born child shall put his hand upon the dragon's lair, he shall lead the lions by their manes.

SECOND SOLDIER: Make him be silent. He is always saying ridiculous things.

FIRST SOLDIER: No, no. He is a holy man. He is very gentle, too. Every day, when I give him to eat he thanks me.

THE CAPPADOCIAN: Who is he?

FIRST SOLDIER: A prophet.

THE CAPPADOCIAN: What is his name?

FIRST SOLDIER: Jokanaan.

THE CAPPADOCIAN: Whence comes he?

FIRST SOLDIER: From the desert, where he fed on locusts and wild honey. He was clothed in camel's hair, and round his loins he had a leathern belt. He was very terrible to look upon. A great multitude used to follow him. He even had disciples.

THE CAPPADOCIAN: What is he talking of?

FIRST SOLDIER: We can never tell. Sometimes he says terrible things, but it is impossible to understand what he says.

THE CAPPADOCIAN: May one see him?

FIRST SOLDIER: No. The Tetrarch has forbidden it.

THE YOUNG SYRIAN: The Princess has hidden her face behind her fan! Her little white hands are fluttering like doves that fly to their dove-cots. They are like white butterflies. They are just like white butterflies.

THE PAGE OF HERODIAS: What is that to you? Why do you look at her? You must not look at her . . . Something terrible may happen.

THE CAPPADOCIAN [*pointing to the cistern*]: What a strange prison!

SECOND SOLDIER: It is an old cistern.

THE CAPPADOCIAN: An old cistern! It must be very unhealthy.

SECOND SOLDIER: Oh no! For instance, the Tetrarch's brother, the elder brother, the first husband of Herodias the Queen, was imprisoned there for twelve years. It did not kill him. At the end of the twelve years he had to be strangled.

THE CAPPADOCIAN: Strangled? Who dared to do that?

SECOND SOLDIER [*pointing to the* EXECUTIONER, *a huge Negro*]: That man yonder, Naaman.

THE CAPPADOCIAN: He was not afraid?

SECOND SOLDIER: Oh no! The Tetrarch sent him the ring.

THE CAPPADOCIAN: What ring?

SECOND SOLDIER: The death-ring. So he was not afraid.

THE CAPPADOCIAN: Yet it is a terrible thing to strangle a king.

FIRST SOLDIER: Why? Kings have but one neck, like other folk.

THE CAPPADOCIAN: I think it terrible.

THE YOUNG SYRIAN: The Princess rises! She is leaving the table! She looks very troubled. Ah, she is coming this way. Yes, she is coming towards us. How pale she is! Never have I seen her so pale.

THE PAGE OF HERODIAS: Do not look at her. I pray you not to look at her.

THE YOUNG SYRIAN: She is like a dove that has strayed . . . She is like a narcissus trembling in the wind . . . She is like a silver flower.

[*Enter* SALOMÉ.]

SALOMÉ: I will not stay. I cannot stay. Why does the Tetrarch look at me all the while with his mole's eyes under his shaking eyelids? It is strange that the husband of my mother looks at me like that. I know not what it means. In truth, yes, I know it.

THE YOUNG SYRIAN: You have just left the feast, Princess?

SALOMÉ: How sweet the air is here! I can breathe here! Within there are Jews from Jerusalem who are tearing each other in pieces over their foolish ceremonies, and barbarians who drink and drink, and spill their wine on the pavement, and Greeks from Smyrna[9] with painted eyes and painted cheeks, and frizzed hair curled in twisted coils, and silent, subtle Egyptians, with long nails of jade and russet cloaks, and Romans brutal and coarse, with their uncouth jargon. Ah! how I loathe the Romans! They are rough and common, and they give themselves the airs of noble lords.[10]

THE YOUNG SYRIAN: Will you be seated, Princess?

THE PAGE OF HERODIAS: Why do you speak to her? Why do you look at her? Oh! something terrible will happen.

SALOMÉ: How good to see the moon! She is like a little piece of money, you would think she was a little silver flower. The moon is cold and chaste. I am sure she is a virgin, she has a virgin's beauty. Yes, she is a virgin. She has never defiled herself. She has never abandoned herself to men, like the other goddesses.

THE VOICE OF JOKANAAN: The Lord hath come. The son of man hath come. The centaurs have hidden themselves in the rivers, and the sirens[11] have left the rivers, and are lying beneath the leaves of the forest.

SALOMÉ: Who was that who cried out?

SECOND SOLDIER: The prophet, Princess.

SALOMÉ: Ah, the prophet! He of whom the Tetrarch is afraid?

SECOND SOLDIER: We know nothing of that, Princess. It was the prophet Jokanaan who cried out.

THE YOUNG SYRIAN: Is it your pleasure that I bid them bring your litter, Princess? The night is fair in the garden.

SALOMÉ: He says terrible things about my mother, does he not?

SECOND SOLDIER: We never understand what he says, Princess.

SALOMÉ: Yes; he says terrible things about her.

[*Enter a* SLAVE.]

THE SLAVE: Princess, the Tetrarch prays you to return to the feast.

SALOMÉ: I will not go back.

THE YOUNG SYRIAN: Pardon me, Princess, but if you do not return some misfortune may happen.

SALOMÉ: Is he an old man, this prophet?

THE YOUNG SYRIAN: Princess, it were better to return. Suffer me to lead you in.

SALOMÉ: This prophet . . . is he an old man?

FIRST SOLDIER: No, Princess, he is quite a young man.

SECOND SOLDIER: You cannot be sure. There are those who say he is Elias.[12]

SALOMÉ: Who is Elias?

SECOND SOLDIER: A very ancient prophet of this country, Princess.

THE SLAVE: What answer may I give the Tetrarch from the Princess?

THE VOICE OF JOKANAAN: Rejoice not thou, land of Palestine, because the rod of him who smote thee is broken. For from the seed of the serpent shall come forth a basilisk,[13] and that which is born of it shall devour the birds.

SALOMÉ: What a strange voice! I would speak with him.

FIRST SOLDIER: I fear it is impossible, Princess. The Tetrarch does not wish anyone to speak with him. He has even forbidden the high priest to speak with him.

SALOMÉ: I desire to speak with him.

FIRST SOLDIER: It is impossible, Princess.

SALOMÉ: I will speak with him.

THE YOUNG SYRIAN: Would it not be better to return to the banquet?

SALOMÉ: Bring forth this prophet.

[*Exit the* SLAVE.]

FIRST SOLDIER: We dare not, Princess.

SALOMÉ [*approaching the cistern and looking down into it*]: How black it is, down there! It must be terrible to be in so black a pit! It is like a tomb . . . [*To the* SOLDIERS.] Did you not hear me? Bring out the prophet. I wish to see him.

SECOND SOLDIER: Princess, I beg you do not require this of us.

SALOMÉ: You keep me waiting!

FIRST SOLDIER: Princess, our lives belong to you, but we cannot do what you have asked of us. And indeed, it is not of us that you should ask this thing.

SALOMÉ [*looking at the* YOUNG SYRIAN]: Ah!

THE PAGE OF HERODIAS: Oh! what is going to happen? I am sure that some misfortune will happen.

SALOMÉ [*going up to the* YOUNG SYRIAN]: You will do this thing for me, will you not, Narraboth? You will do this thing for me. I have always been kind to you. You will do it for me. I would but look at this strange prophet. Men have talked so much of him. Often have I heard the Tetrarch talk of him. I think the Tetrarch is afraid of him. Are you, even you, also afraid of him, Narraboth?

THE YOUNG SYRIAN: I fear him not, Princess; there is no man I fear. But the Tetrarch has formally forbidden that any man should raise the cover of this well.

SALOMÉ: You will do this thing for me, Narraboth, and tomorrow when I pass in my litter beneath the gateway of the idol-sellers I will let fall for you a little flower, a little green flower.

THE YOUNG SYRIAN: Princess, I cannot, I cannot.

SALOMÉ [*smiling*]: You will do this thing for me, Narraboth. You know that you will do this thing for me. And tomorrow when I pass in my litter by the bridge of the idol-buyers, I will look at you through the muslin veils, I will look at you, Narraboth, it may be I will smile at you. Look at me, Narraboth, look at me. Ah! you know that you will do what I ask of you. You know it well ... I know that you will do this thing.

THE YOUNG SYRIAN [*signing to the* THIRD SOLDIER]: Let the prophet come forth ... The Princess Salomé desires to see him.

SALOMÉ: Ah!

THE PAGE OF HERODIAS: Oh! How strange the moon looks. You would think it was the hand of a dead woman who is seeking to cover herself with a shroud.

THE YOUNG SYRIAN: She has a strange look! She is like a little princess, whose eyes are eyes of amber. Through the clouds of muslin she is smiling like a little princess.

[*The* PROPHET *comes out of the cistern.* SALOMÉ *looks at him and steps slowly back.*]

JOKANAAN: Where is he whose cup of abominations is now full? Where is he, who in a robe of silver shall one day die in the face of all the people? Bid him come forth, that he may hear the voice of him who hath cried in the waste places and in the houses of kings.

SALOMÉ: Of whom is he speaking?

THE YOUNG SYRIAN: You can never tell, Princess.

JOKANAAN: Where is she who having seen the images of men painted on the walls, the images of the Chaldeans limned in colours, gave herself up unto the lust of her eyes, and sent ambassadors into Chaldea?[14]

SALOMÉ: It is of my mother that he speaks.

THE YOUNG SYRIAN: Oh, no, Princess.

SALOMÉ: Yes; it is of my mother that he speaks.

JOKANAAN: Where is she who gave herself unto the Captains of Assyria,[15] who have baldricks[16] on their loins, and tiaras of divers colours on their heads? Where is she who hath given herself to the young men of Egypt, who are clothed in fine linen and purple, whose shields are of gold, whose helmets are of silver, whose bodies are mighty? Bid her rise up from the bed of her abominations, from the bed of her incestuousness, that she may hear the words of him who prepareth the way of the Lord, that she may repent her of her iniquities. Though she will never repent, but will stick fast in her abominations; bid her come, for the fan of the Lord is in his hand.[17]

SALOMÉ: But he is terrible, he is terrible!

THE YOUNG SYRIAN: Do not stay here, Princess, I beseech you.

SALOMÉ: It is his eyes above all that are terrible. They are like black holes burned by torches in a Tyrian[18] tapestry. They are like black caverns where dragons dwell. They are like the black caverns of Egypt in which the dragons make their lairs. They are like black lakes troubled by fantastic moons . . . Do you think he will speak again?

THE YOUNG SYRIAN: Do not stay here, Princess. I pray you do not stay here.

SALOMÉ: How wasted he is! He is like a thin ivory statue. He is like an image of silver. I am sure he is chaste as the moon is. He is like a moonbeam, like a shaft of silver. His flesh must be cool like ivory. I would look closer at him.

THE YOUNG SYRIAN: No, no, Princess.

SALOMÉ: I must look at him closer.

THE YOUNG SYRIAN: Princess! Princess!

JOKANAAN: Who is this woman who is looking at me? I will not have her look at me. Wherefore doth she look at me with her golden eyes, under her gilded eyelids? I know not who she is. I do not wish to know who she is. Bid her begone. It is not to her that I would speak.

SALOMÉ: I am Salomé, daughter of Herodias, Princess of Judaea.

JOKANAAN: Back! Daughter of Babylon![19] Come not near the chosen of the Lord. Thy mother hath filled the earth with the wine of her iniquities, and the cry of her sins hath come up to the ears of God.

SALOMÉ: Speak again, Jokanaan. Thy voice is wine to me.

THE YOUNG SYRIAN: Princess! Princess! Princess!

SALOMÉ: Speak again! Speak again, Jokanaan, and tell me what I must do.

JOKANAAN: Daughter of Sodom,[20] come not near me! But cover thy face with a veil, and scatter ashes upon thine head, and get thee to the desert and seek out the son of man.

SALOMÉ: Who is he, the son of man? Is he as beautiful as thou art, Jokanaan?

JOKANAAN: Get thee behind me! I hear in the palace the beatings of the wings of the angel of death.

THE YOUNG SYRIAN: Princess, I beseech thee to go within.

JOKANAAN: Angel of the Lord God, what dost thou here with thy sword? Whom seekest thou in this foul palace? The day of him who shall die in a robe of silver has not yet come.

SALOMÉ: Jokanaan!

JOKANAAN: Who speaketh?

SALOMÉ: Jokanaan, I am amorous of thy body! Thy body is white like the lilies of a field that the mower hath never mowed. Thy body is white like the snows that lie on the mountains, like the snows that lie on the mountains of Judaea, and come down into the valleys. The roses in the garden of the Queen of Arabia are not so white as thy body. Neither the roses in the garden of the Queen of Arabia, the perfumed garden of spices of the Queen of Arabia, nor the feet of the dawn when they light on the leaves, nor the breast of the moon when she lies on the breast of the sea . . . There is nothing in the world so white as thy body. Let me touch thy body.

JOKANAAN: Back! Daughter of Babylon! By woman came evil into the world.[21] Speak not to me. I will not listen to thee. I listen but to the voice of the Lord God.

SALOMÉ: Thy body is hideous. It is like the body of a leper. It is like a plastered wall where vipers have crawled; like a plastered wall where the scorpions have made their nest. It is like a whitened sepulchre full of loathsome things. It is horrible, thy body is horrible. It is of thy hair that I am enamoured, Jokanaan. Thy hair is like clusters of grapes, like the clusters of black grapes that hang from the vine trees of Edom[22] in the land of the Edomites. Thy hair is like the cedars of Lebanon,[23] like the great cedars of Lebanon that give their shade to the lions and to the robbers who would hide themselves by day. The long black nights, when the moon hides her face, when the stars are afraid, are not so black. The silence that dwells in the forest is not so black. There is nothing in the world so black as thy hair . . . Let me touch thy hair.

JOKANAAN: Back, daughter of Sodom! Touch me not. Profane not the temple of the Lord God.

SALOMÉ: Thy hair is horrible. It is covered with mire and dust. It is like a crown of thorns which they have placed on thy forehead. It is like a knot of black serpents writhing round thy neck. I love not thy hair . . . It is thy mouth that I desire, Jokanaan. Thy mouth is like a band of scarlet on a tower of ivory. It is like a pomegranate cut with a knife of ivory. The pomegranate-flowers that blossom in the gardens of Tyre, and are redder than roses, are not so red. The red blasts of trumpets that herald the approach of kings, and make afraid the enemy, are not so red. Thy mouth is redder than the feet of those who tread the wine in the wine-press. Thy mouth is redder than the feet of the doves who haunt the temples and are fed by the priests. It is redder than the feet of him who cometh from a forest where he hath slain a lion, and seen gilded tigers. Thy mouth is like a branch of coral that fishers have found in the twilight of the sea, the coral that they keep for the kings! . . . It is like the vermilion that the Moabites find in the mines of Moab,[24] the vermilion that the kings take from them. It is like the bow of the King of the Persians, that is painted with vermilion, and is tipped with coral. There is nothing in the world so red as thy mouth . . . Let me kiss thy mouth.

JOKANAAN: Never! Daughter of Babylon! Daughter of Sodom! Never.

SALOMÉ: I will kiss thy mouth, Jokanaan. I will kiss thy mouth.

THE YOUNG SYRIAN: Princess, Princess, thou who art like a garden of myrrh, thou who art the dove of all doves, look not at this man, look not at him! Do not speak such words to him. I cannot suffer them . . . Princess, Princess, do not speak these things.

SALOMÉ: I will kiss thy mouth, Jokanaan.

THE YOUNG SYRIAN: Ah!

[*He kills himself and falls between* SALOMÉ *and* JOKANAAN.]

THE PAGE OF HERODIAS: The young Syrian has slain himself! The young captain has slain himself! He has slain himself who was my friend! I gave him a little box of perfumes and earrings wrought in silver, and now he has killed himself! Ah, did he not foretell that some misfortune would happen? I, too, foretold it, and it has happened. Well, I knew that the moon was seeking a dead thing, but I knew not that it was he whom she sought. Ah! why did I not hide him from the moon? If I had hidden him in a cavern she would not have seen him.

FIRST SOLDIER: Princess, the young captain has just killed himself.

SALOMÉ: Let me kiss thy mouth, Jokanaan.

JOKANAAN: Art thou not afraid, daughter of Herodias? Did I not tell thee that I had heard in the palace the beatings of the wings of the angel of death, and hath he not come, the angel of death?

SALOMÉ: Let me kiss thy mouth.

JOKANAAN: Daughter of adultery, there is but one who can save thee, it is he of whom I spake. Go seek him. He is in a boat on the sea of Galilee, and he talketh with his disciples. Kneel down on the shore of the sea, and call unto him by his name. When he cometh to thee (and to all who call on him he cometh), bow thyself at his feet and ask of him the remission of thy sins.

SALOMÉ: Let me kiss thy mouth.

JOKANAAN: Cursed be thou! Daughter of an incestuous mother, be thou accursed!

SALOMÉ: I will kiss thy mouth, Jokanaan.

JOKANAAN: I do not wish to look at thee. I will not look at thee, thou art accursed, Salomé, thou art accursed.

[*He goes down into the cistern.*]

SALOMÉ: I will kiss thy mouth, Jokanaan; I will kiss thy mouth.

FIRST SOLDIER: We must bear away the body to another place. The Tetrarch does not care to see dead bodies, save the bodies of those whom he himself has slain.

THE PAGE OF HERODIAS: He was my brother, and nearer to me than a brother. I gave him a little box full of perfumes, and a ring of agate that he wore always on his hand. In the evening we used to walk by the river, among the almond trees, and he would tell me of the things of his country. He spake ever very low. The sound of his voice was like the sound of the flute, of a flute player. Also he much loved to gaze at himself in the river. I used to reproach him for that.

SECOND SOLDIER: You are right; we must hide the body. The Tetrarch must not see it.

FIRST SOLDIER: The Tetrarch will not come to this place. He never comes on the terrace. He is too much afraid of the prophet.

[*Enter* HEROD, HERODIAS, *and all the Court.*]

HEROD: Where is Salomé? Where is the Princess? Why did she not return to the banquet as I commanded her? Ah! There she is!

HERODIAS: You must not look at her! You are always looking at her!

HEROD: The moon has a strange look tonight. Has she not a strange look? She is like a mad woman, a mad woman who is seeking everywhere for lovers. She is naked, too. She is quite naked. The clouds are seeking to clothe her nakedness, but she will not let them. She shows herself naked in the sky. She reels through the clouds like a drunken woman . . . I am sure she is looking for lovers. Does she not reel like a drunken woman? She is like a mad woman, is she not?

HERODIAS: No; the moon is like the moon, that is all. Let us go within . . . You have nothing to do here.

HEROD: I will stay here! Manasseh, lay carpets there. Light torches, bring forth the ivory tables, and the tables of jasper. The air here is delicious. I will drink more wine with my guests. We must show all honours to the ambassadors of Caesar.

HERODIAS: It is not because of them that you remain.

HEROD: Yes; the air is delicious. Come, Herodias, our guests await us. Ah! I have slipped! I have slipped in blood! It is an ill omen. It is a very evil omen. Wherefore is there blood here? . . . and this body, what does this body here? Think you I am like the King of Egypt, who gives no feast to his guests but that he shows them a corpse? Whose is it? I will not look on it.

FIRST SOLDIER: It is our captain, sire. He is the young Syrian whom you made captain only three days ago.

HEROD: I gave no order that he should be slain.

SECOND SOLDIER: He killed himself, sire.

HEROD: For what reason? I had made him captain.

SECOND SOLDIER: We do not know, sire. But he killed himself.

HEROD: That seems strange to me. I thought it was only the Roman philosophers who killed themselves. Is it not true, Tigellinus, that the philosophers at Rome kill themselves?

TIGELLINUS: There are some who kill themselves, sire. They are the Stoics.[25] The Stoics are coarse people. They are ridiculous people. I myself regard them as being perfectly ridiculous.

HEROD: I also. It is ridiculous to kill oneself.

TIGELLINUS: Everybody at Rome laughs at them. The Emperor[26] has written a satire against them. It is recited everywhere.

HEROD: Ah! he has written a satire against them? Caesar is wonderful. He can do everything . . . It is strange that the young Syrian has killed himself. I am sorry he has killed himself. I am very sorry, for he was fair to look upon. He was even very fair. He had very languorous eyes. I remember that I saw he looked languorously at Salomé. Truly, I thought he looked too much at her.

HERODIAS: There are others who look at her too much.

HEROD: His father was a king. I drove him from his kingdom. And you made a slave of his mother, who was a queen, Herodias. So he was here as my guest, as it were, and for that reason I made him my captain. I am sorry he is dead. Ho! Why have you left the body here? I will not look at it – away with it! [*They take away the body.*] It is cold here. There is a wind blowing. Is there not a wind blowing?

HERODIAS: No; there is no wind.

HEROD: I tell you there is a wind that blows . . . And I hear in the air something that is like the beating of wings, like the beating of vast wings. Do you not hear it?

HERODIAS: I hear nothing.

HEROD: I hear it no longer. But I heard it. It was the blowing of the wind, no doubt. It has passed away. But no, I hear it again. Do you not hear it? It is just like the beating of wings.

HERODIAS: I tell you there is nothing. You are ill. Let us go within.

HEROD: I am not ill. It is your daughter who is sick. She has the mien of a sick person. Never have I seen her so pale.

HERODIAS: I have told you not to look at her.

HEROD: Pour me forth wine. [*Wine is brought.*] Salomé, come drink a little wine with me. I have here a wine that is exquisite. Caesar himself sent it me. Dip into it thy little red lips, that I may drain the cup.

SALOMÉ: I am not thirsty, Tetrarch.

HEROD: You hear how she answers me, this daughter of yours?

HERODIAS: She does right. Why are you always gazing at her?

HEROD: Bring me ripe fruits. [*Fruits are brought.*] Salomé, come and eat fruit with me. I love to see in a fruit the mark of thy little teeth. Bite but a little of this fruit and then I will eat what is left.

SALOMÉ: I am not hungry, Tetrarch.

HEROD [*to* HERODIAS]: You see how you have brought up this daughter of yours.

HERODIAS: My daughter and I come of a royal race. As for thee, thy father was a camel driver! He was also a robber!

HEROD: Thou liest!

HERODIAS: Thou knowest well that it is true.

HEROD: Salomé, come and sit next to me. I will give thee the throne of thy mother.

SALOMÉ: I am not tired, Tetrarch.

HERODIAS: You see what she thinks of you.

HEROD: Bring me – what is it that I desire? I forget. Ah! ah! I remember.

THE VOICE OF JOKANAAN: Lo! The time is come! That which I fore-

told has come to pass, saith the Lord God. Lo! The day of which
I spoke.

HERODIAS: Bid him be silent. I will not listen to his voice. This man
is for ever vomiting insults against me.

HEROD: He has said nothing against you. Besides, he is a very great
prophet.

HERODIAS: I do not believe in prophets. Can a man tell what will
come to pass? No man knows it. Moreover, he is for ever insulting
me. But I think you are afraid of him . . . I know well that you are
afraid of him.

HEROD: I am not afraid of him. I am afraid of no man.

HERODIAS: I tell you, you are afraid of him. If you are not afraid of
him why do you not deliver him to the Jews, who for these six
months past have been clamouring for him?

A JEW: Truly, my lord, it were better to deliver him into our hands.

HEROD: Enough on this subject. I have already given you my answer.
I will not deliver him into your hands. He is a holy man. He is a
man who has seen God.

A JEW: That cannot be. There is no man who hath seen God since
the prophet Elias. He is the last man who saw God. In these days
God doth not show himself. He hideth himself. Therefore great
evils have come upon the land.

ANOTHER JEW: Verily, no man knoweth if Elias the prophet did indeed
see God. Peradventure it was but the shadow of God that he saw.

A THIRD JEW: God is at no time hidden. He showeth himself at all
times and in everything. God is in what is evil even as he is what
is good.

A FOURTH JEW: That must not be said. It is a very dangerous doctrine.
It is a doctrine that cometh from the schools at Alexandria,[27] where
men teach the philosophy of the Greeks. And the Greeks are
Gentiles. They are not even circumcised.

A FIFTH JEW: No one can tell how God worketh. His ways are very
mysterious. It may be that the things which we call evil are good,
and that the things which we call good are evil. There is no
knowledge of any thing. We must needs submit to everything, for

God is very strong. He breaketh in pieces the strong together with the weak, for he regardeth not any man.

FIRST JEW: Thou speakest truly. God is terrible; he breaketh the strong and the weak as a man brays[28] corn in a mortar. But this man hath never seen God. No man hath seen God since the prophet Elias.

HERODIAS: Make them be silent. They weary me.

HEROD: But I have heard it said that Jokanaan himself is your prophet Elias.

THE JEW: That cannot be. It is more than three hundred years since the days of the prophet Elias.

HEROD: There be some who say that this man is the prophet Elias.

A NAZARENE:[29] I am sure that he is the prophet Elias.

THE JEW: Nay, but he is not the prophet Elias.

THE VOICE OF JOKANAAN: So the day is come, the day of the Lord, and I hear upon the mountains the feet of him who shall be the saviour of the world.

HEROD: What does that mean? The saviour of the world.

TIGELLINUS: It is a title that Caesar takes.

HEROD: But Caesar is not coming into Judaea. Only yesterday I received letters from Rome. They contained nothing concerning this matter. And you, Tigellinus, who were at Rome during the winter, you heard nothing concerning this matter, did you?

TIGELLINUS: Sire, I heard nothing concerning the matter. I was explaining the title. It is one of Caesar's titles.

HEROD: But Caesar cannot come. He is too gouty. They say that his feet are like the feet of an elephant. Also there are reasons of State. He who leaves Rome loses Rome. He will not come. Howbeit, Caesar is lord, he will come if he wishes. Nevertheless, I do not think he will come.

FIRST NAZARENE: It was not concerning Caesar that the prophet spake these words, sire.

HEROD: Not of Caesar?

FIRST NAZARENE: No, sire.

HEROD: Concerning whom then did he speak?

FIRST NAZARENE: Concerning Messias[30] who has come.

A JEW: Messias hath not come.

FIRST NAZARENE: He hath come, and everywhere he worketh miracles.

HERODIAS: Ho! ho! miracles! I do not believe in miracles. I have seen too many. [*To the page.*] My fan!

FIRST NAZARENE: This man worketh true miracles. Thus, at a marriage which took place in a little town of Galilee, a town of some importance, he changed water into wine.[31] Certain persons who were present related it to me. Also he healed two lepers that were seated before the Gate of Capernaum simply by touching them.

SECOND NAZARENE: Nay, it was blind men that he healed at Capernaum.

FIRST NAZARENE: Nay; they were lepers. But he hath healed blind people also, and he was seen on a mountain talking with angels.

A SADDUCEE: Angels do not exist.

A PHARISEE: Angels exist, but I do not believe that this man has talked with them.

FIRST NAZARENE: He was seen by a great multitude of people talking with angels.

A SADDUCEE: Not with angels.

HERODIAS: How these men weary me! They are ridiculous! [*To the page.*] Well! my fan! [*The page gives her the fan.*] You have a dreamer's look; you must not dream. It is only sick people who dream. [*She strikes the page with her fan.*]

SECOND NAZARENE: There is also the miracle of the daughter of Jairus.[32]

FIRST NAZARENE: Yes, that is sure. No man can gainsay it.

HERODIAS: These men are mad. They have looked too long on the moon. Command them to be silent.

HEROD: What is this miracle of the daughter of Jairus?

FIRST NAZARENE: The daughter of Jairus was dead. He raised her from the dead.

HEROD: He raises the dead?

FIRST NAZARENE: Yes, sire, he raiseth the dead.

HEROD: I do not wish him to do that. I forbid him to do that. I allow no man to raise the dead. This man must be found and told that I forbid him to raise the dead. Where is this man at present?

SECOND NAZARENE: He is in every place, my lord, but it is hard to find him.

FIRST NAZARENE: It is said that he is now in Samaria.[33]

A JEW: It is easy to see that this is not Messias, if he is in Samaria. It is not to the Samaritans that Messias shall come. The Samaritans are accursed. They bring no offerings to the Temple.

SECOND NAZARENE: He left Samaria a few days since. I think that at the present moment he is in the neighbourhood of Jerusalem.

FIRST NAZARENE: No; he is not there. I have just come from Jerusalem. For two months they have had no tidings of him.

HEROD: No matter! But let them find him, and tell him from me, I will not allow him to raise the dead! To change water into wine, to heal the lepers and the blind . . . He may do these things if he will. I say nothing against these things. In truth I hold it a good deed to heal a leper. But I allow no man to raise the dead. It would be terrible if the dead came back.

THE VOICE OF JOKANAAN: Ah! the wanton! The harlot! Ah! the daughter of Babylon with her golden eyes and her gilded eyelids! Thus saith the Lord God, Let there come up against her a multitude of men. Let the people take stones and stone her . . .[34]

HERODIAS: Command him to be silent.

THE VOICE OF JOKANAAN: Let the war captains pierce her with their swords, let them crush her beneath their shields.

HERODIAS: Nay, but it is infamous.

THE VOICE OF JOKANAAN: It is thus that I will wipe out all wickedness from the earth, and that all women shall learn not to imitate her abominations.

HERODIAS: You hear what he says against me? You allow him to revile your wife?

HEROD: He did not speak your name.

HERODIAS: What does that matter? You know well that it is I whom he seeks to revile. And I am your wife, am I not?

HEROD: Of a truth, dear and noble Herodias, you are my wife, and before that you were the wife of my brother.

HERODIAS: It was you who tore me from his arms.

HEROD: Of a truth I was stronger . . . But let us not talk of that matter.

I do not desire to talk of it. It is the cause of the terrible words that the prophet has spoken. Peradventure on account of it a misfortune will come. Let us not speak of this matter. Noble Herodias, we are not mindful of our guests. Fill thou my cup, my well-beloved. Fill with wine the great goblets of silver, and the great goblets of glass. I will drink to Caesar. There are Romans here, we must drink to Caesar.

ALL: Caesar! Caesar!

HEROD: Do you not see your daughter, how pale she is?

HERODIAS: What is it to you if she be pale or not?

HEROD: Never have I seen her so pale.

HERODIAS: You must not look at her.

THE VOICE OF JOKANAAN: In that day the sun shall become black like sackcloth of hair, and the moon shall become like blood, and the stars of the heavens shall fall upon the earth like ripe figs that fall from the fig tree, and the kings of the earth shall be afraid.

HERODIAS: Ah! Ah! I should like to see that day of which he speaks, when the moon shall become like blood, and when the stars shall fall upon the earth like ripe figs. This prophet talks like a drunken man . . . But I cannot suffer the sound of his voice. I hate his voice. Command him to be silent.

HEROD: I will not. I cannot understand what it is that he saith, but it may be an omen.

HERODIAS: I do not believe in omens. He speaks like a drunken man.

HEROD: It may be he is drunk with the wine of God.

HERODIAS: What wine is that, the wine of God? From what vineyards is it gathered? In what wine-press may one find it?

HEROD [*from this point he looks all the while at* SALOMÉ]: Tigellinus, when you were at Rome of late, did the Emperor speak with you on the subject of . . . ?

TIGELLINUS: On what subject, sire?

HEROD: On what subject? Ah! I asked you a question, did I not? I have forgotten what I would have asked you.

HERODIAS: You are looking again at my daughter. You must not look at her. I have already said so.

HEROD: You say nothing else.

HERODIAS: I say it again.

HEROD: And that restoration of the Temple about which they have talked so much, will anything be done? They say the veil of the Sanctuary has disappeared, do they not?

HERODIAS: It was thyself didst steal it. Thou speakest at random. I will not stay here. Let us go within.

HEROD: Dance for me, Salomé.

HERODIAS: I will not have her dance.

SALOMÉ: I have no desire to dance, Tetrarch.

HEROD: Salomé, daughter of Herodias, dance for me.

HERODIAS: Let her alone.

HEROD: I command thee to dance, Salomé.

SALOMÉ: I will not dance, Tetrarch.[35]

HERODIAS [*laughing*]: You see how she obeys you.

HEROD: What is it to me whether she dance or not? It is naught to me. Tonight I am happy, I am exceeding happy. Never have I been so happy.

FIRST SOLDIER: The Tetrarch has a sombre look. Has he not a sombre look?

SECOND SOLDIER: Yes, he has a sombre look.

HEROD: Wherefore should I not be happy? Caesar, who is lord of the world, who is lord of all things, loves me well. He has just sent me most precious gifts. Also he has promised me to summon to Rome the King of Cappadocia, who is my enemy. It may be that at Rome he will crucify him, for he is able to do all things that he wishes. Verily, Caesar is lord. Thus you see I have a right to be happy. Indeed, I am happy. I have never been so happy. There is nothing in the world that can mar my happiness.

THE VOICE OF JOKANAAN: He shall be seated on his throne. He shall be clothed in scarlet and purple. In his hand he shall bear a golden cup full of his blasphemies. And the angel of the Lord shall smite him. He shall be eaten of worms.

HERODIAS: You hear what he says about you. He says that you will be eaten of worms.

HEROD: It is not of me that he speaks. He speaks never against me. It is of the King of Cappadocia that he speaks; the King of Cappadocia, who is mine enemy. It is he who shall be eaten of worms. It is not I. Never has he spoken word against me, this prophet, save that I sinned in taking to wife the wife of my brother. It may be he is right. For, of a truth, you are sterile.

HERODIAS: I am sterile, I? You say that, you that are ever looking at my daughter, you that would have her dance for your pleasure? It is absurd to say that. I have borne a child. You have gotten no child, no, not even from one of your slaves. It is you who are sterile, not I.

HEROD: Peace, woman! I say that you are sterile. You have borne me no child, and the prophet says that our marriage is not a true marriage. He says that it is an incestuous marriage, a marriage that will bring evils . . . I fear he is right; I am sure that he is right. But it is not the moment to speak of such things. I would be happy at this moment. Of a truth, I am happy. There is nothing I lack.

HERODIAS: I am glad you are of so fair a humour tonight. It is not your custom. But it is late. Let us go within. Do not forget that we hunt at sunrise. All honours must be shown to Caesar's ambassadors, must they not?

SECOND SOLDIER: What a sombre look the Tetrarch wears.

FIRST SOLDIER: Yes, he wears a sombre look.

HEROD: Salomé, Salomé, dance for me. I pray thee dance for me. I am sad tonight. Yes; I am passing sad tonight. When I came hither I slipped in blood, which is an evil omen; and I heard, I am sure I heard in the air a beating of wings, a beating of giant wings. I cannot tell what they mean . . . I am sad tonight. Therefore dance for me. Dance for me, Salomé, I beseech you. If you dance for me you may ask of me what you will, and I will give it you, even unto the half of my kingdom.

SALOMÉ [rising]: Will you indeed give me whatsoever I shall ask, Tetrarch?

HERODIAS: Do not dance, my daughter.

HEROD: Everything, even the half of my kingdom.

SALOMÉ: You swear it, Tetrarch?

HEROD: I swear it, Salomé.

HERODIAS: Do not dance, my daughter.

SALOMÉ: By what will you swear, Tetrarch?

HEROD: By my life, by my crown, by my gods. Whatsoever you desire I will give it you, even to the half of my kingdom, if you will but dance for me. O, Salomé, Salomé, dance for me!

SALOMÉ: You have sworn, Tetrarch.

HEROD: I have sworn, Salomé.

SALOMÉ: All that I ask, even the half of your kingdom.

HERODIAS: My daughter, do not dance.

HEROD: Even to the half of my kingdom. Thou wilt be passing fair as a queen, Salomé, if it please thee to ask for the half of my kingdom. Will she not be fair as a queen? Ah! it is cold here! There is an icy wind, and I hear . . . wherefore do I hear in the air this beating of wings? Ah! one might fancy a bird, a huge black bird that hovers over the terrace. Why can I not see it, this bird? The beat of its wings is terrible. The breath of the wind of its wings is terrible. It is a chill wind. Nay, but it is not cold, it is hot. I am choking. Pour water on my hands. Give me snow to eat. Loosen my mantle. Quick! quick! loosen my mantle. Nay, but leave it. It is my garland that hurts me, my garland of roses. The flowers are like fire. They have burned my forehead. [*He tears the wreath from his head and throws it on the table.*] Ah! I can breathe now. How red those petals are! They are like stains of blood on the cloth. That does not matter. You must not find symbols in everything you see. It makes life impossible. It were better to say that stains of blood are as lovely as rose petals. It were better far to say that . . . But we will not speak of this. Now I am happy, I am passing happy. Have I not the right to be happy? Your daughter is going to dance for me. Will you not dance for me, Salomé? You have promised to dance for me.

HERODIAS: I will not have her dance.

SALOMÉ: I will dance for you, Tetrarch.

HEROD: You hear what your daughter says. She is going to dance for me. You do well to dance for me, Salomé. And when you have danced for me, forget not to ask of me whatsoever you wish. Whatsoever you wish I will give it you, even to the half of my kingdom. I have sworn it, have I not?

SALOMÉ: You have sworn it, Tetrarch.

HEROD: And I have never broken my word. I am not of those who break their oaths. I know not how to lie. I am the slave of my word, and my word is the word of a king. The King of Cappadocia always lies, but he is no true king. He is a coward. Also he owes me money that he will not repay. He has even insulted my ambassadors. He has spoken words that were wounding. But Caesar will crucify him when he comes to Rome. I am sure that Caesar will crucify him. And if not, yet will he die, being eaten of worms. The prophet has prophesied it. Well, wherefore dost thou tarry, Salomé?

SALOMÉ: I am waiting until my slaves bring perfumes to me and the seven veils, and take off my sandals.

[*Slaves bring perfumes and the seven veils, and take off the sandals of* SALOMÉ.]

HEROD: Ah, you are going to dance with naked feet. 'Tis well! 'Tis well. Your little feet will be like white doves. They will be like little white flowers that dance upon the trees . . . No, no, she is going to dance on blood. There is blood spilt on the ground. She must not dance on blood. It were an evil omen.

HERODIAS: What is it to you if she dance on blood? Thou hast waded deep enough therein . . .

HEROD: What is it to me? Ah! look at the moon! She has become red.[36] She has become red as blood. Ah! the prophet prophesied truly. He prophesied that the moon would become red as blood. Did he not prophesy it? All of you heard him. And now the moon has become red as blood. Do ye not see it?

HERODIAS: Oh, yes, I see it well, and the stars are falling like ripe figs, are they not? And the sun is becoming black like sackcloth of hair, and the kings of the earth are afraid. That at least one can see. The prophet, for once in his life, was right; the kings of the earth are afraid . . . Let us go within. You are sick. They will say at Rome that you are mad. Let us go within, I tell you.

THE VOICE OF JOKANAAN: Who is this who cometh from Edom, who is this who cometh from Bozra,[37] whose raiment is dyed with purple, who shineth in the beauty of his garments, who walketh mighty in his greatness? Wherefore is thy raiment stained with scarlet?

HERODIAS: Let us go within. The voice of that man maddens me. I will not have my daughter dance while he is continually crying out. I will not have her dance while you look at her in this fashion. In a word, I will not have her dance.

HEROD: Do not rise, my wife, my queen, it will avail thee nothing. I will not go within till she hath danced. Dance, Salomé, dance for me.

HERODIAS: Do not dance, my daughter.

SALOMÉ: I am ready, Tetrarch.

[SALOMÉ *dances the dance of the seven veils.*][38]

HEROD: Ah! wonderful! wonderful! You see that she has danced for me, your daughter. Come near, Salomé, come near, that I may give you your reward. Ah! I pay the dancers well. I will pay thee royally. I will give thee whatsoever thy soul desireth. What wouldst thou have? Speak.

SALOMÉ [*kneeling*]: I would that they presently bring me in a silver charger . . .

HEROD [*laughing*]: In a silver charger? Surely yes, in a silver charger. She is charming, is she not? What is it you would have in a silver charger, O sweet and fair Salomé, you who are fairer than all the daughters of Judaea? What would you have them bring thee in a silver charger? Tell me. Whatsoever it may be, they shall give it you. My treasures belong to thee. What is it, Salomé?

SALOMÉ [*rising*]: The head of Jokanaan.

HERODIAS: Ah! that is well said, my daughter.

HEROD: No, no!

HERODIAS: That is well said, my daughter.

HEROD: No, no, Salomé. You do not ask me that. Do not listen to your mother's voice. She is ever giving you evil counsel. Do not heed her.

SALOMÉ: I do not heed my mother. It is for mine own pleasure that I ask the head of Jokanaan in a silver charger. You have sworn, Herod. Forget not that you have sworn an oath.

HEROD: I know it. I have sworn by my gods. I know it well. But I pray you, Salomé, ask of me something else. Ask of me the half of my kingdom, and I will give it you. But ask not of me what you have asked.

SALOMÉ: I ask of you the head of Jokanaan.

HEROD: No, no, I do not wish it.

SALOMÉ: You have sworn, Herod.

HERODIAS: Yes, you have sworn. Everybody heard you. You swore it before everybody.

HEROD: Be silent! It is not to you I speak.

HERODIAS: My daughter has done well to ask the head of Jokanaan. He has covered me with insults. He has said monstrous things against me. One can see that she loves her mother well. Do not yield, my daughter. He has sworn, he has sworn.

HEROD: Be silent, speak not to me! . . . Come, Salomé, be reasonable. I have never been hard to you. I have ever loved you . . . It may be that I have loved you too much. Therefore ask not this thing of me. This is a terrible thing, an awful thing to ask of me. Surely, I think you are jesting. The head of a man that is cut from his body is ill to look upon, is it not? It is not meet that the eyes of a virgin should look upon such a thing. What pleasure could you have in it? None. No, no, it is not what you desire. Hearken to me. I have an emerald, a great round emerald, which Caesar's minion sent me. If you look through this emerald you can see things which happen at a great distance. Caesar himself carries such an emerald when he goes to the circus. But my emerald is larger. I know well that it is larger. It is the largest emerald in the whole world. You would like that, would you not? Ask it of me and I will give it you.

SALOMÉ: I demand the head of Jokanaan.

HEROD: You are not listening. You are not listening. Suffer me to speak, Salomé.

SALOMÉ: The head of Jokanaan.

HEROD: No, no, you would not have that. You say that to trouble me, because I have looked at you all this evening. It is true, I have looked at you all this evening. Your beauty troubled me. Your beauty has grievously troubled me, and I have looked at you too much. But I will look at you no more. Neither at things, nor at people should one look. Only in mirrors should one look, for mirrors do but show us masks. Oh! oh! bring wine! I thirst . . . Salomé, Salomé, let us be friends. Come now! . . . Ah! what would I say? What was't? Ah! I remember! . . . Salomé – nay, but come nearer to me; I fear you will not hear me – Salomé, you know my white peacocks, my beautiful white peacocks, that walk in the garden between the myrtles and the tall cypress trees. Their beaks are gilded with gold, and the grains that they eat are gilded with gold also, and their feet are stained with purple. When they cry out the rain comes, and the moon shows herself in the heavens when they spread their tails. Two by two they walk between the cypress trees and the black myrtles, and each has a slave to tend it. Sometimes they fly across the trees, and anon they crouch in the grass, and round the lake. There are not in all the world birds so wonderful. There is no king in all the world who possesses such wonderful birds. I am sure that Caesar himself has no birds so fine as my birds. I will give you fifty of my peacocks. They will follow you whither-soever you go, and in the midst of them you will be like the moon in the midst of a great white cloud . . . I will give them all to you. I have but a hundred, and in the whole world there is no king who has peacocks like unto my peacocks. But I will give them all to you. Only you must loose me from my oath, and must not ask of me that which you have asked of me.

[*He empties the cup of wine.*]

SALOMÉ: Give me the head of Jokanaan.

HERODIAS: Well said, my daughter! As for you, you are ridiculous with your peacocks.

HEROD: Be silent! You cry out always; you cry out like a beast of prey. You must not. Your voice wearies me. Be silent, I say . . . Salomé, think of what you are doing. This man comes perchance from God. He is a holy man. The finger of God has touched him. God has put into his mouth terrible words. In the palace as in the desert God is always with him . . . At least it is possible. One does not know. It is possible that God is for him and with him. Furthermore, if he died some misfortune might happen to me. In any case, he said that the day he dies a misfortune will happen to someone.

That could only be to me. Remember, I slipped in blood when I entered. Also, I heard a beating of wings in the air, a beating of mighty wings. These are very evil omens, and there were others. I am sure there were others though I did not see them. Well, Salomé, you do not wish a misfortune to happen to me? You do not wish that. Listen to me, then.

SALOMÉ: Give me the head of Jokanaan.

HEROD: Ah! you are not listening to me. Be calm. I – I am calm. I am quite calm. Listen. I have jewels hidden in this place – jewels that your mother even has never seen; jewels that are marvellous. I have a collar of pearls, set in four rows. They are like unto moons chained with rays of silver. They are like fifty moons caught in a golden net. On the ivory of her breast a queen has worn it. Thou shalt be as fair as a queen when thou wearest it. I have amethysts of two kinds, one that is black like wine, and one that is red like wine which has been coloured with water. I have topazes, yellow as are the eyes of tigers, and topazes that are pink as the eyes of a wood-pigeon, and green topazes that are as the eyes of cats. I have opals that burn always, with an icelike flame, opals that make sad men's minds, and are fearful of the shadows. I have onyxes like the eyeballs of a dead woman. I have moonstones that change when the moon changes, and are wan when they see the sun. I have sapphires big like eggs, and as blue as blue flowers. The sea wanders within them and the moon comes never to trouble the blue of their waves. I have chrysolites and beryls and chrysoprases and rubies. I have sardonyx and hyacinth stones, and stones of chalcedony,[39] and I will give them all to you, all, and other things will I add to them. The King of the Indies has but even now sent me four fans fashioned from the feathers of parrots, and the King of Numidia[40] a garment of ostrich feathers. I have a crystal, into which it is not lawful for a woman to look, nor may young men behold it until they have been beaten with rods. In a coffer of nacre[41] I have three wondrous turquoises. He who wears them on his forehead can imagine things which are not, and he who carries them in his hand can make women sterile. These are great treasures above all price. They are treasures without price. But this is not all. In an ebony coffer I have two cups of amber, that are like apples of gold. If an enemy pour poison into these cups, they become like an apple of silver. In a coffer incrusted with amber I have sandals incrusted with glass. I have mantles that have been brought from the land of the Seres,[42] and bracelets decked about with carbuncles and with jade that come from the city of Euphrates . . . What desirest thou more than this, Salomé? Tell me the thing that thou desirest, and I will give it thee. All that thou askest I will give thee, save one thing. I will give thee all that is mine, save one life. I will give thee the mantle of the high priest. I will give thee the veil of the sanctuary.

THE JEWS: Oh! oh!

SALOMÉ: Give me the head of Jokanaan.

HEROD [*sinking back in his seat*]: Let her be given what she asks! Of a truth she is her mother's child! [*The* FIRST SOLDIER *approaches.* HERODIAS *draws from the hand of the* TETRARCH *the ring of death and gives it to the* SOLDIER, *who straightway bears it to the* EXECUTIONER. *The* EXECUTIONER *looks scared.*] Who has taken my ring? There was a ring on my right hand. Who has drunk my wine? There was wine in my cup. It was full of wine. Some one has drunk it! Oh! surely some evil will befall some one. [*The* EXECUTIONER *goes down into the cistern.*] Ah! Wherefore did I give my oath? Kings ought never to pledge their word. If they keep it not, it is terrible, and if they keep it, it is terrible also.

HERODIAS: My daughter has done well.

HEROD: I am sure that some misfortune will happen.

SALOMÉ [*she leans over the cistern and listens*]: There is no sound. I hear nothing. Why does he not cry out, this man? Ah, if any man sought to kill me, I would cry out, I would struggle, I would not suffer . . . Strike, strike, Naaman, strike, I tell you . . . No, I hear nothing. There is a silence, a terrible silence. Ah! something has fallen upon the ground. I heard something fall. It is the sword of the headsman. He is afraid, this slave. He has let his sword fall. He dare not kill him. He is a coward, this slave! Let soldiers be sent. [*She sees the* PAGE OF HERODIAS *and addresses him.*] Come hither, thou wert the friend of him who is dead, is it not so? Well, I tell thee, there are not dead men enough. Go to the soldiers and bid them go down and bring me the thing I ask, the thing the Tetrarch has promised me, the thing that is mine. [*The* PAGE *recoils. She turns to the* SOLDIERS.] Hither, ye soldiers. Get ye down into this cistern and bring me the head of this man. [*The* SOLDIERS *recoil.*] Tetrarch, Tetrarch, command your soldiers that they bring me the head of Jokanaan.

[*A huge black arm, the arm of the* EXECUTIONER, *comes forth from the cistern, bearing on a silver shield the head of* JOKANAAN. SALOMÉ *seizes it.* HEROD *hides his face with his cloak.* HERODIAS *smiles and fans herself. The* NAZARENES *fall on their knees and begin to pray.*]

Ah! Thou wouldst not suffer me to kiss thy mouth, Jokanaan. Well! I will kiss it now. I will bite it with my teeth as one bites a ripe fruit. Yes, I will kiss thy mouth, Jokannan. I said it. Did I not say it? I said it. Ah! I will kiss it now . . . But wherefore dost thou not look at me, Jokanaan? Thine eyes that were so terrible, so full of rage and scorn, are shut now. Wherefore are they shut? Open thine eyes! Lift up thine eyelids, Jokanaan! Wherefore dost thou not look at me? Art thou afraid of me, Jokanaan, that thou wilt not look at me? . . . And thy tongue, that was like a red snake darting poison, it moves no more, it says nothing now, Jokanaan, that scarlet viper that spat its venom upon me. It is strange, is it not? How is it that the red viper stirs no longer? . . . Thou wouldst have none of me, Jokanaan. Thou didst reject me. Thou didst speak evil words against me. Thou didst reject me as a harlot, as a wanton, me, Salomé, daughter of Herodias, Princess of Judaea! Well, Jokanaan, I still live, but thou, thou art dead, and thy head belongs to me. I can do with it what I will. I can throw it to the dogs and to the birds of the air.[43] That which the dogs leave, the birds of the air shall devour . . . Ah, Jokanaan, Jokanaan, thou wert the only man that I have loved. All other men are hateful to me. But thou, thou wert beautiful! Thy body was a column of ivory set on a silver socket. It was a garden full of doves and of silver lilies. It was a tower of silver decked with shields of ivory. There was nothing in the world so white as thy body. There was nothing in the world so black as thy hair. In the whole world there was nothing so red as thy mouth.

Thy voice was a censer that scattered strange perfumes, and when I looked on thee I heard a strange music. Ah! Wherefore didst thou not look at me, Jokanaan? Behind thine hands and thy curses thou didst hide thy face. Thou didst put upon thine eyes the covering of him who would see his God. Well, thou hast seen thy God, Jokanaan, but me, me, thou didst never see. If thou hadst seen me thou wouldst have loved me. I, I saw thee, Jokanaan, and I loved thee. Oh, how I loved thee! I love thee yet, Jokanaan, I love thee only . . . I am athirst for thy beauty; I am hungry for thy body; and neither wine nor fruits can appease my desire. What shall I do now, Jokanaan? Neither the floods nor the great waters can quench my passion. I was a princess, and thou didst scorn me. I was a virgin, and thou didst take my virginity from me. I was chaste, and thou didst fill my veins with fire . . . Ah! Ah! Wherefore didst thou not look at me, Jokanaan? If thou hadst looked at me thou hadst loved me. Well I know that thou wouldst have loved me, and the mystery of love is greater than the mystery of death. Love only should one consider.

HEROD: She is monstrous, thy daughter, she is altogether monstrous. In truth, what she has done is a great crime. I am sure that it was a crime against an unknown God.

HERODIAS: I approve of what my daughter has done. And I will stay here now.

HEROD [*rising*]: Ah! There speaks the incestuous wife! Come! I will not stay here. Come, I tell thee. Surely some terrible thing will befall. Manasseh, Issachar, Ozias, put out the torches. I will not look at things, I will not suffer things to look at me. Put out the torches! Hide the moon! Hide the stars! Let us hide ourselves in our palace, Herodias. I begin to be afraid.

[*The* SLAVES *put out the torches. The stars disappear. A great black cloud crosses the moon and conceals it completely. The stage becomes very dark.*[44] The TETRARCH *begins to climb the staircase.*]

THE VOICE OF SALOMÉ: Ah! I have kissed thy mouth, Jokanaan, I have kissed thy mouth. There was a bitter taste on thy lips. Was it the taste of blood? . . . But perchance it is the taste of love . . . They

say that love hath a bitter taste . . . But what of that? What of that?
I have kissed thy mouth, Jokanaan.

[*A moonbeam falls on* SALOMÉ *covering her with light.*]

HEROD [*turning round and seeing* SALOMÉ]: Kill that woman!

[*The* SOLDIERS *rush forward and crush beneath their shields* SALOMÉ,
daughter of HERODIAS, *Princess of Judaea.*]

CURTAIN

A Woman of No Importance

TO
GLADYS[1]
COUNTESS DE GREY
[MARCHIONESS OF RIPON]

The Persons of the Play

LORD ILLINGWORTH

SIR JOHN PONTEFRACT

LORD ALFRED RUFFORD

MR KELVIL, M.P.

THE VEN. ARCHDEACON DAUBENY, D.D.

GERALD ARBUTHNOT

FARQUHAR, *Butler*

FRANCIS, *Footman*

LADY HUNSTANTON

LADY CAROLINE PONTEFRACT

LADY STUTFIELD

MRS ALLONBY

MISS HESTER WORSLEY

ALICE, *Maid*

MRS ARBUTHNOT

TIME
The present

PLACE
The Shires

The action of the play takes place within twenty-four hours

FIRST ACT

SCENE
Lawn in front of the terrace at Hunstanton.

[SIR JOHN *and* LADY CAROLINE PONTEFRACT, MISS WORSLEY, *on chairs under large yew tree.*]

LADY CAROLINE: I believe this is the first English country house you have stayed at, Miss Worsley?

HESTER: Yes, Lady Caroline.

LADY CAROLINE: You have no country houses, I am told, in America?

HESTER: We have not many.

LADY CAROLINE: Have you any country? What we should call country?

HESTER [*smiling*]: We have the largest country in the world, Lady Caroline. They used to tell us at school that some of our states are as big as France and England put together.

LADY CAROLINE: Ah! you must find it very draughty, I should fancy. [*To* SIR JOHN.] John, you should have your muffler. What is the use of my always knitting mufflers for you if you won't wear them?

SIR JOHN: I am quite warm, Caroline, I assure you.

LADY CAROLINE: I think not, John. Well, you couldn't come to a more charming place than this, Miss Worsley, though the house is excessively damp, quite unpardonably damp, and dear Lady Hunstanton is sometimes a little lax about the people she asks down here. [*To* SIR JOHN.] Jane mixes too much. Lord Illingworth, of course, is a man of high distinction. It is a privilege to meet him. And that member of Parliament, Mr Kettle –

SIR JOHN: Kelvil, my love, Kelvil.

LADY CAROLINE: He must be quite respectable. One has never heard his name before in the whole course of one's life, which speaks volumes for a man, nowadays. But Mrs Allonby is hardly a very suitable person.

HESTER: I dislike Mrs Allonby. I dislike her more than I can say.

LADY CAROLINE: I am not sure, Miss Worsley, that foreigners like yourself should cultivate likes or dislikes about the people they are invited to meet. Mrs Allonby is very well born. She is a niece of Lord Brancaster's. It is said, of course, that she ran away twice before she was married. But you know how unfair people often are. I myself don't believe she ran away more than once.[1]

HESTER: Mr Arbuthnot is very charming.

LADY CAROLINE: Ah, yes! the young man who has a post in a bank. Lady Hunstanton is most kind in asking him here, and Lord Illingworth seems to have taken quite a fancy to him. I am not sure, however, that Jane is right in taking him out of his position. In my young days, Miss Worsley, one never met anyone in society who worked for their living.[2] It was not considered the thing.

HESTER: In America those are the people we respect most.

LADY CAROLINE: I have no doubt of it.

HESTER: Mr Arbuthnot has a beautiful nature! He is so simple, so sincere.[3] He has one of the most beautiful natures I have ever come across. It is a privilege to meet *him*.

LADY CAROLINE: It is not customary in England, Miss Worsley, for a young lady to speak with such enthusiasm of any person of the opposite sex. Englishwomen conceal their feelings till after they are married. They show them then.

HESTER: Do you, in England, allow no friendship to exist between a young man and a young girl?

[*Enter* LADY HUNSTANTON, *followed by Footman with shawls and a cushion.*]

LADY CAROLINE: We think it very inadvisable. Jane, I was just saying what a pleasant party you have asked us to meet. You have a wonderful power of selection. It is quite a gift.

LADY HUNSTANTON: Dear Caroline, how kind of you! I think we all do fit in very nicely together. And I hope our charming American visitor will carry back pleasant recollections of our English country life. [*To Footman.*] The cushion, there, Francis. And my shawl. The Shetland. Get the Shetland.

[*Exit Footman for shawl.*]

[*Enter* GERALD ARBUTHNOT.]

GERALD: Lady Hunstanton, I have such good news to tell you. Lord Illingworth has just offered to make me his secretary.

LADY HUNSTANTON: His secretary? That is good news indeed, Gerald. It means a very brilliant future in store for you. Your dear mother will be delighted. I really must try and induce her to come up here tonight. Do you think she would, Gerald? I know how difficult it is to get her to go anywhere.

GERALD: Oh! I am sure she would, Lady Hunstanton, if she knew Lord Illingworth had made me such an offer.

[*Enter Footman with shawl.*]

LADY HUNSTANTON: I will write and tell her about it, and ask her to come up and meet him. [*To Footman.*] Just wait, Francis.

[*Writes letter.*]

LADY CAROLINE: That is a very wonderful opening for so young a man as you are, Mr Arbuthnot.

GERALD: It is indeed, Lady Caroline. I trust I shall be able to show myself worthy of it.

LADY CAROLINE: I trust so.

GERALD [*to* HESTER]: *You* have not congratulated me yet, Miss Worsley.

HESTER: Are you very pleased about it?

GERALD: Of course I am. It means everything to me – things that were out of the reach of hope before may be within hope's reach now.

HESTER: Nothing should be out of the reach of hope. Life is a hope.

LADY HUNSTANTON: I fancy, Caroline, that Diplomacy is what Lord Illingworth is aiming at. I heard that he was offered Vienna.[4] But that may not be true.

LADY CAROLINE: I don't think that England should be represented abroad by an unmarried man, Jane. It might lead to complications.[5]

LADY HUNSTANTON: You are too nervous, Caroline. Believe me, you are too nervous. Besides, Lord Illingworth may marry any day. I was in hopes he would have married Lady Kelso. But I believe he said her family was too large. Or was it her feet? I forget which.[6] I regret it very much. She was made to be an ambassador's wife.

LADY CAROLINE: She certainly has a wonderful faculty of remembering people's names, and forgetting their faces.

LADY HUNSTANTON: Well, that is very natural, Caroline, is it not? [*To Footman.*] Tell Henry to wait for an answer. I have written a line to your dear mother, Gerald, to tell her your good news, and to say she really must come to dinner.

[*Exit Footman.*]

GERALD: That is awfully kind of you, Lady Hunstanton. [*To* HESTER.] Will you come for a stroll, Miss Worsley?

HESTER: With pleasure.

[*Exit with* GERALD.]

LADY HUNSTANTON: I am very much gratified at Gerald Arbuthnot's good fortune. He is quite a *protégé* of mine. And I am particularly pleased that Lord Illingworth should have made the offer of his own accord without my suggesting anything. Nobody likes to be asked favours. I remember poor Charlotte Pagden making herself quite unpopular one season, because she had a French governess she wanted to recommend to everyone.

LADY CAROLINE: I saw the governess, Jane. Lady Pagden sent her to me. It was before Eleanor came out. She was far too good-looking to be in any respectable household. I don't wonder Lady Pagden was so anxious to get rid of her.

LADY HUNSTANTON: Ah, that explains it.

LADY CAROLINE: John, the grass is too damp for you. You had better go and put on your overshoes at once.

SIR JOHN: I am quite comfortable, Caroline, I assure you.

LADY CAROLINE: You must allow me to be the best judge of that, John. Pray do as I tell you.

[SIR JOHN *gets up and goes off.*]

LADY HUNSTANTON: You spoil him, Caroline, you do indeed!

[*Enter* MRS ALLONBY *and* LADY STUTFIELD.]

[*To* MRS ALLONBY]: Well, dear, I hope you like the park. It is said to be well timbered.

MRS ALLONBY: The trees are wonderful, Lady Hunstanton.

LADY STUTFIELD: Quite, quite wonderful.

MRS ALLONBY: But somehow, I feel sure that if I lived in the country for six months, I should become so unsophisticated that no one would take the slightest notice of me.

LADY HUNSTANTON: I assure you, dear, that the country has not that effect at all. Why, it was from Melthorpe, which is only two miles from here, that Lady Belton eloped with Lord Fethersdale. I remember the occurrence perfectly. Poor Lord Belton died three days afterwards of joy, or gout. I forget which. We had a large party staying here at the time, so we were all very much interested in the whole affair.

MRS ALLONBY: I think to elope is cowardly. It's running away from danger. And danger has become so rare in modern life.

LADY CAROLINE: As far as I can make out, the young women of the present day seem to make it the sole object of their lives to be always playing with fire.

MRS ALLONBY: The one advantage of playing with fire, Lady Caroline, is that one never gets even singed. It is the people who don't know how to play with it who get burned up.

LADY STUTFIELD: Yes; I see that. It is very, very helpful.

LADY HUNSTANTON: I don't know how the world would get on with such a theory as that, dear Mrs Allonby.

LADY STUTFIELD: Ah! The world was made for men and not for women.

MRS ALLONBY: Oh, don't say that, Lady Stutfield. We have a much better time than they have. There are far more things forbidden to us than are forbidden to them.

LADY STUTFIELD: Yes; that is quite, quite true. I had not thought of that.

[*Enter* SIR JOHN *and* MR KELVIL.]

LADY HUNSTANTON: Well, Mr Kelvil, have you got through your work?

KELVIL: I have finished my writing for the day, Lady Hunstanton. It has been an arduous task. The demands on the time of a public man are very heavy nowadays, very heavy indeed. And I don't think they meet with adequate recognition.

LADY CAROLINE: John, have you got your overshoes on?

SIR JOHN: Yes, my love.

LADY CAROLINE: I think you had better come over here, John. It is more sheltered.

SIR JOHN: I am quite comfortable, Caroline.

LADY CAROLINE: I think not, John. You had better sit beside me.

[SIR JOHN *rises and goes across.*][7]

LADY STUTFIELD: And what have you been writing about this morning, Mr Kelvil?

KELVIL: On the usual subject, Lady Stutfield. On Purity.

LADY STUTFIELD: That must be such a very, very interesting thing to write about.

KELVIL: It is the one subject of really national importance, nowadays, Lady Stutfield. I purpose addressing my constituents on the question before Parliament meets. I find that the poorer classes of this country display a marked desire for a higher ethical standard.

LADY STUTFIELD: How quite, quite nice of them.

LADY CAROLINE: Are you in favour of women taking part in politics, Mr Kettle?

SIR JOHN: Kelvil, my love, Kelvil.

KELVIL: The growing influence of women is the one reassuring thing in our political life, Lady Caroline. Women are always on the side of morality, public and private.

LADY STUTFIELD: It is so very, very gratifying to hear you say that.

LADY HUNSTANTON: Ah, yes! the moral qualities in women – that is the important thing. I am afraid, Caroline, that dear Lord Illingworth doesn't value the moral qualities in women as much as he should.

[*Enter* LORD ILLINGWORTH.]

LADY STUTFIELD: The world says that Lord Illingworth is very, very wicked.

LORD ILLINGWORTH: But what world says that, Lady Stutfield? It must be the next world. This world and I are on excellent terms.

[*Sits down beside* MRS ALLONBY.]

LADY STUTFIELD: Everyone *I* know says you are very, very wicked.

LORD ILLINGWORTH: It is perfectly monstrous the way people go about, nowadays, saying things against one behind one's back that are absolutely and entirely true.

LADY HUNSTANTON: Dear Lord Illingworth is quite hopeless, Lady Stutfield. I have given up trying to reform him. It would take a Public Company with a Board of Directors and a paid Secretary to do that. But you have the secretary already, Lord Illingworth, haven't you? Gerald Arbuthnot has told us of his good fortune; it is really most kind of you.

LORD ILLINGWORTH: Oh, don't say that, Lady Hunstanton. Kind is a dreadful word. I took a great fancy to young Arbuthnot the moment I met him, and he'll be of considerable use to me in something I am foolish enough to think of doing.

LADY HUNSTANTON: He is an admirable young man. And his mother is one of my dearest friends. He has just gone for a walk with our pretty American. She is very pretty, is she not?

LADY CAROLINE: Far too pretty. These American girls carry off all the good matches. Why can't they stay in their own country? They are always telling us it is the Paradise of women.

LORD ILLINGWORTH: It is, Lady Caroline. That is why, like Eve, they are so extremely anxious to get out of it.

LADY CAROLINE: Who are Miss Worsley's parents?

LORD ILLINGWORTH: American women are wonderfully clever in concealing their parents.

LADY HUNSTANTON: My dear Lord Illingworth, what do you mean? Miss Worsley, Caroline, is an orphan. Her father was a very wealthy millionaire or philanthropist, or both, I believe, who entertained my son quite hospitably when he visited Boston. I don't know how he made his money, originally.

KELVIL: I fancy in American dry goods.

LADY HUNSTANTON: What are American dry goods?

LORD ILLINGWORTH: American novels.

LADY HUNSTANTON: How very singular! . . . Well, from whatever source her large fortune came, I have a great esteem for Miss Worsley. She dresses exceedingly well. All Americans do dress well. They get their clothes in Paris.

MRS ALLONBY: They say, Lady Hunstanton, that when good Americans die they go to Paris.

LADY HUNSTANTON: Indeed? And when bad Americans die, where do they go to?

LORD ILLINGWORTH: Oh, they go to America.

KELVIL: I am afraid you don't appreciate America, Lord Illingworth. It is a very remarkable country, especially considering its youth.

LORD ILLINGWORTH: The youth of America is their oldest tradition. It has been going on now for three hundred years. To hear them talk one would imagine they were in their first childhood. As far as civilization goes they are in their second.

KELVIL: There is undoubtedly a great deal of corruption in American politics. I suppose you allude to that?

LORD ILLINGWORTH: I wonder.

LADY HUNSTANTON: Politics are in a sad way everywhere, I am told. They certainly are in England. Dear Mr Cardew is ruining the country. I wonder Mrs Cardew allows him. I am sure, Lord Illingworth, you don't think that uneducated people should be allowed to have votes?

LORD ILLINGWORTH: I think they are the only people who should.

KELVIL: Do you take no side then in modern politics, Lord Illingworth?

LORD ILLINGWORTH: One should never take sides in anything, Mr Kelvil. Taking sides is the beginning of sincerity, and earnestness follows shortly afterwards, and the human being becomes a bore. However, the House of Commons really does very little harm. You can't make people good by Act of Parliament, – that is something.

KELVIL: You cannot deny that the House of Commons has always shown great sympathy with the sufferings of the poor.

LORD ILLINGWORTH: That is its special vice. That is the special vice of the age. One should sympathize with the joy, the beauty, the colour of life. The less said about life's sores the better, Mr Kelvil.

KELVIL: Still our East End is a very important problem.

LORD ILLINGWORTH: Quite so. It is the problem of slavery. And we are trying to solve it by amusing the slaves.

LADY HUNSTANTON: Certainly, a great deal may be done by means of cheap entertainments, as you say, Lord Illingworth. Dear Dr Daubeny, our rector here, provides, with the assistance of his curates, really admirable recreations for the poor during the winter. And much good may be done by means of a magic lantern, or a missionary, or some popular amusement of that kind.[8]

LADY CAROLINE: I am not at all in favour of amusements for the poor, Jane. Blankets and coals are sufficient. There is too much love of pleasure amongst the upper classes as it is. Health is what we want in modern life. The tone is not healthy, not healthy at all.

KELVIL: You are quite right, Lady Caroline.

LADY CAROLINE: I believe I am usually right.

MRS ALLONBY: Horrid word 'health'.

LORD ILLINGWORTH: Silliest word in our language, and one knows so well the popular idea of health. The English country gentleman galloping after a fox – the unspeakable in full pursuit of the uneatable.

KELVIL: May I ask, Lord Illingworth, if you regard the House of Lords as a better institution than the House of Commons?

LORD ILLINGWORTH: A much better institution, of course. We in the House of Lords are never in touch with public opinion. That makes us a civilized body.

KELVIL: Are you serious in putting forward such a view?

LORD ILLINGWORTH: Quite serious, Mr Kelvil. [*To* MRS ALLONBY.] Vulgar habit that is people have nowadays of asking one, after one has given them an idea, whether one is serious or not. Nothing is serious except passion. The intellect is not a serious thing, and never has been. It is an instrument on which one plays, that is all. The only serious form of intellect I know is the British intellect. And on the British intellect the illiterates play the drum.

LADY HUNSTANTON: What are you saying, Lord Illingworth, about the drum?

LORD ILLINGWORTH: I was merely talking to Mrs Allonby about the leading articles in the London newspapers.

LADY HUNSTANTON: But do you believe all that is written in the newspapers?

LORD ILLINGWORTH: I do. Nowadays it is only the unreadable that occurs.

[*Rises with* MRS ALLONBY.]

LADY HUNSTANTON: Are you going, Mrs Allonby?

MRS ALLONBY: Just as far as the conservatory. Lord Illingworth told me this morning that there was an orchid there as beautiful as the seven deadly sins.

LADY HUNSTANTON: My dear, I hope there is nothing of the kind, I will certainly speak to the gardener.

[*Exit* MRS ALLONBY *and* LORD ILLINGWORTH.]

LADY CAROLINE: Remarkable type, Mrs Allonby.

LADY HUNSTANTON: She lets her clever tongue run away with her sometimes.

LADY CAROLINE: Is that the only thing, Jane, Mrs Allonby allows to run away with her?

LADY HUNSTANTON: I hope so, Caroline, I am sure. [*Enter* LORD ALFRED.] Dear Lord Alfred, do join us. [LORD ALFRED[9] *sits down beside* LADY STUTFIELD.]

LADY CAROLINE: You believe good of everyone, Jane. It is a great fault.

LADY STUTFIELD: Do you really, really think, Lady Caroline, that one should believe evil of everyone?

LADY CAROLINE: I think it is much safer to do so, Lady Stutfield. Until, of course, people are found out to be good. But that requires a great deal of investigation, nowadays.

LADY STUTFIELD: But there is so much unkind scandal in modern life.

LADY CAROLINE: Lord Illingworth remarked to me last night at dinner that the basis of every scandal is an absolutely immoral certainty.

KELVIL: Lord Illingworth is, of course, a very brilliant man, but he seems to me to be lacking in that fine faith in the nobility and purity of life which is so important in this century.

LADY STUTFIELD: Yes, quite, quite important, is it not?

KELVIL: He gives me the impression of a man who does not appreciate the beauty of our English home-life. I would say that he was tainted with foreign ideas on the subject.

LADY STUTFIELD: There is nothing, nothing like the beauty of home-life, is there?

KELVIL: It is the mainstay of our moral system in England, Lady Stutfield. Without it we would become like our neighbours.

LADY STUTFIELD: That would be so, so sad, would it not?

KELVIL: I am afraid, too, that Lord Illingworth regards woman simply as a toy. Now, I have never regarded woman as a toy. Woman is the intellectual helpmeet of man in public as in private life. Without her we should forget the true ideals.

[*Sits down beside* LADY STUTFIELD.]

LADY STUTFIELD: I am so very, very glad to hear you say that.

LADY CAROLINE: You a married man, Mr Kettle?

SIR JOHN: Kelvil, dear, Kelvil.

KELVIL: I am married, Lady Caroline.

LADY CAROLINE: Family?

KELVIL: Yes.

LADY CAROLINE: How many?

KELVIL: Eight.

[LADY STUTFIELD *turns her attention to* LORD ALFRED.]

LADY CAROLINE: Mrs Kettle and the children are, I suppose, at the seaside?

[SIR JOHN *shrugs his shoulders.*]

KELVIL: My wife is at the seaside with the children, Lady Caroline.

LADY CAROLINE: You will join them later on, no doubt?

KELVIL: If my public engagements permit me.

LADY CAROLINE: Your public life must be a great source of gratification to Mrs Kettle.[10]

SIR JOHN: Kelvil, my love, Kelvil.

LADY STUTFIELD [*to* LORD ALFRED]: How very, very charming those gold-tipped cigarettes of yours are, Lord Alfred.

LORD ALFRED: They are awfully expensive. I can only afford them when I'm in debt.

LADY STUTFIELD: It must be terribly, terribly distressing to be in debt.

LORD ALFRED: One must have some occupation nowadays. If I hadn't my debts I shouldn't have anything to think about. All the chaps I know are in debt.

LADY STUTFIELD: But don't the people to whom you owe the money give you a great, great deal of annoyance?

[*Enter Footman.*]

LORD ALFRED: Oh, no, they write; I don't.

LADY STUTFIELD: How very, very strange.

LADY HUNSTANTON: Ah, here is a letter, Caroline, from dear Mrs Arbuthnot. She won't dine. I am so sorry. But she will come in the evening. I am very pleased indeed. She is one of the sweetest of women. Writes a beautiful hand,[11] too, so large, so firm.

[*Hands letter to* LADY CAROLINE.]

LADY CAROLINE [*looking at it*]: A little lacking in femininity, Jane. Femininity is the quality I admire most in women.

LADY HUNSTANTON [*taking back letter and leaving it on table*]: Oh! she is very feminine, Caroline, and so good too. You should hear what the Archdeacon says of her. He regards her as his right hand in the parish. [*Footman speaks to her.*] In the Yellow Drawing-room. Shall we all go in? Lady Stutfield, shall we go in to tea?

LADY STUTFIELD: With pleasure, Lady Hunstanton.

[*They rise and proceed to go off.* SIR JOHN *offers to carry* LADY STUTFIELD'S *cloak.*]

LADY CAROLINE: John! If you would allow your nephew to look after Lady Stutfield's cloak, you might help me with my work-basket.

[*Enter* LORD ILLINGWORTH *and* MRS ALLONBY.]

SIR JOHN: Certainly, my love.

[*Exeunt.*]

MRS ALLONBY: Curious thing, plain women are always jealous of their husbands, beautiful women never are!

LORD ILLINGWORTH: Beautiful women never have time. They are always so occupied in being jealous of other people's husbands.

MRS ALLONBY: I should have thought Lady Caroline would have grown tired of conjugal anxiety by this time! Sir John is her fourth!

LORD ILLINGWORTH: So much marriage is certainly not becoming. Twenty years of romance make a woman look like a ruin; but twenty years of marriage make her something like a public building.

MRS ALLONBY: Twenty years of romance! Is there such a thing?

LORD ILLINGWORTH: Not in our day. Women have become too brilliant. Nothing spoils a romance so much as a sense of humour in the woman.

MRS ALLONBY: Or the want of it in the man.[12]

LORD ILLINGWORTH: You are quite right. In a Temple everyone should be serious, except the thing that is worshipped.

MRS ALLONBY: And that should be man?

LORD ILLINGWORTH: Women kneel so gracefully; men don't.

MRS ALLONBY: You are thinking of Lady Stutfield!

LORD ILLINGWORTH: I assure you I have not thought of Lady Stutfield for the last quarter of an hour.

MRS ALLONBY: Is she such a mystery?

LORD ILLINGWORTH: She is more than a mystery – she is a mood.

MRS ALLONBY: Moods don't last.

LORD ILLINGWORTH: It is their chief charm.

[*Enter* HESTER *and* GERALD.]

GERALD: Lord Illingworth, everyone has been congratulating me, Lady Hunstanton and Lady Caroline, and . . . everyone. I hope I shall make a good secretary.

LORD ILLINGWORTH: You will be the pattern secretary, Gerald.

[*Talks to him.*]

MRS ALLONBY: You enjoy country life, Miss Worsley?

HESTER: Very much indeed.

MRS ALLONBY: Don't find yourself longing for a London dinner-party?

HESTER: I dislike London dinner-parties.

MRS ALLONBY: I adore them. The clever people never listen, and the stupid people never talk.

HESTER: I think the stupid people talk a great deal.

MRS ALLONBY: Ah, I never listen!

LORD ILLINGWORTH: My dear boy, if I didn't like you I wouldn't have made you the offer. It is because I like you so much that I want to have you with me. [*Exit* HESTER *with* GERALD.] Charming fellow, Gerald Arbuthnot!

MRS ALLONBY: He is very nice; very nice indeed. But I can't stand the American young lady.

LORD ILLINGWORTH: Why?

MRS ALLONBY: She told me yesterday, and in quite a loud voice too, that she was only eighteen. It was most annoying.

LORD ILLINGWORTH: One should never trust a woman who tells one her real age. A woman who would tell one that, would tell one anything.

MRS ALLONBY: She is a Puritan besides –

LORD ILLINGWORTH: Ah, that is inexcusable. I don't mind plain women being Puritans. It is the only excuse they have for being plain. But she is decidedly pretty. I admire her immensely.

[*Looks steadfastly at* MRS ALLONBY.][13]

MRS ALLONBY: What a thoroughly bad man you must be!

LORD ILLINGWORTH: What do you call a bad man?

MRS ALLONBY: The sort of man who admires innocence.

LORD ILLINGWORTH: And a bad woman?

MRS ALLONBY: Oh! the sort of woman a man never gets tired of.

LORD ILLINGWORTH: You are severe – on yourself.

MRS ALLONBY: Define us as a sex.

LORD ILLINGWORTH: Sphinxes[14] without secrets.

MRS ALLONBY: Does that include the Puritan women?

LORD ILLINGWORTH: Do you know, I don't believe in the existence of Puritan women! I don't think there is a woman in the world who would not be a little flattered if one made love[15] to her. It is that which makes women so irresistibly adorable.

MRS ALLONBY: You think there is no woman in the world who would object to being kissed?

LORD ILLINGWORTH: Very few.

MRS ALLONBY: Miss Worsley would not let you kiss her.

LORD ILLINGWORTH: Are you sure?

MRS ALLONBY: Quite.

LORD ILLINGWORTH: What do you think she'd do if I kissed her?

MRS ALLONBY: Either marry you, or strike you across the face with her glove. What would you do if she struck you across the face with her glove?

LORD ILLINGWORTH: Fall in love with her, probably.

MRS ALLONBY: Then it is lucky you are not going to kiss her!

LORD ILLINGWORTH: Is that a challenge?

MRS ALLONBY: It is an arrow shot into the air.

LORD ILLINGWORTH: Don't you know that I always succeed in whatever I try?

MRS ALLONBY: I am sorry to hear it. We women adore failures. They lean on us.

LORD ILLINGWORTH: You worship successes. You cling to them.

MRS ALLONBY: We are the laurels to hide their baldness.

LORD ILLINGWORTH: And they need you always, except at the moment of triumph.

MRS ALLONBY: They are uninteresting then.

LORD ILLINGWORTH: How tantalizing you are!

[*A pause.*]

MRS ALLONBY: Lord Illingworth, there is one thing I shall always like you for.

LORD ILLINGWORTH: Only one thing? And I have so many bad qualities.

MRS ALLONBY: Ah, don't be too conceited about them. You may lose them as you grow old.

LORD ILLINGWORTH: I never intend to grow old. The soul is born old but grows young. That is the comedy of life.

MRS ALLONBY: And the body is born young and grows old. That is life's tragedy.

LORD ILLINGWORTH: It's comedy also, sometimes. But what is the mysterious reason why you will always like me?

MRS ALLONBY: It is that you have never made love to me.

LORD ILLINGWORTH: I have never done anything else.

MRS ALLONBY: Really? I have not noticed it.

LORD ILLINGWORTH: How fortunate! It might have been a tragedy for both of us.

MRS ALLONBY: We should each have survived.

LORD ILLINGWORTH: One can survive everything nowadays, except death, and live down anything except a good reputation.

MRS ALLONBY: Have you tried a good reputation?

LORD ILLINGWORTH: It is one of the many annoyances to which I have never been subjected.

MRS ALLONBY: It may come.

LORD ILLINGWORTH: Why do you threaten me?

MRS ALLONBY: I will tell you when you have kissed the Puritan.

[*Enter Footman.*]

FRANCIS: Tea is served in the Yellow Drawing-room, my lord.

LORD ILLINGWORTH: Tell her ladyship we are coming in.

FRANCIS: Yes, my lord.

[*Exit.*]

LORD ILLINGWORTH: Shall we go in to tea?

MRS ALLONBY: Do you like such simple pleasures?

LORD ILLINGWORTH: I adore simple pleasures. They are the last refuge of the complex. But, if you wish, let us stay here. Yes, let us stay here. The Book of Life begins with a man and a woman in a garden.

MRS ALLONBY: It ends with Revelations.

LORD ILLINGWORTH: You fence divinely. But the button has come off your foil.

MRS ALLONBY: I have still the mask.

LORD ILLINGWORTH: It makes your eyes lovelier.

MRS ALLONBY: Thank you. Come.

LORD ILLINGWORTH [*sees* MRS ARBUTHNOT'S *letter on table, and takes it up and looks at envelope*]: What a curious handwriting! It reminds me of the handwriting of a woman I used to know years ago.

MRS ALLONBY: Who?

LORD ILLINGWORTH: Oh! no one. No one in particular. A woman of no importance.[16]

[*Throws letter down, and passes up the steps of the terrace with* MRS ALLONBY. *They smile at each other.*]

ACT DROP

SECOND ACT

SCENE

Drawing-room at Hunstanton, after dinner, lamps lit.
Door L. C. Door R. C.

[*Ladies seated on sofas.*][1]

MRS ALLONBY: What a comfort it is to have got rid of the men for a little!

LADY STUTFIELD: Yes; men persecute us dreadfully, don't they?

MRS ALLONBY: Persecute us? I wish they did.

LADY HUNSTANTON: My dear!

MRS ALLONBY: The annoying thing is that the wretches can be perfectly happy without us. That is why I think it is every woman's duty never to leave them alone for a single moment, except during this short breathing space after dinner; without which I believe we poor women would be absolutely worn to shadows.

[*Enter Servants with coffee.*]

LADY HUNSTANTON: Worn to shadows, dear?

MRS ALLONBY: Yes, Lady Hunstanton. It is such a strain keeping men up to the mark. They are always trying to escape from us.

LADY STUTFIELD: It seems to me that it is we who are always trying to escape from them. Men are so very, very heartless. They know their power and use it.

LADY CAROLINE [*takes coffee from Servant*]: What stuff and nonsense all this about men is! The thing to do is to keep men in their proper place.

MRS ALLONBY: But what is their proper place, Lady Caroline?

LADY CAROLINE: Looking after their wives, Mrs Allonby.

MRS ALLONBY [*takes coffee from Servant*]: Really? And if they're not married?

LADY CAROLINE: If they are not married, they should be looking after a wife. It's perfectly scandalous the amount of bachelors who are going about society. There should be a law passed to compel them all to marry within twelve months.

LADY STUTFIELD [*refuses coffee*]: But if they're in love with someone who, perhaps, is tied to another?

LADY CAROLINE: In that case, Lady Stutfield, they should be married off in a week to some plain respectable girl, in order to teach them not to meddle with other people's property.

MRS ALLONBY: I don't think that we should ever be spoken of as other people's property. All men are married women's property. That is the only true definition of what married women's property really is. But we don't belong to anyone.[2]

LADY STUTFIELD: Oh, I am so very, very glad to hear you say so.

LADY HUNSTANTON: But do you really think, dear Caroline, that legislation would improve matters in any way? I am told that, nowadays, all the married men live like bachelors, and all the bachelors like married men.

MRS ALLONBY: I certainly never know one from the other.

LADY STUTFIELD: Oh, I think one can always know at once whether a man has home claims upon his life or not. I have noticed a very, very sad expression in the eyes of so many married men.

MRS ALLONBY: Ah, all that I have noticed is that they are horribly tedious when they are good husbands, and abominably conceited when they are not.

LADY HUNSTANTON: Well, I suppose the type of husband has completely changed since my young days, but I'm bound to state that poor dear Hunstanton was the most delightful of creatures, and as good as gold.

MRS ALLONBY: Ah, my husband is a sort of promissory note;[3] I'm tired of meeting him.

LADY CAROLINE: But you renew him from time to time, don't you?

MRS ALLONBY: Oh no, Lady Caroline. I have only had one husband as yet. I suppose you look upon me as quite an amateur.

LADY CAROLINE: With your views on life I wonder you married at all.

MRS ALLONBY: So do I.

LADY HUNSTANTON: My dear child, I believe you are really very happy in your married life, but that you like to hide your happiness from others.

MRS ALLONBY: I assure you I was horribly deceived in Ernest.

LADY HUNSTANTON: Oh, I hope not, dear. I knew his mother quite well. She was a Stratton, Caroline, one of Lord Crowland's daughters.

LADY CAROLINE: Victoria Stratton? I remember her perfectly. A silly fair-haired woman with no chin.

MRS ALLONBY: Ah, Ernest has a chin. He has a very strong chin, a square chin. Ernest's chin is far too square.

LADY STUTFIELD: But do you really think a man's chin can be too square? I think a man should look very, very strong, and that his chin should be quite, quite square.

MRS ALLONBY: Then you should certainly know Ernest, Lady Stutfield. It is only fair to tell you beforehand he has got no conversation at all.

LADY STUTFIELD: I adore silent men.

MRS ALLONBY: Oh, Ernest isn't silent. He talks the whole time. But he has got no conversation. What he talks about I don't know. I haven't listened to him for years.

LADY STUTFIELD: Have you never forgiven him then? How sad that seems! But all life is very, very sad, is it not?

MRS ALLONBY: Life, Lady Stutfield, is simply a *mauvais quart d'heure*[4] made up of exquisite moments.

LADY STUTFIELD: Yes, there are moments, certainly. But was it something very, very wrong that Mr Allonby did? Did he become angry with you, and say anything that was unkind or true?

MRS ALLONBY: Oh dear, no. Ernest is invariably calm. That is one of the reasons he always gets on my nerves. Nothing is so aggravating as calmness. There is something positively brutal about the good temper of most modern men. I wonder we women stand it as well as we do.

LADY STUTFIELD: Yes; men's good temper shows they are not so sensitive as we are, not so finely strung. It makes a great barrier often between husband and wife, does it not? But I would so much like to know what was the wrong thing Mr Allonby did.

MRS ALLONBY: Well, I will tell you, if you solemnly promise to tell everybody else.

LADY STUTFIELD: Thank you, thank you. I will make a point of repeating it.

MRS ALLONBY: When Ernest and I were engaged, he swore to me positively on his knees that he had never loved anyone before in the whole course of his life. I was very young at the time, so I didn't believe him, I needn't tell you. Unfortunately, however, I made no inquiries of any kind till after I had been actually married four or five months. I found out then that what he had told me was perfectly true. And that sort of thing makes a man so absolutely uninteresting.[5]

LADY HUNSTANTON: My dear!

MRS ALLONBY: Men always want to be a woman's first love. That is their clumsy vanity. We women have a more subtle instinct about things. What we like is to be a man's last romance.

LADY STUTFIELD: I see what you mean. It's very, very beautiful.

LADY HUNSTANTON: My dear child, you don't mean to tell me that you won't forgive your husband because he never loved anyone else? Did you ever hear such a thing, Caroline? I am quite surprised.

LADY CAROLINE: Oh, women have become so highly educated, Jane, that nothing should surprise us nowadays, except happy marriages. They apparently are getting remarkably rare.

MRS ALLONBY: Oh, they're quite out of date.

LADY STUTFIELD: Except amongst the middle classes, I have been told.

MRS ALLONBY: How like the middle classes!

LADY STUTFIELD: Yes – is it not? – very, very like them.

LADY CAROLINE: If what you tell us about the middle classes is true, Lady Stutfield, it redounds greatly to their credit. It is much to be regretted that in our rank of life the wife should be so persistently frivolous, under the impression apparently that it is the proper thing to be. It is to that I attribute the unhappiness of so many marriages we all know of in society.

MRS ALLONBY: Do you know, Lady Caroline, I don't think the frivolity of the wife has ever anything to do with it. More marriages are ruined nowadays by the common sense of the husband than by anything else. How can a woman be expected to be happy with a man who insists on treating her as if she were a perfectly rational being?

LADY HUNSTANTON: My dear!

MRS ALLONBY: Man, poor, awkward, reliable, necessary man belongs to a sex that has been rational for millions and millions of years. He can't help himself. It is in his race. The History of Woman is very different. We have always been picturesque protests against the mere existence of common sense. We saw its dangers from the first.

LADY STUTFIELD: Yes, the common sense of husbands is certainly most, most trying. Do tell me your conception of the Ideal Husband. I think it would be so very, very helpful.

MRS ALLONBY: The Ideal Husband? There couldn't be such a thing. The institution is wrong.

LADY STUTFIELD: The Ideal Man, then, in his relations to *us*.

LADY CAROLINE: He would probably be extremely realistic.

MRS ALLONBY: The Ideal Man! Oh, the Ideal Man should talk to us as if we were goddesses, and treat us as if we were children. He should refuse all our serious requests, and gratify every one of our whims. He should encourage us to have caprices, and forbid us to have missions. He should always say much more than he means, and always mean much more than he says.

LADY HUNSTANTON: But how could he do both, dear?

MRS ALLONBY: He should never run down other pretty women. That would show he had no taste, or make one suspect that he had too much. No; he should be nice about them all, but say that somehow they don't attract him.

LADY STUTFIELD: Yes, that is always very, very pleasant to hear about other women.

MRS ALLONBY: If we ask him a question about anything, he should give us an answer all about ourselves. He should invariably praise us for whatever qualities he knows we haven't got. But he should be pitiless, quite pitiless, in reproaching us for the virtues that we have never dreamed of possessing. He should never believe that we know the use of useful things. That would be unforgivable. But he should shower on us everything we don't want.

LADY CAROLINE: As far as I can see, he is to do nothing but pay bills and compliments.

MRS ALLONBY: He should persistently compromise us in public, and treat us with absolute respect when we are alone. And yet he should be always ready to have a perfectly terrible scene, whenever we want one, and to become miserable, absolutely miserable, at a moment's notice, and to overwhelm us with just reproaches in less than twenty minutes, and to be positively violent at the end of half an hour, and to leave us for ever at a quarter to eight, when we have to go and dress for dinner. And when, after that, one has seen him for really the last time, and he has refused to take back the little things he has given one, and promised never to communicate with one again, or to write one any foolish letters, he should be perfectly broken-hearted, and telegraph to one all day long, and send one little notes every half-hour by a private hansom, and dine quite alone at the club, so that every one should know how unhappy he was. And after a whole dreadful week, during which one has gone about everywhere with one's husband, just to show how absolutely lonely one was, he may be given a third last parting, in the evening, and then, if his conduct has been quite irreproachable, and one has behaved really badly to him, he should be allowed to admit that he has been entirely in the wrong, and when he has admitted that, it becomes a woman's duty to forgive, and one can do it all over again from the beginning, with variations.

LADY HUNSTANTON: How clever you are, my dear! You never mean a single word you say.

LADY STUTFIELD: Thank you, thank you. It has been quite, quite entrancing. I must try and remember it all. There are such a number of details that are so very, very important.

LADY CAROLINE: But you have not told us yet what the reward of the Ideal Man is to be.

MRS ALLONBY: His reward? Oh, infinite expectation. That is quite enough for him.

LADY STUTFIELD: But men are so terribly, terribly, exacting, are they not?

MRS ALLONBY: That makes no matter. One should never surrender.

LADY STUTFIELD: Not even to the Ideal Man?

MRS ALLONBY: Certainly not to him. Unless, of course, one wants to grow tired of him.

LADY STUTFIELD: Oh! . . . yes. I see that. It is very, very helpful. Do you think, Mrs Allonby, I shall ever meet the Ideal Man? Or are there more than one?

MRS ALLONBY: There are just four in London, Lady Stutfield.

LADY HUNSTANTON: Oh, my dear!

MRS ALLONBY [*going over to her*]: What has happened? Do tell me.

LADY HUNSTANTON [*in a low voice*]: I had completely forgotten that the American young lady has been in the room all the time. I am afraid some of this clever talk may have shocked her a little.

MRS ALLONBY: Ah, that will do her so much good!

LADY HUNSTANTON: Let us hope she didn't understand much. I think I had better go over and talk to her. [*Rises and goes across to* HESTER WORSLEY.] Well, dear Miss Worsley. [*Sitting down beside her.*] How quiet you have been in your nice little corner all this time! I suppose you have been reading a book? There are so many books here in the library.

HESTER: No, I have been listening to the conversation.

LADY HUNSTANTON: You mustn't believe everything that was said, you know, dear.

HESTER: I didn't believe any of it.

LADY HUNSTANTON: That is quite right, dear.

HESTER [*continuing*]: I couldn't believe that any women could really hold such views of life as I have heard tonight from some of your guests.

[*An awkward pause.*]

LADY HUNSTANTON: I hear you have such pleasant society in America. Quite like our own in places, my son wrote to me.

HESTER: There are cliques in America as elsewhere, Lady Hunstanton. But true American society consists simply of all the good women and good men we have in our country.[6]

LADY HUNSTANTON: What a sensible system, and I dare say quite pleasant too. I am afraid in England we have too many artificial social barriers. We don't see as much as we should of the middle and lower classes.

HESTER: In America we have no lower classes.

LADY HUNSTANTON: Really? What a very strange arrangement!

MRS ALLONBY: What is that dreadful girl talking about?

LADY STUTFIELD: She is painfully natural, is she not?

LADY CAROLINE: There are a great many things you haven't got in America, I am told, Miss Worsley. They say you have no ruins, and no curiosities.

MRS ALLONBY [*to* LADY STUTFIELD]: What nonsense! They have their mothers and their manners.

HESTER: The English aristocracy supply us with our curiosities, Lady Caroline. They are sent over to us every summer, regularly, in the steamers, and propose to us the day after they land. As for ruins, we are trying to build up something that will last longer than brick or stone.

[*Gets up to take her fan from table.*]

LADY HUNSTANTON: What is that, dear? Ah, yes, an iron Exhibition, is it not, at that place that has the curious name?[7]

HESTER [*standing by table*]: We are trying to build up life, Lady Hunstanton, on a better, truer, purer basis than life rests on here. This sounds strange to you all, no doubt. How could it sound other than strange? You rich people in England, you don't know how you are living. How could you know? You shut out from your society the gentle and the good. You laugh at the simple and the pure. Living, as you all do, on others and by them, you sneer at self-sacrifice, and if you throw bread to the poor, it is merely to keep them quiet for a season. With all your pomp and wealth and art you don't know how to live – you don't even know that. You love the beauty that you can see and touch and handle, the beauty that you can destroy, and do destroy, but of the unseen beauty of life, of the unseen beauty of a higher life, you know nothing. You have lost life's secret. Oh, your English society seems to me shallow, selfish, foolish. It has blinded its eyes, and stopped its ears. It lies like a leper in purple. It sits like a dead thing smeared with gold. It is all wrong, all wrong.

LADY STUTFIELD: I don't think one should know of these things. It is not very, very nice, is it?

LADY HUNSTANTON: My dear Miss Worsley, I thought you liked English society so much. You were such a success in it. And you were so much admired by the best people. I quite forget what Lord Henry Weston said of you – but it was most complimentary, and you know what an authority he is on beauty.

HESTER: Lord Henry Weston! I remember him, Lady Hunstanton. A man with a hideous smile and a hideous past. He is asked everywhere. No dinner-party is complete without him.[8] What of those whose ruin is due to him? They are outcasts. They are nameless. If you met them in the street you would turn your head away. I don't complain of their punishment. Let all women who have sinned be punished.

[MRS ARBUTHNOT *enters from terrace behind in a cloak with a lace veil over her head. She hears the last words and starts.*]

LADY HUNSTANTON: My dear young lady!

HESTER: It is right that they should be punished, but don't let them be the only ones to suffer. If a man and woman have sinned, let them both go forth into the desert to love or loathe each other there. Let them both be branded. Set a mark, if you wish, on each, but don't punish the one and let the other go free.[9] Don't have one law for men and another for women. You are unjust to women in England. And till you count what is a shame in a woman to be an infamy in a man, you will always be unjust, and Right, that pillar of fire, and Wrong, that pillar of cloud, will be made dim to your eyes, or be not seen at all, or if seen, not regarded.

LADY CAROLINE: Might I, dear Miss Worsley, as you are standing up, ask you for my cotton that is just behind you? Thank you.[10]

LADY HUNSTANTON: My dear Mrs Arbuthnot! I am so pleased you have come up. But I didn't hear you announced.

MRS ARBUTHNOT: Oh, I came straight in from the terrace, Lady Hunstanton, just as I was. You didn't tell me you had a party.

LADY HUNSTANTON: Not a party. Only a few guests who are staying in the house, and whom you must know. Allow me. [*Tries to help her. Rings bell.*] Caroline, this is Mrs Arbuthnot, one of my sweetest friends. Lady Caroline Pontefract, Lady Stutfield, Mrs Allonby, and my young American friend, Miss Worsley, who has just been telling us all how wicked we are.

HESTER: I am afraid you think I spoke too strongly, Lady Hunstanton. But there are some things in England –

LADY HUNSTANTON: My dear young lady, there was a great deal of truth, I dare say, in what you said, and you looked very pretty while you said it, which is much more important, Lord Illingworth would tell us. The only point where I thought you were a little hard was about Lady Caroline's brother, about poor Lord Henry. He is really such good company. [*Enter Footman.*] Take Mrs Arbuthnot's things.

[*Exit Footman with wraps.*]

HESTER: Lady Caroline, I had no idea it was your brother. I am sorry for the pain I must have caused you – I –

LADY CAROLINE: My dear Miss Worsley, the only part of your little speech, if I may so term it, with which I thoroughly agreed, was the part about my brother. Nothing that you could possibly say could be too bad for him. I regard Henry as infamous, absolutely infamous. But I am bound to state, as you were remarking, Jane, that he is excellent company, and he has one of the best cooks in London, and after a good dinner one can forgive anybody, even one's own relations.

LADY HUNSTANTON [*to* MISS WORSLEY]: Now, do come, dear, and make friends with Mrs Arbuthnot. She is one of the good, sweet, simple people you told us we never admitted into society. I am sorry to say Mrs Arbuthnot comes very rarely to me. But that is not my fault.

MRS ALLONBY: What a bore it is the men staying so long after dinner! I expect they are saying the most dreadful things about us.

LADY STUTFIELD: Do you really think so?

MRS ALLONBY: I am sure of it.

LADY STUTFIELD: How very, very horrid of them! Shall we go on to the terrace?

MRS ALLONBY: Oh, anything to get away from the dowagers and the dowdies. [*Rises and goes with* LADY STUTFIELD *to door L. C.*] We are only going to look at the stars, Lady Hunstanton.

LADY HUNSTANTON: You will find a great many, dear, a great many. But don't catch cold. [*To* MRS ARBUTHNOT.] We shall all miss Gerald so much, dear Mrs Arbuthnot.

MRS ARBUTHNOT: But has Lord Illingworth really offered to make Gerald his secretary?

LADY HUNSTANTON: Oh, yes! He has been most charming about it. He has the highest possible opinion of your boy. You don't know Lord Illingworth, I believe, dear.

MRS ARBUTHNOT: I have never met him.

LADY HUNSTANTON: You know him by name, no doubt?

MRS ARBUTHNOT: I am afraid I don't. I live so much out of the world, and see so few people. I remember hearing years ago of an old Lord Illingworth who lived in Yorkshire, I think.

LADY HUNSTANTON: Ah, yes. That would be the last Earl but one. He was a very curious man. He wanted to marry beneath him. Or wouldn't, I believe. There was some scandal about it. The present Lord Illingworth is quite different. He is very distinguished. He does – well, he does nothing, which I am afraid our pretty American visitor here thinks very wrong of anybody, and I don't know that he cares much for the subjects in which you are so interested, dear Mrs Arbuthnot. Do you think, Caroline, that Lord Illingworth is interested in the Housing of the Poor?

LADY CAROLINE: I should fancy not at all, Jane.

LADY HUNSTANTON: We all have our different tastes, have we not? But Lord Illingworth has a very high position, and there is nothing he couldn't get if he chose to ask for it. Of course, he is comparatively a young man still, and he has only come to his title within – how long exactly is it, Caroline, since Lord Illingworth succeeded?

LADY CAROLINE: About four years, I think, Jane. I know it was the same year in which my brother had his last exposure in the evening newspapers.

LADY HUNSTANTON: Ah, I remember. That would be about four years ago. Of course, there were a great many people between the present Lord Illingworth and the title, Mrs Arbuthnot. There was – who was there, Caroline?

LADY CAROLINE: There was poor Margaret's baby. You remember how anxious she was to have a boy, and it was a boy, but it died and her husband died shortly afterwards, and she married almost immediately one of Lord Ascot's sons, who, I am told, beats her.

LADY HUNSTANTON: Ah, that is in the family, dear, that is in the family. And there was also, I remember, a clergyman who wanted to be a lunatic, or a lunatic who wanted to be a clergyman, I forget which, but I know the Court of Chancery investigated the matter, and decided that he was quite sane. And I saw him afterwards at poor Lord Plumstead's with straws in his hair, or something very odd about him. I can't recall what. I often regret, Lady Caroline, that dear Lady Cecilia never lived to see her son get the title.

MRS ARBUTHNOT: Lady Cecilia?

LADY HUNSTANTON: Lord Illingworth's mother, dear Mrs Arbuthnot, was one of the Duchess of Jerningham's pretty daughters, and she married Sir Thomas Harford, who wasn't considered a very good match for her at the time, though he was said to be the handsomest man in London. I knew them all quite intimately, and both the sons, Arthur and George.

MRS ARBUTHNOT: It was the eldest son who succeeded, of course, Lady Hunstanton?

LADY HUNSTANTON: No, dear, he was killed in the hunting field. Or was it fishing, Caroline? I forget. But George came in for everything. I always tell him that no younger son has ever had such good luck as he has had.

MRS ARBUTHNOT: Lady Hunstanton, I want to speak to Gerald at once. Might I see him? Can he be sent for?

LADY HUNSTANTON: Certainly, dear. I will send one of the servants into the dining-room to fetch him. I don't know what keeps the gentlemen so long. [*Rings bell.*] When I knew Lord Illingworth first as plain George Harford, he was simply a very brilliant young man about town, with not a penny of money except what poor dear

Lady Cecilia gave him. She was quite devoted to him. Chiefly, I fancy, because he was on bad terms with his father.[11] Oh, here is the dear Archdeacon. [*To Servant.*] It doesn't matter.

[*Enter* SIR JOHN *and* DOCTOR DAUBENY. SIR JOHN *goes over to* LADY STUTFIELD, DOCTOR DAUBENY *to* LADY HUNSTANTON.]

THE ARCHDEACON: Lord Illingworth has been most entertaining. I have never enjoyed myself more. [*Sees* MRS ARBUTHNOT.] Ah, Mrs Arbuthnot.

LADY HUNSTANTON [*to* DOCTOR DAUBENY]: You see I have got Mrs Arbuthnot to come to me at last.

THE ARCHDEACON: That is a great honour, Lady Hunstanton. Mrs Daubeny will be quite jealous of you.

LADY HUNSTANTON: Ah, I am so sorry Mrs Daubeny could not come with you tonight. Headache as usual, I suppose?

THE ARCHDEACON: Yes, Lady Hunstanton; a perfect martyr. But she is happiest alone. She is happiest alone.

LADY CAROLINE [*to her husband*]: John!

[SIR JOHN *goes over to his wife.* DOCTOR DAUBENY *talks to* LADY HUNSTANTON *and* MRS ARBUTHNOT.]

[MRS ARBUTHNOT *watches* LORD ILLINGWORTH *the whole time. He has passed across the room without noticing her, and approaches* MRS ALLONBY, *who with* LADY STUTFIELD *is standing by the door looking on to the terrace.*]

LORD ILLINGWORTH: How is the most charming woman in the world?

MRS ALLONBY [*taking* LADY STUTFIELD *by the hand*]: We are both quite well, thank you, Lord Illingworth. But what a short time you have been in the dining-room! It seems as if we had only just left.

LORD ILLINGWORTH: I was bored to death. Never opened my lips the whole time. Absolutely longing to come in to you.

MRS ALLONBY: You should have. The American girl has been giving us a lecture.

LORD ILLINGWORTH: Really? All Americans lecture,[12] I believe. I suppose it is something in their climate. What did she lecture about?

MRS ALLONBY: Oh, Puritanism, of course.

LORD ILLINGWORTH: I am going to convert her, am I not? How long do you give me?

MRS ALLONBY: A week.

LORD ILLINGWORTH: A week is more than enough.

[*Enter* GERALD *and* LORD ALFRED.]

GERALD [*going to* MRS ARBUTHNOT]: Dear mother.

MRS ARBUTHNOT: Gerald, I don't feel at all well. See me home, Gerald. I shouldn't have come.

GERALD: I am so sorry, mother. Certainly. But you must know Lord Illingworth first.

[*Goes across room.*]

MRS ARBUTHNOT: Not tonight, Gerald.

GERALD: Lord Illingworth, I want you so much to know my mother.[13]

LORD ILLINGWORTH: With the greatest pleasure. [*To* MRS ALLONBY.] I'll be back in a moment. People's mothers always bore me to death. All women become like their mothers. That is their tragedy.

MRS ALLONBY: No man does. That is his.[14]

LORD ILLINGWORTH: What a delightful mood you are in tonight!

[*Turns round and goes across with* GERALD *to* MRS ARBUTHNOT. *When he sees her, he starts back in wonder. Then slowly his eyes turn towards* GERALD.]

GERALD: Mother, this is Lord Illingworth, who has offered to take me as his private secretary. [MRS ARBUTHNOT *bows coldly*.] It is a wonderful opening for me, isn't it? I hope he won't be disappointed in me, that is all. You'll thank Lord Illingworth, mother, won't you?

MRS ARBUTHNOT: Lord Illingworth is very good, I am sure, to interest himself in you for the moment.

LORD ILLINGWORTH [*putting his hand on* GERALD's *shoulder*]: Oh, Gerald and I are great friends already, Mrs . . . Arbuthnot.

MRS ARBUTHNOT: There can be nothing in common between you and my son, Lord Illingworth.

GERALD: Dear mother, how can you say so? Of course Lord Illingworth is awfully clever and that sort of thing. There is nothing Lord Illingworth doesn't know.

LORD ILLINGWORTH: My dear boy!

GERALD: He knows more about life than anyone I have ever met. I feel an awful duffer when I am with you, Lord Illingworth. Of course, I have had so few advantages. I have not been to Eton or Oxford[15] like other chaps. But Lord Illingworth doesn't seem to mind that. He has been awfully good to me, mother.

MRS ARBUTHNOT: Lord Illingworth may change his mind. He may not really want you as his secretary.

GERALD: Mother!

MRS ARBUTHNOT: You must remember, as you said yourself, you have had so few advantages.

MRS ALLONBY: Lord Illingworth, I want to speak to you for a moment. Do come over.

LORD ILLINGWORTH: Will you excuse me, Mrs Arbuthnot? Now, don't let your charming mother make any more difficulties, Gerald. The thing is quite settled, isn't it?

GERALD: I hope so.

[LORD ILLINGWORTH *goes across to* MRS ALLONBY.]

MRS ALLONBY: I thought you were never going to leave the lady in black velvet.[16]

LORD ILLINGWORTH: She is excessively handsome.

[*Looks at* MRS ARBUTHNOT.]

LADY HUNSTANTON: Caroline, shall we all make a move to the music-room? Miss Worsley is going to play. You'll come too, dear Mrs Arbuthnot, won't you? You don't know what a treat is in store for you. [*To* DOCTOR DAUBENY.] I must really take Miss Worsley down some afternoon to the rectory. I should so much like dear Mrs Daubeny to hear her on the violin. Ah, I forgot. Dear Mrs Daubeny's hearing is a little defective, is it not?

THE ARCHDEACON: Her deafness is a great privation to her. She can't even hear my sermons now. She reads them at home. But she has many resources in herself, many resources.

LADY HUNSTANTON: She reads a good deal, I suppose?

THE ARCHDEACON: Just the very largest print. The eyesight is rapidly going. But she's never morbid, never morbid.

GERALD [*to* LORD ILLINGWORTH]: Do speak to my mother, Lord Illingworth, before you go into the music-room. She seems to think, somehow, you don't mean what you said to me.

MRS ALLONBY: Aren't you coming?

LORD ILLINGWORTH: In a few moments. Lady Hunstanton, if Mrs Arbuthnot would allow me, I would like to say a few words to her, and we will join you later on.

LADY HUNSTANTON: Ah, of course. You will have a great deal to say to her, and she will have a great deal to thank you for. It is not every son who gets such an offer, Mrs Arbuthnot. But I know you appreciate that, dear.

LADY CAROLINE: John!

LADY HUNSTANTON: Now, don't keep Mrs Arbuthnot too long, Lord Illingworth. We can't spare her.

[*Exit following the other guests. Sound of violin heard from music-room.*][17]

LORD ILLINGWORTH: So that is our son, Rachel![18] Well, I am very proud of him. He is a Harford, every inch of him. By the way, why Arbuthnot, Rachel?

MRS ARBUTHNOT: One name is as good as another, when one has no right to any name.

LORD ILLINGWORTH: I suppose so – but why Gerald?

MRS ARBUTHNOT: After a man whose heart I broke – after my father.

LORD ILLINGWORTH: Well, Rachel, what is over is over. All I have got to say now is that I am very, very much pleased with our boy. The world will know him merely as my private secretary, but to me he will be something very near, and very dear. It is a curious thing, Rachel; my life seemed to be quite complete. It was not so. It lacked something, it lacked a son. I have found my son now, I am glad I have found him.

MRS ARBUTHNOT: You have no right to claim him, or the smallest part of him. The boy is entirely mine, and shall remain mine.

LORD ILLINGWORTH: My dear Rachel, you have had him to yourself for over twenty years. Why not let me have him for a little now? He is quite as much mine as yours.

MRS ARBUTHNOT: Are you talking of the child you abandoned? Of the child who, as far as you are concerned, might have died of hunger and of want?

LORD ILLINGWORTH: You forget, Rachel, it was you who left me. It was not I who left you.

MRS ARBUTHNOT: I left you because you refused to give the child a name. Before my son was born, I implored you to marry me.

LORD ILLINGWORTH: I had no expectations then. And besides, Rachel, I wasn't much older than you were. I was only twenty-two. I was twenty-one, I believe, when the whole thing began in your father's garden.[19]

MRS ARBUTHNOT: When a man is old enough to do wrong he should be old enough to do right also.

LORD ILLINGWORTH: My dear Rachel, intellectual generalities are always interesting, but generalities in morals mean absolutely nothing. As for saying I left our child to starve, that, of course, is untrue and silly. My mother offered you six hundred a year.[20] But you wouldn't take anything. You simply disappeared, and carried the child away with you.

MRS ARBUTHNOT: I wouldn't have accepted a penny from her. Your father was different. He told you, in my presence, when we were in Paris, that it was your duty to marry me.[21]

LORD ILLINGWORTH: Oh, duty is what one expects from others, it is not what one does oneself. Of course, I was influenced by my mother. Every man is when he is young.

MRS ARBUTHNOT: I am glad to hear you say so. Gerald shall certainly not go away with you.

LORD ILLINGWORTH: What nonsense, Rachel!

MRS ARBUTHNOT: Do you think I would allow my son –

LORD ILLINGWORTH: *Our* son.

MRS ARBUTHNOT: My son [LORD ILLINGWORTH *shrugs his shoulders*] – to go away with the man who spoiled my youth, who ruined my life, who has tainted every moment of my days? You don't realize what my past has been in suffering and in shame.

LORD ILLINGWORTH: My dear Rachel, I must candidly say that I think Gerald's future considerably more important than your past.

MRS ARBUTHNOT: Gerald cannot separate his future from my past.

LORD ILLINGWORTH: That is exactly what he should do. That is exactly what you should help him to do. What a typical woman you are! You talk sentimentally, and you are thoroughly selfish the whole time. But don't let us have a scene. Rachel, I want you to look at this matter from the common-sense point of view, from the point of view of what is best for our son, leaving you and me out of the question. What is our son at present? An underpaid clerk in a small Provincial Bank in a third-rate English town. If you imagine he is quite happy in such a position, you are mistaken. He is thoroughly discontented.

MRS ARBUTHNOT: He was not discontented till he met you. You have made him so.

LORD ILLINGWORTH: Of course, I made him so. Discontent is the first step in the progress of a man or a nation. But I did not leave him with a mere longing for things he could not get. No, I made him a charming offer. He jumped at it, I need hardly say. Any young man would. And now, simply because it turns out that I am the boy's own father and he my own son, you propose practically to ruin his career. That is to say, if I were a perfect stranger, you would allow Gerald to go away with me, but as he is my own flesh and blood you won't. How utterly illogical you are!

MRS ARBUTHNOT: I will not allow him to go.

LORD ILLINGWORTH: How can you prevent it? What excuse can you give to him for making him decline such an offer as mine? I won't tell him in what relations I stand to him, I need hardly say. But you daren't tell him. You know that. Look how you have brought him up.

MRS ARBUTHNOT: I have brought him up to be a good man.

LORD ILLINGWORTH: Quite so. And what is the result? You have educated him to be your judge if he ever finds you out. And a bitter, an unjust judge he will be to you. Don't be deceived, Rachel. Children begin by loving their parents. After a time they judge them. Rarely, if ever, do they forgive them.

MRS ARBUTHNOT: George, don't take my son away from me. I have had twenty years of sorrow, and I have only had one thing to love me, only one thing to love. You have had a life of joy, and pleasure, and success. You have been quite happy, you have never thought of us. There was no reason, according to your views of life, why you should have remembered us at all. Your meeting us was a mere accident, a horrible accident. Forget it. Don't come now, and rob me of . . . of all I have in the whole world. You are so rich in other things. Leave me the little vineyard of my life; leave me the walled-in garden and the well of water; the ewe-lamb God sent me, in pity or in wrath, oh! leave me that.[22] George, don't take Gerald from me.

LORD ILLINGWORTH: Rachel, at the present moment you are not necessary to Gerald's career; I am. There is nothing more to be said on the subject.

MRS ARBUTHNOT: I will not let him go.

LORD ILLINGWORTH: Here is Gerald. He has a right to decide for himself.

[*Enter* GERALD.]

GERALD: Well, dear mother, I hope you have settled it all with Lord Illingworth?

MRS ARBUTHNOT: I have not, Gerald.

LORD ILLINGWORTH: Your mother seems not to like your coming with me, for some reason.

GERALD: Why, mother?

MRS ARBUTHNOT: I thought you were quite happy here with me, Gerald. I didn't know you were so anxious to leave me.

GERALD: Mother, how can you talk like that? Of course I have been quite happy with you. But a man can't stay always with his mother. No chap does. I want to make myself a position, to do something. I thought you would have been proud to see me Lord Illingworth's secretary.

MRS ARBUTHNOT: I do not think you would be suitable as a private secretary to Lord Illingworth. You have no qualifications.

LORD ILLINGWORTH: I don't wish to seem to interfere for a moment,

Mrs Arbuthnot, but as far as your last objection is concerned, I surely am the best judge. And I can only tell you that your son has all the qualifications I had hoped for. He has more, in fact, than I had even thought of. Far more. [MRS ARBUTHNOT *remains silent.*] Have you any other reason, Mrs Arbuthnot, why you don't wish your son to accept this post?[23]

GERALD: Have you, mother? Do answer.

LORD ILLINGWORTH: If you have, Mrs Arbuthnot, pray, pray say it. We are quite by ourselves here. Whatever it is, I need not say I will not repeat it.

GERALD: Mother?

LORD ILLINGWORTH: If you would like to be alone with your son, I will leave you. You may have some other reason you don't wish me to hear.

MRS ARBUTHNOT: I have no other reason.

LORD ILLINGWORTH: Then, my dear boy, we may look on the thing as settled. Come, you and I will smoke a cigarette on the terrace together. And Mrs Arbuthnot, pray let me tell you, that I think you have acted very, very wisely.

[*Exit with* GERALD. MRS ARBUTHNOT *is left alone. She stands immobile with a look of unutterable sorrow on her face.*]

ACT DROP

THIRD ACT

The picture gallery at Hunstanton. Door at back leading on to terrace.

[LORD ILLINGWORTH *and* GERALD, *R. C.* LORD ILLINGWORTH *lolling on a sofa.* GERALD *in a chair.*]¹

LORD ILLINGWORTH: Thoroughly sensible woman, your mother, Gerald. I knew she would come round in the end.

GERALD: My mother is awfully conscientious, Lord Illingworth, and I know she doesn't think I am educated enough to be your secretary. She is perfectly right, too. I was fearfully idle when I was at school, and I couldn't pass an examination now to save my life.

LORD ILLINGWORTH: My dear Gerald, examinations are of no value whatsoever. If a man is a gentleman, he knows quite enough, and if he is not a gentleman, whatever he knows is bad for him.

GERALD: But I am so ignorant of the world, Lord Illingworth.

LORD ILLINGWORTH: Don't be afraid, Gerald. Remember that you've got on your side the most wonderful thing in the world – youth! There is nothing like youth. The middle-aged are mortgaged to Life. The old are in Life's lumber-room. But youth is the Lord of Life. Youth has a kingdom waiting for it. Everyone is born a king, and most people die in exile, like most kings. To win back my youth, Gerald, there is nothing I wouldn't do – except take exercise, get up early or be a useful member of the community.

GERALD: But you don't call yourself old, Lord Illingworth?

LORD ILLINGWORTH: I am old enough to be your father, Gerald.

GERALD: I don't remember my father; he died years ago.

LORD ILLINGWORTH: So Lady Hunstanton told me.

GERALD: It is very curious, my mother never talks to me about my father. I sometimes think she must have married beneath her.

LORD ILLINGWORTH [*winces slightly*]: Really? [*Goes over and puts his hand*

142

on GERALD's *shoulder.*] You have missed not having a father, I suppose, Gerald?

GERALD: Oh, no; my mother has been so good to me. No one ever had such a mother as I have had.

LORD ILLINGWORTH: I am quite sure of that. Still I should imagine that most mothers don't quite understand their sons. Don't realize, I mean, that a son has ambitions, a desire to see life, to make himself a name. After all, Gerald, you couldn't be expected to pass all your life in such a hole as Wrockley, could you?

GERALD: Oh, no! It would be dreadful!

LORD ILLINGWORTH: A mother's love is very touching, of course, but it is often curiously selfish. I mean, there is a good deal of selfishness in it.

GERALD [*slowly*]: I suppose there is.

LORD ILLINGWORTH: Your mother is a thoroughly good woman. But good women have such limited views of life, their horizon is so small, their interests are so petty, aren't they?

GERALD: They are awfully interested, certainly, in things we don't care much about.

LORD ILLINGWORTH: I suppose your mother is very religious, and that sort of thing.

GERALD: Oh, yes, she's always going to church.

LORD ILLINGWORTH: Ah! she is not modern, and to be modern is the only thing worth being nowadays. You want to be modern, don't you, Gerald? You want to know life as it really is. Not to be put off with any old-fashioned theories about life. Well, what you have to do at present is simply to fit yourself for the best society. A man who can dominate a London dinner-table can dominate the world. The future belongs to the dandy. It is the exquisites who are going to rule.

GERALD: I should like to wear nice things awfully, but I have always been told that a man should not think too much about his clothes.[2]

LORD ILLINGWORTH: People nowadays are so absolutely superficial that they don't understand the philosophy of the superficial. By the way, Gerald, you should learn how to tie your tie better. Sentiment is all very well for the buttonhole. But the essential thing for a necktie is style. A well-tied tie is the first serious step in life.

GERALD [*laughing*]: I might be able to learn how to tie a tie, Lord Illingworth, but I should never be able to talk as you do. I don't know how to talk.

LORD ILLINGWORTH: Oh! talk to every woman as if you loved her, and to every man as if he bored you, and at the end of your first season you will have the reputation of possessing the most perfect social tact.

GERALD: But it is very difficult to get into society, isn't it?

LORD ILLINGWORTH: To get into the best society, nowadays, one has either to feed people, amuse people or shock people – that is all!

GERALD: I suppose society is wonderfully delightful!

LORD ILLINGWORTH: To be in it is merely a bore. But to be out of it simply a tragedy. Society is a necessary thing. No man has any real success in this world unless he has got women to back him, and women rule society. If you have not got women on your side you are quite over. You might just as well be a barrister, or a stockbroker, or a journalist at once.

GERALD: It is very difficult to understand women, is it not?

LORD ILLINGWORTH: You should never try to understand them. Women are pictures. Men are problems. If you want to know what a woman really means – which, by the way, is always a dangerous thing to do – look at her, don't listen to her.

GERALD: But women are awfully clever, aren't they?

LORD ILLINGWORTH: One should always tell them so. But, to the philosopher, my dear Gerald, women represent the triumph of matter over mind – just as men represent the triumph of mind over morals.

GERALD: How then can women have so much power as you say they have?

LORD ILLINGWORTH: The history of women is the history of the worst form of tyranny the world has ever known. The tyranny of the weak over the strong. It is the only tyranny that lasts.

GERALD: But haven't women got a refining influence?

LORD ILLINGWORTH: Nothing refines but the intellect.

GERALD: Still, there are many different kinds of women, aren't there?

LORD ILLINGWORTH: Only two kinds in society: the plain and the coloured.[3]

GERALD: But there are good women in society, aren't there?

LORD ILLINGWORTH: Far too many.

GERALD: But do you think women shouldn't be good?

LORD ILLINGWORTH: One should never tell them so, they'd all become good at once. Women are a fascinatingly wilful sex. Every woman is a rebel, and usually in wild revolt against herself.

GERALD: You have never been married, Lord Illingworth, have you?

LORD ILLINGWORTH: Men marry because they are tired; women because they are curious. Both are disappointed.

GERALD: But don't you think one can be happy when one is married?

LORD ILLINGWORTH: Perfectly happy. But the happiness of a married man, my dear Gerald, depends on the people he has not married.

GERALD: But if one is in love?

LORD ILLINGWORTH: One should always be in love. That is the reason one should never marry.

GERALD: Love is a very wonderful thing, isn't it?

LORD ILLINGWORTH: When one is in love one begins by deceiving oneself. And one ends by deceiving others. That is what the world calls a romance. But a really *grande passion* is comparatively rare nowadays. It is the privilege of people who have nothing to do. That is the one use of the idle classes in a country, and the only possible explanation of us Harfords.

GERALD: Harfords, Lord Illingworth?

LORD ILLINGWORTH: That is my family name. You should study the Peerage,[4] Gerald. It is the one book a young man about town should know thoroughly, and it is the best thing in fiction the English have ever done. And now, Gerald, you are going into a perfectly new life with me, and I want you to know how to live. [MRS ARBUTHNOT *appears on terrace behind.*] For the world has been made by fools that wise men should live in it!

[*Enter L. C.* LADY HUNSTANTON *and* DR DAUBENY.]

LADY HUNSTANTON: Ah! here you are, dear Lord Illingworth. Well, I suppose you have been telling our young friend, Gerald, what his new duties are to be, and giving him a great deal of good advice over a pleasant cigarette.

LORD ILLINGWORTH: I have been giving him the best of advice, Lady Hunstanton, and the best of cigarettes.

LADY HUNSTANTON: I am so sorry I was not here to listen to you, but I suppose I am too old now to learn. Except from you, dear Archdeacon, when you are in your nice pulpit. But then I always know what you are going to say, so I don't feel alarmed. [*Sees* MRS ARBUTHNOT.] Ah! dear Mrs Arbuthnot, do come and join us. Come, dear. [*Enter* MRS ARBUTHNOT.] Gerald has been having such a long talk with Lord Illingworth; I am sure you must feel very much flattered at the pleasant way in which everything has turned out for him. Let us sit down. [*They sit down.*] And how is your beautiful embroidery going on?

MRS ARBUTHNOT: I am always at work, Lady Hunstanton.

LADY HUNSTANTON: Mrs Daubeny embroiders a little, too, doesn't she?

THE ARCHDEACON: She was very deft with her needle once, quite a Dorcas. But the gout has crippled her fingers a good deal. She has not touched the tambour frame[5] for nine or ten years. But she has many other amusements. She is very much interested in her own health.

LADY HUNSTANTON: Ah! that is always a nice distraction, is it not? Now, what are you talking about, Lord Illingworth? Do tell us.

LORD ILLINGWORTH: I was on the point of explaining to Gerald that the world has always laughed at its own tragedies, that being the only way in which it has been able to bear them. And that, consequently, whatever the world has treated seriously belongs to the comedy side of things.

LADY HUNSTANTON: Now I am quite out of my depth. I usually am when Lord Illingworth says anything. And the Humane Society[6] is most careless. They never rescue me. I am left to sink. I have a dim idea, dear Lord Illingworth, that you are always on the side of the sinners, and I know I always try to be on the side of the saints, but that is as far as I get. And after all, it may be merely the fancy of a drowning person.

LORD ILLINGWORTH: The only difference between the saint and the sinner is that every saint has a past, and every sinner has a future.

LADY HUNSTANTON: Ah! that quite does for me. I haven't a word to say. You and I, dear Mrs Arbuthnot, are behind the age. We can't follow Lord Illingworth. Too much care was taken with our education, I am afraid. To have been well brought up is a great drawback nowadays. It shuts one out from so much.

MRS ARBUTHNOT: I should be sorry to follow Lord Illingworth in any of his opinions.

LADY HUNSTANTON: You are quite right, dear.

[GERALD *shrugs his shoulders and looks irritably over at his mother.*]

[*Enter* LADY CAROLINE.]

LADY CAROLINE: Jane, have you seen John anywhere?

LADY HUNSTANTON: You needn't be anxious about him, dear. He is with Lady Stutfield; I saw them some time ago, in the Yellow Drawing-room. They seem quite happy together. You are not going, Caroline? Pray sit down.

LADY CAROLINE: I think I had better look after John.

[*Exit* LADY CAROLINE.]

LADY HUNSTANTON: It doesn't do to pay men so much attention. And Caroline has really nothing to be anxious about. Lady Stutfield is very sympathetic. She is just as sympathetic about one thing as she is about another. A beautiful nature. [*Enter* SIR JOHN *and* MRS ALLONBY.] Ah! here is Sir John! And with Mrs Allonby too! I suppose it was Mrs Allonby I saw him with. Sir John, Caroline has been looking everywhere for you.

MRS ALLONBY: We have been waiting for her in the Music-room, dear Lady Hunstanton.

LADY HUNSTANTON: Ah! the Music-room, of course. I thought it was the Yellow Drawing-room, my memory is getting so defective. [*To the* ARCHDEACON.] Mrs Daubeny has a wonderful memory, hasn't she?

THE ARCHDEACON: She used to be quite remarkable for her memory, but since her last attack she recalls chiefly the events of her early childhood. But she finds great pleasure in such retrospections, great pleasure.

[*Enter* LADY STUTFIELD *and* MR KELVIL.]

LADY HUNSTANTON: Ah! dear Lady Stutfield! and what has Mr Kelvil been talking to you about?

LADY STUTFIELD: About Bimetallism,[7] as well as I remember.

LADY HUNSTANTON: Bimetallism! Is that quite a nice subject? However, I know people discuss everything very freely nowadays. What did Sir John talk to you about, dear Mrs Allonby?

MRS ALLONBY: About Patagonia.

LADY HUNSTANTON: Really? What a remote topic! But very improving, I have no doubt.

MRS ALLONBY: He has been most interesting on the subject of Patagonia. Savages seem to have quite the same views as cultured people on almost all subjects. They are excessively advanced.

LADY HUNSTANTON: What do they do?

MRS ALLONBY: Apparently everything.

LADY HUNSTANTON: Well, it is very gratifying, dear Archdeacon, is it not, to find that Human Nature is permanently one. – On the whole, the world is the same world, is it not?

LORD ILLINGWORTH: The world is simply divided into two classes – those who believe the incredible, like the public – and those who do the improbable –

MRS ALLONBY: Like yourself?

LORD ILLINGWORTH: Yes; I am always astonishing myself. It is the only thing that makes life worth living.

LADY STUTFIELD: And what have you been doing lately that astonishes you?

LORD ILLINGWORTH: I have been discovering all kinds of beautiful qualities in my own nature.

MRS ALLONBY: Ah! don't become quite perfect all at once. Do it gradually!

LORD ILLINGWORTH: I don't intend to grow perfect at all. At least, I hope I shan't. It would be most inconvenient. Women love us for our defects. If we have enough of them, they will forgive us everything, even our gigantic intellects.

MRS ALLONBY: It is premature to ask us to forgive analysis. We forgive adoration; that is quite as much as should be expected from us.

[*Enter* LORD ALFRED. *He joins* LADY STUTFIELD.]

LADY HUNSTANTON: Ah! we women should forgive everything, shouldn't we, dear Mrs Arbuthnot? I am sure you agree with me in that.

MRS ARBUTHNOT: I do not, Lady Hunstanton. I think there are many things women should never forgive.

LADY HUNSTANTON: What sort of things?

MRS ARBUTHNOT: The ruin of another woman's life.

[*Moves slowly away to back of stage.*]

LADY HUNSTANTON: Ah! those things are very sad, no doubt, but I believe there are admirable homes where people of that kind are looked after and reformed,[8] and I think on the whole that the secret of life is to take things very, very easily.

MRS ALLONBY: The secret of life is never to have an emotion that is unbecoming.

LADY STUTFIELD: The secret of life is to appreciate the pleasure of being terribly, terribly deceived.

KELVIL: The secret of life is to resist temptation, Lady Stutfield.

LORD ILLINGWORTH: There is no secret of life. Life's aim, if it has one, is simply to be always looking for temptations. There are not nearly enough. I sometimes pass a whole day without coming across a single one. It is quite dreadful. It makes one so nervous about the future.

LADY HUNSTANTON [*shakes her fan at him*]: I don't know how it is, dear Lord Illingworth, but everything you have said today seems to me excessively immoral. It has been most interesting, listening to you.

LORD ILLINGWORTH: All thought is immoral. Its very essence is destruction. If you think of anything, you kill it. Nothing survives being thought of.

LADY HUNSTANTON: I don't understand a word, Lord Illingworth. But I have no doubt it is all quite true. Personally, I have very little to reproach myself with, on the score of thinking. I don't believe in women thinking too much. Women should think in moderation, as they should do all things in moderation.

LORD ILLINGWORTH: Moderation is a fatal thing, Lady Hunstanton. Nothing succeeds like excess.

LADY HUNSTANTON: I hope I shall remember that. It sounds an admirable maxim. But I'm beginning to forget everything. It's a great misfortune.

LORD ILLINGWORTH: It is one of your most fascinating qualities, Lady Hunstanton. No woman should have a memory. Memory in a woman is the beginning of dowdiness. One can always tell from a woman's bonnet whether she has got a memory or not.

LADY HUNSTANTON: How charming you are, dear Lord Illingworth. You always find out that one's most glaring fault is one's most important virtue. You have the most comforting views of life.

[*Enter* FARQUHAR.]

FARQUHAR: Doctor Daubeny's carriage!

LADY HUNSTANTON: My dear Archdeacon! It is only half-past ten.

THE ARCHDEACON [*rising*]: I am afraid I must go, Lady Hunstanton. Tuesday is always one of Mrs Daubeny's bad nights.

LADY HUNSTANTON [*rising*]: Well, I won't keep you from her. [*Goes with him towards door.*] I have told Farquhar to put a brace of partridge into the carriage. Mrs Daubeny may fancy them.

THE ARCHDEACON: It is very kind of you, but Mrs Daubeny never touches solids now. Lives entirely on jellies. But she is wonderfully cheerful, wonderfully cheerful. She has nothing to complain of.

[*Exit with* LADY HUNSTANTON.]

MRS ALLONBY [*goes over to* LORD ILLINGWORTH]: There is a beautiful moon tonight.

LORD ILLINGWORTH: Let us go and look at it. To look at anything
that is inconstant is charming nowadays.

MRS ALLONBY: You have your looking-glass.

LORD ILLINGWORTH: It is unkind. It merely shows me my wrinkles.

MRS ALLONBY: Mine is better behaved. It never tells me the truth.

LORD ILLINGWORTH: Then it is in love with you.

[*Exeunt* SIR JOHN, LADY STUTFIELD, MR KELVIL *and* LORD ALFRED.]

GERALD [*to* LORD ILLINGWORTH]: May I come too?

LORD ILLINGWORTH: Do, my dear boy.

[*Moves towards door with* MRS ALLONBY *and* GERALD.]

[LADY CAROLINE *enters, looks rapidly round and goes out in opposite direction
to that taken by* SIR JOHN *and* LADY STUTFIELD.]

MRS ARBUTHNOT: Gerald!

GERALD: What, mother?

[*Exit* LORD ILLINGWORTH *with* MRS ALLONBY.]

MRS ARBUTHNOT: It is getting late. Let us go home.

GERALD: My dear mother. Do let us wait a little longer. Lord Illingworth is so delightful, and, by the way, mother, I have a great
surprise for you. We are starting for India at the end of this month.

MRS ARBUTHNOT: Let us go home.

GERALD: If you really want to, of course, mother, but I must bid
good-bye to Lord Illingworth first. I'll be back in five minutes.

[*Exit.*]

MRS ARBUTHNOT: Let him leave me if he chooses, but not with him
– not with him! I couldn't bear it.

[*Walks up and down.*]

[*Enter* HESTER.]

HESTER: What a lovely night it is, Mrs Arbuthnot.

MRS ARBUTHNOT: Is it?

HESTER: Mrs Arbuthnot, I wish you would let us be friends. You are so different from the other women here. When you came into the drawing-room this evening, somehow you brought with you a sense of what is good and pure in life. I had been foolish. There are things that are right to say, but that may be said at the wrong time and to the wrong people.

MRS ARBUTHNOT: I heard what you said. I agree with it, Miss Worsley.

HESTER: I didn't know you had heard it. But I knew you would agree with me. A woman who has sinned should be punished, shouldn't she?

MRS ARBUTHNOT: Yes.

HESTER: She shouldn't be allowed to come into the society of good men and women?

MRS ARBUTHNOT: She should not.

HESTER: And the man should be punished in the same way?

MRS ARBUTHNOT: In the same way. And the children, if there are children, in the same way also?

HESTER: Yes, it is right that the sins of the parents should be visited on the children. It is a just law. It is God's law.

MRS ARBUTHNOT: It is one of God's terrible laws.[9]

[Moves away to fireplace.]

HESTER: You are distressed about your son leaving you, Mrs Arbuthnot?

MRS ARBUTHNOT: Yes.

HESTER: Do you like him going away with Lord Illingworth? Of course there is position, no doubt, and money, but position and money are not everything, are they?

MRS ARBUTHNOT: They are nothing; they bring misery.

HESTER: Then why do you let your son go with him?

MRS ARBUTHNOT: He wishes it himself.

HESTER: But if you asked him he would stay, would he not?

MRS ARBUTHNOT: He has set his heart on going.

HESTER: He couldn't refuse you anything. He loves you too much. Ask him to stay. Let me send him in to you. He is on the terrace at this moment with Lord Illingworth. I heard them laughing together as I passed through the Music-room.

MRS ARBUTHNOT: Don't trouble, Miss Worsley, I can wait. It is of no consequence.

HESTER: No, I'll tell him you want him. Do – do ask him to stay.

[*Exit* HESTER.]

MRS ARBUTHNOT: He won't come – I know he won't come.

[*Enter* LADY CAROLINE. *She looks round anxiously. Enter* GERALD.]

LADY CAROLINE: Mr Arbuthnot, may I ask you is Sir John anywhere on the terrace?

GERALD: No, Lady Caroline, he is not on the terrace.

LADY CAROLINE: It is very curious. It is time for him to retire.

[*Exit* LADY CAROLINE.]

GERALD: Dear mother, I am afraid I kept you waiting. I forgot all about it. I am so happy tonight, mother; I have never been so happy.

MRS ARBUTHNOT: At the prospect of going away?

GERALD: Don't put it like that, mother. Of course I am sorry to leave you. Why, you are the best mother in the whole world. But after all, as Lord Illingworth says, it is impossible to live in such a place as Wrockley. You don't mind it. But I'm ambitious; I want something more than that. I want to have a career. I want to do something that will make you proud of me, and Lord Illingworth is going to help me. He is going to do everything for me.

MRS ARBUTHNOT: Gerald, don't go away with Lord Illingworth. I implore you not to. Gerald, I beg you!

GERALD: Mother, how changeable you are! You don't seem to know your own mind for a single moment. An hour and a half ago in the drawing-room you agreed to the whole thing; now you turn round and make objections, and try to force me to give up my one chance in life. Yes, my one chance. You don't suppose that men like Lord Illingworth are to be found every day, do you, mother? It is very strange that when I have had such a wonderful piece of good luck, the one person to put difficulties in my way should be my own mother. Besides, you know, mother, I love Hester Worsley.

Who could help loving her? I love her more than I have ever told you, far more. And if I had a position, if I had prospects, I could – I could ask her to – Don't you understand now, mother, what it means to me to be Lord Illingworth's secretary? To start like that is to find a career ready for one – before one – waiting for one. If I were Lord Illingworth's secretary I could ask Hester to be my wife. As a wretched bank clerk with a hundred a year it would be an impertinence.

MRS ARBUTHNOT: I fear you need have no hopes of Miss Worsley. I know her views on life. She has just told them to me.

[*A pause.*]

GERALD: Then I have my ambition left, at any rate. That is something – I am glad I have that! You have always tried to crush my ambition, mother – haven't you? You have told me that the world is a wicked place, that success is not worth having, that society is shallow, and all that sort of thing – well, I don't believe it, mother. I think the world must be delightful. I think society must be exquisite. I think success is a thing worth having. You have been wrong in all that you taught me, mother, quite wrong. Lord Illingworth is a successful man. He is a fashionable man. He is a man who lives in the world and for it. Well, I would give anything to be just like Lord Illingworth.

MRS ARBUTHNOT: I would sooner see you dead.

GERALD: Mother, what is your objection to Lord Illingworth? Tell me – tell me right out. What is it?

MRS ARBUTHNOT: He is a bad man.

GERALD: In what way bad? I don't understand what you mean.

MRS ARBUTHNOT: I will tell you.

GERALD: I suppose you think him bad, because he doesn't believe the same things as you do. Well, men are different from women, mother. It is natural that they should have different views.

MRS ARBUTHNOT: It is not what Lord Illingworth believes, or what he does not believe, that makes him bad. It is what he is.

GERALD: Mother, is it something you know of him? Something you actually know?

MRS ARBUTHNOT: It is something I know.

GERALD: Something you are quite sure of?

MRS ARBUTHNOT: Quite sure of.

GERALD: How long have you known it?

MRS ARBUTHNOT: For twenty years.

GERALD: Is it fair to go back twenty years in any man's career? And what have you or I to do with Lord Illingworth's early life? What business is it of ours?

MRS ARBUTHNOT: What this man has been, he is now, and will be always.

GERALD: Mother, tell me what Lord Illingworth did. If he did anything shameful, I will not go away with him. Surely you know me well enough for that?

MRS ARBUTHNOT: Gerald, come near to me. Quite close to me, as you used to do when you were a little boy, when you were mother's own boy. [GERALD *sits down beside his mother. She runs her fingers through his hair, and strokes his hands.*][10] Gerald, there was a girl once, she was very young, she was little over eighteen at the time. George Harford – that was Lord Illingworth's name then – George Harford met her. She knew nothing about life. He – knew everything. He made this girl love him. He made her love him so much that she left her father's house with him one morning. She loved him so much, and he had promised to marry her! He had solemnly promised to marry her, and she had believed him. She was very young, and – and ignorant of what life really is. But he put the marriage off from week to week, and month to month. – She trusted in him all the while. She loved him. – Before her child was born – for she had a child – she implored him for the child's sake to marry her, that the child might have a name, that her sin might not be visited on the child, who was innocent. He refused. After the child was born she left him, taking the child away, and her life was ruined, and her soul ruined, and all that was sweet, and good, and pure in her ruined also. She suffered terribly – she suffers now. She will always suffer. For her there is no joy, no peace, no atonement. She is a woman who drags a chain like a guilty thing. She is a woman who wears a mask, like a thing that is a leper. The fire cannot purify her. The waters cannot quench her anguish. Nothing can heal her! no anodyne can give her sleep! no poppies[11] forgetfulness! She is lost! She is a lost soul! – That is why I call Lord Illingworth a bad man. That is why I don't want my boy to be with him.

GERALD: My dear mother, it all sounds very tragic, of course. But I dare say the girl was just as much to blame as Lord Illingworth was. – After all, would a really nice girl, a girl with any nice feelings at all, go away from her home with a man to whom she was not married, and live with him as his wife? No nice girl would.[12]

MRS ARBUTHNOT [*after a pause*]: Gerald, I withdraw all my objections. You are at liberty to go away with Lord Illingworth, when and where you choose.

GERALD: Dear mother, I knew you wouldn't stand in my way. You are the best woman God ever made. And, as for Lord Illingworth, I don't believe he is capable of anything infamous or base. I can't believe it of him – I can't.

HESTER [*outside*]: Let me go! Let me go!

[*Enter* HESTER *in terror, and rushes over to* GERALD *and flings herself in his arms.*]

HESTER: Oh! save me – save me from him!

GERALD: From whom?

HESTER: He has insulted me! Horribly insulted me! Save me!

GERALD: Who? Who has dared –?

[LORD ILLINGWORTH *enters at back of stage.* HESTER *breaks from* GERALD'S *arms and points to him.*]

GERALD [*he is quite beside himself with rage and indignation*]: Lord Illingworth, you have insulted the purest thing on God's earth, a thing as pure as my own mother. You have insulted the woman I love most in the world with my own mother. As there is a God in Heaven, I will kill you!

MRS ARBUTHNOT [*rushing across and catching hold of him*]: No! no!

GERALD [*thrusting her back*]: Don't hold me, mother. Don't hold me – I'll kill him!

MRS ARBUTHNOT: Gerald!

GERALD: Let me go, I say!

MRS ARBUTHNOT: Stop, Gerald, stop! He is your own father!

[GERALD *clutches his mother's hands and looks into her face. She sinks slowly on the ground in shame.* HESTER *steals towards the door.* LORD ILLINGWORTH *frowns and bites his lip. After a time* GERALD *raises his mother up, puts his arm round her and leads her from the room.*][13]

ACT DROP

FOURTH ACT

SCENE

*Sitting-room at Mrs Arbuthnot's. Large open French window at back,
looking on to garden. Doors R. C. and L. C.*[1]

[GERALD ARBUTHNOT *writing at table.*]

[*Enter* ALICE *R. C.* followed by LADY HUNSTANTON *and* MRS
ALLONBY.]

ALICE: Lady Hunstanton and Mrs Allonby.

[*Exit L. C.*]

LADY HUNSTANTON: Good morning, Gerald.

GERALD [*rising*]: Good morning, Lady Hunstanton. Good morning,
Mrs Allonby.

LADY HUNSTANTON [*sitting down*]: We came to inquire for your dear
mother, Gerald. I hope she is better?

GERALD: My mother has not come down yet, Lady Hunstanton.

LADY HUNSTANTON: Ah, I am afraid the heat was too much for her
last night. I think there must have been thunder in the air. Or
perhaps it was the music. Music makes one feel so romantic – at
least it always gets on one's nerves.

MRS ALLONBY: It's the same thing, nowadays.

LADY HUNSTANTON: I am so glad I don't know what you mean,
dear. I am afraid you mean something wrong. Ah, I see you're
examining Mrs Arbuthnot's pretty room. Isn't it nice and old-
fashioned?

MRS ALLONBY [*surveying the room through her lorgnette*]: It looks quite the
happy English home.

LADY HUNSTANTON: That's just the word, dear; that just describes it.
One feels your mother's good influence in everything she has about
her, Gerald.

MRS ALLONBY: Lord Illingworth says that all influence is bad, but that a good influence is the worst in the world.

LADY HUNSTANTON: When Lord Illingworth knows Mrs Arbuthnot better he will change his mind. I must certainly bring him here.

MRS ALLONBY: I should like to see Lord Illingworth in a happy English home.[2]

LADY HUNSTANTON: It would do him a great deal of good, dear. Most women in London, nowadays, seem to furnish their rooms with nothing but orchids, foreigners and French novels. But here we have the room of a sweet saint. Fresh natural flowers, books that don't shock one, pictures that one can look at without blushing.

MRS ALLONBY: But I like blushing.[3]

LADY HUNSTANTON: Well, there *is* a good deal to be said for blushing, if one can do it at the proper moment. Poor dear Hunstanton used to tell me I didn't blush nearly often enough. But then he was so very particular. He wouldn't let me know any of his men friends, except those who were over seventy, like poor Lord Ashton: who afterwards, by the way, was brought into the Divorce Court. A most unfortunate case.

MRS ALLONBY: I delight in men over seventy. They always offer one the devotion of a lifetime. I think seventy an ideal age for a man.

LADY HUNSTANTON: She is quite incorrigible, Gerald, isn't she? By the by, Gerald, I hope your dear mother will come and see me more often now. You and Lord Illingworth start almost immediately, don't you?

GERALD: I have given up my intention of being Lord Illingworth's secretary.

LADY HUNSTANTON: Surely not, Gerald! It would be most unwise of you. What reason can you have?

GERALD: I don't think I should be suitable for the post.

MRS ALLONBY: I wish Lord Illingworth would ask me to be his secretary. But he says I am not serious enough.

LADY HUNSTANTON: My dear, you really mustn't talk like that in this house. Mrs Arbuthnot doesn't know anything about the wicked society in which we all live. She won't go into it. She is far too good. I consider it was a great honour her coming to me last night. It gave quite an atmosphere of respectability to the party.

MRS ALLONBY: Ah, that must have been what you thought was thunder in the air.

LADY HUNSTANTON: My dear, how can you say that? There is no resemblance between the two things at all. But really, Gerald, what do you mean by not being suitable?

GERALD: Lord Illingworth's views of life and mine are too different.

LADY HUNSTANTON: But, my dear Gerald, at your age you shouldn't have any views of life. They are quite out of place. You must be guided by others in this matter. Lord Illingworth has made you the most flattering offer, and travelling with him you would see the world – as much of it, at least, as one should look at – under the best auspices possible, and stay with all the right people, which is so important at this solemn moment in your career.

GERALD: I don't want to see the world: I've seen enough of it.

MRS ALLONBY: I hope you don't think you have exhausted life, Mr Arbuthnot. When a man says that, one knows that life has exhausted him.

GERALD: I don't wish to leave my mother.

LADY HUNSTANTON: Now, Gerald, that is pure laziness on your part. Not leave your mother! If I were your mother I would insist on your going.

[*Enter* ALICE *L. C.*]

ALICE: Mrs Arbuthnot's compliments, my lady, but she has a bad headache, and cannot see anyone this morning.

[*Exit R. C.*]

LADY HUNSTANTON [*rising*]: A bad headache! I am so sorry! Perhaps you'll bring her up to Hunstanton this afternoon, if she is better, Gerald.

GERALD: I am afraid not this afternoon, Lady Hunstanton.

LADY HUNSTANTON: Well, tomorrow, then. Ah, if you had a father, Gerald, he wouldn't let you waste your life here. He would send you off with Lord Illingworth at once. But mothers are so weak.

They give up to their sons in everything. We are all heart, all heart. Come, dear, I must call at the rectory and inquire for Mrs Daubeny, who, I am afraid, is far from well. It is wonderful how the Archdeacon bears up, quite wonderful. He is the most sympathetic of husbands. Quite a model. Good-bye, Gerald, give my fondest love to your mother.

MRS ALLONBY: Good-bye, Mr Arbuthnot.

GERALD: Good-bye.

[*Exit* LADY HUNSTANTON *and* MRS ALLONBY. GERALD *sits down and reads over his letter.*]

GERALD: What name can I sign? I, who have no right to any name.

[*Signs name, puts letter into envelope, addresses it and is about to seal it, when L. C. door opens and* MRS ARBUTHNOT *enters.* GERALD *lays down sealing-wax. Mother and son look at each other.*]

LADY HUNSTANTON [*through French window at the back*]: Good-bye again, Gerald. We are taking the short cut across your pretty garden. Now, remember my advice to you – start at once with Lord Illingworth.

MRS ALLONBY: *Au revoir*, Mr Arbuthnot. Mind you bring me back something nice from your travels – not an Indian shawl – on no account an Indian shawl.

[*Exeunt.*]

GERALD: Mother, I have just written to him.

MRS ARBUTHNOT: To whom?

GERALD: To my father. I have written to tell him to come here at four o'clock this afternoon.

MRS ARBUTHNOT: He shall not come here. He shall not cross the threshold of my house.

GERALD: He must come.

MRS ARBUTHNOT: Gerald, if you are going away with Lord Illingworth, go at once. Go before it kills me: but don't ask me to meet him.

GERALD: Mother, you don't understand. Nothing in the world would induce me to go away with Lord Illingworth, or to leave you. Surely

you know me well enough for that. No: I have written to him to
say –

MRS ARBUTHNOT: What can you have to say to him?

GERALD: Can't you guess, mother, what I have written in this letter?

MRS ARBUTHNOT: No.

GERALD: Mother, surely you can. Think, think what must be done,
now, at once, within the next few days.

MRS ARBUTHNOT: There is nothing to be done.

GERALD: I have written to Lord Illingworth to tell him that he must
marry you.

MRS ARBUTHNOT: Marry me?

GERALD: Mother, I will force him to do it. The wrong that has been
done you must be repaired. Atonement must be made. Justice may
be slow, mother, but it comes in the end. In a few days you shall
be Lord Illingworth's lawful wife.

MRS ARBUTHNOT: But, Gerald –

GERALD: I will insist upon his doing it. I will make him do it: he will
not dare to refuse.

MRS ARBUTHNOT: But, Gerald, it is I who refuse. I will not marry Lord
Illingworth.

GERALD: Not marry him? Mother!

MRS ARBUTHNOT: I will not marry him.

GERALD: But you don't understand: it is for your sake I am talking,
not for mine. This marriage, this necessary marriage, this marriage
that, for obvious reasons, must inevitably take place, will not help
me, will not give me a name that will be really, rightly mine to
bear. But surely it will be something for you, that you, my mother,
should, however late, become the wife of the man who is my father.
Will not that be something?

MRS ARBUTHNOT: I will not marry him.

GERALD: Mother, you must.

MRS ARBUTHNOT: I will not. You talk of atonement for a wrong done.
What atonement can be made to me? There is no atonement
possible. I am disgraced: he is not. That is all. It is the usual history
of a man and a woman as it usually happens, as it always happens.

And the ending is the ordinary ending.[4] The woman suffers. The man goes free.

GERALD: I don't know if that is the ordinary ending, mother: I hope it is not. But your life, at any rate, shall not end like that. The man shall make whatever reparation is possible. It is not enough. It does not wipe out the past, I know that. But at least it makes the future better, better for you, mother.

MRS ARBUTHNOT: I refuse to marry Lord Illingworth.

GERALD: If he came to you himself and asked you to be his wife you would give him a different answer. Remember, he is my father.

MRS ARBUTHNOT: If he came himself, which he will not do, my answer would be the same. Remember I am your mother.

GERALD: Mother, you make it terribly difficult for me by talking like that; and I can't understand why you won't look at this matter from the right, from the only proper standpoint. It is to take away the bitterness out of your life, to take away the shadow that lies on your name, that this marriage must take place. There is no alternative: and after the marriage you and I can go away together. But the marriage must take place first. It is a duty that you owe, not merely to yourself, but to all other women – yes: to all the other women in the world, lest he betray more.

MRS ARBUTHNOT: I owe nothing to other women. There is not one of them to help me. There is not one woman in the world to whom I could go for pity, if I would take it, or for sympathy, if I could win it. Women are hard on each other.[5] That girl, last night, good though she is, fled from the room as though I were a tainted thing. She was right. I am a tainted thing. But my wrongs are my own, and I will bear them alone. I must bear them alone. What have women who have not sinned to do with me, or I with them? We do not understand each other.

[*Enter* HESTER *behind.*][6]

GERALD: I implore you to do what I ask you.

MRS ARBUTHNOT: What son has ever asked of his mother to make so hideous a sacrifice? None.

GERALD: What mother has ever refused to marry the father of her own child? None.

MRS ARBUTHNOT: Let me be the first, then. I will not do it.

GERALD: Mother, you believe in religion, and you brought me up to believe in it also. Well, surely your religion, the religion that you taught me when I was a boy, mother, must tell you that I am right. You know it, you feel it.

MRS ARBUTHNOT: I do not know it. I do not feel it, nor will I ever stand before God's altar and ask God's blessing on so hideous a mockery as a marriage between me and George Harford. I will not say the words the Church bids us to say. I will not say them. I dare not. How could I swear to love the man I loathe, to honour him who wrought you dishonour, to obey him who, in his mastery, made me to sin? No: marriage is a sacrament for those who love each other. It is not for such as him, or such as me. Gerald, to save you from the world's sneers and taunts I have lied to the world. For twenty years I have lied to the world. I could not tell the world the truth. Who can, ever? But not for my own sake will I lie to God, and in God's presence. No, Gerald, no ceremony, Church-hallowed or State-made, shall ever bind me to George Harford. It may be that I am too bound to him already, who, robbing me, yet left me richer, so that in the mire of my life I found the pearl of price,[7] or what I thought would be so.

GERALD: I don't understand you now.

MRS ARBUTHNOT: Men don't understand what mothers are. I am no different from other women except in the wrong done me and the wrong I did, and my very heavy punishments and great disgrace. And yet, to bear you I had to look on death. To nurture you I had to wrestle with it. Death fought with me for you. All women have to fight with death to keep their children. Death, being childless, wants our children from us. Gerald, when you were naked I clothed you, when you were hungry I gave you food.[8] Night and day all that long winter I tended you. No office is too mean, no care too lowly for the thing we women love – and oh! how *I* loved *you*. Not Hannah,[9] Samuel more. And you needed love, for you were weakly, and only love could have kept you alive. Only love can keep anyone alive. And boys are careless often and without thinking give pain, and we always fancy that when they come to man's estate and know us better, they will repay us. But it is not so. The world draws them from our side, and they make friends with whom they are happier than they are with us, and have amusements from which we are barred, and interests that are not ours: and they are unjust to us often, for when they find life bitter they blame us for it, and when they find it sweet we do not taste its sweetness with them . . . You made many friends and went into their houses and were glad with them, and I, knowing my secret, did not dare to follow, but stayed at home and closed the door, shut out the sun and sat in darkness. What should I have done in honest households? My past was ever with me . . . And you thought I didn't care for the pleasant things of life. I tell you I longed for them, but did not dare to touch them, feeling I had no right. You thought I was happier working amongst the poor. That was my mission, you imagined. It was not, but where else was I to go? The sick do not ask if the hand that smoothes their pillow is pure, nor the dying care if the lips that touch their brow have known the kiss of sin. It was you I thought of all the time; I gave to them the love you did not need: lavished on them a love that was not theirs . . . And you thought I spent too much of my time in going to Church, and in Church duties. But where else could I turn? God's house is the only house where sinners are made welcome, and you were always in my heart, Gerald, too much in my heart. For, though day after day, at morn or evensong, I have knelt in God's house, I have never repented of my sin. How could I repent of my sin when you, my love, were its fruit! Even now that you are bitter to me I cannot repent. I do not. You are more to me than innocence. I would rather be your mother – oh! much rather! – than have been always pure . . . Oh, don't you see? don't you understand? It is my dishonour that has made you so dear to me. It is my disgrace that has bound you so closely to me. It is the price I paid for you – the price of soul and body – that makes me love you as I do. Oh, don't ask me to do this horrible thing. Child of my shame, be still the child of my shame!

GERALD: Mother, I didn't know you loved me so much as that. And I will be a better son to you than I have been. And you and I must never leave each other . . . but, mother . . . I can't help it . . . you must become my father's wife. You must marry him. It is your duty.

HESTER [*running forward and embracing* MRS ARBUTHNOT]:[10] No, no; you shall not. That would be real dishonour, the first you have ever known. That would be real disgrace: the first to touch you. Leave him and come with me. There are other countries than England . . . Oh! other countries over sea, better, wiser, and less unjust lands. The world is very wide and very big.

MRS ARBUTHNOT: No, not for me. For me the world is shrivelled to a palm's breadth, and where I walk there are thorns.

HESTER: It shall not be so. We shall somewhere find green valleys and fresh waters, and if we weep, well, we shall weep together. Have we not both loved him?

GERALD: Hester!

HESTER [*waving him back*]: Don't, don't! You cannot love me at all, unless you love her also. You cannot honour me, unless she's holier to you. In her all womanhood is martyred. Not she alone, but all of us are stricken in her house.

GERALD: Hester, Hester, what shall I do?

HESTER: Do you respect the man who is your father?

GERALD: Respect him? I despise him! He is infamous.

HESTER: I thank you for saving me from him last night.

GERALD: Ah, that is nothing. I would die to save you. But you don't tell me what to do now!

HESTER: Have I not thanked you for saving *me*?

GERALD: But what should I do?

HESTER: Ask your own heart, not mine. I never had a mother to save, or shame.

MRS ARBUTHNOT: He is hard – he is hard. Let me go away.

GERALD [*rushes over and kneels down beside his mother*]: Mother, forgive me: I have been to blame.

MRS ARBUTHNOT: Don't kiss my hands: they are cold. My heart is cold: something has broken it.

HESTER: Ah, don't say that. Hearts live by being wounded. Pleasure may turn a heart to stone, riches may make it callous, but sorrow – oh, sorrow cannot break it. Besides, what sorrows have you now? Why, at this moment you are more dear to him than ever, *dear* though you have *been*, and oh! how dear you *have* been always. Ah! be kind to him.

GERALD: You are my mother and my father all in one. I need no second parent. It was for you I spoke, for you alone. Oh, say something, mother. Have I but found one love to lose another? Don't tell me that. O mother, you are cruel.

[*Gets up and flings himself sobbing on a sofa.*]

MRS ARBUTHNOT [*to* HESTER]: But has he found indeed another love?

HESTER: You know I have loved him always.

MRS ARBUTHNOT: But we are very poor.

HESTER: Who, being loved, is poor? Oh, no one. I hate my riches. They are a burden. Let him share it with me.

MRS ARBUTHNOT: But we are disgraced. We rank among the outcasts. Gerald is nameless. The sins of the parents should be visited on the children. It is God's law.

HESTER: I was wrong. God's law is only Love.

MRS ARBUTHNOT [*rises, and taking* HESTER *by the hand, goes slowly over to where* GERALD *is lying on the sofa with his head buried in his hands. She touches him and he looks up*]: Gerald, I cannot give you a father, but I have brought you a wife.

GERALD: Mother, I am not worthy either of her or you.

MRS ARBUTHNOT: So she comes first, you are worthy. And when you are away, Gerald ... with ... her – oh, think of me sometimes. Don't forget me. And when you pray, pray for me. We should pray when we are happiest, and you will be happy, Gerald.

HESTER: Oh, you don't think of leaving us?

GERALD: Mother, you won't leave us?

MRS ARBUTHNOT: I might bring shame upon you!

GERALD: Mother!

MRS ARBUTHNOT: For a little then: and if you let me, near you always.

HESTER [*to* MRS ARBUTHNOT]: Come out with us to the garden.

MRS ARBUTHNOT: Later on, later on.

[*Exeunt* HESTER *and* GERALD.]

[MRS ARBUTHNOT *goes towards door L. C. Stops at looking-glass over mantelpiece and looks into it.*]

[*Enter* ALICE *R. C.*]

ALICE: A gentleman to see you, ma'am.

MRS ARBUTHNOT: Say I am not at home. Show me the card. [*Takes card from salver and looks at it.*] Say I will not see him. [LORD ILLINGWORTH *enters.*[11] MRS ARBUTHNOT *sees him in the glass and starts, but does not turn round. Exit* ALICE.] What can you have to say to me today, George Harford? You can have nothing to say to me. You must leave this house.

LORD ILLINGWORTH: Rachel, Gerald knows everything about you and me now, so some arrangement must be come to that will suit us all three. I assure you, he will find in me the most charming and generous of fathers.

MRS ARBUTHNOT: My son may come in at any moment. I saved you last night. I may not be able to save you again. My son feels my dishonour strongly, terribly strongly. I beg you to go.

LORD ILLINGWORTH [*sitting down*]: Last night was excessively unfortunate. That silly Puritan girl making a scene merely because I wanted to kiss her. What harm is there in a kiss?

MRS ARBUTHNOT [*turning round*]: A kiss may ruin a human life, George Harford. *I* know that. *I* know that too well.

LORD ILLINGWORTH: We won't discuss that at present. What is of importance today, as yesterday, is still our son. I am extremely fond of him, as you know, and odd though it may seem to you, I admired his conduct last night immensely. He took up the cudgels for that pretty prude with wonderful promptitude. He is just what I should have liked a son of mine to be. Except that no son of mine should ever take the side of the Puritans: that is always an error. Now, what I propose is this.

MRS ARBUTHNOT: Lord Illingworth, no proposition of yours interests me.

LORD ILLINGWORTH: According to our ridiculous English laws, I can't legitimize Gerald. But I can leave him my property. Illingworth is entailed,[12] of course, but it is a tedious barrack of a place. He can have Ashby, which is much prettier, Harborough, which has the best shooting in the north of England, and the house in St James's Square. What more can a gentleman desire in this world?

MRS ARBUTHNOT: Nothing more, I am quite sure.

LORD ILLINGWORTH: As for a title, a title is really rather a nuisance in these democratic days. As George Harford I had everything I wanted. Now I have merely everything that other people want, which isn't nearly so pleasant. Well, my proposal is this.

MRS ARBUTHNOT: I told you I was not interested, and I beg you to go.

LORD ILLINGWORTH: The boy is to be with you for six months in the year, and with me for the other six. That is perfectly fair, is it not? You can have whatever allowance you like, and live where you choose. As for your past, no one knows anything about it except myself and Gerald. There is the Puritan, of course, the Puritan in white muslin, but she doesn't count. She couldn't tell the story without explaining that she objected to being kissed, could she? And all the women would think her a fool and the men think her a bore. And you need not be afraid that Gerald won't be my heir. I needn't tell you I have not the slightest intention of marrying.

MRS ARBUTHNOT: You come too late. My son has no need of you. You are not necessary.

LORD ILLINGWORTH: What do you mean, Rachel?

MRS ARBUTHNOT: That you are not necessary to Gerald's career. He does not require you.

LORD ILLINGWORTH: I do not understand you.

MRS ARBUTHNOT: Look into the garden. [LORD ILLINGWORTH *rises and goes towards window.*][13] You had better not let them see you: you bring unpleasant memories. [LORD ILLINGWORTH *looks out and starts.*] She loves him. They love each other. We are safe from you, and we are going away.

LORD ILLINGWORTH: Where?

MRS ARBUTHNOT: We will not tell you, and if you find us we will not know you. You seem surprised. What welcome would you get from the girl whose lips you tried to soil, from the boy whose life you have shamed, from the mother whose dishonour comes from you?

LORD ILLINGWORTH: You have grown hard, Rachel.

MRS ARBUTHNOT: I was too weak once. It is well for me that I have changed.

LORD ILLINGWORTH: I was very young at the time. We men know life too early.

MRS ARBUTHNOT: And we women know life too late. That is the difference between men and women.

[*A pause.*]

LORD ILLINGWORTH: Rachel, I want my son. My money may be of no use to him now. I may be of no use to him, but I want my son. Bring us together, Rachel. You can do it if you choose.[14]

[*Sees letter on table.*]

MRS ARBUTHNOT: There is no room in my boy's life for *you*. He is not interested in *you*.

LORD ILLINGWORTH: Then why does he write to me?

MRS ARBUTHNOT: What do you mean?

LORD ILLINGWORTH: What letter is this?

[*Takes up letter.*]

MRS ARBUTHNOT: That – is nothing. Give it to me.

LORD ILLINGWORTH: It is addressed to *me*.

MRS ARBUTHNOT: You are not to open it. I forbid you to open it.

LORD ILLINGWORTH: And in Gerald's handwriting.

MRS ARBUTHNOT: It was not to have been sent. It is a letter he wrote to you this morning, before he saw me. But he is sorry now he wrote it, very sorry. You are not to open it. Give it to me.

LORD ILLINGWORTH: It belongs to me. [*Opens it, sits down, and reads it slowly.* MRS ARBUTHNOT *watches him all the time.*] You have read this letter, I suppose, Rachel?

MRS ARBUTHNOT: No.

LORD ILLINGWORTH: You know what is in it?

MRS ARBUTHNOT: Yes!

LORD ILLINGWORTH: I don't admit for a moment that the boy is right in what he says. I don't admit that it is any duty of mine to marry you. I deny it entirely. But to get my son back I am ready – yes, I am ready to marry you, Rachel – and to treat you always with the deference and respect due to my wife. I will marry you as soon as you choose. I give you my word of honour.

MRS ARBUTHNOT: You made that promise to me once before and broke it.

LORD ILLINGWORTH: I will keep it now. And that will show you that I love my son, at least as much as you love him. For when I marry you, Rachel, there are some ambitions I shall have to surrender. High ambitions too, if any ambition is high.

MRS ARBUTHNOT: I decline to marry you, Lord Illingworth.

LORD ILLINGWORTH: Are you serious?

MRS ARBUTHNOT: Yes.

LORD ILLINGWORTH: Do tell me your reasons. They would interest me enormously.

MRS ARBUTHNOT: I have already explained them to my son.

LORD ILLINGWORTH: I suppose they were intensely sentimental, weren't they? You women live by your emotions and for them. You have no philosophy of life.

MRS ARBUTHNOT: You are right. We women live by our emotions and for them. By our passions, and for them, if you will. I have two passions, Lord Illingworth; my love of him, my hate of you. You cannot kill those. They feed each other.

LORD ILLINGWORTH: What sort of love is that which needs to have hate as its brother!

MRS ARBUTHNOT: It is the sort of love I have for Gerald. Do you think that terrible? Well, it is terrible. All love is terrible. All love is a tragedy. I loved you once, Lord Illingworth. Oh, what a tragedy for a woman to have loved you!

LORD ILLINGWORTH: So you really refuse to marry me?

MRS ARBUTHNOT: Yes.

LORD ILLINGWORTH: Because you hate me?

MRS ARBUTHNOT: Yes.

LORD ILLINGWORTH: And does my son hate me as you do?

MRS ARBUTHNOT: No.

LORD ILLINGWORTH: I am glad of that, Rachel.

MRS ARBUTHNOT: He merely despises you.

LORD ILLINGWORTH: What a pity! What a pity for him, I mean.

MRS ARBUTHNOT: Don't be deceived, George. Children begin by loving their parents. After a time they judge them. Rarely if ever do they forgive them.[15]

LORD ILLINGWORTH [*reads letter over again, very slowly*]: May I ask by what arguments you made the boy who wrote this letter, this beautiful, passionate letter, believe that you should not marry his father, the father of your own child?

MRS ARBUTHNOT: It was not I who made him see it. It was another.

LORD ILLINGWORTH: What *fin-de-siècle*[16] person?

MRS ARBUTHNOT: The Puritan, Lord Illingworth.

[*A pause.*]

LORD ILLINGWORTH [*winces, then rises slowly and goes over to table where his hat and gloves are.* MRS ARBUTHNOT *is standing close to the table. He picks up one of the gloves, and begins putting it on*]: There is not much then for me to do here, Rachel?

MRS ARBUTHNOT: Nothing.

LORD ILLINGWORTH: It is good-bye, is it?

MRS ARBUTHNOT: For ever, I hope, this time, Lord Illingworth.

LORD ILLINGWORTH: How curious! At this moment you look exactly as you looked the night you left me twenty years ago. You have just the same expression in your mouth. Upon my word, Rachel, no woman ever loved me as you did. Why, you gave yourself to me like a flower, to do anything I liked with. You were the prettiest of playthings, the most fascinating of small romances . . . [*Pulls out watch.*] Quarter to two! Must be strolling back to Hunstanton. Don't suppose I shall see you there again. I'm sorry, I am, really. It's been an amusing experience to have met amongst people of one's own rank, and treated quite seriously too, one's mistress, and one's –

[MRS ARBUTHNOT *snatches up glove and strikes* LORD ILLINGWORTH *across the face with it.* LORD ILLINGWORTH *starts. He is dazed by the insult of his punishment. Then he controls himself, and goes to window and looks out at his son. Sighs and leaves the room.*][17]

MRS ARBUTHNOT [*falls sobbing on the sofa*]: He would have said it. He would have said it.

[*Enter* GERALD *and* HESTER *from the garden.*]

GERALD: Well, dear mother. You never came out after all. So we have come in to fetch you. Mother, you have not been crying?

[*Kneels down beside her.*]

MRS ARBUTHNOT: My boy! My boy! My boy!

[*Running her fingers through his hair.*]

HESTER [*coming over*]: But you have two children now. You'll let me be your daughter?

MRS ARBUTHNOT [*looking up*]: Would you choose me for a mother?

HESTER: You of all women I have ever known.

[*They move towards the door leading into garden with their arms round each other's waists.* GERALD *goes to table L. C. for his hat. On turning round he sees* LORD ILLINGWORTH's *glove lying on the floor, and picks it up.*]

GERALD: Hallo, mother, whose glove is this? You have had a visitor. Who was it?

MRS ARBUTHNOT [*turning round*]: Oh! no one. No one in particular. A man of no importance.[18]

CURTAIN

An Ideal Husband

TO
FRANK HARRIS[1]
A SLIGHT TRIBUTE TO
HIS POWER AND DISTINCTION
AS AN ARTIST
HIS CHIVALRY AND NOBILITY
AS A FRIEND

The Persons of the Play

THE EARL OF CAVERSHAM, K.G.

VISCOUNT GORING, *his son*

SIR ROBERT CHILTERN, *Bart, Under-Secretary for Foreign Affairs*

VICOMTE DE NANJAC, *Attaché at the French Embassy in London*

MR MONTFORD

MASON, *Butler to Sir Robert Chiltern*

PHIPPS, *Lord Goring's servant*

JAMES }
HAROLD } *Footmen*

LADY CHILTERN

LADY MARKBY

THE COUNTESS OF BASILDON

MRS MARCHMONT

MISS MABEL CHILTERN, *Sir Robert Chiltern's sister*

MRS CHEVELEY

TIME
The present

PLACE
London

The action of the play is completed within twenty-four hours

FIRST ACT

The octagon room at Sir Robert Chiltern's house in Grosvenor Square.[1]

[*The room is brilliantly lighted and full of guests. At the top of the staircase stands* LADY CHILTERN, *a woman of grave Greek beauty, about twenty-seven years of age. She receives the guests as they come up. Over the well of the staircase hangs a great chandelier with wax lights, which illumine a large eighteenth-century French tapestry – representing the Triumph of Love, from a design by Boucher – that is stretched on the staircase wall. On the right is the entrance to the music-room. The sound of a string quartette is faintly heard. The entrance on the left leads to other reception-rooms.* MRS MARCHMONT *and* LADY BASILDON, *two very pretty women, are seated together on a Louis Seize sofa. They are types of exquisite fragility. Their affectation of manner has a delicate charm. Watteau would have loved to paint them.*]

MRS MARCHMONT: Going on to the Hartlocks' tonight, Margaret?

LADY BASILDON: I suppose so. Are you?

MRS MARCHMONT: Yes. Horribly tedious parties they give, don't they?

LADY BASILDON: Horribly tedious! Never know why I go. Never know why I go anywhere.

MRS MARCHMONT: I come here to be educated.

LADY BASILDON: Ah! I hate being educated!

MRS MARCHMONT: So do I. It puts one almost on a level with the commercial classes, doesn't it? But dear Gertrude Chiltern is always telling me that I should have some serious purpose in life. So I come here to try to find one.

LADY BASILDON [*looking round through her lorgnette*]: I don't see anybody here tonight whom one could possibly call a serious purpose. The man who took me in to dinner talked to me about his wife the whole time.

MRS MARCHMONT: How very trivial of him!

LADY BASILDON: Terribly trivial! What did your man talk about?

MRS MARCHMONT: About myself.

LADY BASILDON [*languidly*]: And were you interested?

MRS MARCHMONT [*shaking her head*]: Not in the smallest degree.

LADY BASILDON: What martyrs we are, dear Margaret!

MRS MARCHMONT [*rising*]: And how well it becomes us, Olivia!

[*They rise and go towards the music-room. The* VICOMTE DE NANJAC, *a young attaché known for his neckties and his Anglomania, approaches with a low bow, and enters into conversation.*]

MASON [*announcing guests from the top of the staircase*]: Mr and Lady Jane Barford. Lord Caversham.

[*Enter* LORD CAVERSHAM, *an old gentleman of seventy, wearing the riband and star of the Garter. A fine Whig type. Rather like a portrait by Lawrence.*][2]

LORD CAVERSHAM: Good evening, Lady Chiltern! Has my good-for-nothing young son been here?

LADY CHILTERN [*smiling*]: I don't think Lord Goring has arrived yet.

MABEL CHILTERN [*coming up to* LORD CAVERSHAM]: Why do you call Lord Goring good-for-nothing?

[MABEL CHILTERN *is a perfect example of the English type of prettiness, the apple-blossom type. She has all the fragrance and freedom of a flower. There is ripple after ripple of sunlight in her hair, and the little mouth, with its parted lips, is expectant, like the mouth of a child. She has the fascinating tyranny of youth, and the astonishing courage of innocence. To sane people she is not reminiscent of any work of art. But she is really like a Tanagra statuette,[3] and would be rather annoyed if she were told so.*]

LORD CAVERSHAM: Because he leads such an idle life.

MABEL CHILTERN: How can you say such a thing? Why, he rides in the Row[4] at ten o'clock in the morning, goes to the Opera three times a week, changes his clothes at least five times a day and dines out every night of the season. You don't call that leading an idle life, do you?

LORD CAVERSHAM [*looking at her with a kindly twinkle in his eye*]: You are a very charming young lady!

MABEL CHILTERN: How sweet of you to say that, Lord Caversham! Do come to us more often. You know we are always at home on Wednesdays, and you look so well with your star!⁵

LORD CAVERSHAM: Never go anywhere now. Sick of London Society. Shouldn't mind being introduced to my own tailor; he always votes on the right side. But object strongly to being sent down to dinner with my wife's milliner. Never could stand Lady Caversham's bonnets.

MABEL CHILTERN: Oh, I love London Society! I think it has immensely improved. It is entirely composed now of beautiful idiots and brilliant lunatics. Just what Society should be.

LORD CAVERSHAM: Hum! Which is Goring? Beautiful idiot, or the other thing?

MABEL CHILTERN [*gravely*]: I have been obliged for the present to put Lord Goring into a class quite by himself. But he is developing charmingly!

LORD CAVERSHAM: Into what?

MABEL CHILTERN [*with a little curtsey*]: I hope to let you know very soon, Lord Caversham!

MASON [*announcing guests*]: Lady Markby. Mrs Cheveley.

[*Enter* LADY MARKBY *and* MRS CHEVELEY. LADY MARKBY *is a pleasant, kindly, popular woman, with grey hair à la marquise⁶ and good lace.* MRS CHEVELEY, *who accompanies her, is tall and rather slight. Lips very thin and highly-coloured, a line of scarlet on a pallid face. Venetian red hair, aquiline nose and long throat. Rouge accentuates the natural paleness of her complexion. Grey-green eyes that move restlessly. She is in heliotrope, with diamonds.⁷ She looks rather like an orchid, and makes great demands on one's curiosity. In all her movements she is extremely graceful. A work of art, on the whole, but showing the influence of too many schools.*]

LADY MARKBY: Good evening, dear Gertrude! So kind of you to let me bring my friend, Mrs Cheveley. Two such charming women should know each other!

LADY CHILTERN [*advances towards* MRS CHEVELEY *with a sweet smile. Then suddenly stops, and bows rather distantly*]: I think Mrs Cheveley and I have met before. I did not know she had married a second time.

LADY MARKBY [*genially*]: Ah, nowadays people marry as often as they can, don't they? It is most fashionable. [*To* DUCHESS OF MARYBOROUGH] Dear Duchess, and how is the Duke? Brain still weak, I suppose? Well, that is only to be expected, is it not? His good father was just the same. There is nothing like race, is there?

MRS CHEVELEY [*playing with her fan*]: But have we really met before, Lady Chiltern? I can't remember where. I have been out of England for so long.

LADY CHILTERN: We were at school together, Mrs Cheveley.

MRS CHEVELEY [*superciliously*]: Indeed? I have forgotten all about my schooldays. I have a vague impression that they were detestable.

LADY CHILTERN [*coldly*]: I am not surprised!

MRS CHEVELEY [*in her sweetest manner*]: Do you know, I am quite looking forward to meeting your clever husband, Lady Chiltern. Since he has been at the Foreign Office, he has been so much talked of in Vienna.[8] They actually succeed in spelling his name right in the newspapers. That in itself is fame, on the continent.

LADY CHILTERN: I hardly think there will be much in common between you and my husband, Mrs Cheveley!

[*Moves away.*]

VICOMTE DE NANJAC: Ah! chère Madame, quelle surprise! I have not seen you since Berlin!

MRS CHEVELEY: Not since Berlin, Vicomte. Five years ago!

VICOMTE DE NANJAC: And you are younger and more beautiful than ever. How do you manage it?

MRS CHEVELEY: By making it a rule only to talk to perfectly charming people like yourself.

VICOMTE DE NANJAC: Ah! you flatter me. You butter me, as they say here.

MRS CHEVELEY: Do they say that here? How dreadful of them!

VICOMTE DE NANJAC: Yes, they have a wonderful language. It should be more widely known.

[SIR ROBERT CHILTERN *enters. A man of forty, but looking somewhat younger. Clean-shaven, with finely-cut features, dark-haired and dark-eyed. A personality of mark. Not popular – few personalities are. But intensely admired by the few, and deeply respected by the many. The note of his manner is that of perfect distinction, with a slight touch of pride. One feels that he is conscious of the success he has made in life. A nervous temperament, with a tired look. The firmly-chiselled mouth and chin contrast strikingly with the romantic expression in the deep-set eyes. The variance is suggestive of an almost complete separation of passion and intellect, as though thought and emotion were each isolated in its own sphere through some violence of will-power. There is nervousness in the nostrils, and in the pale, thin, pointed hands. It would be inaccurate to call him picturesque. Picturesqueness cannot survive the House of Commons. But Vandyck⁹ would have liked to have painted his head.]*

SIR ROBERT CHILTERN: Good evening, Lady Markby! I hope you have brought Sir John with you?

LADY MARKBY: Oh! I have brought a much more charming person than Sir John. Sir John's temper since he has taken seriously to politics has become quite unbearable. Really, now that the House of Commons is trying to become useful, it does a great deal of harm.

SIR ROBERT CHILTERN: I hope not, Lady Markby. At any rate we do our best to waste the public time, don't we? But who is this charming person you have been kind enough to bring to us?

LADY MARKBY: Her name is Mrs Cheveley. One of the Dorsetshire Cheveleys, I suppose. But I really don't know. Families are so mixed nowadays. Indeed, as a rule, everybody turns out to be somebody else.

SIR ROBERT CHILTERN: Mrs Cheveley? I seem to know the name.

LADY MARKBY: She has just arrived from Vienna.

SIR ROBERT CHILTERN: Ah! yes. I think I know whom you mean.

LADY MARKBY: Oh! she goes everywhere there, and has such pleasant scandals about all her friends. I really must go to Vienna next winter. I hope there is a good chef at the Embassy.

SIR ROBERT CHILTERN: If there is not, the Ambassador will certainly have to be recalled. Pray point out Mrs Cheveley to me. I should like to see her.

LADY MARKBY: Let me introduce you. [*To* MRS CHEVELEY] My dear, Sir Robert Chiltern is dying to know you!

SIR ROBERT CHILTERN [*bowing*]: Every one is dying to know the brilliant Mrs Cheveley. Our attachés at Vienna write to us about nothing else.

MRS CHEVELEY: Thank you, Sir Robert. An acquaintance that begins with a compliment is sure to develop into a real friendship. It starts in the right manner. And I find that I know Lady Chiltern already.

SIR ROBERT CHILTERN: Really?

MRS CHEVELEY: Yes. She has just reminded me that we were at school together. I remember it perfectly now. She always got the good conduct prize. I have a distinct recollection of Lady Chiltern always getting the good conduct prize!

SIR ROBERT CHILTERN [*smiling*]: And what prizes did you get, Mrs Cheveley?

MRS CHEVELEY: My prizes came a little later on in life. I don't think any of them were for good conduct. I forget!

SIR ROBERT CHILTERN: I am sure they were for something charming!

MRS CHEVELEY: I don't know that women are always rewarded for being charming. I think they are usually punished for it! Certainly, more women grow old nowadays through the faithfulness of their admirers than through anything else! At least that is the only way I can account for the terribly haggard look of most of your pretty women in London!

SIR ROBERT CHILTERN: What an appalling philosophy that sounds! To attempt to classify you, Mrs Cheveley, would be an impertinence. But may I ask, at heart, are you an optimist or a pessimist? Those seem to be the only two fashionable religions left to us nowadays.

MRS CHEVELEY: Oh, I'm neither. Optimism begins in a broad grin, and Pessimism ends with blue spectacles.[10] Besides, they are both of them merely poses.

SIR ROBERT CHILTERN: You prefer to be natural?

MRS CHEVELEY: Sometimes. But it is such a very difficult pose to keep up.

SIR ROBERT CHILTERN: What would those modern psychological novelists, of whom we hear so much, say to such a theory as that?

MRS CHEVELEY: Ah! the strength of women comes from the fact that psychology cannot explain us. Men can be analysed, women . . . merely adored.

SIR ROBERT CHILTERN: You think science cannot grapple with the problem of women?

MRS CHEVELEY: Science can never grapple with the irrational. That is why it has no future before it, in this world.

SIR ROBERT CHILTERN: And women represent the irrational.

MRS CHEVELEY: Well-dressed women do.

SIR ROBERT CHILTERN [*with a polite bow*]: I fear I could hardly agree with you there. But do sit down. And now tell me, what makes you leave your brilliant Vienna for our gloomy London – or perhaps the question is indiscreet?

MRS CHEVELEY: Questions are never indiscreet. Answers sometimes are.

SIR ROBERT CHILTERN: Well, at any rate, may I know if it is politics or pleasure?

MRS CHEVELEY: Politics are my only pleasure. You see nowadays it is not fashionable to flirt till one is forty, or to be romantic till one is forty-five, so we poor women who are under thirty, or say we are, have nothing open to us but politics or philanthropy. And philanthropy seems to me to have become simply the refuge of people who wish to annoy their fellow-creatures. I prefer politics. I think they are more . . . becoming!

SIR ROBERT CHILTERN: A political life is a noble career!

MRS CHEVELEY: Sometimes. And sometimes it is a clever game, Sir Robert. And sometimes it is a great nuisance.

SIR ROBERT CHILTERN: Which do you find it?

MRS CHEVELEY: I? A combination of all three.

[*Drops her fan.*]

SIR ROBERT CHILTERN [*picks up fan*]: Allow me!

MRS CHEVELEY: Thanks.

SIR ROBERT CHILTERN: But you have not told me yet what makes you honour London so suddenly. Our season is almost over.

MRS CHEVELEY: Oh! I don't care about the London season! It is too matrimonial. People are either hunting for husbands, or hiding from them. I wanted to meet you. It is quite true. You know what a woman's curiosity is. Almost as great as a man's! I wanted immensely to meet you, and . . . to ask you to do something for me.

SIR ROBERT CHILTERN: I hope it is not a little thing, Mrs Cheveley. I find that little things are so very difficult to do.

MRS CHEVELEY [*after a moment's reflection*]: No, I don't think it is quite a little thing.

SIR ROBERT CHILTERN: I am so glad. Do tell me what it is.

MRS CHEVELEY: Later on. [*Rises.*] And now may I walk through your beautiful house? I hear your pictures are charming. Poor Baron Arnheim – you remember the Baron? – used to tell me you had some wonderful Corots.[11]

SIR ROBERT CHILTERN [*with an almost imperceptible start*]: Did you know Baron Arnheim well?

MRS CHEVELEY [*smiling*]: Intimately. Did you?

SIR ROBERT CHILTERN: At one time.

MRS CHEVELEY: Wonderful man, wasn't he?

SIR ROBERT CHILTERN [*after a pause*]: He was very remarkable, in many ways.

MRS CHEVELEY: I often think it such a pity he never wrote his memoirs. They would have been most interesting.

SIR ROBERT CHILTERN: Yes: he knew men and cities well, like the old Greek.

MRS CHEVELEY: Without the dreadful disadvantage of having a Penelope[12] waiting at home for him.

MASON: Lord Goring.

[*Enter* LORD GORING. *Thirty-four, but always says he is younger. A well-bred, expressionless face. He is clever, but would not like to be thought so. A flawless dandy, he would be annoyed if he were considered romantic. He plays with life, and is on perfectly good terms with the world. He is fond of being misunderstood. It gives him a post of vantage.*]

SIR ROBERT CHILTERN: Good evening, my dear Arthur! Mrs Cheveley, allow me to introduce to you Lord Goring, the idlest man in London.

MRS CHEVELEY: I have met Lord Goring before.

LORD GORING [*bowing*]: I did not think you would remember me, Mrs Cheveley.

MRS CHEVELEY: My memory is under admirable control. And are you still a bachelor?

LORD GORING: I . . . believe so.

MRS CHEVELEY: How very romantic!

LORD GORING: Oh! I am not at all romantic. I am not old enough. I leave romance to my seniors.

SIR ROBERT CHILTERN: Lord Goring is the result of Boodle's Club,[13] Mrs Cheveley.

MRS CHEVELEY: He reflects every credit on the institution.

LORD GORING: May I ask are you staying in London long?

MRS CHEVELEY: That depends partly on the weather, partly on the cooking and partly on Sir Robert.

SIR ROBERT CHILTERN: You are not going to plunge us into a European war, I hope?

MRS CHEVELEY: There is no danger, at present!

[*She nods to* LORD GORING, *with a look of amusement in her eyes, and goes out with* SIR ROBERT CHILTERN. LORD GORING *saunters over to* MABEL CHILTERN.]

MABEL CHILTERN: You are very late!

LORD GORING: Have you missed me?

MABEL CHILTERN: Awfully!

LORD GORING: Then I am sorry I did not stay away longer. I like being missed.

MABEL CHILTERN: How very selfish of you!

LORD GORING: I am very selfish.

MABEL CHILTERN: You are always telling me of your bad qualities, Lord Goring.

LORD GORING: I have only told you half of them as yet, Miss Mabel!

MABEL CHILTERN: Are the others very bad?

LORD GORING: Quite dreadful! When I think of them at night I go to sleep at once.

MABEL CHILTERN: Well, I delight in your bad qualities. I wouldn't have you part with one of them.

LORD GORING: How very nice of you! But then you are always nice. By the way, I want to ask you a question, Miss Mabel. Who brought Mrs Cheveley here? That woman in heliotrope, who has just gone out of the room with your brother?

MABEL CHILTERN: Oh, I think Lady Markby brought her. Why do you ask?

LORD GORING: I haven't seen her for years, that is all.

MABEL CHILTERN: What an absurd reason!

LORD GORING: All reasons are absurd.

MABEL CHILTERN: What sort of a woman is she?

LORD GORING: Oh! a genius in the daytime and a beauty at night!

MABEL CHILTERN: I dislike her already.

LORD GORING: That shows your admirable good taste.

VICOMTE DE NANJAC [*approaching*]: Ah, the English young lady is the dragon of good taste, is she not? Quite the dragon of good taste.

LORD GORING: So the newspapers are always telling us.

VICOMTE DE NANJAC: I read all your English newspapers. I find them so amusing.

LORD GORING: Then, my dear Nanjac, you must certainly read between the lines.

VICOMTE DE NANJAC: I should like to, but my professor objects. [*To* MABEL CHILTERN.] May I have the pleasure of escorting you to the music-room, Mademoiselle?

MABEL CHILTERN [*looking very disappointed*]: Delighted, Vicomte, quite delighted! [*Turning to* LORD GORING] Aren't you coming to the music-room?

LORD GORING: Not if there is any music going on, Miss Mabel.

MABEL CHILTERN [*severely*]: The music is in German. You would not understand it.[14]

[*Goes out with the* VICOMTE DE NANJAC. LORD CAVERSHAM *comes up to his son.*]

LORD CAVERSHAM: Well, sir! what are you doing here? Wasting your life as usual! You should be in bed, sir. You keep too late hours! I heard of you the other night at Lady Rufford's dancing till four o'clock in the morning!

LORD GORING: Only a quarter to four, father.

LORD CAVERSHAM: Can't make out how you stand London Society. The thing has gone to the dogs, a lot of damned nobodies talking about nothing.

LORD GORING: I love talking about nothing, father. It is the only thing I know anything about.

LORD CAVERSHAM: You seem to me to be living entirely for pleasure.

LORD GORING: What else is there to live for, father? Nothing ages like happiness.

LORD CAVERSHAM: You are heartless, sir, very heartless!

LORD GORING: I hope not, father. Good evening, Lady Basildon!

LADY BASILDON [arching two pretty eyebrows]: Are you here? I had no idea you ever came to political parties!

LORD GORING: I adore political parties. They are the only place left to us where people don't talk politics.

LADY BASILDON: I delight in talking politics. I talk them all day long. But I can't bear listening to them. I don't know how the unfortunate men in the House stand these long debates.

LORD GORING: By never listening.

LADY BASILDON: Really?

LORD GORING [in his most serious manner]: Of course. You see, it is a very dangerous thing to listen. If one listens one may be convinced; and a man who allows himself to be convinced by an argument is a thoroughly unreasonable person.

LADY BASILDON: Ah! that accounts for so much in men that I have never understood, and so much in women that their husbands never appreciate in them!

MRS MARCHMONT [with a sigh]: Our husbands never appreciate anything in us. We have to go to others for that!

LADY BASILDON [emphatically]: Yes, always to others, have we not?

LORD GORING [smiling]: And those are the views of the two ladies who are known to have the most admirable husbands in London.

MRS MARCHMONT: That is exactly what we can't stand. My Reginald is quite hopelessly faultless. He is really unendurably so, at times!

There is not the smallest element of excitement in knowing him.

LORD GORING: How terrible! Really, the thing should be more widely known!

LADY BASILDON: Basildon is quite as bad; he is as domestic as if he was a bachelor.

MRS MARCHMONT [*pressing* LADY BASILDON's *hand*]: My poor Olivia! We have married perfect husbands, and we are well punished for it.

LORD GORING: I should have thought it was the husbands who were punished.

MRS MARCHMONT [*drawing herself up*]: Oh dear, no! They are as happy as possible! And as for trusting us, it is tragic how much they trust us.

LADY BASILDON: Perfectly tragic!

LORD GORING: Or comic, Lady Basildon?

LADY BASILDON: Certainly not comic, Lord Goring. How unkind of you to suggest such a thing!

MRS MARCHMONT: I am afraid Lord Goring is in the camp of the enemy, as usual. I saw him talking to that Mrs Cheveley when he came in.

LORD GORING: Handsome woman, Mrs Cheveley!

LADY BASILDON [*stiffly*]: Please don't praise other women in our presence. You might wait for us to do that!

LORD GORING: I did wait.

MRS MARCHMONT: Well, we are not going to praise her. I hear she went to the Opera on Monday night, and told Tommy Rufford at supper that, as far as she could see, London Society was entirely made up of dowdies and dandies.

LORD GORING: She is quite right, too. The men are all dowdies and the women are all dandies, aren't they?

MRS MARCHMONT [*after a pause*]: Oh! do you really think that is what Mrs Cheveley meant?

LORD GORING: Of course. And a very sensible remark for Mrs Cheveley to make, too.

[*Enter* MABEL CHILTERN. *She joins the group.*]

MABEL CHILTERN: Why are you talking about Mrs Cheveley? Every-body is talking about Mrs Cheveley! Lord Goring says – what did you say, Lord Goring, about Mrs Cheveley? Oh! I remember, that she was a genius in the daytime and a beauty at night.

LADY BASILDON: What a horrid combination! So very unnatural!

MRS MARCHMONT [*in her most dreamy manner*]: I like looking at geniuses, and listening to beautiful people.

LORD GORING: Ah! that is morbid[15] of you, Mrs Marchmont!

MRS MARCHMONT [*brightening to a look of real pleasure*]: I am so glad to hear you say that. Marchmont and I have been married for seven years, and he has never once told me that I was morbid. Men are so painfully unobservant!

LADY BASILDON [*turning to her*]: I have always said, dear Margaret, that you were the most morbid person in London.

MRS MARCHMONT: Ah! but you are always sympathetic, Olivia!

MABEL CHILTERN: Is it morbid to have a desire for food? I have a great desire for food. Lord Goring, will you give me some supper?[16]

LORD GORING: With pleasure, Miss Mabel.

[*Moves away with her.*]

MABEL CHILTERN: How horrid you have been! You have never talked to me the whole evening!

LORD GORING: How could I? You went away with the child-diplomatist.

MABEL CHILTERN: You might have followed us. Pursuit would have been only polite. I don't think I like you at all this evening!

LORD GORING: I like you immensely.

MABEL CHILTERN: Well, I wish you'd show it in a more marked way!

[*They go downstairs.*]

MRS MARCHMONT: Olivia, I have a curious feeling of absolute faintness. I think I should like some supper very much. I know I should like some supper.

LADY BASILDON: I am positively dying for supper, Margaret!

MRS MARCHMONT: Men are so horribly selfish, they never think of these things.

LADY BASILDON: Men are grossly material, grossly material!

[*The* VICOMTE DE NANJAC *enters from the music-room with some other guests. After having carefully examined all the people present, he approaches* LADY BASILDON.]

VICOMTE DE NANJAC: May I have the honour of taking you down to supper, Comtesse?

LADY BASILDON [*coldly*]: I never take supper, thank you, Vicomte. [*The* VICOMTE *is about to retire.* LADY BASILDON, *seeing this, rises at once and takes his arm.*] But I will come down with you with pleasure.

VICOMTE DE NANJAC: I am so fond of eating! I am very English in all my tastes.

LADY BASILDON: You look quite English, Vicomte, quite English.

[*They pass out,* MR MONTFORD, *a perfectly groomed young dandy, approaches* MRS MARCHMONT.]

MR MONTFORD: Like some supper, Mrs Marchmont?

MRS MARCHMONT [*languidly*]: Thank you, Mr Montford, I never touch supper. [*Rises hastily and takes his arm.*] But I will sit beside you, and watch you.

MR MONTFORD: I don't know that I like being watched when I am eating!

MRS MARCHMONT: Then I will watch someone else.

MR MONTFORD: I don't know that I should like that either.

MRS MARCHMONT [*severely*]: Pray, Mr Montford, do not make these painful scenes of jealousy in public!

[*They go downstairs with the other guests, passing* SIR ROBERT CHILTERN *and* MRS CHEVELEY, *who now enter.*]

SIR ROBERT CHILTERN: And are you going to any of our country houses before you leave England, Mrs Cheveley?

MRS CHEVELEY: Oh, no! I can't stand your English house-parties. In England people actually try to be brilliant at breakfast. That is so dreadful of them! Only dull people are brilliant at breakfast. And then the family skeleton is always reading family prayers. My stay in England really depends on you, Sir Robert.

[*Sits down on the sofa.*]

SIR ROBERT CHILTERN [*taking a seat beside her*]: Seriously?

MRS CHEVELEY: Quite seriously. I want to talk to you about a great political and financial scheme, about this Argentine Canal Company, in fact.

SIR ROBERT CHILTERN: What a tedious, practical subject for you to talk about, Mrs Cheveley!

MRS CHEVELEY: Oh, I like tedious, practical subjects. What I don't like are tedious, practical people. There is a wide difference. Besides, you are interested, I know, in International Canal schemes. You were Lord Radley's secretary, weren't you, when the Government bought the Suez Canal shares?[17]

SIR ROBERT CHILTERN: Yes. But the Suez Canal was a very great and splendid undertaking. It gave us our direct route to India. It had imperial value. It was necessary that we should have control. This Argentine scheme is a commonplace Stock Exchange swindle.

MRS CHEVELEY: A speculation, Sir Robert! A brilliant, daring speculation.

SIR ROBERT CHILTERN: Believe me, Mrs Cheveley, it is a swindle. Let us call things by their proper names. It makes matters simpler. We have all the information about it at the Foreign Office. In fact, I sent out a special Commission to inquire into the matter privately, and they report that the works are hardly begun, and as for the money already subscribed, no one seems to know what has become of it. The whole thing is a second Panama,[18] and with not a quarter of the chance of success that miserable affair ever had. I hope you have not invested in it. I am sure you are far too clever to have done that.

MRS CHEVELEY: I have invested very largely in it.

SIR ROBERT CHILTERN: Who could have advised you to do such a foolish thing?

MRS CHEVELEY: Your old friend – and mine.

SIR ROBERT CHILTERN: Who?

MRS CHEVELEY: Baron Arnheim.

SIR ROBERT CHILTERN [*frowning*]: Ah! yes. I remember hearing, at the time of his death, that he had been mixed up in the whole affair.

MRS CHEVELEY: It was his last romance. His last but one, to do him justice.

SIR ROBERT CHILTERN [*rising*]: But you have not seen my Corots yet. They are in the music-room. Corots seem to go with music, don't they? May I show them to you?

MRS CHEVELEY [*shaking her head*]: I am not in a mood tonight for silver twilights, or rose-pink dawns. I want to talk business.

[*Motions to him with her fan to sit down again beside her.*]

SIR ROBERT CHILTERN: I fear I have no advice to give you, Mrs Cheveley, except to interest yourself in something less dangerous. The success of the Canal depends, of course, on the attitude of England, and I am going to lay the report of the Commissioners before the House tomorrow night.

MRS CHEVELEY: That you must not do. In your own interests, Sir Robert, to say nothing of mine, you must not do that.

SIR ROBERT CHILTERN [*looking at her in wonder*]: In my own interests? My dear Mrs Cheveley, what do you mean?

[*Sits down beside her.*]

MRS CHEVELEY: Sir Robert, I will be quite frank with you. I want you to withdraw the report that you had intended to lay before the House, on the ground that you have reasons to believe that the Commissioners have been prejudiced or misinformed, or something. Then I want you to say a few words to the effect that the Government is going to reconsider the question, and that you have reason to believe that the Canal, if completed, will be of great international value. You know the sort of things ministers say in cases of this kind. A few ordinary platitudes will do. In modern life nothing produces such an effect as a good platitude. It makes the whole world kin.[19] Will you do that for me?

SIR ROBERT CHILTERN: Mrs Cheveley, you cannot be serious in making me such a proposition!

MRS CHEVELEY: I am quite serious.

SIR ROBERT CHILTERN [*coldly*]: Pray allow me to believe that you are not.

MRS CHEVELEY [*speaking with great deliberation and emphasis*]: Ah! but I am. And if you do what I ask you, I . . . will pay you very handsomely!

SIR ROBERT CHILTERN: Pay me!

MRS CHEVELEY: Yes.

SIR ROBERT CHILTERN: I am afraid I don't understand what you mean.

MRS CHEVELEY [*leaning back on the sofa and looking at him*]: How very disappointing! And I have come all the way from Vienna in order that you should thoroughly understand me.

SIR ROBERT CHILTERN: I fear I don't.

MRS CHEVELEY [*in her most nonchalant manner*]: My dear Sir Robert, you are a man of the world, and you have your price, I suppose. Everybody has nowadays. The drawback is that most people are so dreadfully expensive. I know I am. I hope you will be more reasonable in your terms.

SIR ROBERT CHILTERN [*rises indignantly*]: If you will allow me, I will call your carriage for you. You have lived so long abroad, Mrs Cheveley, that you seem to be unable to realize that you are talking to an English gentleman.

MRS CHEVELEY [*detains him by touching his arm with her fan, and keeping it there while she is talking*]: I realize that I am talking to a man who laid the foundation of his fortune by selling to a Stock Exchange speculator a Cabinet secret.

SIR ROBERT CHILTERN [*biting his lip*]: What do you mean?

MRS CHEVELEY [*rising and facing him*]: I mean that I know the real origin of your wealth and your career, and I have got your letter, too.

SIR ROBERT CHILTERN: What letter?

MRS CHEVELEY [*contemptuously*]: The letter you wrote to Baron Arnheim, when you were Lord Radley's secretary, telling the Baron to buy Suez Canal shares – a letter written three days before the Government announced its own purchase.

SIR ROBERT CHILTERN [*hoarsely*]: It is not true.

MRS CHEVELEY: You thought that letter had been destroyed. How foolish of you! It is in my possession.[20]

ОSCAR WILDE

SIR ROBERT CHILTERN: The affair to which you allude was no more than a speculation. The House of Commons had not yet passed the bill; it might have been rejected.

MRS CHEVELEY: It was a swindle, Sir Robert. Let us call things by their proper names. It makes everything simpler. And now I am going to sell you that letter, and the price I ask for it is your public support of the Argentine scheme. You made your own fortune out of one canal. You must help me and my friends to make our fortunes out of another!

SIR ROBERT CHILTERN: It is infamous, what you propose – infamous!

MRS CHEVELEY: Oh, no! This is the game of life as we all have to play it, Sir Robert, sooner or later!

SIR ROBERT CHILTERN: I cannot do what you ask me.

MRS CHEVELEY: You mean you cannot help doing it. You know you are standing on the edge of a precipice. And it is not for you to make terms. It is for you to accept them. Supposing you refuse –

SIR ROBERT CHILTERN: What then?

MRS CHEVELEY: My dear Sir Robert, what then? You are ruined, that is all! Remember to what a point your Puritanism in England has brought you. In old days nobody pretended to be a bit better than his neighbours. In fact, to be a bit better than one's neighbour was considered excessively vulgar and middle class. Nowadays, with our modern mania for morality, everyone has to pose as a paragon of purity, incorruptibility, and all the other seven deadly virtues – and what is the result? You all go over like ninepins – one after the other. Not a year passes in England without somebody disappearing. Scandals used to lend charm, or at least interest, to a man – now they crush him. And yours is a very nasty scandal. You couldn't survive it. If it were known that as a young man, secretary to a great and important minister, you sold a Cabinet secret for a large sum of money, and that that was the origin of your wealth and career, you would be hounded out of public life, you would disappear completely. And after all, Sir Robert, why should you sacrifice your entire future rather than deal diplomatically with your enemy? For the moment I am your enemy. I admit it! And I am much stronger than you are. The big battalions are on my side. You have a splendid position, but it is your splendid position that makes you so vulnerable. You can't defend it! And I am in attack. Of course I have not talked morality to you. You must admit in fairness that I have spared you that. Years ago you did a clever, unscrupulous thing; it turned out a great success. You owe to it your fortune and position. And now you have got to pay for it. Sooner or later we have all to pay for what we do. You have to pay now. Before I leave you tonight, you have got to promise me to suppress your report, and to speak in the House in favour of this scheme.

SIR ROBERT CHILTERN: What you ask is impossible.

MRS CHEVELEY: You must make it possible. You are going to make it possible. Sir Robert, you know what your English newspapers are like. Suppose that when I leave this house I drive down to some newspaper office, and give them this scandal and the proofs of it! Think of their loathsome joy, of the delight they would have in dragging you down, of the mud and mire they would plunge you in. Think of the hypocrite with his greasy smile penning his leading article, and arranging the foulness of the public placard.

SIR ROBERT CHILTERN: Stop! You want me to withdraw the report and to make a short speech stating that I believe there are possibilities in the scheme?

MRS CHEVELEY [*sitting down on the sofa*]:[21] Those are my terms.

SIR ROBERT CHILTERN [*in a low voice*]: I will give you any sum of money you want.

MRS CHEVELEY: Even you are not rich enough, Sir Robert, to buy back your past. No man is.

SIR ROBERT CHILTERN: I will not do what you ask me. I will not.

MRS CHEVELEY: You have to. If you don't . . .

[*Rises from the sofa.*]

SIR ROBERT CHILTERN [*bewildered and unnerved*]: Wait a moment! What did you propose? You said that you would give me back my letter, didn't you?

MRS CHEVELEY: Yes. That is agreed. I will be in the Ladies' Gallery[22] tomorrow night at half-past eleven. If by that time – and you will have had heaps of opportunity – you have made an announcement to the House in the terms I wish, I shall hand you back your letter with the prettiest thanks, and the best, or at any rate the most suitable, compliment I can think of. I intend to play quite fairly with you. One should always play fairly ... when one has the winning cards. The Baron taught me that ... amongst other things.

SIR ROBERT CHILTERN: You must let me have time to consider your proposal.

MRS CHEVELEY: No; you must settle now!

SIR ROBERT CHILTERN: Give me a week – three days!

MRS CHEVELEY: Impossible! I have got to telegraph to Vienna to-night.

SIR ROBERT CHILTERN: My God! what brought you into my life?

MRS CHEVELEY: Circumstances.

[*Moves towards the door.*]

SIR ROBERT CHILTERN: Don't go. I consent. The report shall be withdrawn. I will arrange for a question to be put to me on the subject.[23]

MRS CHEVELEY: Thank you. I knew we should come to an amicable agreement. I understood your nature from the first. I analysed you, though you did not adore me. And now you can get my carriage for me, Sir Robert. I see the people coming up from supper, and English men always get romantic after a meal, and that bores me dreadfully.

[*Exit* SIR ROBERT CHILTERN.]

[*Enter guests,* LADY CHILTERN, LADY MARKBY, LORD CAVERSHAM, LADY BASILDON, MRS MARCHMONT, VICOMTE DE NANJAC, MR MONTFORD.]

LADY MARKBY: Well, dear Mrs Cheveley, I hope you have enjoyed yourself. Sir Robert is very entertaining, is he not?

MRS CHEVELEY: Most entertaining! I have enjoyed my talk with him immensely.

LADY MARKBY: He has had a very interesting and brilliant career. And he has married a most admirable wife. Lady Chiltern is a woman of the very highest principles, I am glad to say. I am a little too old now, myself, to trouble about setting a good example, but I always admire people who do. And Lady Chiltern has a very ennobling effect on life, though her dinner-parties are rather dull sometimes. But one can't have everything, can one? And now I must go, dear. Shall I call for you tomorrow?

MRS CHEVELEY: Thanks.

LADY MARKBY: We might drive in the Park[24] at five. Everything looks so fresh in the Park now!

MRS CHEVELEY: Except the people!

LADY MARKBY: Perhaps the people are a little jaded. I have often observed that the Season as it goes on produces a kind of softening of the brain. However, I think anything is better than high intellectual pressure. That is the most unbecoming thing there is. It makes the noses of the young girls so particularly large. And there is nothing so difficult to marry as a large nose; men don't like them. Good night, dear! [*To* LADY CHILTERN.] Good night, Gertrude!

[*Goes out on* LORD CAVERSHAM'S *arm.*]

MRS CHEVELEY: What a charming house you have, Lady Chiltern! I have spent a delightful evening. It has been so interesting getting to know your husband.

LADY CHILTERN: Why did you wish to meet my husband, Mrs Cheveley?

MRS CHEVELEY: Oh, I will tell you. I wanted to interest him in this Argentine Canal scheme, of which I dare say you have heard. And I found him most susceptible, – susceptible to reason, I mean. A rare thing in a man. I converted him in ten minutes. He is going to make a speech in the House tomorrow night in favour of the idea. We must go to the Ladies' Gallery and hear him! It will be a great occasion!

LADY CHILTERN: There must be some mistake. That scheme could never have my husband's support.

MRS CHEVELEY: Oh, I assure you it's all settled. I don't regret my tedious journey from Vienna now. It has been a great success. But, of course, for the next twenty-four hours the whole thing is a dead secret.

LADY CHILTERN [*gently*]: A secret? Between whom?

MRS CHEVELEY [*with a flash of amusement in her eyes*]: Between your husband and myself.

SIR ROBERT CHILTERN [*entering*]: Your carriage is here, Mrs Cheveley!

MRS CHEVELEY: Thanks! Good evening, Lady Chiltern! Good night, Lord Goring! I am at Claridge's.[25] Don't you think you might leave a card?

LORD GORING: If you wish, Mrs Cheveley!

MRS CHEVELEY: Oh, don't be so solemn about it, or I shall be obliged to leave a card on you. In England I suppose that would hardly be considered *en règle*.[26] Abroad, we are more civilized. Will you see me down, Sir Robert? Now that we have both the same interests at heart we shall be great friends, I hope!

[*Sails out on* SIR ROBERT CHILTERN'*s arm.* LADY CHILTERN *goes to the top of the staircase and looks down at them as they descend. Her expression is troubled. After a little time she is joined by some of the guests, and passes with them into another reception-room.*]

MABEL CHILTERN: What a horrid woman!

LORD GORING: You should go to bed, Miss Mabel.

MABEL CHILTERN: Lord Goring!

LORD GORING: My father told me to go to bed an hour ago. I don't see why I shouldn't give you the same advice. I always pass on good advice. It is the only thing to do with it. It is never of any use to oneself.

MABEL CHILTERN: Lord Goring, you are always ordering me out of the room. I think it most courageous of you. Especially as I am not going to bed for hours. [*Goes over to the sofa.*] You can come and sit down if you like, and talk about anything in the world, except the Royal Academy, Mrs Cheveley or novels in Scotch dialect. They are not improving subjects. [*Catches sight of something that is lying on the sofa half hidden by the cushion.*][27] What is this? Someone has dropped a diamond brooch! Quite beautiful, isn't it? [*Shows it to him.*] I wish it was mine, but Gertrude won't let me wear anything but pearls, and I am thoroughly sick of pearls. They make one look so plain, so good and so intellectual. I wonder whom the brooch belongs to.

LORD GORING: I wonder who dropped it.

MABEL CHILTERN: It is a beautiful brooch.

LORD GORING: It is a handsome bracelet.

MABEL CHILTERN: It isn't a bracelet. It's a brooch.

LORD GORING: It can be used as a bracelet.

[*Takes it from her, and, pulling out a green letter-case, puts the ornament carefully in it, and replaces the whole thing in his breast-pocket with the most perfect sang-froid.*]

MABEL CHILTERN: What are you doing?

LORD GORING: Miss Mabel, I am going to make a rather strange request to you.

MABEL CHILTERN [*eagerly*]: Oh, pray do! I have been waiting for it all the evening.

LORD GORING [*is a little taken aback, but recovers himself*]: Don't mention to anybody that I have taken charge of this brooch. Should anyone write and claim it, let me know at once.

MABEL CHILTERN: That is a strange request.

LORD GORING: Well, you see I gave this brooch to somebody once, years ago.

MABEL CHILTERN: You did?

LORD GORING: Yes.

[LADY CHILTERN *enters alone. The other guests have gone.*]

MABEL CHILTERN: Then I shall certainly bid you good night. Good night, Gertrude!

[*Exit.*]

LADY CHILTERN: Good night, dear! [*To* LORD GORING.] You saw whom Lady Markby brought here tonight?

LORD GORING: Yes. It was an unpleasant surprise. What did she come here for?

LADY CHILTERN: Apparently to try and lure Robert to uphold some fraudulent scheme in which she is interested. The Argentine Canal, in fact.

LORD GORING: She has mistaken her man, hasn't she?

LADY CHILTERN: She is incapable of understanding an upright nature like my husband's!

LORD GORING: Yes. I should fancy she came to grief if she tried to get Robert into her toils. It is extraordinary what astounding mistakes clever women make.

LADY CHILTERN: I don't call women of that kind clever. I call them stupid!

LORD GORING: Same thing often. Good night, Lady Chiltern!

LADY CHILTERN: Good night!

[*Enter* SIR ROBERT CHILTERN.]

SIR ROBERT CHILTERN: My dear Arthur, you are not going? Do stop a little!

LORD GORING: Afraid I can't, thanks. I have promised to look in at the Hartlocks'. I believe they have got a mauve Hungarian band that plays mauve Hungarian music. See you soon. Good-bye!

[*Exit.*]

SIR ROBERT CHILTERN: How beautiful you look tonight, Gertrude!

LADY CHILTERN: Robert, it is not true, is it? You are not going to lend your support to this Argentine speculation? You couldn't!

SIR ROBERT CHILTERN [*starting*]: Who told you I intended to do so?

LADY CHILTERN: That woman who has just gone out, Mrs Cheveley, as she calls herself now. She seemed to taunt me with it. Robert, I know this woman. You don't. We were at school together. She was untruthful, dishonest, an evil influence on everyone whose trust or friendship she could win. I hated, I despised her. She stole things, she was a thief. She was sent away for being a thief. Why do you let her influence you?

SIR ROBERT CHILTERN: Gertrude, what you tell me may be true, but it happened many years ago. It is best forgotten! Mrs Cheveley may have changed since then. No one should be entirely judged by their past.

LADY CHILTERN [*sadly*]: One's past is what one is. It is the only way by which people should be judged.

SIR ROBERT CHILTERN: That is a hard saying, Gertrude!

LADY CHILTERN: It is a true saying, Robert. And what did she mean by boasting that she had got you to lend your support, your name, to a thing I have heard you describe as the most dishonest and fraudulent scheme there has ever been in political life?

SIR ROBERT CHILTERN [*biting his lip*]: I was mistaken in the view I took. We all may make mistakes.

LADY CHILTERN: But you told me yesterday that you had received the report from the Commission, and that it entirely condemned the whole thing.

SIR ROBERT CHILTERN [*walking up and down*]: I have reasons now to believe that the Commission was prejudiced, or, at any rate, misinformed. Besides, Gertrude, public and private life are different things. They have different laws, and move on different lines.[28]

LADY CHILTERN: They should both represent man at his highest. I see no difference between them.

SIR ROBERT CHILTERN [*stopping*]: In the present case, on a matter of practical politics, I have changed my mind. That is all.

LADY CHILTERN: All!

SIR ROBERT CHILTERN [*sternly*]: Yes!

LADY CHILTERN: Robert! Oh! it is horrible that I should have to ask you such a question – Robert, are you telling me the whole truth?

SIR ROBERT CHILTERN: Why do you ask me such a question?

LADY CHILTERN [*after a pause*]: Why do you not answer it?

SIR ROBERT CHILTERN [*sitting down*]: Gertrude, truth is a very complex thing, and politics is a very complex business. There are wheels within wheels. One may be under certain obligations to people that one must pay. Sooner or later in political life one has to compromise. Everyone does.

LADY CHILTERN: Compromise? Robert, why do you talk so differently tonight from the way I have always heard you talk? Why are you changed?

SIR ROBERT CHILTERN: I am not changed. But circumstances alter things.

LADY CHILTERN: Circumstances should never alter principles!

SIR ROBERT CHILTERN: But if I told you –

LADY CHILTERN: What?

SIR ROBERT CHILTERN: That it was necessary, vitally necessary?

LADY CHILTERN: It can never be necessary to do what is not honourable. Or if it be necessary, then what is it that I have loved! But it is not, Robert; tell me it is not. Why should it be? What gain would you get? Money? We have no need of that! And money that comes from a tainted source is a degradation. Power? But power is nothing in itself. It is power to do good that is fine – that, and that only. What is it, then? Robert, tell me why you are going to do this dishonourable thing!

SIR ROBERT CHILTERN: Gertrude, you have no right to use that word. I told you it was a question of rational compromise. It is no more than that.

LADY CHILTERN: Robert, that is all very well for other men, for men who treat life simply as a sordid speculation; but not for you, Robert, not for you. You are different. All your life you have stood apart from others. You have never let the world soil you. To the world, as to myself, you have been an ideal always. Oh! be that ideal still. That great inheritance throw not away – that tower of ivory do not destroy.²⁹ Robert, men can love what is beneath them – things unworthy, stained, dishonoured. We women worship when we love; and when we lose our worship, we lose everything. Oh! don't kill my love for you, don't kill that!

SIR ROBERT CHILTERN: Gertrude!

LADY CHILTERN: I know that there are men with horrible secrets in their lives – men who have done some shameful thing, and who in some critical moment have to pay for it, by doing some other act of shame – oh! don't tell me you are such as they are! Robert, is there in your life any secret dishonour or disgrace? Tell me, tell me at once, that –

SIR ROBERT CHILTERN: That what?

LADY CHILTERN [*speaking very slowly*]: That our lives may drift apart.

SIR ROBERT CHILTERN: Drift apart?

LADY CHILTERN: That they may be entirely separate. It would be better for us both.

SIR ROBERT CHILTERN: Gertrude, there is nothing in my past life that you might not know.

LADY CHILTERN: I was sure of it, Robert, I was sure of it. But why did you say those dreadful things, things so unlike your real self? Don't let us ever talk about the subject again. You will write, won't you, to Mrs Cheveley, and tell her that you cannot support this scandalous scheme of hers? If you have given her any promise you must take it back, that is all!

SIR ROBERT CHILTERN: Must I write and tell her that?

LADY CHILTERN: Surely, Robert! What else is there to do?

SIR ROBERT CHILTERN: I might see her personally. It would be better.

LADY CHILTERN: You must never see her again, Robert. She is not a woman you should ever speak to. She is not worthy to talk to a man like you. No; you must write to her at once, now, this moment, and let your letter show her that your decision is quite irrevocable!

SIR ROBERT CHILTERN: Write this moment!

LADY CHILTERN: Yes.

SIR ROBERT CHILTERN: But it is so late. It is close on twelve.

LADY CHILTERN: That makes no matter. She must know at once that she has been mistaken in you – and that you are not a man to do anything base or underhand or dishonourable. Write here, Robert. Write that you decline to support this scheme of hers, as you hold it to be a dishonest scheme. Yes – write the word dishonest. She knows what that word means. [SIR ROBERT CHILTERN *sits down and writes a letter. His wife takes it up and reads it.*] Yes; that will do. [*Rings bell.*] And now the envelope. [*He writes the envelope slowly. Enter* MASON.] Have this letter sent at once to Claridge's Hotel. There is no answer. [*Exit* MASON. LADY CHILTERN *kneels down beside her husband and puts her arms around him.*] Robert, love gives one an instinct to things. I feel tonight that I have saved you from something that might have been a danger to you, from something that might have made men honour you less than they do. I don't think you realize sufficiently, Robert, that you have brought into the political life of our time a nobler atmosphere, a finer attitude towards life, a freer air of purer aims and higher ideals – I know it, and for that I love you, Robert.

SIR ROBERT CHILTERN: Oh, love me always, Gertrude, love me always!

LADY CHILTERN: I will love you always, because you will always be worthy of love. We needs must love the highest when we see it![30]

[*Kisses him and rises and goes out.*]

[SIR ROBERT CHILTERN *walks up and down for a moment; then sits down and buries his face in his hands. The Servant enters and begins putting out the lights.* SIR ROBERT CHILTERN *looks up.*]

SIR ROBERT CHILTERN: Put out the lights, Mason, put out the lights![31]

[*The Servant puts out the lights. The room becomes almost dark. The only light there is comes from the great chandelier that hangs over the staircase and illumines the tapestry of the Triumph of Love.*]

ACT DROP

SECOND ACT

Morning-room at Sir Robert Chiltern's house.

[LORD GORING, *dressed in the height of fashion, is lounging in an armchair.*[1] SIR ROBERT CHILTERN *is standing in front of the fireplace. He is evidently in a state of great mental excitement and distress. As the scene progresses he paces nervously up and down the room.*]

LORD GORING: My dear Robert, it's a very awkward business, very awkward indeed. You should have told your wife the whole thing. Secrets from other people's wives are a necessary luxury in modern life. So, at least, I am always told at the club by people who are bald enough to know better. But no man should have a secret from his own wife. She invariably finds it out. Women have a wonderful instinct about things. They can discover everything except the obvious.

SIR ROBERT CHILTERN: Arthur, I couldn't tell my wife. When could I have told her? Not last night. It would have made a lifelong separation between us, and I would have lost the love of the one woman in the world I worship, of the only woman who has ever stirred love within me. Last night it would have been quite impossible. She would have turned from me in horror . . . in horror and in contempt.

LORD GORING: Is Lady Chiltern as perfect as all that?

SIR ROBERT CHILTERN: Yes, my wife is as perfect as all that.

LORD GORING [*taking off his left-hand glove*]: What a pity! I beg your pardon, my dear fellow, I didn't quite mean that. But if what you tell me is true, I should like to have a serious talk about life with Lady Chiltern.

SIR ROBERT CHILTERN: It would be quite useless.

LORD GORING: May I try?

SIR ROBERT CHILTERN: Yes; but nothing could make her alter her views.

LORD GORING: Well, at the worst it would simply be a psychological experiment.

SIR ROBERT CHILTERN: All such experiments are terribly dangerous.

LORD GORING: Everything is dangerous, my dear fellow. If it wasn't so, life wouldn't be worth living . . . Well, I am bound to say that I think you should have told her years ago.

SIR ROBERT CHILTERN: When? When we were engaged? Do you think she would have married me if she had known that the origin of my fortune is such as it is, the basis of my career such as it is, and that I had done a thing that I suppose most men would call shameful and dishonourable?

LORD GORING [*slowly*]: Yes; most men would call it ugly names. There is no doubt of that.

SIR ROBERT CHILTERN [*bitterly*]: Men who every day do something of the same kind themselves. Men who, each one of them, have worse secrets in their own lives.

LORD GORING: That is the reason they are so pleased to find out other people's secrets. It distracts public attention from their own.

SIR ROBERT CHILTERN: And, after all, whom did I wrong by what I did? No one.

LORD GORING [*looking at him steadily*]: Except yourself, Robert.

SIR ROBERT CHILTERN [*after a pause*]: Of course I had private information about a certain transaction contemplated by the Government of the day, and I acted on it. Private information is practically the source of every large modern fortune.

LORD GORING [*tapping his boot with his cane*]: And public scandal invariably the result.

SIR ROBERT CHILTERN [*pacing up and down the room*]: Arthur, do you think that what I did nearly eighteen years ago should be brought up against me now? Do you think it fair that a man's whole career should be ruined for a fault done in one's boyhood almost? I was twenty-two at the time, and I had the double misfortune of being well-born and poor, two unforgivable things nowadays. Is it fair that the folly, the sin of one's youth, if men choose to call it a sin, should wreck a life like mine, should place me in the pillory,[2] should shatter all that I have worked for, all that I have built up? Is it fair, Arthur?

LORD GORING: Life is never fair, Robert. And perhaps it is a good thing for most of us that it is not.

SIR ROBERT CHILTERN: Every man of ambition has to fight his century with its own weapons. What this century worships is wealth. The god of this century is wealth.[3] To succeed one must have wealth. At all costs one must have wealth.

LORD GORING: You underrate yourself, Robert. Believe me, without wealth you could have succeeded just as well.

SIR ROBERT CHILTERN: When I was old, perhaps. When I had lost my passion for power, or could not use it. When I was tired, worn out, disappointed. I wanted my success when I was young. Youth is the time for success. I couldn't wait.

LORD GORING: Well, you certainly have had your success while you are still young. No one in our day has had such a brilliant success. Under-Secretary for Foreign Affairs at the age of forty – that's good enough for anyone, I should think.

SIR ROBERT CHILTERN: And if it is all taken away from me now? If I lose everything over a horrible scandal? If I am hounded from public life?

LORD GORING: Robert, how could you have sold yourself for money?

SIR ROBERT CHILTERN [*excitedly*]: I did not sell myself for money. I bought success at a great price. That is all.

LORD GORING [*gravely*]: Yes; you certainly paid a great price for it. But what first made you think of doing such a thing?

SIR ROBERT CHILTERN: Baron Arnheim.

LORD GORING: Damned scoundrel!

SIR ROBERT CHILTERN: No; he was a man of a most subtle and refined intellect. A man of culture, charm and distinction. One of the most intellectual men I ever met.

LORD GORING: Ah! I prefer a gentlemanly fool any day. There is more to be said for stupidity than people imagine. Personally I have a great admiration for stupidity. It is a sort of fellow-feeling, I suppose. But how did he do it? Tell me the whole thing.

SIR ROBERT CHILTERN [*throws himself into an armchair by the writing-table*]: One night after dinner at Lord Radley's the Baron began talking about success in modern life as something that one could reduce to an absolutely definite science. With that wonderfully fascinating quiet voice of his he expounded to us the most terrible of all philosophies, the philosophy of power, preached to us the most marvellous of all gospels, the gospel of gold. I think he saw the effect he had produced on me, for some days afterwards he wrote and asked me to come and see him. He was living then in Park Lane, in the house Lord Woolcomb has now. I remember so well how, with a strange smile on his pale, curved lips, he led me through his wonderful picture gallery, showed me his tapestries, his enamels, his jewels, his carved ivories, made me wonder at the strange loveliness of the luxury in which he lived; and then told me that luxury was nothing but a background, a painted scene in a play, and that power, power over other men, power over the world, was the one thing worth having, the one supreme pleasure worth knowing, the one joy one never tired of, and that in our century only the rich possessed it.

LORD GORING [*with great deliberation*]: A thoroughly shallow creed.[4]

SIR ROBERT CHILTERN [*rising*]: I didn't think so then. I don't think so now. Wealth has given me enormous power. It gave me at the very outset of my life freedom, and freedom is everything. You have never been poor, and never known what ambition is. You cannot understand what a wonderful chance the Baron gave me. Such a chance as few men get.

LORD GORING: Fortunately for them, if one is to judge by results. But tell me definitely, how did the Baron finally persuade you to – well, to do what you did?

SIR ROBERT CHILTERN: When I was going away he said to me that if I ever could give him any private information of real value he would make me a very rich man. I was dazed at the prospect he held out to me, and my ambition and my desire for power were at that time boundless. Six weeks later certain private documents passed through my hands.

LORD GORING [*keeping his eyes steadily fixed on the carpet*]: State documents?

SIR ROBERT CHILTERN: Yes.

[LORD GORING *sighs, then passes his hand across his forehead and looks up.*]

LORD GORING: I had no idea that you, of all men in the world, could have been so weak, Robert, as to yield to such a temptation as Baron Arnheim held out to you.

SIR ROBERT CHILTERN: Weak? Oh, I am sick of hearing that phrase. Sick of using it about others. Weak? Do you really think, Arthur, that it is weakness that yields to temptation? I tell you that there are terrible temptations that it requires strength, strength and courage, to yield to. To stake all one's life on a single moment, to risk everything on one throw, whether the stake be power or pleasure, I care not – there is no weakness in that. There is a horrible, a terrible courage. I had that courage. I sat down the same afternoon and wrote Baron Arnheim the letter this woman now holds. He made three-quarters of a million over the transaction.

LORD GORING: And you?

SIR ROBERT CHILTERN: I received from the Baron £110,000.

LORD GORING: You were worth more, Robert.

SIR ROBERT CHILTERN: No; that money gave me exactly what I wanted, power over others. I went into the House immediately. The Baron advised me in finance from time to time. Before five years I had almost trebled my fortune. Since then everything that I have touched has turned out a success. In all things connected with money I have had a luck so extraordinary that sometimes it has made me almost afraid. I remember having read somewhere, in some strange book,[5] that when the gods wish to punish us they answer our prayers.

LORD GORING: But tell me, Robert, did you ever suffer any regret for what you had done?

SIR ROBERT CHILTERN: No. I felt that I had fought the century with its own weapons, and won.

LORD GORING [*sadly*]: You thought you had won.

SIR ROBERT CHILTERN: I thought so. [*After a long pause.*] Arthur, do you despise me for what I have told you?

LORD GORING [*with deep feeling in his voice*]: I am very sorry for you, Robert, very sorry indeed.

SIR ROBERT CHILTERN: I don't say that I suffered any remorse. I didn't. Not remorse in the ordinary, rather silly sense of the word. But I have paid conscience money many times. I had a wild hope that I might disarm destiny. The sum Baron Arnheim gave me I have distributed twice over in public charities since then.

LORD GORING [*looking up*]: In public charities? Dear me! what a lot of harm you must have done, Robert!

SIR ROBERT CHILTERN: Oh, don't say that, Arthur; don't talk like that!

LORD GORING: Never mind what I say, Robert! I am always saying what I shouldn't say. In fact, I usually say what I really think. A great mistake nowadays. It makes one so liable to be misunderstood. As regards this dreadful business, I will help you in whatever way I can. Of course, you know that.

SIR ROBERT CHILTERN: Thank you, Arthur, thank you. But what is to be done? What can be done?

LORD GORING [*leaning back with his hands in his pockets*]: Well, the English can't stand a man who is always saying he is in the right, but they are very fond of a man who admits that he has been in the wrong. It is one of the best things in them. However, in your case, Robert, a confession would not do. The money, if you will allow me to say so, is . . . awkward. Besides, if you did make a clean breast of the whole affair, you would never be able to talk morality again. And in England a man who can't talk morality twice a week to a large, popular, immoral audience is quite over as a serious politician. There would be nothing left for him as a profession except Botany or the Church. A confession would be of no use. It would ruin you.

SIR ROBERT CHILTERN: It would ruin me. Arthur, the only thing for me to do now is to fight the thing out.

LORD GORING [*rising from his chair*]: I was waiting for you to say that, Robert. It is the only thing to do now. And you must begin by telling your wife the whole story.

SIR ROBERT CHILTERN: That I will not do.

LORD GORING: Robert, believe me, you are wrong.

SIR ROBERT CHILTERN: I couldn't do it. It would kill her love for me. And now about this woman, this Mrs Cheveley. How can I defend myself against her? You knew her before, Arthur, apparently.

LORD GORING: Yes.

SIR ROBERT CHILTERN: Did you know her well?

LORD GORING [*arranging his necktie*]: So little that I got engaged to be married to her once, when I was staying at the Tenbys'. The affair lasted for three days . . . nearly.

SIR ROBERT CHILTERN: Why was it broken off?

LORD GORING [*airily*]: Oh, I forget. At least, it makes no matter. By the way, have you tried her with money? She used to be confoundedly fond of money.

SIR ROBERT CHILTERN: I offered her any sum she wanted. She refused.

LORD GORING: Then the marvellous gospel of gold breaks down sometimes. The rich can't do everything, after all.

SIR ROBERT CHILTERN: Not everything. I suppose you are right. Arthur, I feel that public disgrace is in store for me. I feel certain of it. I never knew what terror was before. I know it now. It is as if a hand of ice were laid upon one's heart. It is as if one's heart were beating itself to death in some empty hollow.[6]

LORD GORING [*striking the table*]: Robert, you must fight her. You must fight her.

SIR ROBERT CHILTERN: But how?

LORD GORING: I can't tell you how at present. I have not the smallest idea. But everyone has some weak point. There is some flaw in each one of us. [*Strolls over to the fireplace and looks at himself in the glass.*] My father tells me that even I have faults. Perhaps I have. I don't know.

SIR ROBERT CHILTERN: In defending myself against Mrs Cheveley, I have a right to use any weapon I can find, have I not?

LORD GORING [*still looking in the glass*]: In your place I don't think I should have the smallest scruple in doing so. She is thoroughly well able to take care of herself.

SIR ROBERT CHILTERN [*sits down at the table and takes a pen in his hand*]: Well, I shall send a cipher telegram to the Embassy at Vienna to inquire if there is anything known against her. There may be some secret scandal she might be afraid of.

LORD GORING [*settling his buttonhole*]: Oh, I should fancy Mrs Cheveley is one of those very modern women of our time who find a new scandal as becoming as a new bonnet, and air them both in the Park every afternoon at five-thirty. I am sure she adores scandals, and that the sorrow of her life at present is that she can't manage to have enough of them.

SIR ROBERT CHILTERN [*writing*]: Why do you say that?

LORD GORING [*turning round*]: Well, she wore far too much rouge last night, and not quite enough clothes. That is always a sign of despair in a woman.

SIR ROBERT CHILTERN [*striking a bell*]: But it is worth while my wiring to Vienna, is it not?

LORD GORING: It is always worth while asking a question, though it is not always worth while answering one.

[*Enter* MASON.]

SIR ROBERT CHILTERN: Is Mr Trafford in his room?

MASON: Yes, Sir Robert.

SIR ROBERT CHILTERN [*puts what he has written into an envelope, which he then carefully closes*]: Tell him to have this sent off in cipher at once. There must not be a moment's delay.

MASON: Yes, Sir Robert.

SIR ROBERT CHILTERN: Oh! just give that back to me again.

[*Writes something on the envelope.* MASON *then goes out with the letter.*]

SIR ROBERT CHILTERN: She must have had some curious hold over Baron Arnheim. I wonder what it was.

LORD GORING [*smiling*]: I wonder.

SIR ROBERT CHILTERN: I will fight her to the death, as long as my wife knows nothing.

LORD GORING [*strongly*]: Oh, fight in any case – in any case.

SIR ROBERT CHILTERN [*with a gesture of despair*]: If my wife found out, there would be little left to fight for. Well, as soon as I hear from Vienna, I shall let you know the result. It is a chance, just a chance, but I believe in it. And as I fought the age with its own weapons, I will fight her with her weapons. It is only fair, and she looks like a woman with a past, doesn't she?

LORD GORING: Most pretty women do. But there is a fashion in pasts just as there is a fashion in frocks. Perhaps Mrs Cheveley's past is merely a slightly *décolleté* one, and they are excessively popular nowadays. Besides, my dear Robert, I should not build too high hopes on frightening Mrs Cheveley. I should not fancy Mrs Cheveley is a woman who would be easily frightened. She has survived all her creditors, and she shows wonderful presence of mind.

SIR ROBERT CHILTERN: Oh! I live on hopes now. I clutch at every chance. I feel like a man on a ship that is sinking. The water is round my feet, and the very air is bitter with storm. Hush! I hear my wife's voice.

[*Enter* LADY CHILTERN *in walking dress.*]

LADY CHILTERN: Good afternoon, Lord Goring!

LORD GORING: Good afternoon, Lady Chiltern! Have you been in the Park?

LADY CHILTERN: No; I have just come from the Woman's Liberal Association, where, by the way, Robert, your name was received with loud applause, and now I have come in to have my tea. [*To* LORD GORING] You will wait and have some tea, won't you?

LORD GORING: I'll wait for a short time, thanks.

LADY CHILTERN: I will be back in a moment. I am only going to take my hat off.

LORD GORING [*in his most earnest manner*]: Oh! please don't. It is so pretty. One of the prettiest hats I ever saw. I hope the Woman's Liberal Association received it with loud applause.

LADY CHILTERN [*with a smile*]: We have much more important work to do than to look at each other's bonnets, Lord Goring.

LORD GORING: Really? What sort of work?

LADY CHILTERN: Oh! dull, useful, delightful things, Factory Acts, Female Inspectors, the Eight Hours' Bill, the Parliamentary Franchise[7]. . . Everything, in fact, that you would find thoroughly uninteresting.

LORD GORING: And never bonnets?

LADY CHILTERN [*with mock indignation*]: Never bonnets, never!

[LADY CHILTERN *goes through the door leading to her boudoir*.]

SIR ROBERT CHILTERN [*takes* LORD GORING's *hand*]: You have been a good friend to me, Arthur, a thoroughly good friend.

LORD GORING: I don't know that I have been able to do much for you, Robert, as yet. In fact, I have not been able to do anything for you, as far as I can see. I am thoroughly disappointed with myself.

SIR ROBERT CHILTERN: You have enabled me to tell you the truth. That is something. The truth has always stifled me.

LORD GORING: Ah! the truth is a thing I get rid of as soon as possible! Bad habit, by the way. Makes one very unpopular at the club . . . with the older members. They call it being conceited. Perhaps it is.

SIR ROBERT CHILTERN: I would to God that I had been able to tell the truth . . . to live the truth. Ah! that is the great thing in life, to live the truth. [*Sighs, and goes towards the door*.] I'll see you soon again, Arthur, shan't I?

LORD GORING: Certainly. Whenever you like. I'm going to look in at the Bachelors' Ball[8] tonight, unless I find something better to do. But I'll come round tomorrow morning. If you should want me tonight by any chance, send round a note to Curzon Street.

SIR ROBERT CHILTERN: Thank you.

[*As he reaches the door*, LADY CHILTERN *enters from her boudoir*.]

LADY CHILTERN: You are not going, Robert?

SIR ROBERT CHILTERN: I have some letters to write, dear.

LADY CHILTERN [*going to him*]: You work too hard, Robert. You seem never to think of yourself, and you are looking so tired.

SIR ROBERT CHILTERN: It is nothing, dear, nothing.

[*He kisses her and goes out*.]

LADY CHILTERN [*to* LORD GORING]: Do sit down. I am so glad you have called. I want to talk to you about . . . well, not about bonnets, or the Woman's Liberal Association. You take far too much interest in the first subject, and not nearly enough in the second.

LORD GORING: You want to talk to me about Mrs Cheveley?

LADY CHILTERN: Yes. You have guessed it. After you left last night I found out that what she had said was really true. Of course I made Robert write her a letter at once, withdrawing his promise.

LORD GORING: So he gave me to understand.

LADY CHILTERN: To have kept it would have been the first stain on a career that has been stainless always. Robert must be above reproach. He is not like other men. He cannot afford to do what other men do. [*She looks at* LORD GORING, *who remains silent.*] Don't you agree with me? You are Robert's greatest friend. You are our greatest friend, Lord Goring. No one, except myself, knows Robert better than you do. He has no secrets from me, and I don't think he has any from you.

LORD GORING: He certainly has no secrets from me. At least I don't think so.

LADY CHILTERN: Then am I not right in my estimate of him? I know I am right. But speak to me frankly.

LORD GORING [*looking straight at her*]: Quite frankly?

LADY CHILTERN: Surely. You have nothing to conceal have you?

LORD GORING: Nothing. But, my dear Lady Chiltern, I think, if you will allow me to say so, that in practical life –

LADY CHILTERN [*smiling*]: Of which you know so little, Lord Goring –

LORD GORING: Of which I know nothing by experience, though I know something by observation. I think that in practical life there is something about success, actual success, that is a little unscrupulous, something about ambition that is unscrupulous always. Once a man has set his heart and soul on getting to a certain point, if he has to climb the crag, he climbs the crag; if he has to walk in the mire –

LADY CHILTERN: Well?

LORD GORING: He walks in the mire. Of course I am only talking generally about life.

LADY CHILTERN [*gravely*]: I hope so. Why do you look at me so strangely, Lord Goring?

LORD GORING: Lady Chiltern, I have sometimes thought that . . . perhaps you are a little hard in some of your views on life. I think that . . . often you don't make sufficient allowances. In every nature there are elements of weakness, or worse than weakness. Supposing, for instance, that – that any public man, my father, or Lord Merton, or Robert, say, had, years ago, written some foolish letter to someone . . .

LADY CHILTERN: What do you mean by a foolish letter?

LORD GORING: A letter gravely compromising one's position. I am only putting an imaginary case.

LADY CHILTERN: Robert is as incapable of doing a foolish thing as he is of doing a wrong thing.

LORD GORING [*after a long pause*]: Nobody is incapable of doing a foolish thing. Nobody is incapable of doing a wrong thing.

LADY CHILTERN: Are you a Pessimist? What will the other dandies say? They will all have to go into mourning.

LORD GORING [*rising*]: No, Lady Chiltern, I am not a Pessimist. Indeed I am not sure that I quite know what Pessimism really means. All I do know is that life cannot be understood without much charity, cannot be lived without much charity. It is love, and not German philosophy, that is the true explanation of this world, whatever may be the explanation of the next. And if you are ever in trouble, Lady Chiltern, trust me absolutely, and I will help you in every way I can. If you ever want me, come to me for my assistance, and you shall have it. Come at once to me.[9]

LADY CHILTERN [*looking at him in surprise*]: Lord Goring, you are talking quite seriously. I don't think I ever heard you talk seriously before.

LORD GORING [*laughing*]: You must excuse me, Lady Chiltern. It won't occur again, if I can help it.

LADY CHILTERN: But I like you to be serious.

[*Enter* MABEL CHILTERN, *in the most ravishing frock.*][10]

MABEL CHILTERN: Dear Gertrude, don't say such a dreadful thing to Lord Goring. Seriousness would be very unbecoming to him. Good afternoon, Lord Goring! Pray be as trivial as you can.

LORD GORING: I should like to, Miss Mabel, but I am afraid I am . . .

a little out of practice this morning; and besides, I have to be going now.

MABEL CHILTERN: Just when I have come in! What dreadful manners you have! I am sure you were very badly brought up.

LORD GORING: I was.

MABEL CHILTERN: I wish I had brought you up!

LORD GORING: I am so sorry you didn't.

MABEL CHILTERN: It is too late now, I suppose?

LORD GORING [smiling]: I am not so sure.

MABEL CHILTERN: Will you ride tomorrow morning?

LORD GORING: Yes, at ten.

MABEL CHILTERN: Don't forget.

LORD GORING: Of course I shan't. By the way, Lady Chiltern, there is no list of your guests in *The Morning Post*[11] of today. It has apparently been crowded out by the County Council, or the Lambeth Conference, or something equally boring. Could you let me have a list? I have a particular reason for asking you.

LADY CHILTERN: I am sure Mr Trafford will be able to give you one.

LORD GORING: Thanks, so much.

MABEL CHILTERN: Tommy is the most useful person in London.

LORD GORING [turning to her]: And who is the most ornamental?

MABEL CHILTERN [triumphantly]: I am.

LORD GORING: How clever of you to guess it! [Takes up his hat and cane.] Good-bye, Lady Chiltern! You will remember what I said to you, won't you?

LADY CHILTERN: Yes; but I don't know why you said it to me.

LORD GORING: I hardly know myself. Good-bye, Miss Mabel!

MABEL CHILTERN [with a little moue[12] of disappointment]: I wish you were not going. I have had four wonderful adventures this morning; four and a half, in fact. You might stop and listen to some of them.

LORD GORING: How very selfish of you to have four and a half! There won't be any left for me.

MABEL CHILTERN: I don't want you to have any. They would not be good for you.

LORD GORING: That is the first unkind thing you have ever said to me. How charmingly you said it! Ten tomorrow.

MABEL CHILTERN: Sharp.

LORD GORING: Quite sharp. But don't bring Mr Trafford.

MABEL CHILTERN [*with a little toss of the head*]: Of course I shan't bring Tommy Trafford. Tommy Trafford is in great disgrace.

LORD GORING: I am delighted to hear it.

[*Bows and goes out.*]

MABEL CHILTERN: Gertrude, I wish you would speak to Tommy Trafford.

LADY CHILTERN: What has poor Mr Trafford done this time? Robert says he is the best secretary he has ever had.

MABEL CHILTERN: Well, Tommy has proposed to me again. Tommy really does nothing but propose to me. He proposed to me last night in the music-room, when I was quite unprotected, as there was an elaborate trio going on. I didn't dare to make the smallest repartee, I need hardly tell you. If I had, it would have stopped the music at once. Musical people are so absurdly unreasonable. They always want one to be perfectly dumb at the very moment when one is longing to be absolutely deaf. Then he proposed to me in broad daylight this morning, in front of that dreadful statue of Achilles. Really, the things that go on in front of that work of art are quite appalling. The police should interfere. At luncheon I saw by the glare in his eye that he was going to propose again, and I just managed to check him in time by assuring him that I was a bimetallist.[13] Fortunately I don't know what bimetallism means. And I don't believe anybody else does either. But the observation crushed Tommy for ten minutes. He looked quite shocked. And then Tommy is so annoying in the way he proposes. If he proposed at the top of his voice, I should not mind so much. That might produce some effect on the public. But he does it in a horrid confidential way. When Tommy wants to be romantic he talks to one just like a doctor. I am very fond of Tommy, but his methods of proposing are quite out of date. I wish, Gertrude, you would speak to him, and tell him that once a week is quite often enough to propose to anyone, and that it should always be done in a manner that attracts some attention.

LADY CHILTERN: Dear Mabel, don't talk like that. Besides, Robert thinks very highly of Mr Trafford. He believes he has a brilliant future before him.

MABEL CHILTERN: Oh! I wouldn't marry a man with a future before him for anything under the sun.

LADY CHILTERN: Mabel!

MABEL CHILTERN: I know, dear. You married a man with a future, didn't you? But then Robert was a genius, and you have a noble, self-sacrificing character. You can stand geniuses. I have no character at all, and Robert is the only genius I could ever bear. As a rule, I think they are quite impossible. Geniuses talk so much, don't they? Such a bad habit! And they are always thinking about themselves, when I want them to be thinking about me. I must go round now and rehearse at Lady Basildon's. You remember, we are having *tableaux*,[14] don't you? The Triumph of something, I don't know what! I hope it will be triumph of me. Only triumph I am really interested in at present. [*Kisses* LADY CHILTERN *and goes out; then comes running back.*] Oh, Gertrude, do you know who is coming to see you? That dreadful Mrs Cheveley, in a most lovely gown. Did you ask her?

LADY CHILTERN [*rising*]: Mrs Cheveley! Coming to see me? Impossible!

MABEL CHILTERN: I assure you she is coming upstairs, as large as life and not nearly so natural.

LADY CHILTERN: You need not wait, Mabel. Remember, Lady Basildon is expecting you.

MABEL CHILTERN: Oh! I must shake hands with Lady Markby. She is delightful. I love being scolded by her.

[*Enter* MASON.]

MASON: Lady Markby. Mrs Cheveley.

[*Enter* LADY MARKBY *and* MRS CHEVELEY.]

LADY CHILTERN [*advancing to meet them*]: Dear Lady Markby, how nice of you to come and see me! [*Shakes hands with her, and bows somewhat distantly to* MRS CHEVELEY.] Won't you sit down, Mrs Cheveley?

MRS CHEVELEY: Thanks. Isn't that Miss Chiltern? I should like so much to know her.

LADY CHILTERN: Mabel, Mrs Cheveley wishes to know you.

[MABEL CHILTERN *gives a little nod*.]

MRS CHEVELEY [*sitting down*]: I thought your frock so charming last
night, Miss Chiltern. So simple and . . . suitable.

MABEL CHILTERN: Really? I must tell my dressmaker. It will be such
a surprise to her. Good-bye, Lady Markby!

LADY MARKBY: Going already?

MABEL CHILTERN: I am so sorry but I am obliged to. I am just off to
rehearsal. I have got to stand on my head in some *tableaux*.

LADY MARKBY: On your head, child? Oh! I hope not. I believe it is
most unhealthy.

[*Takes a seat on the sofa next* LADY CHILTERN.]

MABEL CHILTERN: But it is for an excellent charity: in aid of the
Undeserving,[15] the only people I am really interested in. I am the
secretary, and Tommy Trafford is treasurer.

MRS CHEVELEY: And what is Lord Goring?

MABEL CHILTERN: Oh! Lord Goring is president.

MRS CHEVELEY: The post should suit him admirably, unless he has
deteriorated since I knew him first.

LADY MARKBY [*reflecting*]: You are remarkably modern, Mabel. A little
too modern, perhaps. Nothing is so dangerous as being too modern.
One is apt to grow old-fashioned quite suddenly. I have known
many instances of it.

MABEL CHILTERN: What a dreadful prospect!

LADY MARKBY: Ah! my dear, you need not be nervous. You will always
be as pretty as possible. That is the best fashion there is, and the
only fashion that England succeeds in setting.

MABEL CHILTERN [*with a curtsey*]: Thank you so much, Lady Markby,
for England . . . and myself.

[*Goes out.*]

LADY MARKBY [*turning to* LADY CHILTERN]: Dear Gertrude, we just
called to know if Mrs Cheveley's diamond brooch has been found.

LADY CHILTERN: Here?

MRS CHEVELEY: Yes. I missed it when I got back to Claridge's, and I thought I might possibly have dropped it here.

LADY CHILTERN: I have heard nothing about it. But I will send for the butler and ask.

[*Touches the bell.*]

MRS CHEVELEY: Oh, pray don't trouble, Lady Chiltern. I dare say I lost it at the Opera, before we came on here.

LADY MARKBY: Ah yes, I suppose it must have been at the Opera. The fact is, we all scramble and jostle so much nowadays that I wonder we have anything at all left on us at the end of an evening. I know myself that, when I am coming back from the Drawing Room,[16] I always feel as if I hadn't a shred on me, except a small shred of decent reputation, just enough to prevent the lower classes making painful observations through the windows of the carriage. The fact is that our Society is terribly over-populated. Really, someone should arrange a proper scheme of assisted emigration.[17] It would do a great deal of good.

MRS CHEVELEY: I quite agree with you, Lady Markby. It is nearly six years since I have been in London for the Season, and I must say Society has become dreadfully mixed. One sees the oddest people everywhere.

LADY MARKBY: That is quite true, dear. But one needn't know them. I'm sure I don't know half the people who come to my house. Indeed, from all I hear, I shouldn't like to.

[*Enter* MASON.]

LADY CHILTERN: What sort of a brooch was it that you lost, Mrs Cheveley?

MRS CHEVELEY: A diamond snake-brooch with a ruby, a rather large ruby.

LADY MARKBY: I thought you said there was a sapphire on the head, dear?

MRS CHEVELEY [*smiling*]: No, Lady Markby – a ruby.

LADY MARKBY [*nodding her head*]: And very becoming, I am quite sure.

LADY CHILTERN: Has a ruby and diamond brooch been found in any of the rooms this morning, Mason?

MASON: No, my lady.

MRS CHEVELEY: It really is of no consequence, Lady Chiltern. I am so sorry to have put you to any inconvenience.

LADY CHILTERN [*coldly*]: Oh, it has been no inconvenience. That will do, Mason. You can bring tea.

[*Exit* MASON.]

LADY MARKBY: Well, I must say it is most annoying to lose anything. I remember once at Bath, years ago, losing in the Pump Room[18] an exceedingly handsome cameo bracelet that Sir John had given me. I don't think he has ever given me anything since, I am sorry to say. He has sadly degenerated. Really, this horrid House of Commons quite ruins our husbands for us. I think the Lower House by far the greatest blow to a happy married life that there has been since that terrible thing called the Higher Education of Women[19] was invented.

LADY CHILTERN: Ah! it is heresy to say that in this house, Lady Markby. Robert is a great champion of the Higher Education of Women, and so, I am afraid, am I.

MRS CHEVELEY: The higher education of men is what I should like to see. Men need it so sadly.

LADY MARKBY: They do, dear. But I am afraid such a scheme would be quite unpractical. I don't think man has much capacity for development. He has got as far as he can, and that is not far, is it? With regard to women, well, dear Gertrude, you belong to the younger generation, and I am sure it is all right if you approve of it. In my time, of course, we were taught not to understand anything. That was the old system, and wonderfully interesting it was. I assure you that the amount of things I and my poor dear sister were taught not to understand was quite extraordinary. But modern women understand everything, I am told.

MRS CHEVELEY: Except their husbands. That is the one thing the modern woman never understands.

LADY MARKBY: And a very good thing too, dear, I dare say. It might break up many a happy home if they did. Not yours, I need hardly say, Gertrude. You have married a pattern husband. I wish I could say as much for myself. But since Sir John has taken to attending the debates regularly, which he never used to do in the good old days, his language has become quite impossible. He always seems to think that he is addressing the House, and consequently whenever he discusses the state of the agricultural labourer, or the Welsh Church,[20] or something quite improper of that kind, I am obliged to send all the servants out of the room. It is not pleasant to see one's own butler, who has been with one for twenty-three years, actually blushing at the sideboard, and the footmen making contortions in corners like persons in circuses. I assure you my life will be quite ruined unless they send John at once to the Upper House. He won't take any interest in politics then, will he? The House of Lords is so sensible. An assembly of gentlemen. But in his present state, Sir John is really a great trial. Why, this morning before breakfast was half-over, he stood up on the hearthrug, put his hands in his pockets, and appealed to the country at the top of his voice. I left the table as soon as I had my second cup of tea, I need hardly say. But his violent language could be heard all over the house! I trust, Gertrude, that Sir Robert is not like that?

LADY CHILTERN: But I am very much interested in politics, Lady Markby. I love to hear Robert talk about them.

LADY MARKBY: Well, I hope he is not as devoted to Blue Books as Sir John is. I don't think they can be quite improving reading for anyone.

MRS CHEVELEY [*languidly*]: I have never read a Blue Book. I prefer books . . . in yellow covers.[21]

LADY MARKBY [*genially unconscious*]: Yellow is a gayer colour, is it not? I used to wear yellow a good deal in my early days, and would do so now if Sir John was not so painfully personal in his observations, and a man on the question of dress is always ridiculous, is he not?

MRS CHEVELEY: Oh, no! I think men are the only authorities on dress.

LADY MARKBY: Really? One wouldn't say so from the sort of hats they wear, would one?

[*The butler enters, followed by the footman. Tea is set on a small table close to* LADY CHILTERN.]

LADY CHILTERN: May I give you some tea, Mrs Cheveley?

MRS CHEVELEY: Thanks.

[*The butler hands* MRS CHEVELEY *a cup of tea on a salver.*]

LADY CHILTERN: Some tea, Lady Markby?

LADY MARKBY: No thanks, dear. [*The servants go out.*] The fact is, I have promised to go round for ten minutes to see poor Lady Brancaster, who is in very great trouble. Her daughter, quite a well-brought-up girl, too, has actually become engaged to be married to a curate in Shropshire. It is very sad, very sad indeed. I can't understand this modern mania for curates. In my time we girls saw them, of course, running about the place like rabbits. But we never took any notice of them, I need hardly say. But I am told that nowadays country society is quite honeycombed with them. I think it most irreligious. And then the eldest son has quarrelled with his father, and it is said that when they meet at the club Lord Brancaster always hides himself behind the money article in *The Times*. However, I believe that is quite a common occurrence nowadays and that they have to take in extra copies of *The Times* at all the clubs in St James's Street; there are so many sons who won't have anything to do with their fathers, and so many fathers who won't speak to their sons. I think myself, it is very much to be regretted.

MRS CHEVELEY: So do I. Fathers have so much to learn from their sons nowadays.

LADY MARKBY: Really, dear? What?

MRS CHEVELEY: The art of living. The only really Fine Art we have produced in modern times.

LADY MARKBY [*shaking her head*]: Ah! I am afraid Lord Brancaster knew a good deal about that. More than his poor wife ever did. [*Turning to* LADY CHILTERN.] You know Lady Brancaster, don't you, dear?

LADY CHILTERN: Just slightly. She was staying at Langton last autumn, when we were there.

LADY MARKBY: Well, like all stout women, she looks the very picture of happiness, as no doubt you noticed. But there are many tragedies in her family, besides this affair of the curate. Her own sister, Mrs Jekyll, had a most unhappy life; through no fault of her own, I am sorry to say. She ultimately was so broken-hearted that she went into a convent, or on to the operatic stage, I forget which. No; I think it was decorative art-needlework she took up.[22] I know she had lost all sense of pleasure in life. [Rising.] And now, Gertrude, if you will allow me, I shall leave Mrs Cheveley in your charge and call back for her in a quarter of an hour. Or perhaps, dear Mrs Cheveley, you wouldn't mind waiting in the carriage while I am with Lady Brancaster. As I intend it to be a visit of condolence, I shan't stay long.

MRS CHEVELEY [rising]: I don't mind waiting in the carriage at all, provided there is somebody to look at one.

LADY MARKBY: Well, I hear the curate is always prowling about the house.

MRS CHEVELEY: I am afraid I am not fond of girl friends.

LADY CHILTERN [rising]: Oh, I hope Mrs Cheveley will stay here a little. I should like to have a few minutes' conversation with her.

MRS CHEVELEY: How very kind of you, Lady Chiltern! Believe me, nothing would give me greater pleasure.

LADY MARKBY: Ah! no doubt you both have many pleasant reminiscences of your schooldays to talk over together. Good-bye, dear Gertrude! Shall I see you at Lady Bonar's tonight? She has discovered a wonderful new genius.[23] He does . . . nothing at all, I believe. That is a great comfort, is it not?

LADY CHILTERN: Robert and I are dining at home by ourselves tonight, and I don't think I shall go anywhere afterwards. Robert, of course, will have to be in the House. But there is nothing interesting on.

LADY MARKBY: Dining at home by yourselves? Is that quite prudent? Ah, I forgot, your husband is an exception. Mine is the general rule, and nothing ages a woman so rapidly as having married the general rule.

[Exit LADY MARKBY.]

MRS CHEVELEY: Wonderful woman, Lady Markby, isn't she? Talks more and says less than anybody I ever met. She is made to be a public speaker. Much more so than her husband, though he is a typical Englishman, always dull and usually violent.

LADY CHILTERN [*makes no answer, but remains standing. There is a pause. Then the eyes of the two women meet.* LADY CHILTERN *looks stern and pale.* MRS CHEVELEY *seems rather amused*]: Mrs Cheveley, I think it is right to tell you quite frankly that, had I known who you really were, I should not have invited you to my house last night.

MRS CHEVELEY [*with an impertinent smile*]: Really?

LADY CHILTERN: I could not have done so.

MRS CHEVELEY: I see that after all these years you have not changed a bit, Gertrude.

LADY CHILTERN: I never change.

MRS CHEVELEY [*elevating her eyebrows*]: Then life has taught you nothing?

LADY CHILTERN: It has taught me that a person who has once been guilty of a dishonest and dishonourable action may be guilty of it a second time, and should be shunned.

MRS CHEVELEY: Would you apply that rule to everyone?

LADY CHILTERN: Yes, to everyone, without exception.

MRS CHEVELEY: Then I am sorry for you, Gertrude, very sorry for you.

LADY CHILTERN: You see now, I am sure, that for many reasons any further acquaintance between us during your stay in London is quite impossible?

MRS CHEVELEY [*leaning back in her chair*]: Do you know, Gertrude, I don't mind your talking morality a bit. Morality is simply the attitude we adopt towards people whom we personally dislike. You dislike me. I am quite aware of that. And I have always detested you. And yet I have come here to do you a service.

LADY CHILTERN [*contemptuously*]: Like the service you wished to render my husband last night, I suppose. Thank heaven, I saved him from that.

MRS CHEVELEY [*starting to her feet*]: It was you who made him write that insolent letter to me? It was you who made him break his promise?

LADY CHILTERN: Yes.

MRS CHEVELEY: Then you must make him keep it. I give you till tomorrow morning – no more. If by that time your husband does not solemnly bind himself to help me in this great scheme in which I am interested –

LADY CHILTERN: This fraudulent speculation –

MRS CHEVELEY: Call it what you choose. I hold your husband in the hollow of my hand, and if you are wise you will make him do what I tell him.

LADY CHILTERN [*rising and going towards her*]: You are impertinent. What has my husband to do with you? With a woman like you?

MRS CHEVELEY [*with a bitter laugh*]: In this world like meets like. It is because your husband is himself fraudulent and dishonest that we pair so well together. Between you and him there are chasms. He and I are closer than friends. We are enemies linked together. The same sin binds us.

LADY CHILTERN: How dare you class my husband with yourself? How dare you threaten him or me? Leave my house. You are unfit to enter it.

[SIR ROBERT CHILTERN *enters from behind. He hears his wife's last words, and sees to whom they are addressed. He grows deadly pale.*]

MRS CHEVELEY: Your house! A house bought with the price of dishonour. A house, everything in which has been paid for by fraud. [*Turns round and sees* SIR ROBERT CHILTERN.] Ask him what the origin of his fortune is! Get him to tell you how he sold to a stockbroker a Cabinet secret. Learn from him to what you owe your position.

LADY CHILTERN: It is not true! Robert! It is not true!

MRS CHEVELEY [*pointing at him with outstretched finger*]: Look at him! Can he deny it? Does he dare to?

SIR ROBERT CHILTERN: Go! Go at once. You have done your worst now.

MRS CHEVELEY: My worst? I have not yet finished with you, with either of you. I give you both till tomorrow at noon. If by then you don't do what I bid you to do, the whole world shall know the origin of Robert Chiltern.[24]

[SIR ROBERT CHILTERN *strikes the bell. Enter* MASON.]

SIR ROBERT CHILTERN: Show Mrs Cheveley out.

[MRS CHEVELEY *starts; then bows with somewhat exaggerated politeness to* LADY CHILTERN, *who makes no sign of response. As she passes by* SIR ROBERT CHILTERN, *who is standing close to the door, she pauses for a moment and looks him straight in the face. She then goes out, followed by the servant, who closes the door after him. The husband and wife are left alone.* LADY CHILTERN *stands like someone in a dreadful dream. Then she turns round and looks at her husband. She looks at him with strange eyes, as though she was seeing him for the first time.*]

LADY CHILTERN: You sold a Cabinet secret for money! You began your life with fraud! You built up your career on dishonour! Oh, tell me it is not true! Lie to me! Lie to me! Tell me it is not true!

SIR ROBERT CHILTERN: What this woman said is quite true. But, Gertrude, listen to me. You don't realize how I was tempted. Let me tell you the whole thing.

[*Goes towards her.*]

LADY CHILTERN: Don't come near me. Don't touch me. I feel as if you had soiled me for ever. Oh! what a mask you have been wearing all these years! A horrible painted mask! You sold yourself for money.[25] Oh! a common thief were better. You put yourself up to sale to the highest bidder! You were bought in the market. You lie to the whole world. And yet you will not lie to me.

SIR ROBERT CHILTERN [*rushing towards her*]: Gertrude! Gertrude!

LADY CHILTERN [*thrusting him back with outstretched hands*]: No, don't speak! Say nothing! Your voice wakes terrible memories – memories of things that made me love you – memories of words that made me love you – memories that now are horrible to me. And how I worshipped you! You were to me something apart from common life, a thing pure, noble, honest, without stain. The world seemed to me finer because you were in it, and goodness more real because you lived. And now – oh, when I think that I made of a man like you my ideal! the ideal of my life![26]

SIR ROBERT CHILTERN: There was your mistake. There was your

error. The error all women commit. Why can't you women love us, faults and all? Why do you place us on monstrous pedestals? We have all feet of clay, women as well as men: but when we men love women, we love them knowing their weaknesses, their follies, their imperfections, love them all the more, it may be, for that reason. It is not the perfect, but the imperfect, who have need of love. It is when we are wounded by our own hands, or by the hands of others, that love should come to cure us – else what use is love at all? All sins, except a sin against itself, Love should forgive. All lives, save loveless lives, true Love should pardon. A man's love is like that. It is wider, larger, more human than a woman's. Women think that they are making ideals of men. What they are making of us are false idols merely. You made your false idol of me, and I had not the courage to come down, show you my wounds, tell you my weaknesses. I was afraid that I might lose your love, as I have lost it now. And so, last night you ruined my life for me – yes, ruined it! What this woman asked of me was nothing compared to what she offered to me. She offered security, peace, stability. The sin of my youth, that I had thought was buried, rose up in front of me, hideous, horrible, with its hands at my throat. I could have killed it for ever, sent it back into its tomb, destroyed its record, burned the one witness against me. You prevented me.[27] No one but you, you know it. And now what is there before me but public disgrace, ruin, terrible shame, the mockery of the world, a lonely dishonoured life, a lonely dishonoured death, it may be, some day? Let women make no more ideals of men! let them not put them on altars and bow before them, or they may ruin other lives as completely as you – you whom I have so wildly loved – have ruined mine!

[*He passes from the room.* LADY CHILTERN *rushes towards him, but the door is closed when she reaches it. Pale with anguish, bewildered, helpless, she sways like a plant in the water. Her hands, outstretched, seem to tremble in the air like blossoms in the wind. Then she flings herself down beside a sofa and buries her face. Her sobs are like the sobs of a child.*]

ACT DROP

THIRD ACT

*The Library in Lord Goring's house. An Adam room.[1] On the right is the
door leading into the hall. On the left, the door of the smoking-room. A
pair of folding doors at the back open into the drawing-room. The fire is
lit. Phipps, the Butler, is arranging some newspapers on the writing-table.
The distinction of Phipps is his impassivity. He has been termed by
enthusiasts the Ideal Butler. The Sphinx is not so incommunicable. He is
a mask with a manner. Of his intellectual or emotional life, history
knows nothing. He represents the dominance of form.*

[*Enter* LORD GORING *in evening dress with a buttonhole. He is wearing a
silk hat and Inverness cape. White-gloved, he carries a Louis Seize cane. His
are all the delicate fopperies of Fashion. One sees that he stands in immediate
relation to modern life, makes it indeed, and so masters it. He is the first
well-dressed philosopher in the history of thought.*]

LORD GORING: Got my second buttonhole for me, Phipps?

PHIPPS: Yes, my lord.

[*Takes his hat, cane and cape, and presents new buttonhole on salver.*]

LORD GORING: Rather distinguished thing, Phipps. I am the only
person of the smallest importance in London at present who wears
a buttonhole.

PHIPPS: Yes, my lord. I have observed that.

LORD GORING [*taking out old buttonhole*]: You see, Phipps, Fashion is
what one wears oneself. What is unfashionable is what other people
wear.

PHIPPS: Yes, my lord.

LORD GORING: Just as vulgarity is simply the conduct of other people.

PHIPPS: Yes, my lord.

LORD GORING [*putting in new buttonhole*]: And falsehoods the truths of other people.

PHIPPS: Yes, my lord.

LORD GORING: Other people are quite dreadful. The only possible society is oneself.

PHIPPS: Yes, my lord.

LORD GORING: To love oneself is the beginning of a lifelong romance, Phipps.

PHIPPS: Yes, my lord.

LORD GORING [*looking at himself in the glass*]: Don't think I quite like this buttonhole, Phipps. Makes me look a little too old. Makes me almost in the prime of life, eh, Phipps?

PHIPPS: I don't observe any alteration in your lordship's appearance.

LORD GORING: You don't, Phipps?

PHIPPS: No, my lord.

LORD GORING: I am not quite sure. For the future a more trivial buttonhole, Phipps, on Thursday evenings.

PHIPPS: I will speak to the florist, my lord. She has had a loss in her family lately, which perhaps accounts for the lack of triviality your lordship complains of in the buttonhole.

LORD GORING: Extraordinary thing about the lower class in England – they are always losing their relations.

PHIPPS: Yes, my lord! They are extremely fortunate in that respect.

LORD GORING [*turns round and looks at him.*[2] PHIPPS *remains impassive*]: Hum! Any letters, Phipps?

PHIPPS: Three, my lord.

[*Hands letters on a salver.*]

LORD GORING [*takes letters*]: Want my cab round in twenty minutes.

PHIPPS: Yes, my lord.

[*Goes towards door.*]

LORD GORING [*holds up letter in pink envelope*]: Ahem! Phipps, when did this letter arrive?

PHIPPS: It was brought by hand just after your lordship went to the club.

LORD GORING: That will do. [*Exit* PHIPPS.] Lady Chiltern's handwriting on Lady Chiltern's pink notepaper. That is rather curious. I thought Robert was to write. Wonder what Lady Chiltern has got to say to me? [*Sits at bureau, opens letter and reads it.*] 'I want you. I trust you. I am coming to you. Gertrude.' [*Puts down the letter with a puzzled look. Then takes it up, and reads it again slowly.*] 'I want you. I trust you. I am coming to you.' So she has found out everything! Poor woman! Poor woman! [*Pulls out watch and looks at it.*] But what an hour to call! Ten o'clock! I shall have to give up going to the Berkshires. However, it is always nice to be expected, and not to arrive. I am not expected at the Bachelors', so I shall certainly go there. Well, I will make her stand by her husband. That is the only thing for her to do. That is the only thing for any woman to do. It is the growth of the moral sense in women that makes marriage such a hopeless, one-sided institution. Ten o'clock. She should be here soon. I must tell Phipps I am not in to anyone else.

[*Goes towards bell.*]

[*Enter* PHIPPS.]

PHIPPS: Lord Caversham.

LORD GORING: Oh, why will parents always appear at the wrong time? Some extraordinary mistake in nature, I suppose. [*Enter* LORD CAVERSHAM.] Delighted to see you, my dear father.

[*Goes to meet him.*]

LORD CAVERSHAM: Take my cloak off.

LORD GORING: Is it worth while, father?

LORD CAVERSHAM: Of course it is worth while, sir. Which is the most comfortable chair?

LORD GORING: This one, father. It is the chair I use myself, when I have visitors.

LORD CAVERSHAM: Thank ye. No draught, I hope, in this room?

LORD GORING: No, father.

LORD CAVERSHAM [*sitting down*]: Glad to hear it. Can't stand draughts. No draughts at home.

LORD GORING: Good many breezes,[3] father.

LORD CAVERSHAM: Eh? Eh? Don't understand what you mean. Want to have a serious conversation with you, sir.

LORD GORING: My dear father! At this hour?

LORD CAVERSHAM: Well, sir, it is only ten o'clock. What is your objection to the hour? I think the hour is an admirable hour!

LORD GORING: Well, the fact is, father, this is not my day for talking seriously. I am very sorry, but it is not my day.

LORD CAVERSHAM: What do you mean, sir?

LORD GORING: During the season, father, I only talk seriously on the first Tuesday in every month, from four to seven.

LORD CAVERSHAM: Well, make it Tuesday, sir, make it Tuesday.

LORD GORING: But it is after seven, father, and my doctor says I must not have any serious conversation after seven. It makes me talk in my sleep.

LORD CAVERSHAM: Talk in your sleep, sir? What does that matter? You are not married.

LORD GORING: No, father, I am not married.

LORD CAVERSHAM: Hum! That is what I have come to talk to you about, sir. You have got to get married, and at once. Why, when I was your age, sir, I had been an inconsolable widower for three months, and was already paying my addresses to your admirable mother. Damme, sir, it is your duty to get married. You can't be always living for pleasure. Every man of position is married nowadays. Bachelors are not fashionable any more. They are a damaged lot. Too much is known about them. You must get a wife, sir. Look where your friend Robert Chiltern has got to by probity, hard work and a sensible marriage with a good woman. Why don't you imitate him, sir? Why don't you take him for your model?

LORD GORING: I think I shall, father.

LORD CAVERSHAM: I wish you would, sir. Then I should be happy. At present I make your mother's life miserable on your account. You are heartless, sir, quite heartless.

LORD GORING: I hope not, father.

LORD CAVERSHAM: And it is high time for you to get married. You are thirty-four years of age, sir.

LORD GORING: Yes, father, but I only admit to thirty-two – thirty-one and a half when I have a really good buttonhole. This buttonhole is not . . . trivial enough.

LORD CAVERSHAM: I tell you you are thirty-four, sir. And there is a draught in your room, besides, which makes your conduct worse. Why did you tell me there was no draught, sir? I feel a draught, sir, I feel it distinctly.

LORD GORING: So do I, father. It is a dreadful draught. I will come and see you tomorrow, father. We can talk over anything you like. Let me help you on with your cloak, father.

LORD CAVERSHAM: No, sir; I have called this evening for a definite purpose, and I am going to see it through at all costs to my health or yours. Put down my cloak, sir.

LORD GORING: Certainly, father. But let us go into another room. [*Rings bell.*] There is a dreadful draught here. [*Enter* PHIPPS.] Phipps, is there a good fire in the smoking-room?

PHIPPS: Yes, my lord.

LORD GORING: Come in there, father. Your sneezes are quite heart-rending.

LORD CAVERSHAM: Well, sir, I suppose I have a right to sneeze when I choose?

LORD GORING [*apologetically*]: Quite so, father. I was merely expressing sympathy.

LORD CAVERSHAM: Oh, damn sympathy. There is a great deal too much of that sort of thing going on nowadays.

LORD GORING: I quite agree with you, father. If there was less sympathy in the world there would be less trouble in the world.

LORD CAVERSHAM [*going towards the smoking-room*]: That is a paradox, sir. I hate paradoxes.

LORD GORING: So do I, father. Everybody one meets is a paradox nowadays. It is a great bore. It makes society so obvious.

LORD CAVERSHAM [*turning round, and looking at his son beneath his bushy eyebrows*]: Do you always really understand what you say, sir?

LORD GORING [*after some hesitation*]: Yes, father, if I listen attentively.

LORD CAVERSHAM [*indignantly*]: If you listen attentively! . . . Conceited young puppy!

[*Goes off grumbling into the smoking-room.* PHIPPS *enters.*]

LORD GORING: Phipps, there is a lady coming to see me this evening on particular business. Show her into the drawing-room when she arrives. You understand?

PHIPPS: Yes, my lord.

LORD GORING: It is a matter of the gravest importance, Phipps.

PHIPPS: I understand, my lord.

LORD GORING: No one else is to be admitted, under any circumstances.

PHIPPS: I understand, my lord.

[*Bell rings.*]

LORD GORING: Ah! that is probably the lady. I shall see her myself.

[*Just as he is going towards the door* LORD CAVERSHAM *enters from the smoking-room.*]

LORD CAVERSHAM: Well, sir? am I to wait attendance on you?

LORD GORING [*considerably perplexed*]: In a moment, father. Do excuse me. [LORD CAVERSHAM *goes back.*] Well, remember my instructions, Phipps – into that room.

PHIPPS: Yes, my lord.

[LORD GORING *goes into the smoking-room.* HAROLD, *the footman, shows* MRS CHEVELEY *in. Lamia-like,*[4] *she is in green and silver. She has a cloak of black satin, lined with dead rose-leaf silk.*]

HAROLD: What name, madam?

MRS CHEVELEY [*to* PHIPPS, *who advances towards her*]: Is Lord Goring not here? I was told he was at home?

PHIPPS: His lordship is engaged at present with Lord Caversham, madam.

[*Turns a cold, glassy eye on* HAROLD, *who at once retires.*]

MRS CHEVELEY [*to herself*]: How very filial!

PHIPPS: His lordship told me to ask you, madam, to be kind enough to wait in the drawing-room for him. His lordship will come to you there.

MRS CHEVELEY [*with a look of surprise*]: Lord Goring expects me?

PHIPPS: Yes, madam.

MRS CHEVELEY: Are you quite sure?

PHIPPS: His lordship told me that if a lady called I was to ask her to wait in the drawing-room. [*Goes to the door of the drawing-room and opens it.*] His lordship's directions on the subject were very precise.

MRS CHEVELEY [*to herself*]: How thoughtful of him! To expect the unexpected shows a thoroughly modern intellect. [*Goes towards the drawing-room and looks in.*] Ugh! How dreary a bachelor's drawing-room always looks. I shall have to alter all this.[5] [PHIPPS *brings the lamp from the writing-table.*] No, I don't care for that lamp. It is far too glaring. Light some candles.

PHIPPS [*replaces lamp*]: Certainly, madam.

MRS CHEVELEY: I hope the candles have very becoming shades.

PHIPPS: We have had no complaints about them, madam, as yet.

[*Passes into the drawing-room and begins to light the candles.*]

MRS CHEVELEY [*to herself*]: I wonder what woman he is waiting for tonight. It will be delightful to catch him. Men always look so silly when they are caught. And they are always being caught. [*Looks about room and approaches the writing-table.*] What a very interesting room! What a very interesting picture! Wonder what his correspondence is like. [*Takes up letters.*] Oh, what a very uninteresting correspondence! Bills and cards, debts and dowagers! Who on earth writes to him on pink paper? How silly to write on pink paper! It looks like the beginning of a middle-class romance. Romance should never begin with sentiment. It should begin with science and end with a settlement. [*Puts letter down, then takes it up again.*] I know that handwriting. That is Gertrude Chiltern's. I remember it perfectly. The ten commandments in every stroke of the pen, and the moral law all over the page. Wonder what Gertrude is writing to him about? Something horrid about me, I suppose. How I detest that woman! [*Reads it.*] 'I trust you. I want you. I am coming to you. Gertrude.' 'I trust you. I want you. I am coming to you.'

[*A look of triumph comes over her face. She is just about to steal the letter, when* PHIPPS *comes in.*]

PHIPPS: The candles in the drawing-room are lit, madam, as you directed.

MRS CHEVELEY: Thank you.

[*Rises hastily and slips the letter under a large silver-cased blotting-book that is lying on the table.*]

PHIPPS: I trust the shades will be to your liking, madam. They are the most becoming we have. They are the same as his lordship uses himself when he is dressing for dinner.

MRS CHEVELEY [*with a smile*]: Then I am sure they will be perfectly right.

PHIPPS [*gravely*]: Thank you, madam.

[MRS CHEVELEY *goes into the drawing-room.* PHIPPS *closes the door and retires. The door is then slowly opened and* MRS CHEVELEY *comes out and creeps stealthily towards the writing-table. Suddenly voices are heard from the smoking-room.* MRS CHEVELEY *grows pale, and stops. The voices grow louder, and she goes back into the drawing-room, biting her lip.*]

[*Enter* LORD GORING *and* LORD CAVERSHAM.]

LORD GORING [*expostulating*]: My dear father, if I am to get married, surely you will allow me to choose the time, place and person? Particularly the person.

LORD CAVERSHAM [*testily*]: That is a matter for me, sir. You would probably make a very poor choice. It is I who should be consulted, not you. There is property at stake. It is not a matter for affection. Affection comes later on in married life.

LORD GORING: Yes. In married life affection comes when people thoroughly dislike each other, father, doesn't it?

[*Puts on* LORD CAVERSHAM'S *cloak for him.*]

LORD CAVERSHAM: Certainly, sir. I mean certainly not, sir. You are talking very foolishly tonight. What I say is that marriage is a matter for common sense.

LORD GORING: But women who have common sense are so curiously plain, father, aren't they? Of course I only speak from hearsay.

LORD CAVERSHAM: No woman, plain or pretty, has any common sense at all, sir. Common sense is the privilege of our sex.

LORD GORING: Quite so. And we men are so self-sacrificing that we never use it, do we, father?

LORD CAVERSHAM: I use it, sir. I use nothing else.

LORD GORING: So my mother tells me.

LORD CAVERSHAM: It is the secret of your mother's happiness. You are very heartless, sir, very heartless.

LORD GORING: I hope not, father.

[*Goes out for a moment with* LORD CAVERSHAM. *Then returns, looking rather put out, with* SIR ROBERT CHILTERN.]

SIR ROBERT CHILTERN: My dear Arthur, what a piece of good luck meeting you on the doorstep! Your servant had just told me you were not at home. How extraordinary!

LORD GORING: The fact is, I am horribly busy tonight, Robert, and I gave orders I was not at home to anyone. Even my father had a comparatively cold reception. He complained of a draught the whole time.

SIR ROBERT CHILTERN: Ah! you must be at home to me, Arthur. You are my best friend. Perhaps by tomorrow you will be my only friend. My wife has discovered everything.

LORD GORING: Ah! I guessed as much!

SIR ROBERT CHILTERN [*looking at him*]: Really! How?

LORD GORING [*after some hesitation*]: Oh, merely by something in the expression of your face as you came in. Who told her?

SIR ROBERT CHILTERN: Mrs Cheveley herself. And the woman I love knows that I began my career with an act of low dishonesty, that I built up my life upon sands of shame[6] – that I sold, like a common huckster, the secret that had been entrusted to me as a man of honour. I thank heaven poor Lord Radley died without knowing that I betrayed him. I would to God I had died before I had been so horribly tempted, or had fallen so low.

[*Burying his face in his hands.*]

LORD GORING [*after a pause*]: You have heard nothing from Vienna
yet, in answer to your wire?

SIR ROBERT CHILTERN [*looking up*]: Yes; I got a telegram from the first
secretary at eight o'clock tonight.

LORD GORING: Well?

SIR ROBERT CHILTERN: Nothing is absolutely known against her.
On the contrary, she occupies a rather high position in society.
It is a sort of open secret that Baron Arnheim left her the
greater portion of his immense fortune. Beyond that I can learn
nothing.

LORD GORING: She doesn't turn out to be a spy, then?

SIR ROBERT CHILTERN: Oh! spies are of no use nowadays. Their
profession is over. The newspapers do their work instead.

LORD GORING: And thunderingly well they do it.

SIR ROBERT CHILTERN: Arthur, I am parched with thirst. May I ring
for something? Some hock and seltzer?[7]

LORD GORING: Certainly. Let me.

[*Rings the bell.*]

SIR ROBERT CHILTERN: Thanks! I don't know what to do, Arthur, I
don't know what to do, and you are my only friend. But what a
friend you are – the one friend I can trust. I can trust you absolutely,
can't I?

[*Enter* PHIPPS.]

LORD GORING: My dear Robert, of course. Oh! [*To* PHIPPS.] Bring
some hock and seltzer.

PHIPPS: Yes, my lord.

LORD GORING: And Phipps!

PHIPPS: Yes, my lord.

LORD GORING: Will you excuse me for a moment, Robert? I want to
give some directions to my servant.

SIR ROBERT CHILTERN: Certainly.

LORD GORING: When that lady calls, tell her that I am not expected
home this evening. Tell her that I have been suddenly called out
of town. You understand?

OSCAR WILDE

PHIPPS: The lady is in that room, my lord. You told me to show her into that room, my lord.

LORD GORING: You did perfectly right. [*Exit* PHIPPS.] What a mess I am in. No; I think I shall get through it. I'll give her a lecture through the door. Awkward thing to manage, though.

SIR ROBERT CHILTERN: Arthur, tell me what I should do. My life seems to have crumbled about me, I am a ship without a rudder in a night without a star.

LORD GORING: Robert, you love your wife, don't you?

SIR ROBERT CHILTERN: I love her more than anything in the world. I used to think ambition the great thing. It is not. Love is the great thing in the world. There is nothing but love, and I love her. But I am defamed in her eyes. I am ignoble in her eyes. There is a wide gulf between us now. She has found me out, Arthur, she has found me out.

LORD GORING: Has she never in her life done some folly – some indiscretion – that she should not forgive your sin?

SIR ROBERT CHILTERN: My wife! Never! She does not know what weakness or temptation is. I am of clay like other men. She stands apart as good women do – pitiless in her perfection – cold and stern and without mercy. But I love her, Arthur. We are childless, and I have no one else to love, no one else to love me. Perhaps if God had sent us children she might have been kinder to me. But God has given us a lonely house. And she has cut my heart in two. Don't let us talk of it. I was brutal to her this evening. But I suppose when sinners talk to saints they are brutal always. I said to her things that were hideously true, on my side, from my standpoint, from the standpoint of men. But don't let us talk of that.

LORD GORING: Your wife will forgive you. Perhaps at this moment she is forgiving you. She loves you, Robert. Why should she not forgive?

SIR ROBERT CHILTERN: God grant it! God grant it! [*Buries his face in his hands.*] But there is something more I have to tell you, Arthur.

[*Enter* PHIPPS *with drinks.*]

PHIPPS [*hands hock and seltzer to* SIR ROBERT CHILTERN]: Hock and seltzer, sir.

SIR ROBERT CHILTERN: Thank you.

LORD GORING: Is your carriage here, Robert?

SIR ROBERT CHILTERN: No; I walked from the club.

LORD GORING: Sir Robert will take my cab, Phipps.

PHIPPS: Yes, my lord.

[*Exit.*]

LORD GORING: Robert, you don't mind my sending you away?

SIR ROBERT CHILTERN: Arthur, you must let me stay for five minutes. I have made up my mind what I am going to do tonight in the House. The debate on the Argentine Canal is to begin at eleven. [*A chair falls in the drawing-room.*] What is that?

LORD GORING: Nothing.

SIR ROBERT CHILTERN: I heard a chair fall in the next room. Someone has been listening.

LORD GORING: No, no; there is no one there.

SIR ROBERT CHILTERN: There is someone. There are lights in the room, and the door is ajar. Someone has been listening to every secret of my life. Arthur, what does this mean?

LORD GORING: Robert, you are excited, unnerved. I tell you there is no one in that room. Sit down, Robert.

SIR ROBERT CHILTERN: Do you give me your word that there is no one there?

LORD GORING: Yes.

SIR ROBERT CHILTERN: Your word of honour?

[*Sits down.*]

LORD GORING: Yes.

SIR ROBERT CHILTERN [*rises*]: Arthur, let me see for myself.

LORD GORING: No, no.

SIR ROBERT CHILTERN: If there is no one there why should I not look in that room? Arthur, you must let me go into that room and satisfy myself. Let me know that no eavesdropper has heard my life's secret. Arthur, you don't realize what I am going through.

LORD GORING: Robert, this must stop. I have told you that there is
no one in that room – that is enough.

SIR ROBERT CHILTERN [*rushes to the door of the room*]: It is not enough.
I insist on going into this room. You have told me there is no one
there, so what reason can you have for refusing me?

LORD GORING: For God's sake, don't! There is someone there. Someone whom you must not see.

SIR ROBERT CHILTERN: Ah, I thought so!

LORD GORING: I forbid you to enter that room.

SIR ROBERT CHILTERN: Stand back. My life is at stake. And I don't
care who is there. I will know who it is to whom I have told my
secret and my shame.

[*Enters room.*]

LORD GORING: Great heaven! his own wife!

[SIR ROBERT CHILTERN *comes back, with a look of scorn and anger on his
face.*]

SIR ROBERT CHILTERN: What explanation have you to give me for
the presence of that woman here?

LORD GORING: Robert, I swear to you on my honour that that lady
is stainless and guiltless of all offence towards you.

SIR ROBERT CHILTERN: She is a vile, an infamous thing!

LORD GORING: Don't say that, Robert! It was for your sake she came
here. It was to try and save you she came here. She loves you and
no one else.

SIR ROBERT CHILTERN: You are mad. What have I to do with her
intrigues with you? Let her remain your mistress! You are well
suited to each other. She, corrupt and shameful – you, false as a
friend, treacherous as an enemy even –

LORD GORING: It is not true, Robert. Before heaven, it is not true. In
her presence and in yours I will explain all.

SIR ROBERT CHILTERN: Let me pass, sir. You have lied enough upon
your word of honour.

[SIR ROBERT CHILTERN *goes out.* LORD GORING *rushes to the door of the drawing-room, when* MRS CHEVELEY *comes out, looking radiant and much amused.*]

MRS CHEVELEY [*with a mock curtsey*]: Good evening, Lord Goring!

LORD GORING: Mrs Cheveley! Great heavens! . . . May I ask what you were doing in my drawing-room?

MRS CHEVELEY: Merely listening. I have a perfect passion for listening through keyholes. One always hears such wonderful things through them.

LORD GORING: Doesn't that sound rather like tempting Providence?

MRS CHEVELEY: Oh! surely Providence can resist temptation by this time.

[*Makes a sign to him to take her cloak off, which he does.*]

LORD GORING: I am glad you have called. I am going to give you some good advice.

MRS CHEVELEY: Oh! pray don't. One should never give a woman anything that she can't wear in the evening.

LORD GORING: I see you are quite as wilful as you used to be.

MRS CHEVELEY: Far more! I have greatly improved. I have had more experience.

LORD GORING: Too much experience is a dangerous thing. Pray have a cigarette. Half the pretty women in London smoke cigarettes. Personally I prefer the other half.

MRS CHEVELEY: Thanks. I never smoke. My dressmaker wouldn't like it, and a woman's first duty in life is to her dressmaker, isn't it? What the second duty is, no one has as yet discovered.

LORD GORING: You have come here to sell me Robert Chiltern's letter, haven't you?

MRS CHEVELEY: To offer it to you on conditions. How did you guess that?

LORD GORING: Because you haven't mentioned the subject. Have you got it with you?

MRS CHEVELEY [*sitting down*]: Oh, no! A well-made dress has no pockets.

LORD GORING: What is your price for it?

MRS CHEVELEY: How absurdly English you are! The English think that a cheque-book can solve every problem in life. Why, my dear Arthur, I have very much more money than you have, and quite as much as Robert Chiltern has got hold of. Money is not what I want.

LORD GORING: What do you want then, Mrs Cheveley?

MRS CHEVELEY: Why don't you call me Laura?[8]

LORD GORING: I don't like the name.

MRS CHEVELEY: You used to adore it.

LORD GORING: Yes: that's why.

[MRS CHEVELEY *motions to him to sit down beside her. He smiles, and does so.*]

MRS CHEVELEY: Arthur, you loved me once.

LORD GORING: Yes.

MRS CHEVELEY: And you asked me to be your wife.

LORD GORING: That was the natural result of my loving you.

MRS CHEVELEY: And you threw me over because you saw, or said you saw, poor old Lord Mortlake trying to have a violent flirtation with me in the conservatory at Tenby.

LORD GORING: I am under the impression that my lawyer settled that matter with you on certain terms . . . dictated by yourself.[9]

MRS CHEVELEY: At the time I was poor; you were rich.

LORD GORING: Quite so. That is why you pretended to love me.

MRS CHEVELEY [*shrugging her shoulders*]: Poor old Lord Mortlake, who had only two topics of conversation, his gout and his wife! I never could quite make out which of the two he was talking about. He used the most horrible language about them both. Well, you were silly, Arthur. Why, Lord Mortlake was never anything more to me than amusement. One of those utterly tedious amusements one only finds at an English country house on an English country Sunday. I don't think anyone at all morally responsible for what he or she does at an English country house.

LORD GORING: Yes. I know lots of people think that.[10]

MRS CHEVELEY: I loved you, Arthur.

LORD GORING: My dear Mrs Cheveley, you have always been far too clever to know anything about love.

MRS CHEVELEY: I did love you. And you loved me. You know you loved me; and love is a very wonderful thing. I suppose that when a man has once loved a woman, he will do anything for her, except continue to love her?

[*Puts her hand on his.*]

LORD GORING [*taking his hand away quietly*]: Yes: except that.

MRS CHEVELEY [*after a pause*]: I am tired of living abroad. I want to come back to London. I want to have a charming house here. I want to have a salon. If one could only teach the English how to talk, and the Irish how to listen, society here would be quite civilized. Besides, I have arrived at the romantic stage. When I saw you last night at the Chilterns', I knew you were the only person I had ever cared for, if I ever have cared for anybody, Arthur. And so, on the morning of the day you marry me, I will give you Robert Chiltern's letter. That is my offer. I will give it to you now, if you promise to marry me.

LORD GORING: Now?

MRS CHEVELEY [*smiling*]: Tomorrow.

LORD GORING: Are you really serious?

MRS CHEVELEY: Yes, quite serious.

LORD GORING: I should make you a very bad husband.

MRS CHEVELEY: I don't mind bad husbands. I have had two. They amused me immensely.

LORD GORING: You mean that you amused yourself immensely, don't you?

MRS CHEVELEY: What do you know about my married life?

LORD GORING: Nothing: but I can read it like a book.

MRS CHEVELEY: What book?

LORD GORING [*rising*]: The Book of Numbers.[11]

MRS CHEVELEY: Do you think it is quite charming of you to be so rude to a woman in your own house?

LORD GORING: In the case of very fascinating women, sex is a challenge, not a defence.

MRS CHEVELEY: I suppose that is meant for a compliment. My dear Arthur, women are never disarmed by compliments. Men always are. That is the difference between the two sexes.

LORD GORING: Women are never disarmed by anything, as far as I know them.

MRS CHEVELEY [*after a pause*]: Then you are going to allow your greatest friend, Robert Chiltern, to be ruined, rather than marry someone who really has considerable attractions left. I thought you would have risen to some great height of self-sacrifice, Arthur. I think you should. And the rest of your life you could spend in contemplating your own perfections.

LORD GORING: Oh! I do that as it is. And self-sacrifice is a thing that should be put down by law. It is so demoralizing to the people for whom one sacrifices oneself. They always go to the bad.[12]

MRS CHEVELEY: As if anything could demoralize Robert Chiltern! You seem to forget that I know his real character.

LORD GORING: What you know about him is not his real character. It was an act of folly done in his youth, dishonourable, I admit, shameful, I admit, unworthy of him, I admit, and therefore . . . not his true character.

MRS CHEVELEY: How you men stand up for each other!

LORD GORING: How you women war against each other!

MRS CHEVELEY [*bitterly*]: I only war against one woman, against Gertrude Chiltern. I hate her. I hate her now more than ever.

LORD GORING: Because you have brought a real tragedy into her life, I suppose?

MRS CHEVELEY [*with a sneer*]: Oh, there is only one real tragedy in a woman's life. The fact that her past is always her lover, and her future invariably her husband.

LORD GORING: Lady Chiltern knows nothing of the kind of life to which you are alluding.

MRS CHEVELEY: A woman whose size in gloves is seven and three-quarters never knows much about anything. You know Gertrude has always worn seven and three-quarters? That is one of the reasons why there was never any moral sympathy between us . . . Well, Arthur, I suppose this romantic interview may be regarded as at an end. You admit it was romantic, don't you? For the privilege of being your wife I was ready to surrender a great prize, the climax of my diplomatic career. You decline. Very well.

If Sir Robert doesn't uphold my Argentine scheme, I expose him. *Voilà tout.*[13]

LORD GORING: You mustn't do that. It would be vile, horrible, infamous.

MRS CHEVELEY [*shrugging her shoulders*]: Oh! don't use big words. They mean so little. It is a commercial transaction. That is all. There is no good mixing up sentimentality in it. I offered to sell Robert Chiltern a certain thing. If he won't pay me my price, he will have to pay the world a greater price. There is no more to be said. I must go. Good-bye. Won't you shake hands?

LORD GORING: With you? No. Your transaction with Robert Chiltern may pass as a loathsome commercial transaction of a loathsome commercial age; but you seem to have forgotten that you who came here tonight to talk of love, you whose lips desecrated the word love, you to whom the thing is a book closely sealed, went this afternoon to the house of one of the most noble and gentle women in the world to degrade her husband in her eyes, to try and kill her love for him, to put poison in her heart, and bitterness in her life, to break her idol, and, it may be, spoil her soul. That I cannot forgive you. That was horrible. For that there can be no forgiveness.

MRS CHEVELEY: Arthur, you are unjust to me. Believe me, you are quite unjust to me. I didn't go to taunt Gertrude at all. I had no idea of doing anything of the kind when I entered. I called with Lady Markby simply to ask whether an ornament, a jewel, that I lost somewhere last night, had been found at the Chilterns'. If you don't believe me, you can ask Lady Markby. She will tell you it is true. The scene that occurred happened after Lady Markby had left, and was really forced on me by Gertrude's rudeness and sneers. I called, oh! – a little out of malice if you like – but really to ask if a diamond brooch of mine had been found. That was the origin of the whole thing.

LORD GORING: A diamond snake-brooch with a ruby?

MRS CHEVELEY: Yes. How do you know?

LORD GORING: Because it is found. In point of fact, I found it myself, and stupidly forgot to tell the butler anything about it as I was leaving. [*Goes over to the writing-table and pulls out the drawers.*] It is in this drawer. No, that one. This is the brooch, isn't it?

[*Holds up the brooch.*]

MRS CHEVELEY: Yes. I am so glad to get it back. It was . . . a present.

LORD GORING: Won't you wear it?

MRS CHEVELEY: Certainly, if you pin it in. [LORD GORING *suddenly clasps it on her arm.*] Why do you put it on as a bracelet? I never knew it could be worn as a bracelet.

LORD GORING: Really?

MRS CHEVELEY [*holding out her handsome arm*]: No; but it looks very well on me as a bracelet, doesn't it?

LORD GORING: Yes; much better than when I saw it last.

MRS CHEVELEY: When did you see it last?

LORD GORING [*calmly*]: Oh, ten years ago, on Lady Berkshire, from whom you stole it.

MRS CHEVELEY [*starting*]: What do you mean?

LORD GORING: I mean that you stole that ornament from my cousin, Mary Berkshire, to whom I gave it when she was married. Suspicion fell on a wretched servant, who was sent away in disgrace. I recognized it last night. I determined to say nothing about it till I had found the thief. I have found the thief now, and I have heard her own confession.

MRS CHEVELEY [*tossing her head*]: It is not true.

LORD GORING: You know it is true. Why, thief is written across your face at this moment.

MRS CHEVELEY: I will deny the whole affair from beginning to end. I will say that I have never seen this wretched thing, that it was never in my possession.

[MRS CHEVELEY *tries to get the bracelet off her arm, but fails.* LORD GORING *looks on amused. Her thin fingers tear at the jewel to no purpose. A curse breaks from her.*]

LORD GORING: The drawback of stealing a thing, Mrs Cheveley, is that one never knows how wonderful the thing that one steals is. You can't get that bracelet off, unless you know where the spring is. And I see you don't know where the spring is. It is rather difficult to find.

MRS CHEVELEY: You brute! You coward!

[*She tries again to unclasp the bracelet, but fails.*]

LORD GORING: Oh! don't use big words. They mean so little.

MRS CHEVELEY [*again tears at the bracelet in a paroxysm of rage, with inarticulate sounds. Then stops, and looks at* LORD GORING]: What are you going to do?

LORD GORING: I am going to ring for my servant. He is an admirable servant. Always comes in the moment one rings for him. When he comes I will tell him to fetch the police.

MRS CHEVELEY [*trembling*]: The police? What for?

LORD GORING: Tomorrow the Berkshires will prosecute you. That is what the police are for.

MRS CHEVELEY [*is now in an agony of physical terror. Her face is distorted. Her mouth awry. A mask has fallen from her. She is, for the moment, dreadful to look at*]: Don't do that. I will do anything you want. Anything in the world you want.

LORD GORING: Give me Robert Chiltern's letter.

MRS CHEVELEY: Stop! Stop! Let me have time to think.

LORD GORING: Give me Robert Chiltern's letter.

MRS CHEVELEY: I have not got it with me. I will give it to you tomorrow.

LORD GORING: You know you are lying. Give it to me at once. [MRS CHEVELEY *pulls the letter out, and hands it to him. She is horribly pale.*] This is it?

MRS CHEVELEY [*in a hoarse voice*]: Yes.

LORD GORING [*takes the letter, examines it, sighs, and burns it over the lamp*]: For so well-dressed a woman, Mrs Cheveley, you have moments of admirable common sense. I congratulate you.

MRS CHEVELEY [*catches sight of* LADY CHILTERN'S *letter, the cover of which is just showing from under the blotting-book*]: Please get me a glass of water.

LORD GORING: Certainly.

[*Goes to the corner of the room and pours out a glass of water. While his back is turned* MRS CHEVELEY *steals* LADY CHILTERN'S *letter. When* LORD GORING *returns with the glass she refuses it with a gesture.*]

MRS CHEVELEY: Thank you. Will you help me on with my cloak?
LORD GORING: With pleasure.

[*Puts her cloak on.*]

MRS CHEVELEY: Thanks. I am never going to try to harm Robert Chiltern again.
LORD GORING: Fortunately you have not the chance, Mrs Cheveley.
MRS CHEVELEY: Well, even if I had the chance, I wouldn't. On the contrary, I am going to render him a great service.
LORD GORING: I am charmed to hear it. It is a reformation.
MRS CHEVELEY: Yes. I can't bear so upright a gentleman, so honourable an English gentleman, being so shamefully deceived, and so —
LORD GORING: Well?
MRS CHEVELEY: I find that somehow Gertrude Chiltern's dying speech and confession has strayed into my pocket.
LORD GORING: What do you mean?
MRS CHEVELEY [*with a bitter note of triumph in her voice*]: I mean that I am going to send Robert Chiltern the love-letter his wife wrote to you tonight.
LORD GORING: Love-letter?
MRS CHEVELEY [*laughing*]: 'I want you. I trust you, I am coming to you. Gertrude.'

[LORD GORING *rushes to the bureau and takes up the envelope, finds it empty, and turns round.*]

LORD GORING: You wretched woman, must you always be thieving? Give me back that letter. I'll take it from you by force. You shall not leave my room till I have got it.

[*He rushes towards her, but* MRS CHEVELEY *at once puts her hand on the electric bell that is on the table. The bell sounds with shrill reverberations, and* PHIPPS *enters.*]

MRS CHEVELEY [*after a pause*]: Lord Goring merely rang that you should show me out. Good night, Lord Goring!

[*Goes out followed by* PHIPPS. *Her face is illumined with evil triumph. There is joy in her eyes. Youth seems to have come back to her. Her last glance is like a swift arrow.*[14] LORD GORING *bites his lip, and lights a cigarette.*]

ACT DROP

FOURTH ACT

SCENE

Same as Act II

[LORD GORING *is standing by the fireplace with his hands in his pockets. He is looking rather bored.*]

LORD GORING [*pulls out his watch, inspects it and rings the bell*]: It is a great nuisance. I can't find anyone in this house to talk to. And I am full of interesting information. I feel like the latest edition of something or other.

[*Enter servant.*]

JAMES: Sir Robert is still at the Foreign Office, my lord.
LORD GORING: Lady Chiltern not down yet?
JAMES: Her ladyship has not yet left her room. Miss Chiltern has just come in from riding.
LORD GORING [*to himself*]: Ah! that is something.
JAMES: Lord Caversham has been waiting for some time in the library for Sir Robert. I told him your lordship was here.
LORD GORING: Thank you. Would you kindly tell him I've gone?
JAMES [*bowing*]: I shall do so, my lord.

[*Exit servant.*]

LORD GORING: Really, I don't want to meet my father three days running. It is a great deal too much excitement for any son. I hope to goodness he won't come up. Fathers should be neither seen nor heard. That is the only proper basis for family life. Mothers are different. Mothers are darlings.

[*Throws himself down into a chair, picks up a paper and begins to read it.*]

[*Enter* LORD CAVERSHAM.]

254

LORD CAVERSHAM: Well, sir, what are you doing here? Wasting your time as usual, I suppose?

LORD GORING [*throws down paper and rises*]: My dear father, when one pays a visit it is for the purpose of wasting other people's time, not one's own.

LORD CAVERSHAM: Have you been thinking over what I spoke to you about last night?

LORD GORING: I have been thinking about nothing else.

LORD CAVERSHAM: Engaged to be married yet?

LORD GORING [*genially*]: Not yet; but I hope to be before lunch-time.

LORD CAVERSHAM [*caustically*]: You can have till dinner-time if it would be of any convenience to you.

LORD GORING: Thanks awfully, but I think I'd sooner be engaged before lunch.

LORD CAVERSHAM: Humph! Never know when you are serious or not.

LORD GORING: Neither do I, father.

[*A pause.*]

LORD CAVERSHAM: I suppose you have read *The Times* this morning?

LORD GORING [*airily*]: *The Times*? Certainly not. I only read *The Morning Post*. All that one should know about modern life is where the Duchesses are; anything else is quite demoralizing.

LORD CAVERSHAM: Do you mean to say you have not read *The Times* leading article on Robert Chiltern's career?

LORD GORING: Good heavens! No. What does it say?

LORD CAVERSHAM: What should it say, sir? Everything complimentary, of course. Chiltern's speech last night on this Argentine Canal scheme was one of the finest pieces of oratory ever delivered in the House since Canning.[1]

LORD GORING: Ah! Never heard of Canning. Never wanted to. And did . . . did Chiltern uphold the scheme?

LORD CAVERSHAM: Uphold it, sir? How little you know him! Why, he denounced it roundly, and the whole system of modern political finance. This speech is the turning-point in his career, as *The Times* points out. You should read this article, sir. [*Opens* The Times.] 'Sir Robert Chiltern . . . most rising of our young statesmen . . .

Brilliant orator . . . Unblemished career . . . Well-known integrity of character . . . Represents what is best in English public life . . . Noble contrast to the lax morality so common among foreign politicians.' They will never say that of you, sir.

LORD GORING: I sincerely hope not, father. However, I am delighted at what you tell me about Robert, thoroughly delighted. It shows he has got pluck.

LORD CAVERSHAM: He has got more than pluck, sir, he has got genius.

LORD GORING: Ah! I prefer pluck. It is not so common, nowadays, as genius is.

LORD CAVERSHAM: I wish you would go into Parliament.

LORD GORING: My dear father, only people who look dull ever get into the House of Commons, and only people who are dull ever succeed there.

LORD CAVERSHAM: Why don't you try to do something useful in life?

LORD GORING: I am far too young.

LORD CAVERSHAM [*testily*]: I hate this affectation of youth, sir. It is a great deal too prevalent nowadays.

LORD GORING: Youth isn't an affectation. Youth is an art.

LORD CAVERSHAM: Why don't you propose to that pretty Miss Chiltern?

LORD GORING: I am of a very nervous disposition, especially in the morning.

LORD CAVERSHAM: I don't suppose there is the smallest chance of her accepting you.

LORD GORING: I don't know how the betting stands today.

LORD CAVERSHAM: If she did accept you she would be the prettiest fool in England.

LORD GORING: That is just what I should like to marry. A thoroughly sensible wife would reduce me to a condition of absolute idiocy in less than six months.

LORD CAVERSHAM: You don't deserve her, sir.

LORD GORING: My dear father, if we men married the women we deserved, we should have a very bad time of it.

[*Enter* MABEL CHILTERN.]

MABEL CHILTERN: Oh! . . . How do you do, Lord Caversham? I hope Lady Caversham is quite well?

LORD CAVERSHAM: Lady Caversham is as usual, as usual.

LORD GORING: Good morning, Miss Mabel!

MABEL CHILTERN [*taking no notice at all of* LORD GORING, *and addressing herself exclusively to* LORD CAVERSHAM]: And Lady Caversham's bonnets . . . are they at all better?

LORD CAVERSHAM: They have had a serious relapse, I am sorry to say.

LORD GORING: Good morning, Miss Mabel!

MABEL CHILTERN [*to* LORD CAVERSHAM]: I hope an operation will not be necessary.

LORD CAVERSHAM [*smiling at her pertness*]: If it is, we shall have to give Lady Caversham a narcotic. Otherwise she would never consent to have a feather touched.

LORD GORING [*with increased emphasis*]: Good morning, Miss Mabel!

MABEL CHILTERN [*turning round with feigned surprise*]: Oh, are you here? Of course you understand that after your breaking your appointment I am never going to speak to you again.

LORD GORING: Oh, please don't say such a thing. You are the one person in London I really like to have to listen to me.

MABEL CHILTERN: Lord Goring, I never believe a single word that either you or I say to each other.

LORD CAVERSHAM: You are quite right, my dear, quite right . . . as far as he is concerned, I mean.

MABEL CHILTERN: Do you think you could possibly make your son behave a little better occasionally? Just as a change.

LORD CAVERSHAM: I regret to say, Miss Chiltern, that I have no influence at all over my son. I wish I had. If I had, I know what I would make him do.

MABEL CHILTERN: I am afraid that he has one of those terribly weak natures that are not susceptible to influence.

LORD CAVERSHAM: He is very heartless, very heartless.

LORD GORING: It seems to me that I am a little in the way here.

MABEL CHILTERN: It is very good for you to be in the way, and to know what people say of you behind your back.

OSCAR WILDE

LORD GORING: I don't at all like knowing what people say of me behind my back. It makes me far too conceited.

LORD CAVERSHAM: After that, my dear, I really must bid you good morning.

MABEL CHILTERN: Oh! I hope you are not going to leave me all alone with Lord Goring? Especially at such an early hour in the day.

LORD CAVERSHAM: I am afraid I can't take him with me to Downing Street. It is not the Prime Minister's day for seeing the unemployed.[2]

[Shakes hands with MABEL CHILTERN, takes up his hat and stick, and goes out, with a parting glare of indignation at LORD GORING.]

MABEL CHILTERN [takes up roses and begins to arrange them in a bowl on the table]: People who don't keep their appointments in the Park are horrid.

LORD GORING: Detestable.

MABEL CHILTERN: I am glad you admit it. But I wish you wouldn't look so pleased about it.

LORD GORING: I can't help it. I always look pleased when I am with you.

MABEL CHILTERN [sadly]: Then I suppose it is my duty to remain with you?

LORD GORING: Of course it is.

MABEL CHILTERN: Well, my duty is a thing I never do, on principle. It always depresses me. So I am afraid I must leave you.

LORD GORING: Please don't, Miss Mabel. I have something very particular to say to you.

MABEL CHILTERN [rapturously]: Oh, is it a proposal?

LORD GORING [somewhat taken aback]: Well, yes, it is – I am bound to say it is.

MABEL CHILTERN [with a sigh of pleasure]: I am so glad. That makes the second today.

LORD GORING [indignantly]: The second today? What conceited ass has been impertinent enough to dare to propose to you before I had proposed to you?

MABEL CHILTERN: Tommy Trafford, of course. It is one of Tommy's

258

days for proposing. He always proposes on Tuesdays and Thursdays, during the season.

LORD GORING: You didn't accept him, I hope?

MABEL CHILTERN: I make it a rule never to accept Tommy. That is why he goes on proposing. Of course, as you didn't turn up this morning, I very nearly said yes. It would have been an excellent lesson both for him and for you if I had. It would have taught you both better manners.

LORD GORING: Oh! bother Tommy Trafford. Tommy is a silly little ass. I love you.

MABEL CHILTERN: I know. And I think you might have mentioned it before. I am sure I have given you heaps of opportunities.[3]

LORD GORING: Mabel, do be serious. Please be serious.

MABEL CHILTERN: Ah! that is the sort of thing a man always says to a girl before he has been married to her. He never says it afterwards.

LORD GORING [taking hold of her hand]: Mabel, I have told you that I love you. Can't you love me a little in return?

MABEL CHILTERN: You silly Arthur! If you knew anything about . . . anything, which you don't, you would know that I adore you. Everyone in London knows it except you. It is a public scandal the way I adore you. I have been going about for the last six months telling the whole of society that I adore you. I wonder you consent to have anything to say to me. I have no character left at all. At least, I feel so happy that I am quite sure I have no character left at all.

LORD GORING [catches her in his arms and kisses her. Then there is a pause of bliss]: Dear! Do you know I was awfully afraid of being refused!

MABEL CHILTERN [looking up at him]: But you never have been refused yet by anybody, have you, Arthur? I can't imagine anyone refusing you.

LORD GORING [after kissing her again]: Of course I'm not nearly good enough for you, Mabel.

MABEL CHILTERN [nestling close to him]: I am so glad, darling. I was afraid you were.

LORD GORING [after some hesitation]: And I'm . . . I'm a little over thirty.

MABEL CHILTERN: Dear, you look weeks younger than that.

LORD GORING [*enthusiastically*]: How sweet of you to say so! . . . And it is only fair to tell you frankly that I am fearfully extravagant.

MABEL CHILTERN: But so am I, Arthur. So we're sure to agree. And now I must go and see Gertrude.

LORD GORING: Must you really?

[*Kisses her.*]

MABEL CHILTERN: Yes.

LORD GORING: Then do tell her I want to talk to her particularly. I have been waiting here all the morning to see either her or Robert.

MABEL CHILTERN: Do you mean to say you didn't come here expressly to propose to me?

LORD GORING [*triumphantly*]: No; that was a flash of genius.

MABEL CHILTERN: Your first.

LORD GORING [*with determination*]: My last.

MABEL CHILTERN: I am delighted to hear it.[4] Now don't stir. I'll be back in five minutes. And don't fall into any temptations while I am away.

LORD GORING: Dear Mabel, while you are away, there are none. It makes me horribly dependent on you.

[*Enter* LADY CHILTERN.]

LADY CHILTERN: Good morning, dear! How pretty you are looking!

MABEL CHILTERN: How pale you are looking, Gertrude! It is most becoming!

LADY CHILTERN: Good morning, Lord Goring!

LORD GORING [*bowing*]: Good morning, Lady Chiltern.

MABEL CHILTERN [*aside to* LORD GORING]: I shall be in the conservatory, under the second palm tree on the left.

LORD GORING: Second on the left?

MABEL CHILTERN [*with a look of mock surprise*]: Yes; the usual palm tree.

[*Blows a kiss to him, unobserved by* LADY CHILTERN, *and goes out.*]

LORD GORING: Lady Chiltern, I have a certain amount of very good news to tell you. Mrs Cheveley gave me up Robert's letter last night, and I burned it. Robert is safe.

LADY CHILTERN [*sinking on the sofa*]: Safe! Oh! I am so glad of that. What a good friend you are to him – to us!

LORD GORING: There is only one person now that could be said to be in any danger.

LADY CHILTERN: Who is that?

LORD GORING [*sitting down beside her*]: Yourself.

LADY CHILTERN: I! In danger? What do you mean?

LORD GORING: Danger is too great a word. It is a word I should not have used. But I admit I have something to tell you that may distress you, that terribly distresses me. Yesterday evening you wrote me a very beautiful, womanly letter, asking me for my help. You wrote to me as one of your oldest friends, one of your husband's oldest friends. Mrs Cheveley stole that letter from my rooms.

LADY CHILTERN: Well, what use is it to her? Why should she not have it?

LORD GORING [*rising*]: Lady Chiltern, I will be quite frank with you. Mrs Cheveley puts a certain construction on that letter and proposes to send it to your husband.

LADY CHILTERN: But what construction could she put on it? . . . Oh! not that! not that! If I in – in trouble, and wanting your help, trusting you, propose to come to you . . . that you may advise me . . . assist me . . . Oh! are there women so horrible as that . . . ? And she proposes to send it to my husband? Tell me what happened. Tell me all that happened.

LORD GORING: Mrs Cheveley was concealed in a room adjoining my library, without my knowledge. I thought that the person who was waiting in that room to see me was yourself. Robert came in unexpectedly. A chair or something fell in the room. He forced his way in, and he discovered her. We had a terrible scene. I still thought it was you. He left me in anger. At the end of everything Mrs Cheveley got possession of your letter – she stole it, when or how, I don't know.

LADY CHILTERN: At what hour did this happen?

LORD GORING: At half-past ten. And now I propose that we tell Robert the whole thing at once.

LADY CHILTERN [*looking at him with amazement that is almost terror*]: You want me to tell Robert that the woman you expected was not Mrs Cheveley, but myself? That it was I whom you thought was concealed in a room in your house, at half-past ten o'clock at night? You want me to tell him that?

LORD GORING: I think it is better that he should know the exact truth.

LADY CHILTERN [*rising*]: Oh, I couldn't, I couldn't!

LORD GORING: May I do it?

LADY CHILTERN: No.

LORD GORING [*gravely*]: You are wrong, Lady Chiltern.

LADY CHILTERN: No. The letter must be intercepted. That is all. But how can I do it? Letters arrive for him every moment of the day. His secretaries open them and hand them to him. I dare not ask the servants to bring me his letters. It would be impossible. Oh! why don't you tell me what to do?

LORD GORING: Pray be calm, Lady Chiltern, and answer the questions I am going to put to you. You said his secretaries open his letters.

LADY CHILTERN: Yes.

LORD GORING: Who is with him today? Mr Trafford, isn't it?

LADY CHILTERN: No. Mr Montford, I think.

LORD GORING: You can trust him?

LADY CHILTERN [*with a gesture of despair*]: Oh! how do I know?

LORD GORING: He would do what you asked him, wouldn't he?

LADY CHILTERN: I think so.

LORD GORING: Your letter was on pink paper. He could recognize it without reading it, couldn't he? By the colour?

LADY CHILTERN: I suppose so.

LORD GORING: Is he in the house now?

LADY CHILTERN: Yes.

LORD GORING: Then I will go and see him myself, and tell him that a certain letter, written on pink paper, is to be forwarded to Robert today, and that at all costs it must not reach him. [*Goes to the door, and opens it.*] Oh! Robert is coming upstairs with the letter in his hand. It has reached him already.

LADY CHILTERN [*with a cry of pain*]: Oh! you have saved his life; what have you done with mine?

[*Enter* SIR ROBERT CHILTERN. *He has the letter in his hand, and is reading it. He comes towards his wife, not noticing* LORD GORING's *presence.*]

SIR ROBERT CHILTERN: 'I want you. I trust you. I am coming to you. Gertrude.' Oh, my love! is this true? Do you indeed trust me, and want me? If so, it was for me to come to you, not for you to write of coming to me. This letter of yours, Gertrude, makes me feel that nothing that the world may do can hurt me now. You want me, Gertrude?

[LORD GORING, *unseen by* SIR ROBERT CHILTERN, *makes an imploring sign to* LADY CHILTERN *to accept the situation and* SIR ROBERT's *error.*]

LADY CHILTERN: Yes.

SIR ROBERT CHILTERN: You trust me, Gertrude?

LADY CHILTERN: Yes.

SIR ROBERT CHILTERN: Ah! why did you not add you loved me?

LADY CHILTERN [*taking his hand*]: Because I loved you.

[LORD GORING *passes into the conservatory.*]

SIR ROBERT CHILTERN [*kisses her*]: Gertrude, you don't know what I feel. When Montford passed me your letter across the table – he had opened it by mistake, I suppose, without looking at the handwriting on the envelope – and I read it – oh! I did not care what disgrace or punishment was in store for me, I only thought you loved me still.

LADY CHILTERN: There is no disgrace in store for you, nor any public shame. Mrs Cheveley has handed over to Lord Goring the document that was in her possession, and he has destroyed it.

SIR ARTHUR CHILTERN: Are you sure of this, Gertrude?

LADY CHILTERN: Yes; Lord Goring has just told me.

SIR ROBERT CHILTERN: Then I am safe! Oh! What a wonderful thing to be safe! For two days I have been in terror. I am safe now. How did Arthur destroy my letter? Tell me.

LADY CHILTERN: He burned it.

SIR ROBERT CHILTERN: I wish I had seen that one sin of my youth burning to ashes. How many men there are in modern life who would like to see their past burning to white ashes before them! Is Arthur still here?

LADY CHILTERN: Yes; he is in the conservatory.

SIR ROBERT CHILTERN: I am so glad now I made that speech last night in the House, so glad. I made it thinking that public disgrace might be the result. But it has not been so.

LADY CHILTERN: Public honour has been the result.

SIR ROBERT CHILTERN: I think so. I fear so, almost. For although I am safe from detection, although every proof against me is destroyed, I suppose, Gertrude . . . I suppose I should retire from public life?

[*He looks anxiously at his wife.*]

LADY CHILTERN [*eagerly*]: Oh yes, Robert, you should do that. It is your duty to do that.

SIR ROBERT CHILTERN: It is much to surrender.

LADY CHILTERN: No; it will be much to gain.

[SIR ROBERT CHILTERN *walks up and down the room with a troubled expression. Then comes over to his wife, and puts his hand on her shoulder.*]

SIR ROBERT CHILTERN: And you would be happy living somewhere alone with me, abroad perhaps, or in the country away from London, away from public life? You would have no regrets?

LADY CHILTERN: Oh! none, Robert.

SIR ROBERT CHILTERN [*sadly*]: And your ambition for me? You used to be ambitious for me.

LADY CHILTERN: Oh, my ambition! I have none now, but that we two may love each other. It was your ambition that led you astray. Let us not talk about ambition.

[LORD GORING *returns from the conservatory, looking very pleased with himself, and with an entirely new buttonhole that someone has made for him.*]

SIR ROBERT CHILTERN [*going towards him*]: Arthur, I have to thank you for what you have done for me. I don't know how I can repay you.

[*Shakes hands with him.*]

LORD GORING: My dear fellow, I'll tell you at once. At the present moment, under the usual palm tree ... I mean in the conservatory ...

[*Enter* MASON.]

MASON: Lord Caversham.

LORD GORING: That admirable father of mine really makes a habit of turning up at the wrong moment. It is very heartless of him, very heartless indeed.

[*Enter* LORD CAVERSHAM. MASON *goes out.*]

LORD CAVERSHAM: Good morning, Lady Chiltern! Warmest congratulations to you, Chiltern, on your brilliant speech last night. I have just left the Prime Minister, and you are to have the vacant seat in the Cabinet.

SIR ROBERT CHILTERN [*with a look of joy and triumph*]: A seat in the Cabinet?

LORD CAVERSHAM: Yes; here is the Prime Minister's letter.

[*Hands letter.*]

SIR ROBERT CHILTERN [*takes letter and reads it*]: A seat in the Cabinet!

LORD CAVERSHAM: Certainly, and you well deserve it too. You have got what we want so much in political life nowadays – high character, high moral tone, high principles. [*To* LORD GORING] Everything that you have not got, sir, and never will have.

LORD GORING: I don't like principles, father. I prefer prejudices.

[SIR ROBERT CHILTERN *is on the brink of accepting the Prime Minister's offer, when he sees his wife looking at him with clear, candid eyes. He then realizes that it is impossible.*]

SIR ROBERT CHILTERN: I cannot accept this offer, Lord Caversham. I have made up my mind to decline it.

LORD CAVERSHAM: Decline it, sir!

SIR ROBERT CHILTERN: My intention is to retire at once from public life.

LORD CAVERSHAM [*angrily*]: Decline a seat in the Cabinet, and retire from public life? Never heard such damned nonsense in the whole course of my existence. I beg your pardon, Lady Chiltern. Chiltern, I beg your pardon. [*To* LORD GORING.] Don't grin like that, sir.

LORD GORING: No, father.

LORD CAVERSHAM: Lady Chiltern, you are a sensible woman, the most sensible woman in London, the most sensible woman I know. Will you kindly prevent your husband from making such a . . . from talking such . . . Will you kindly do that, Lady Chiltern?

LADY CHILTERN: I think my husband is right in his determination, Lord Caversham. I approve of it.

LORD CAVERSHAM: You approve of it? Good heavens!

LADY CHILTERN [*taking her husband's hand*]: I admire him for it. I admire him immensely for it. I have never admired him so much before. He is finer than even I thought him. [*To* SIR ROBERT CHILTERN] You will go and write your letter to the Prime Minister now, won't you? Don't hesitate about it, Robert.

SIR ROBERT CHILTERN [*with a touch of bitterness*]: I suppose I had better write it at once. Such offers are not repeated. I will ask you to excuse me for a moment, Lord Caversham.

LADY CHILTERN: I may come with you, Robert, may I not?

SIR ROBERT CHILTERN: Yes, Gertrude.

[LADY CHILTERN *goes out with him.*]

LORD CAVERSHAM: What is the matter with the family? Something wrong here, eh? [*Tapping his forehead.*] Idiocy? Hereditary, I suppose. Both of them, too. Wife as well as husband. Very sad. Very sad indeed! And they are not an old family. Can't understand it.

LORD GORING: It is not idiocy, father, I assure you.

LORD CAVERSHAM: What is it then, sir.

LORD GORING [*after some hesitation*]: Well, it is what is called nowadays a high moral tone, father. That is all.

LORD CAVERSHAM: Hate these new-fangled names. Same thing as we used to call idiocy fifty years ago. Shan't stay in this house any longer.

LORD GORING [*taking his arm*]: Oh! just go in here for a moment, father. Second palm tree[5] to the left, the usual palm tree.

LORD CAVERSHAM: What, sir?

LORD GORING: I beg your pardon, father, I forgot. The conservatory, father, the conservatory – there is someone there I want you to talk to.

LORD CAVERSHAM: What about, sir?

LORD GORING: About me, father.

LORD CAVERSHAM [*grimly*]: Not a subject on which much eloquence is possible.

LORD GORING: No, father; but the lady is like me. She doesn't care much for eloquence in others. She thinks it a little loud.

[LORD CAVERSHAM *goes into the conservatory.* LADY CHILTERN *enters.*]

LORD GORING: Lady Chiltern, why are you playing Mrs Cheveley's cards?

LADY CHILTERN [*startled*]: I don't understand you.

LORD GORING: Mrs Cheveley made an attempt to ruin your husband. Either to drive him from public life, or to make him adopt a dishonourable position. From the latter tragedy you saved him. The former you are now thrusting on him. Why should you do him the wrong Mrs Cheveley tried to do and failed?

LADY CHILTERN: Lord Goring?

LORD GORING [*pulling himself together for a great effort, and showing the philosopher that underlies the dandy*]: Lady Chiltern, allow me. You wrote me a letter last night in which you said you trusted me and wanted my help. Now is the moment when you really want my help, now is the time when you have got to trust me, to trust in my counsel and judgement. You love Robert. Do you want to kill his love for you? What sort of existence will he have if you rob him of the fruits of his ambition, if you take him from the splendour of a great political career, if you close the doors of public life against him, if you condemn him to sterile failure, he who was made for triumph and success? Women are not meant to judge us, but to forgive us when we need forgiveness. Pardon, not punishment, is their mission. Why should you scourge him with rods for a sin done in his youth, before he knew you, before he knew himself? A man's life is of more value than a woman's. It has larger issues, wider scope, greater ambitions. A woman's life revolves in curves of emotions. It is upon lines of intellect that a man's life progresses. Don't make any terrible mistake, Lady Chiltern. A woman who can keep a man's love, and love him in return, has done all the world wants of women, or should want of them.[6]

LADY CHILTERN [*troubled and hesitating*]: But it is my husband himself who wishes to retire from public life. He feels it is his duty. It was he who first said so.

LORD GORING: Rather than lose your love, Robert would do anything, wreck his whole career, as he is on the brink of doing now. He is making for you a terrible sacrifice. Take my advice, Lady Chiltern, and do not accept a sacrifice so great. If you do, you will live to repent it bitterly. We men and women are not made to accept such sacrifices from each other. We are not worthy of them. Besides, Robert has been punished enough.

LADY CHILTERN: We have both been punished. I set him up too high.

LORD GORING [*with deep feeling in his voice*]: Do not for that reason set him down now too low. If he has fallen from his altar, do not thrust him into the mire. Failure to Robert would be the very mire of shame. Power is his passion. He would lose everything, even his power to feel love. Your husband's life is at this moment in your hands, your husband's love is in your hands. Don't mar both for him.

[*Enter* SIR ROBERT CHILTERN.]

SIR ROBERT CHILTERN: Gertrude, here is the draft of my letter. Shall I read it to you?

LADY CHILTERN: Let me see it.

[SIR ROBERT *hands her the letter. She reads it, and then, with a gesture of passion, tears it up.*]

SIR ROBERT CHILTERN: What are you doing?

LADY CHILTERN: A man's life is of more value than a woman's. It has larger issues, wider scope, greater ambitions. Our lives revolve in curves of emotions. It is upon lines of intellect that a man's life progresses. I have just learnt this, and much else with it, from Lord

Goring. And I will not spoil your life for you, nor see you spoil it as a sacrifice to me, a useless sacrifice![7]

SIR ROBERT CHILTERN: Gertrude! Gertrude!

LADY CHILTERN: You can forget. Men easily forget. And I forgive. That is how women help the world. I see that now.

SIR ROBERT CHILTERN [*deeply overcome by emotion, embraces her*]: My wife! my wife! [*To* LORD GORING] Arthur, it seems that I am always to be in your debt.

LORD GORING: Oh dear no, Robert. Your debt is to Lady Chiltern, not to me!

SIR ROBERT CHILTERN: I owe you much. And now tell me what you were going to ask me just now as Lord Caversham came in.

LORD GORING: Robert, you are your sister's guardian, and I want your consent to my marriage with her. That is all.

LADY CHILTERN: Oh, I am so glad! I am so glad!

[*Shakes hands with* LORD GORING.]

LORD GORING: Thank you, Lady Chiltern.

SIR ROBERT CHILTERN [*with a troubled look*]: My sister to be your wife?

LORD GORING: Yes.

SIR ROBERT CHILTERN [*speaking with great firmness*]: Arthur, I am very sorry, but the thing is quite out of the question. I have to think of Mabel's future happiness. And I don't think her happiness would be safe in your hands. And I cannot have her sacrificed!

LORD GORING: Sacrificed!

SIR ROBERT CHILTERN: Yes, utterly sacrificed. Loveless marriages are horrible. But there is one thing worse than an absolutely loveless marriage. A marriage in which there is love, but on one side only; faith, but on one side only; devotion, but on one side only, and in which of the two hearts one is sure to be broken.

LORD GORING: But I love Mabel. No other woman has any place in my life.

LADY CHILTERN: Robert, if they love each other, why should they not be married?

SIR ROBERT CHILTERN: Arthur cannot bring Mabel the love that she deserves.

LORD GORING: What reason have you for saying that?

SIR ROBERT CHILTERN [*after a pause*]: Do you really require me to tell you?

LORD GORING: Certainly I do.

SIR ROBERT CHILTERN: As you choose. When I called on you yesterday evening I found Mrs Cheveley concealed in your rooms. It was between ten and eleven o'clock at night. I do not wish to say anything more. Your relations with Mrs Cheveley have, as I said to you last night, nothing whatsoever to do with me. I know you were engaged to be married to her once. The fascination she exercised over you then seems to have returned. You spoke to me last night of her as of a woman pure and stainless, a woman whom you respected and honoured. That may be so. But I cannot give my sister's life into your hands. It would be wrong of me. It would be unjust, infamously unjust to her.

LORD GORING: I have nothing more to say.

LADY CHILTERN: Robert, it was not Mrs Cheveley whom Lord Goring expected last night.

SIR ROBERT CHILTERN: Not Mrs Cheveley! Who was it then?

LORD GORING: Lady Chiltern!

LADY CHILTERN: It was your own wife. Robert, yesterday afternoon Lord Goring told me that if ever I was in trouble I could come to him for help, as he was our oldest and best friend. Later on, after that terrible scene in this room, I wrote to him telling him that I trusted him, that I had need of him, that I was coming to him for help and advice. [SIR ROBERT CHILTERN *takes the letter out of his pocket.*] Yes, that letter. I didn't go to Lord Goring's, after all. I felt that it is from ourselves alone that help can come. Pride made me think that. Mrs Cheveley went. She stole my letter and sent it anonymously to you this morning, that you should think . . . Oh! Robert, I cannot tell you what she wished you to think . . .

SIR ROBERT CHILTERN: What! Had I fallen so low in your eyes that you thought that even for a moment I could have doubted your goodness? Gertrude, Gertrude, you are to me the white image of all good things, and sin can never touch you. Arthur, you can go to Mabel, and you have my best wishes! Oh! stop a moment. There is no name at the beginning of this letter. The brilliant Mrs Cheveley does not seem to have noticed that. There should be a name.

LADY CHILTERN: Let me write yours. It is you I trust and need. You and none else.

LORD GORING: Well, really, Lady Chiltern, I think I should have back my own letter.

LADY CHILTERN [*smiling*]: No; you shall have Mabel. [*Takes the letter and writes her husband's name on it.*]

LORD GORING: Well, I hope she hasn't changed her mind. It's nearly twenty minutes since I saw her last. [*Enter* MABEL CHILTERN *and* LORD CAVERSHAM.]

MABEL CHILTERN: Lord Goring, I think your father's conversation much more improving than yours. I am only going to talk to Lord Caversham in the future, and always under the usual palm tree.

LORD GORING: Darling!

[*Kisses her.*]

LORD CAVERSHAM [*considerably taken aback*]: What does this mean, sir? You don't mean to say that this charming, clever young lady has been so foolish as to accept you?

LORD GORING: Certainly, father! And Chiltern's been wise enough to accept the seat in the Cabinet.

LORD CAVERSHAM: I am very glad to hear that, Chiltern . . . I congratulate you, sir. If the country doesn't go to the dogs or the Radicals, we shall have you Prime Minister, some day.

[*Enter* MASON.]

MASON: Luncheon is on the table, my Lady!

[MASON *goes out.*]

MABEL CHILTERN: You'll stop to luncheon, Lord Caversham, won't you?

LORD CAVERSHAM: With pleasure, and I'll drive you down to Downing Street afterwards, Chiltern. You have a great future before you, a great future. [*To* LORD GORING] Wish I could say the same for you, sir. But your career will have to be entirely domestic.

LORD GORING: Yes, father, I prefer it domestic.

LORD CAVERSHAM: And if you don't make this young lady an ideal husband, I'll cut you off with a shilling.

MABEL CHILTERN: An ideal husband! Oh, I don't think I should like that. It sounds like something in the next world.

LORD CAVERSHAM: What do you want him to be then, dear?

MABEL CHILTERN: He can be what he chooses. All I want is to be . . . to be . . . oh! a real wife to him.

LORD CAVERSHAM: Upon my word, there is a good deal of common sense in that, Lady Chiltern.

[*They all go out except* SIR ROBERT CHILTERN. *He sinks into a chair, wrapt in thought. After a little time* LADY CHILTERN *returns to look for him.*]

LADY CHILTERN [*leaning over the back of the chair*]: Aren't you coming in, Robert?

SIR ROBERT CHILTERN [*taking her hand*]: Gertrude, is it love you feel for me, or is it pity merely?

LADY CHILTERN [*kisses him*]: It is love, Robert. Love, and only love. For both of us a new life is beginning.[8]

CURTAIN

A Florentine Tragedy

The Persons of the Play

SIMONE, *the husband*
BIANCA, *the wife*
GUIDO BARDI, *son to the Duke of Florence*

[*Enter* THE HUSBAND].

SIMONE: My good wife, you come slowly, were it not better
    To run to meet your lord? Here, take my cloak.
    Take this pack first. 'Tis heavy. I have sold nothing:
    Save a furred robe unto the Cardinal's son,
    Who hopes to wear it when his father dies,
    And hopes that will be soon.
                        But who is this?
    Why you have here some friend. Some kinsman doubtless,
    Newly returned from foreign lands and fallen
    Upon a house without a host to greet him?
    I crave your pardon, kinsman. For a house
    Lacking a host is but an empty thing
    And void of honour; a cup without its wine,
    A scabbard without steel to keep it straight,
    A flowerless garden widowed of the sun.
    Again I crave your pardon, my sweet cousin.
BIANCA: This is no kinsman and no cousin neither.
SIMONE: No kinsman, and no cousin! You amaze me.
    Who is it then who with such courtly grace
    Deigns to accept our hospitalities?
GUIDO: My name is Guido Bardi.
SIMONE: What! The son
    Of that great Lord of Florence whose dim towers
    Like shadows silvered by the wandering moon
    I see from out my casement every night!
    Sir Guido Bardi, you are welcome here,
    Twice welcome. For I trust my honest wife,
    Most honest if uncomely to the eye,

Hath not with foolish chatterings wearied you,
As is the wont of women.

GUIDO: Your gracious lady,
Whose beauty is a lamp that pales the stars
And robs Diana's quiver of her beams
Has welcomed me with such sweet courtesies
That if it be her pleasure, and your own,
I will come often to your simple house.
And when your business bids you walk abroad
I will sit here and charm her loneliness
Lest she might sorrow for you overmuch.
What say you, good Simone?

SIMONE: My noble Lord,
You bring me such high honour that my tongue
Like a slave's tongue is tied, and cannot say
The word it would. Yet not to give you thanks
Were to be too unmannerly. So, I thank you,
From my heart's core.

                    It is such things as these
That knit a state together, when a Prince
So nobly born and of such fair address,
Forgetting unjust Fortune's differences,
Comes to an honest burgher's honest home
As a most honest friend.[1]

                    And yet, my Lord,
I fear I am too bold. Some other night
We trust that you will come here as a friend,
Tonight you come to buy my merchandise.
Is it not so? Silks, velvets, what you will,
I doubt not but I have some dainty wares
Will woo your fancy. True, the hour is late,
But we poor merchants toil both night and day
To make our scanty gains. The tolls are high,
And every city levies its own toll,
And prentices are unskilful, and wives even
Lack sense and cunning, though Bianca here

Has brought me a rich customer tonight.
Is it not so, Bianca? But I waste time.
Where is my pack? Where is my pack, I say?
Open it, my good wife. Unloose the cords.
Kneel down upon the floor. You are better so.
Nay not that one, the other. Despatch, despatch!
Buyers will grow impatient oftentimes.
We dare not keep them waiting. Ay! 'tis that,
Give it to me; with care. It is most costly.
Touch it with care. And now, my noble Lord –
Nay, pardon, I have here a Lucca damask,[2]
The very web of silver and the roses
So cunningly wrought that they lack perfume merely
To cheat the wanton sense. Touch it, my Lord.
Is it not soft as water, strong as steel?
And then the roses! Are they not finely woven?
I think the hillsides that best love the rose,
At Bellosguardo or at Fiesole,[3]
Throw no such blossoms on the lap of spring,
Or if they do their blossoms droop and die.
Such is the fate of all the dainty things
That dance in wind and water. Nature herself
Makes war on her own loveliness and slays
Her children like Medea.[4] Nay but, my Lord,
Look closer still. Why in this damask here
It is summer always, and no winter's tooth
Will ever blight these blossoms. For every ell[5]
I paid a piece of gold. Red gold, and good,
The fruit of careful thrift.

GUIDO: Honest Simone,
Enough, I pray you. I am well content,
Tomorrow I will send my servant to you,
Who will pay twice your price.

SIMONE: My generous Prince!
I kiss your hands. And now I do remember
Another treasure hidden in my house

Which you must see. It is a robe of state:
Woven by a Venetian: the stuff, cut-velvet:[6]
The pattern, pomegranates: each separate seed
Wrought of a pearl: the collar all of pearls,
As thick as moths in summer streets at night,
And whiter than the moons that madmen see
Through prison bars at morning. A male ruby[7]
Burns like a lighted coal within the clasp.
The Holy Father has not such a stone,
Nor could the Indies show a brother to it.
The brooch itself is of most curious art,
Cellini never made a fairer thing
To please the great Lorenzo.[8] You must wear it.
There is none worthier in our city here,
And it will suit you well. Upon one side
A slim and horned satyr leaps in gold
To catch some nymph of silver. Upon the other
Stands Silence with a crystal in her hand,
No bigger than the smallest ear of corn,
That wavers at the passing of a bird,
And yet so cunningly wrought that one would say
It breathed, or held its breath.
                              Worthy Bianca,
Would not this noble and most costly robe
Suit young Lord Guido well?
                              Nay, but entreat him;
He will refuse you nothing, though the price
Be as a prince's ransom. And your profit
Shall not be less than mine.
BIANCA: Am I your prentice?
Why should I chaffer for your velvet robe?
GUIDO: Nay, fair Bianca, I will buy your robe,
And all things that the honest merchant has
I will buy also. Princes must be ransomed,
And fortunate are all high lords who fall
Into the white hands of so fair a foe.

SIMONE: I stand rebuked. But you will buy my wares?
   Will you not buy them? Fifty thousand crowns
   Would scarce repay me. But you, my Lord, shall have them
   For forty thousand. Is that price too high?
   Name your own price. I have a curious fancy
   To see you in this wonder of the loom
   Amidst the noble ladies of the court,
   A flower among flowers.
                They say, my lord,
   These highborn dames do so affect your Grace
   That where you go they throng like flies around you,
   Each seeking for your favour.
               I have heard also
   Of husbands that wear horns,[9] and wear them bravely,
   A fashion most fantastical.
GUIDO: Simone,
   Your reckless tongue needs curbing; and besides,
   You do forget this gracious lady here
   Whose delicate ears are surely not attuned
   To such coarse music.
SIMONE: True: I had forgotten,
   Nor will offend again. Yet, my sweet Lord,
   You'll buy the robe of state. Will you not buy it?
   But forty thousand crowns. 'Tis but a trifle,
   To one who is Giovanni Bardi's heir.
GUIDO: Settle this thing tomorrow with my steward
   Antonio Costa. He will come to you.
   And you will have a hundred thousand crowns
   If that will serve your purpose.
SIMONE: A hundred thousand!
   Said you a hundred thousand? Oh! be sure
   That will for all time, and in everything
   Make me your debtor. Ay! from this time forth
   My house, with everything my house contains
   Is yours, and only yours.
           A hundred thousand!

My brain is dazed. I will be richer far
Than all the other merchants. I will buy
Vineyards, and lands, and gardens. Every loom
From Milan down to Sicily shall be mine,
And mine the pearls that the Arabian seas
Store in their silent caverns.

                             Generous Prince,
This night shall prove the herald of my love,
Which is so great that whatsoe'er you ask
It will not be denied you.

GUIDO: What if I asked
For white Bianca here?

SIMONE: You jest, my Lord,
She is not worthy of so great a Prince.
She is but made to keep the house and spin.
Is it not so, good wife? It is so. Look!
Your distaff[10] waits for you. Sit down and spin.
Women should not be idle in their homes.
For idle fingers make a thoughtless heart.
Sit down, I say.

BIANCA: What shall I spin?

SIMONE: Oh! spin
Some robe which, dyed in purple, sorrow might wear
For her own comforting: or some long-fringed cloth
In which a new-born and unwelcome babe
Might wail unheeded; or a dainty sheet
Which, delicately perfumed with sweet herbs,
Might serve to wrap a dead man. Spin what you will;
I care not, I.

BIANCA: The brittle thread is broken,
The dull wheel wearies of its ceaseless round,
The duller distaff sickens of its load;
I will not spin tonight.

SIMONE: It matters not.
Tomorrow you shall spin, and every day
Shall find you at your distaff. So, Lucretia

Was found by Tarquin.[11] So, perchance, Lucretia
Waited for Tarquin. Who knows? I have heard
Strange things about men's wives. And now, my lord,
What news abroad? I heard today at Pisa
That certain of the English merchants there
Would sell their woollens at a lower rate
Than the just laws allow, and have entreated
The Signory to hear them.

                           Is this well?
Should merchant be to merchant as a wolf?
And should the stranger living in our land
Seek by enforced privilege or craft
To rob us of our profits?

GUIDO: What should I do
With merchants or their profits? Shall I go
And wrangle with the Signory on your count?
And wear the gown in which you buy from fools,
Or sell to sillier bidders? Honest Simone,
Wool-selling or wool-gathering is for you.
My wits have other quarries.

BIANCA: Noble Lord,
I pray you pardon my good husband here,
His soul stands ever in the market-place,
And his heart beats but at the price of wool.
Yet he is honest in his common way.

[*To* SIMONE.]

And you, have you no shame? A gracious Prince
Comes to our house, and you must weary him
With most misplaced assurance. Ask his pardon.

SIMONE: I ask it humbly. We will talk tonight
Of other things. I hear the Holy Father
Has sent a letter to the King of France
Bidding him cross that shield of snow, the Alps,
And make a peace in Italy, which will be
Worse than war of brothers, and more bloody

Than civil rapine or intestine feuds.

GUIDO: Oh! we are weary of that King of France,
Who never comes, but ever talks of coming.
What are these things to me? There are other things
Closer, and of more import, good Simone.

BIANCA [*to* SIMONE]: I think you tire our most gracious guest.
What is the King of France to us? As much
As are your English merchants with their wool.[12]

*   *   *   *   *   *   *

SIMONE: Is it so then? Is all this mighty world
Narrowed into the confines of this room
With but three souls for poor inhabitants?
Ay! There are times when the great universe,
Like cloth in some unskilful dyer's vat,
Shrivels into a handsbreadth, and perchance
That time is now! Well! Let that time be now.
Let this mean room be as that mighty stage
Whereon kings die, and our ignoble lives
Become the stakes God plays for.
                                   I do not know
Why I speak thus. My ride has wearied me.
And my horse stumbled thrice, which is an omen
That bodes not good to any.
                                   Alas! my lord,
How poor a bargain is this life of man,
And in how mean a market are we sold!
When we are born our mothers weep, but when
We die there is none weep for us. No, not one.

[*Passes to back of stage.*]

BIANCA: How like a common chapman[13] does he speak!
I hate him, soul and body. Cowardice
Has set her pale seal on his brow. His hands
Whiter than poplar leaves in windy springs,
Shake with some palsy; and his stammering mouth

282

Blurts out a foolish froth of empty words
Like water from a conduit.
GUIDO: Sweet Bianca,
He is not worthy of your thought or mine.
The man is but a very honest knave
Full of fine phrases for life's merchandise,
Selling most dear what he must hold most cheap,
A windy brawler in a world of words.
I never met so eloquent a fool.
BIANCA: Oh, would that Death might take him where he stands!
SIMONE [*turning round*]: Who spake of Death? Let no one speak of
    Death.
What should Death do in such a merry house,
With but a wife, a husband and a friend
To give it greeting? Let Death go to houses
Where there are vile, adulterous things, chaste wives
Who grow weary of their noble lords
Draw back the curtains of their marriage beds,
And in polluted and dishonoured sheets
Feed some unlawful lust. Ay! 'tis so
Strange, and yet so. *You* do not know the world.
You are too single and too honourable.
I know it well. And would it were not so,
But wisdom comes with winters. My hair grows grey,
And youth has left my body. Enough of that.
Tonight is ripe for pleasure, and indeed,
I would be merry, as beseems a host
Who finds a gracious and unlooked-for guest
Waiting to greet him. [*Takes up a lute.*]
                              But what is this, my lord?
Why, you have brought a lute to play to us.
Oh! play, sweet Prince. And, if I am bold,
Pardon, but play.
GUIDO: I will not play tonight.
Some other night, Simone.

                    [*To* BIANCA]   You and I

Together, with no listeners but the stars,
Or the more jealous moon.

SIMONE: Nay, but my lord!
Nay, but I do beseech you. For I have heard
That by the simple fingering of a string,
Or delicate breath breathed along hollowed reeds,
Or blown into cold mouths of cunning bronze,
Those who are curious in this art can draw
Poor souls from prison-houses. I have heard also
How such strange magic lurks within these shells
And innocence puts vine-leaves in her hair,
And wantons like a maenad. Let that pass.
Your lute I know is chaste. And therefore play:
Ravish my ears with some sweet melody;
My soul is in a prison-house, and needs
Music to cure its madness. Good Bianca,
Entreat our guest to play.

BIANCA: Be not afraid,
Our well-loved guest will choose his place and moment:
That moment is not now. You weary him
With your uncouth insistence.

GUIDO: Honest Simone,
Some other night. Tonight I am content
With the low music of Bianca's voice,
Who, when she speaks, charms the too amorous air,
And makes the reeling earth stand still, or fix
His cycle round her beauty.[14]

SIMONE: You flatter her.
She has her virtues as most women have,
But beauty is a gem she may not wear.
It is better so, perchance.

Well, my dear lord,
If you will not draw melodies from your lute
To charm my moody and o'er-troubled soul
You'll drink with me at least? [*Sees table.*]

Your place is laid.

Fetch me a stool, Bianca. Close the shutters.
Set the great bar across. I would not have
The curious world with its small prying eyes
To peer upon our pleasure.
                              Now, my lord,
Give us a toast from a full brimming cup. [*Starts back.*]
What is this stain upon the cloth? It looks
As purple as a wound upon Christ's side.
Wine merely is it? I have heard it said
When wine is spilt blood is spilt also,
But that's a foolish tale.
                          My lord, I trust
My grape is to your liking? The wine of Naples
Is fiery like its mountains. Our Tuscan vineyards
Yield a more wholesome juice.
GUIDO: I like it well,
Honest Simone; and, with your good leave,
Will toast the fair Bianca when her lips
Have like red rose-leaves floated on this cup
And left its vintage sweeter. Taste, Bianca. [BIANCA *drinks.*]
Oh, all the honey of Hyblean bees,[15]
Matched with this draught were bitter!
                                      Good Simone,
You do not share the feast.
SIMONE: It is strange, my lord,
I cannot eat or drink with you tonight.
Some humour, or some fever in my blood,
At other seasons temperate, or some thought
That like an adder creeps from point to point,
That like a madman crawls from cell to cell,
Poisons my palate and makes appetite
A loathing, not a longing. [*Goes aside.*]
GUIDO: Sweet Bianca,
This common chapman wearies me with words.
I must go hence. Tomorrow I will come.
Tell me the hour.

BIANCA:　　　　　Come with the youngest dawn!
　Until I see you all my life is vain.
GUIDO: Ah! loose the falling midnight of your hair,
　And in those stars, your eyes, let me behold
　Mine image, as in mirrors. Dear Bianca,
　Though it be but a shadow, keep me there,
　Nor gaze at anything that does not show
　Some symbol of my semblance. I am jealous
　Of what your vision feasts on.
BIANCA:　　　　　　　Oh! be sure
　Your image will be with me always. Dear,
　Love can translate the very meanest thing
　Into a sign of sweet remembrances.
　But come before the lark with its shrill song
　Has waked a world of dreamers. I will stand
　Upon the balcony.
GUIDO:　　　　And by a ladder
　Wrought out of scarlet silk and sewn with pearls
　Will come to meet me. White foot after foot,
　Like snow upon a rose-tree.
BIANCA:　　　　　　As you will.
　You know that I am yours for love or Death.
GUIDO: Simone, I must go to mine house.
SIMONE: So soon? Why should you? the great Duomo's bell[16]
　Has not yet tolled its midnight, and the watchmen
　Who with their hollow horns mock the pale moon,
　Lie drowsy in their towers. Stay awhile.
　I fear we may not see you here again,
　And that fear saddens my too simple heart.
GUIDO: Be not afraid, Simone. I will stand
　Most constant in my friendship. But tonight
　I go to mine own home, and that at once.
　Tomorrow, sweet Bianca.
SIMONE:　　　　Well, well, so be it.
　I would have wished for fuller converse with you,
　My new friend, my honourable guest,

But that it seems may not be.

                    And besides,
I do not doubt your father waits for you,
Wearying for voice or footstep. You, I think,
Are his one child? He has no other child.
You are the gracious pillar of his house,
The flower of a garden full of weeds.
Your father's nephews do not love him well.
So run folk's tongues in Florence. I meant but that;
Men say they envy your inheritance
And look upon your vineyard with fierce eyes
As Ahab looked on Naboth's goodly field.[17]
But that is but the chatter of a town
Where women talk too much.

                       Good night, my lord.
Fetch a pine torch, Bianca. The old staircase
Is full of pitfalls, and the churlish moon
Grows, like a miser, niggard of her beams,
And hides her face behind a muslin mask
As harlots do when they go forth to snare
Some wretched soul in sin. Now, I will get
Your cloak and sword. Nay, pardon, my good Lord,
It is but meet that I should wait on you
Who have so honoured my poor burgher's house,
Drunk of my wine, and broken bread, and made
Yourself a sweet familiar. Oftentimes
My wife and I will talk of this fair night
And its great issues.

                  Why, what a sword is this!
Ferrara's[18] temper, pliant as a snake,
And deadlier, I doubt not. With such steel
One need fear nothing in the moil of life.
I never touched so delicate a blade.
I have a sword too, somewhat rusted now.
We men of peace are taught humility,
And to bear many burdens on our backs,

And not to murmur at an unjust world,
And to endure unjust indignities.
We are taught that, and like the patient Jew
Find profit in our pain.
                        Yet I remember
How once upon the road to Padua
A robber sought to take my pack-horse from me,
I slit his throat and left him. I can bear
Dishonour, public insult, many shames,
Shrill scorn and open contumely, but he
Who filches from me something that is mine,
Ay! though it be the meanest trencher-plate
From which I feed mine appetite – oh! he
Perils his soul and body in the theft
And dies for his small sin. From what strange clay
We men are moulded!

GUIDO: Why do you speak like this?

SIMONE: I wonder, my Lord Guido, if my sword
    Is better tempered than this steel of yours?
    Shall we make trial? Or is my state too low
    For you to cross your rapier against mine,
    In jest, or earnest?

GUIDO: Naught would please me better
    Than to stand fronting you with naked blade
    In jest, or earnest. Give me mine own sword.
    Fetch yours. Tonight will settle the great issue
    Whether the Prince's or the merchant's steel
    Is better tempered. Was not that your word?
    Fetch your own sword. Why do you tarry, sir?

SIMONE: My lord, of all the gracious courtesies
    That you have showered on my barren house
    This is the highest.
                        Bianca, fetch my sword.
    Thrust back that stool and table. We must have
    An open circle for our match at arms,
    And good Bianca here shall hold the torch

Lest what is but a jest grow serious.

BIANCA [*to* GUIDO]: Oh! kill him, kill him!

SIMONE: Hold the torch, Bianca. [*They begin to fight.*]

Have at you! Ah! Ha! would you?

[*He is wounded by* GUIDO.]

A scratch, no more. The torch was in mine eyes.

Do not look sad, Bianca. It is nothing.

Your husband bleeds, 'tis nothing. Take a cloth,

Bind it about mine arm. Nay, not so tight.

More softly, my good wife. And be not sad,

I pray you be not sad. No: take it off.

What matter if I bleed? [*Tears bandage off.*]

Again! again!

[SIMONE *disarms* GUIDO.]

My gentle Lord, you see that I was right.

My sword is better tempered, finer steel,

But let us match our daggers.

BIANCA [*to* GUIDO]: Kill him! kill him!

SIMONE: Put out the torch, Bianca. [BIANCA: *puts out torch.*]

Now, my good Lord,

Now to the death of one, or both of us,

Or all the three it may be. [*They fight.*]

There and there.

Ah, devil! do I hold thee in my grip?

[SIMONE *overpowers* GUIDO *and throws him down over table.*]

GUIDO: Fool! take your strangling fingers from my throat.

I am my father's only son; the State

Has but one heir, and that false enemy France

Waits for the ending of my father's line

To fall upon our city.

SIMONE: Hush! your father

When he is childless will be happier.

As for the State, I think our state of Florence

Needs no adulterous pilot at its helm.
Your life would soil its lilies.

GUIDO: Take off your hands.
Take off your damned hands. Loose me, I say!

SIMONE: Nay, you are caught in such a cunning vice
That nothing will avail you, and your life
Narrowed into a single point of shame
Ends with that shame and ends most shamefully.[19]

GUIDO: Oh! let me have a priest before I die!

SIMONE: What wouldst thou have a priest for? Tell thy sins
To God, whom thou shalt see this very night
And then no more for ever. Tell thy sins
To Him who is most just, being pitiless,
Most pitiful being just. As for myself . . .

GUIDO: Oh! help me, sweet Bianca! help me, Bianca,
Thou knowest I am innocent of harm.

SIMONE: What, is there life yet in those lying lips?
Die like a dog with lolling tongue! Die! Die!
And the dumb river shall receive your corse
And wash it all unheeded to the sea.

GUIDO: Lord Christ receive my wretched soul tonight! [*He dies*].

SIMONE: Amen to that. Now for the other.

[SIMONE *rises and looks at* BIANCA.[20] *She comes towards him as one dazed with wonder and with outstretched arms.*]

BIANCA: Why
Did you not tell me you were so strong?

SIMONE: Why
Did you not tell me you were beautiful?

[*He kisses her on the mouth.*]

CURTAIN

The Importance of Being Earnest

A TRIVIAL COMEDY
FOR SERIOUS PEOPLE

TO
ROBERT BALDWIN ROSS[1]
IN APPRECIATION
AND
AFFECTION

The Persons of the Play

JOHN WORTHING, J.P.

ALGERNON MONCRIEFF

REV. CANON CHASUBLE, D.D.

MERRIMAN, *Butler*

LANE, *Manservant*

LADY BRACKNELL

HON. GWENDOLEN FAIRFAX

CECILY CARDEW

MISS PRISM, *Governess*

FIRST ACT

Morning-room in Algernon's flat in Half-Moon Street.[1] *The room is*
luxuriously and artistically furnished. The sound of a piano is heard in
the adjoining room.

[LANE *is arranging afternoon tea on the table and, after the music has ceased,*
ALGERNON *enters.*]

ALGERNON: Did you hear what I was playing, Lane?

LANE: I didn't think it polite to listen, sir.

ALGERNON: I'm sorry for that, for your sake. I don't play accurately
– anyone can play accurately – but I play with wonderful expression.
As far as the piano is concerned, sentiment is my forte. I keep
science for Life.

LANE: Yes, sir.

ALGERNON: And, speaking of the science of Life, have you got the
cucumber sandwiches cut for Lady Bracknell?

LANE: Yes, sir. [*Hands them on a salver.*]

ALGERNON [*Inspects them, takes two and sits down on the sofa*]: Oh! . . . by
the way, Lane, I see from your book that on Thursday night, when
Lord Shoreman and Mr Worthing were dining with me, eight
bottles of champagne are entered as having been consumed.

LANE: Yes, sir; eight bottles and a pint.

ALGERNON: Why is it that at a bachelor's establishment the servants
invariably drink the champagne? I ask merely for information.

LANE: I attribute it to the superior quality of the wine, sir. I have often
observed that in married households the champagne is rarely of a
first-rate brand.

ALGERNON: Good heavens! Is marriage so demoralizing as that?[2]

LANE: I believe it *is* a very pleasant state, sir. I have had very little
experience of it myself up to the present. I have only been married

once. That was in consequence of a misunderstanding between myself and a young person.

ALGERNON [*languidly*]: I don't know that I am much interested in your family life, Lane.

LANE: No, sir; it is not a very interesting subject. I never think of it myself.

ALGERNON: Very natural, I am sure. That will do, Lane, thank you.[3]

LANE: Thank you, sir.

[LANE *goes out.*]

ALGERNON: Lane's views on marriage seem somewhat lax. Really, if the lower orders don't set us a good example, what on earth is the use of them? They seem, as a class, to have absolutely no sense of moral responsibility.

[*Enter* LANE.]

LANE: Mr Ernest Worthing.

[*Enter* JACK. LANE *goes out.*]

ALGERNON: How are you, my dear Ernest? What brings you up to town?

JACK: Oh, pleasure, pleasure! What else should bring one anywhere? Eating as usual, I see, Algy!

ALGERNON [*stiffly*]: I believe it is customary in good society to take some slight refreshment at five o'clock.[4] Where have you been since last Thursday?

JACK [*sitting down on the sofa*]: In the country.

ALGERNON: What on earth do you do there?

JACK [*pulling off his gloves*]: When one is in town one amuses oneself. When one is in the country one amuses other people. It is excessively boring.

ALGERNON: And who are the people you amuse?

JACK [*airily*]: Oh, neighbours, neighbours.

ALGERNON: Got nice neighbours in your part of Shropshire?

JACK: Perfectly horrid! Never speak to one of them.

ALGERNON: How immensely you must amuse them! [*Goes over and takes sandwich.*] By the way, Shropshire is your county, is it not?

JACK: Eh? Shropshire? Yes, of course. Hallo! Why all these cups? Why cucumber sandwiches? Why such reckless extravagance in one so young? Who is coming to tea?

ALGERNON: Oh! merely Aunt Augusta and Gwendolen.

JACK: How perfectly delightful!

ALGERNON: Yes, that is all very well; but I am afraid Aunt Augusta won't quite approve of your being here.

JACK: May I ask why?

ALGERNON: My dear fellow, the way you flirt with Gwendolen is perfectly disgraceful. It is almost as bad as the way Gwendolen flirts with you.

JACK: I am in love with Gwendolen. I have come up to town expressly to propose to her.

ALGERNON: I thought you had come up for pleasure? . . . I call that business.[5]

JACK: How utterly unromantic you are!

ALGERNON: I really don't see anything romantic in proposing. It is very romantic to be in love. But there is nothing romantic about a definite proposal. Why, one may be accepted. One usually is, I believe. Then the excitement is all over. The very essence of romance is uncertainty. If ever I get married, I'll certainly try to forget the fact.

JACK: I have no doubt about that, dear Algy. The Divorce Court was specially invented for people whose memories are so curiously constituted.

ALGERNON: Oh, there is no use speculating on that subject. Divorces are made in Heaven – [JACK *puts out his hand to take a sandwich.* ALGERNON *at once interferes.*] Please don't touch the cucumber sand-wiches. They are ordered specially for Aunt Augusta. [*Takes one and eats it.*]

JACK: Well, you have been eating them all the time.

ALGERNON: That is quite a different matter. She is my aunt. [*Takes plate from below.*] Have some bread and butter. The bread and butter is for Gwendolen. Gwendolen is devoted to bread and butter.

JACK [*advancing to table and helping himself*]: And very good bread and butter it is too.

ALGERNON: Well, my dear fellow, you need not eat as if you were going to eat it all. You behave as if you were married to her already. You are not married to her already, and I don't think you ever will be.

JACK: Why on earth do you say that?

ALGERNON: Well, in the first place, girls never marry the men they flirt with. Girls don't think it right.

JACK: Oh, that is nonsense!

ALGERNON: It isn't. It is a great truth. It accounts for the extraordinary number of bachelors that one sees all over the place. In the second place, I don't give my consent.

JACK: Your consent!

ALGERNON: My dear fellow, Gwendolen is my first cousin. And before I allow you to marry her, you will have to clear up the whole question of Cecily. [*Rings bell.*]

JACK: Cecily! What on earth do you mean? What do you mean, Algy, by Cecily! I don't know anyone of the name of Cecily.

[*Enter* LANE.]

ALGERNON: Bring me that cigarette case Mr Worthing left in the smoking-room the last time he dined here.

LANE: Yes, sir.

[LANE *goes out.*]

JACK: Do you mean to say you have had my cigarette case all this time? I wish to goodness you had let me know. I have been writing frantic letters to Scotland Yard[6] about it. I was very nearly offering a large reward.

ALGERNON: Well, I wish you would offer one. I happen to be more than usually hard up.

JACK: There is no good offering a large reward now that the thing is found.

[*Enter* LANE *with the cigarette case on a salver.* ALGERNON *takes it at once.* LANE *goes out.*]

ALGERNON: I think that is rather mean of you, Ernest, I must say.

[*Opens case and examines it.*] However, it makes no matter, for, now that I look at the inscription inside, I find that the thing isn't yours after all.

JACK: Of course it's mine. [*Moving to him.*] You have seen me with it a hundred times, and you have no right whatsoever to read what is written inside. It is a very ungentlemanly thing to read a private cigarette case.

ALGERNON: Oh! it is absurd to have a hard and fast rule about what one should read and what one shouldn't. More than half of modern culture depends on what one shouldn't read.[7]

JACK: I am quite aware of the fact, and I don't propose to discuss modern culture. It isn't the sort of thing one should talk of in private. I simply want my cigarette case back.

ALGERNON: Yes; but this isn't your cigarette case. This cigarette case is a present from someone of the name of Cecily, and you said you didn't know anyone of that name.

JACK: Well, if you want to know, Cecily happens to be my aunt.

ALGERNON: Your aunt!

JACK: Yes. Charming old lady she is, too. Lives at Tunbridge Wells.[8] Just give it back to me, Algy.

ALGERNON [*retreating to back of sofa*]: But why does she call herself little Cecily if she is your aunt and lives at Tunbridge Wells? [*Reading.*] 'From little Cecily with her fondest love'.

JACK [*moving to sofa and kneeling upon it*]: My dear fellow, what on earth is there in that? Some aunts are tall, some aunts are not tall. That is a matter that surely an aunt may be allowed to decide for herself. You seem to think that every aunt should be exactly like your aunt! That is absurd. For Heaven's sake give me back my cigarette case. [*Follows* ALGERNON *round the room.*]

ALGERNON: Yes. But why does your aunt call you her uncle? 'From little Cecily, with her fondest love to her dear Uncle Jack.' There is no objection, I admit, to an aunt being a small aunt, but why an aunt, no matter what her size may be, should call her own nephew her uncle, I can't quite make out. Besides, your name isn't Jack at all; it is Ernest.

JACK: It isn't Ernest; it's Jack.

ALGERNON: You have always told me it was Ernest. I have introduced you to every one as Ernest. You answer to the name of Ernest. You look as if your name was Ernest. You are the most earnest-looking person I ever saw in my life. It is perfectly absurd your saying that your name isn't Ernest. It's on your cards. Here is one of them. [*Taking it from case.*] 'Mr Ernest Worthing, B.4, The Albany.'⁹ I'll keep this as a proof that your name is Ernest if ever you attempt to deny it to me, or to Gwendolen, or to anyone else. [*Puts the card in his pocket.*]

JACK: Well, my name is Ernest in town and Jack in the country, and the cigarette case was given to me in the country.

ALGERNON: Yes, but that does not account for the fact that your small Aunt Cecily, who lives at Tunbridge Wells, calls you her dear uncle. Come, old boy, you had much better have the thing out at once.

JACK: My dear Algy, you talk exactly as if you were a dentist. It is very vulgar to talk like a dentist when one isn't a dentist. It produces a false impression.

ALGERNON: Well, that is exactly what dentists always do. Now, go on! Tell me the whole thing. I may mention that I have always suspected you of being a confirmed and secret Bunburyist; and I am quite sure of it now.

JACK: Bunburyist? What on earth do you mean by a Bunburyist?

ALGERNON: I'll reveal to you the meaning of that incomparable expression as soon as you are kind enough to inform me why you are Ernest in town and Jack in the country.

JACK: Well, produce my cigarette case first.

ALGERNON: Here it is. [*Hands cigarette case.*] Now produce your explanation, and pray make it improbable. [*Sits on sofa.*]

JACK: My dear fellow, there is nothing improbable about my explanation at all. In fact it's perfectly ordinary. Old Mr Thomas Cardew, who adopted me when I was a little boy, made me in his will guardian to his granddaughter, Miss Cecily Cardew. Cecily, who addresses me as her uncle from motives of respect that you could not possibly appreciate, lives at my place in the country under the charge of her admirable governess, Miss Prism.

ALGERNON: Where is that place in the country, by the way?

JACK: That is nothing to you, dear boy. You are not going to be invited . . . I may tell you candidly that the place is not in Shropshire.

ALGERNON: I suspected that, my dear fellow! I have Bunburyed all over Shropshire on two separate occasions. Now, go on. Why are you Ernest in town and Jack in the country?

JACK: My dear Algy, I don't know whether you will be able to understand my real motives. You are hardly serious enough. When one is placed in the position of guardian, one has to adopt a very high moral tone on all subjects. It's one's duty to do so. And as a high moral tone can hardly be said to conduce very much to either one's health or one's happiness, in order to get up to town I have always pretended to have a younger brother of the name of Ernest, who lives in the Albany, and gets into the most dreadful scrapes. That, my dear Algy, is the whole truth pure and simple.

ALGERNON: The truth is rarely pure and never simple.[10] Modern life would be very tedious if it were either, and modern literature a complete impossibility!

JACK: That wouldn't be at all a bad thing.

ALGERNON: Literary criticism is not your forte, my dear fellow. Don't try it. You should leave that to people who haven't been at a University. They do it so well in the daily papers. What you really are is a Bunburyist. I was quite right in saying you were a Bunburyist. You are one of the most advanced Bunburyists I know.

JACK: What on earth do you mean?

ALGERNON: You have invented a very useful younger brother called Ernest, in order that you may be able to come up to town as often as you like. I have invented an invaluable permanent invalid called Bunbury, in order that I may be able to go down into the country whenever I choose. Bunbury is perfectly invaluable. If it wasn't for Bunbury's extraordinary bad health, for instance, I wouldn't be able to dine with you at Willis's[11] tonight, for I have been really engaged to Aunt Augusta for more than a week.

JACK: I haven't asked you to dine with me anywhere tonight.

ALGERNON: I know. You are absurdly careless about sending out invitations. It is very foolish of you. Nothing annoys people so much as not receiving invitations.

JACK: You had much better dine with your Aunt Augusta.

ALGERNON: I haven't the smallest intention of doing anything of the kind. To begin with, I dined there on Monday, and once a week is quite enough to dine with one's own relations. In the second place, whenever I do dine there I am always treated as a member of the family, and sent down with either no woman at all, or two.[12] In the third place, I know perfectly well whom she will place me next to, tonight. She will place me next Mary Farquhar, who always flirts with her own husband across the dinner-table. That is not very pleasant. Indeed, it is not even decent – and that sort of thing is enormously on the increase. The amount of women in London who flirt with their own husbands is perfectly scandalous. It looks so bad. It is simply washing one's clean linen in public. Besides, now that I know you to be a confirmed Bunburyist I naturally want to talk to you about Bunburying. I want to tell you the rules.

JACK: I'm not a Bunburyist at all. If Gwendolen accepts me, I am going to kill my brother,[13] indeed I think I'll kill him in any case. Cecily is a little too much interested in him. It is rather a bore. So I am going to get rid of Ernest. And I strongly advise you to do the same with Mr . . . with your invalid friend who has the absurd name.

ALGERNON: Nothing will induce me to part with Bunbury, and if you ever get married, which seems to me extremely problematic, you will be very glad to know Bunbury. A man who marries without knowing Bunbury has a very tedious time of it.

JACK: That is nonsense. If I marry a charming girl like Gwendolen, and she is the only girl I ever saw in my life that I would marry, I certainly won't want to know Bunbury.

ALGERNON: Then your wife will. You don't seem to realize, that in married life three is company and two is none.

JACK [*sententiously*]: That, my dear young friend, is the theory that the corrupt French Drama[14] has been propounding for the last fifty years.

ALGERNON: Yes; and that the happy English home has proved in half the time.

JACK: For heaven's sake, don't try to be cynical. It's perfectly easy to be cynical.

ALGERNON: My dear fellow, it isn't easy to be anything nowadays. There's such a lot of beastly competition about. [*The sound of an electric bell is heard.*] Ah! that must be Aunt Augusta. Only relatives, or creditors, ever ring in that Wagnerian manner.[15] Now, if I get her out of the way for ten minutes, so that you can have an opportunity for proposing to Gwendolen, may I dine with you tonight at Willis's?

JACK: I suppose so, if you want to.

ALGERNON: Yes, but you must be serious about it. I hate people who are not serious about meals. It is so shallow of them.

[*Enter* LANE.]

LANE: Lady Bracknell and Miss Fairfax.

[ALGERNON *goes forward to meet them. Enter* LADY BRACKNELL *and* GWENDOLEN.]

LADY BRACKNELL: Good afternoon, dear Algernon, I hope you are behaving very well.

ALGERNON: I'm feeling very well, Aunt Augusta.

LADY BRACKNELL: That's not quite the same thing. In fact the two things rarely go together. [*Sees* JACK *and bows to him with icy coldness.*][16]

ALGERNON [*to* GWENDOLEN]: Dear me, you are smart!

GWENDOLEN: I am always smart! Am I not, Mr Worthing?

JACK: You're quite perfect, Miss Fairfax.

GWENDOLEN: Oh! I hope I am not that. It would leave no room for developments, and I intend to develop in many directions.

[GWENDOLEN *and* JACK *sit down together in the corner.*]

LADY BRACKNELL: I'm sorry if we are a little late, Algernon, but I was obliged to call on dear Lady Harbury.[17] I hadn't been there since her poor husband's death. I never saw a woman so altered; she looks quite twenty years younger. And now I'll have a cup of tea, and one of those nice cucumber sandwiches you promised me.

ALGERNON: Certainly, Aunt Augusta. [*Goes over to tea-table.*]

LADY BRACKNELL: Won't you come and sit here, Gwendolen?

GWENDOLEN: Thanks, mamma, I'm quite comfortable where I am.

ALGERNON [*picking up empty plate in horror*]: Good heavens! Lane! Why are there no cucumber sandwiches? I ordered them specially.

LANE [*gravely*]: There were no cucumbers in the market this morning, sir. I went down twice.

ALGERNON: No cucumbers!

LANE: No, sir. Not even for ready money.

ALGERNON: That will do, Lane, thank you.

LANE: Thank you, sir. [*Goes out.*]

ALGERNON: I am greatly distressed, Aunt Augusta, about there being no cucumbers, not even for ready money.

LADY BRACKNELL: It really makes no matter, Algernon. I had some crumpets with Lady Harbury, who seems to me to be living entirely for pleasure now.

ALGERNON: I hear her hair has turned quite gold from grief.

LADY BRACKNELL: It certainly has changed its colour. From what cause I, of course, cannot say. [ALGERNON *crosses and hands tea.*] Thank you. I've quite a treat for you tonight, Algernon. I am going to send you down with Mary Farquhar. She is such a nice woman, and so attentive to her husband. It's delightful to watch them.

ALGERNON: I am afraid, Aunt Augusta, I shall have to give up the pleasure of dining with you tonight after all.

LADY BRACKNELL [*frowning*]: I hope not, Algernon. It would put my table completely out.[18] Your uncle would have to dine upstairs. Fortunately he is accustomed to that.

ALGERNON: It is a great bore, and, I need hardly say, a terrible disappointment to me, but the fact is I have just had a telegram to say that my poor friend Bunbury is very ill again. [*Exchanges glances with* JACK.] They seem to think I should be with him.

LADY BRACKNELL: It is very strange. This Mr Bunbury seems to suffer from curiously bad health.

ALGERNON: Yes; poor Bunbury is a dreadful invalid.

LADY BRACKNELL: Well, I must say, Algernon, that I think it is high time that Mr Bunbury made up his mind whether he was going to live or to die. This shilly-shallying with the question is absurd. Nor do I in any way approve of the modern sympathy with invalids. I consider it morbid. Illness of any kind is hardly a thing to be encouraged in others. Health is the primary duty of life. I am always telling that to your poor uncle, but he never seems to take much notice . . . as far as any improvement in his ailment goes. I should be much obliged if you would ask Mr Bunbury, from me, to be kind enough not to have a relapse on Saturday, for I rely on you to arrange my music for me. It is my last reception, and one wants something that will encourage conversation, particularly at the end of the season when everyone has practically said whatever they had to say, which, in most cases, was probably not much.

ALGERNON: I'll speak to Bunbury, Aunt Augusta, if he is still conscious, and I think I can promise you he'll be all right by Saturday. Of course the music is a great difficulty. You see, if one plays good music, people don't listen, and if one plays bad music people don't talk. But I'll run over the programme I've drawn out, if you will kindly come into the next room for a moment.

LADY BRACKNELL: Thank you, Algernon. It is very thoughtful of you. [*Rising, and following* ALGERNON.] I'm sure the programme will be delightful, after a few expurgations. French songs I cannot possibly allow. People always seem to think that they are improper, and either look shocked, which is vulgar, or laugh, which is worse. But German sounds a thoroughly respectable language, and, indeed I believe is so. Gwendolen, you will accompany me.

GWENDOLEN: Certainly, mamma.

[LADY BRACKNELL *and* ALGERNON *go into the music-room,* GWENDOLEN *remains behind.*]

JACK: Charming day it has been, Miss Fairfax.

GWENDOLEN: Pray don't talk to me about the weather, Mr Worthing. Whenever people talk to me about the weather, I always feel quite certain that they mean something else. And that makes me so nervous.

JACK: I do mean something else.

GWENDOLEN: I thought so. In fact, I am never wrong.

JACK: And I would like to be allowed to take advantage of Lady Bracknell's temporary absence . . .

GWENDOLEN: I would certainly advise you to do so. Mamma has a way of coming back suddenly into a room that I have often had to speak to her about.[19]

JACK [*nervously*]: Miss Fairfax, ever since I met you I have admired you more than any girl . . . I have ever met since . . . I met you.

GWENDOLEN: Yes, I am quite well aware of the fact. And I often wish that in public, at any rate, you had been more demonstrative. For me you have always had an irresistible fascination. Even before I met you I was far from indifferent to you. [JACK *looks at her in amazement.*] We live, as I hope you know, Mr Worthing, in an age of ideals. The fact is constantly mentioned in the more expensive monthly magazines, and has reached the provincial pulpits, I am told; and my ideal has always been to love someone of the name of Ernest. There is something in that name that inspires absolute confidence. The moment Algernon first mentioned to me that he had a friend called Ernest, I knew I was destined to love you.

JACK: You really love me, Gwendolen?[20]

GWENDOLEN: Passionately!

JACK: Darling! You don't know how happy you've made me.

GWENDOLEN: My own Ernest!

JACK: But you don't really mean to say that you couldn't love me if my name wasn't Ernest?

GWENDOLEN: But your name is Ernest.

JACK: Yes, I know it is. But supposing it was something else? Do you mean to say you couldn't love me then?

GWENDOLEN [*glibly*]: Ah! that is clearly a metaphysical speculation, and like most metaphysical speculations has very little reference at all to the actual facts of real life, as we know them.

JACK: Personally, darling, to speak quite candidly, I don't much care about the name of Ernest . . . I don't think the name suits me at all.

GWENDOLEN: It suits you perfectly. It is a divine name. It has a music of its own. It produces vibrations.

JACK: Well, really, Gwendolen, I must say that I think there are lots of other much nicer names. I think Jack, for instance, a charming name.

GWENDOLEN: Jack? . . . No, there is very little music in the name Jack,

if any at all, indeed. It does not thrill. It produces absolutely no
vibrations . . . I have known several Jacks, and they all, without
exception, were more than usually plain. Besides, Jack is a notorious
domesticity for John! And I pity any woman who is married to a
man called John. She would probably never be allowed to know
the entrancing pleasure of a single moment's solitude. The only
really safe name is Ernest.

JACK: Gwendolen, I must get christened at once – I mean we must
get married at once. There is no time to be lost.

GWENDOLEN: Married, Mr Worthing?

JACK [*astounded*]: Well . . . surely. You know that I love you, and you
led me to believe, Miss Fairfax, that you were not absolutely
indifferent to me.

GWENDOLEN: I adore you. But you haven't proposed to me yet.
Nothing has been said at all about marriage. The subject has not
even been touched on.

JACK: Well . . . may I propose to you now?

GWENDOLEN: I think it would be an admirable opportunity. And to
spare you any possible disappointment, Mr Worthing, I think it
only fair to tell you quite frankly beforehand that I am fully
determined to accept you.

JACK: Gwendolen!

GWENDOLEN: Yes, Mr Worthing, what have you got to say to me?

JACK: You know what I have got to say to you.

GWENDOLEN: Yes, but you don't say it.

JACK: Gwendolen, will you marry me? [*Goes on his knees.*]

GWENDOLEN: Of course I will, darling. How long you have been about
it! I am afraid you have had very little experience in how to propose.

JACK: My own one, I have never loved anyone in the world but you.

GWENDOLEN: Yes, but men often propose for practice. I know my
brother Gerald does. All my girl-friends tell me so. What wonderfully blue eyes you have, Ernest! They are quite, quite blue. I hope
you will always look at me just like that, especially when there are
other people present.

[*Enter* LADY BRACKNELL.]

LADY BRACKNELL: Mr Worthing! Rise, sir, from this semi-recumbent posture. It is most indecorous.

GWENDOLEN: Mamma! [*He tries to rise; she restrains him.*]²¹ I must beg you to retire. This is no place for you. Besides, Mr Worthing has not quite finished yet.

LADY BRACKNELL: Finished what, may I ask?

GWENDOLEN: I am engaged to Mr Worthing, mamma. [*They rise together.*]

LADY BRACKNELL: Pardon me, you are not engaged to anyone. When you do become engaged to someone, I, or your father, should his health permit him, will inform you of the fact. An engagement should come on a young girl as a surprise, pleasant or unpleasant, as the case may be. It is hardly a matter that she could be allowed to arrange for herself . . . And now I have a few questions to put to you, Mr Worthing. While I am making these inquiries, you, Gwendolen, will wait for me below in the carriage.

GWENDOLEN [*reproachfully*]: Mamma!

LADY BRACKNELL: In the carriage, Gwendolen! [GWENDOLEN *goes to the door. She and* JACK *blow kisses to each other behind* LADY BRACKNELL'S *back.* LADY BRACKNELL *looks vaguely about as if she could not understand what the noise was. Finally turns round.*] Gwendolen, the carriage!

GWENDOLEN: Yes, mamma. [*Goes out, looking back at* JACK.]

LADY BRACKNELL [*sitting down*]: You can take a seat, Mr Worthing.

[*Looks in her pocket for notebook and pencil.*]

JACK: Thank you, Lady Bracknell, I prefer standing.

LADY BRACKNELL [*pencil and notebook in hand*]: I feel bound to tell you that you are not down on my list of eligible young men, although I have the same list as the dear Duchess of Bolton has. We work together, in fact. However, I am quite ready to enter your name, should your answers be what a really affectionate mother requires. Do you smoke?

JACK: Well, yes, I must admit I smoke.

LADY BRACKNELL: I am glad to hear it. A man should always have an occupation of some kind. There are far too many idle men in London as it is. How old are you?

JACK: Twenty-nine.

LADY BRACKNELL: A very good age to be married at. I have always been of opinion that a man who desires to get married should know either everything or nothing. Which do you know?

JACK [*after some hesitation*]: I know nothing, Lady Bracknell.

LADY BRACKNELL: I am pleased to hear it. I do not approve of anything that tampers with natural ignorance. Ignorance is like a delicate exotic fruit; touch it and the bloom is gone. The whole theory of modern education is radically unsound. Fortunately in England, at any rate, education produces no effect whatsoever. If it did, it would prove a serious danger to the upper classes, and probably lead to acts of violence in Grosvenor Square.[22] What is your income?

JACK: Between seven and eight thousand a year.[23]

LADY BRACKNELL [*makes a note in her book*]: In land, or in investments?

JACK: In investments, chiefly.

LADY BRACKNELL: That is satisfactory. What between the duties expected of one during one's lifetime, and the duties exacted from one after one's death, land has ceased to be either a profit or a pleasure. It gives one position, and prevents one from keeping it up. That's all that can be said about land.

JACK: I have a country house with some land, of course, attached to it, about fifteen hundred acres, I believe; but I don't depend on that for my real income. In fact, as far as I can make out, the poachers are the only people who make anything out of it.

LADY BRACKNELL: A country house! How many bedrooms? Well, that point can be cleared up afterwards. You have a town house, I hope? A girl with a simple, unspoiled nature, like Gwendolen, could hardly be expected to reside in the country.

JACK: Well, I own a house in Belgrave Square, but it is let by the year to Lady Bloxham. Of course, I can get it back whenever I like, at six months' notice.

LADY BRACKNELL: Lady Bloxham? I don't know her.

JACK: Oh, she goes about very little. She is a lady considerably advanced in years.

LADY BRACKNELL: Ah, nowadays that is no guarantee of respectability of character. What number in Belgrave Square?

JACK: 149.

LADY BRACKNELL [*shaking her head*]: The unfashionable side. I thought there was something. However, that could easily be altered.

JACK: Do you mean the fashion, or the side?

LADY BRACKNELL [*sternly*]: Both, if necessary, I presume. What are your politics?

JACK: Well, I am afraid I really have none. I am a Liberal Unionist.[24]

LADY BRACKNELL: Oh, they count as Tories. They dine with us. Or come in the evening, at any rate. Now to minor matters. Are your parents living?

JACK: I have lost both my parents.

LADY BRACKNELL: Both? To lose one parent may be regarded as a misfortune; to lose *both* looks like carelessness.[25] Who was your father? He was evidently a man of some wealth. Was he born in what the Radical papers call the purple of commerce, or did he rise from the ranks of the aristocracy?

JACK: I am afraid I really don't know. The fact is, Lady Bracknell, I said I had lost my parents. It would be nearer the truth to say that my parents seem to have lost me . . . I don't actually know who I am by birth. I was . . . well, I was found.

LADY BRACKNELL: Found!

JACK: The late Mr Thomas Cardew, an old gentleman of a very charitable and kindly disposition, found me, and gave me the name of Worthing, because he happened to have a first-class ticket for Worthing in his pocket at the time. Worthing is a place in Sussex. It is a seaside resort.

LADY BRACKNELL: Where did the charitable gentleman who had a first-class ticket for this seaside resort find you?

JACK [*gravely*]: In a hand-bag.

LADY BRACKNELL: A hand-bag?

JACK [*very seriously*]: Yes, Lady Bracknell. I was in a hand-bag – a somewhat large, black leather hand-bag, with handles to it – an ordinary hand-bag in fact.

LADY BRACKNELL: In what locality did this Mr James, or Thomas, Cardew come across this ordinary hand-bag?

JACK: In the cloak-room at Victoria Station. It was given to him in mistake for his own.

LADY BRACKNELL: The cloak-room at Victoria Station?

JACK: Yes. The Brighton line.

LADY BRACKNELL: The line is immaterial. Mr Worthing, I confess I feel somewhat bewildered by what you have just told me. To be born, or at any rate bred, in a hand-bag, whether it had handles or not, seems to me to display a contempt for the ordinary decencies of family life that reminds one of the worst excesses of the French Revolution. And I presume you know what that unfortunate movement led to? As for the particular locality in which the hand-bag was found, a cloak-room at a railway station might serve to conceal a social indiscretion – has probably, indeed, been used for that purpose before now – but it could hardly be regarded as an assured basis for a recognized position in good society.

JACK: May I ask you then what you would advise me to do? I need hardly say I would do anything in the world to ensure Gwendolen's happiness.

LADY BRACKNELL: I would strongly advise you, Mr Worthing, to try and acquire some relations as soon as possible, and to make a definite effort to produce at any rate one parent, of either sex, before the season is quite over.

JACK: Well, I don't see how I could possibly manage to do that. I can produce the hand-bag at any moment. It is in my dressing-room at home. I really think that should satisfy you, Lady Bracknell.

LADY BRACKNELL: Me, sir! What has it to do with me? You can hardly imagine that I and Lord Bracknell would dream of allowing our only daughter – a girl brought up with the utmost care – to marry into a cloak-room, and form an alliance with a parcel. Good morning, Mr Worthing!

[LADY BRACKNELL *sweeps out in majestic indignation.*]

JACK: Good morning! [ALGERNON, *from the other room, strikes up the Wedding March.*[26] JACK *looks perfectly furious, and goes to the door.*] For goodness' sake don't play that ghastly tune, Algy! How idiotic you are!

[*The music stops and* ALGERNON *enters cheerily.*]

ALGERNON: Didn't it go off all right, old boy? You don't mean to say Gwendolen refused you? I know it is a way she has. She is always refusing people. I think it is most ill-natured of her.

JACK: Oh, Gwendolen is as right as a trivet. As far as she is concerned, we are engaged. Her mother is perfectly unbearable. Never met such a Gorgon[27]. . . I don't really know what a Gorgon is like, but I am quite sure that Lady Bracknell is one. In any case, she is a monster, without being a myth, which is rather unfair . . . I beg your pardon, Algy, I suppose I shouldn't talk about your own aunt in that way before you.

ALGERNON: My dear boy, I love hearing my relations abused. It is the only thing that makes me put up with them at all. Relations are simply a tedious pack of people, who haven't got the remotest knowledge of how to live, nor the smallest instinct about when to die.

JACK: Oh, that is nonsense!

ALGERNON: It isn't!

JACK: Well, I won't argue about the matter. You always want to argue about things.

ALGERNON: That is exactly what things were originally made for.

JACK: Upon my word, if I thought that, I'd shoot myself . . . [*A pause.*] You don't think there is any chance of Gwendolen becoming like her mother in about a hundred and fifty years, do you, Algy?

ALGERNON: All women become like their mothers. That is their tragedy. No man does. That's his.

JACK: Is that clever?

ALGERNON: It is perfectly phrased! and quite as true as any observation in civilized life should be.

JACK: I am sick to death of cleverness. Everybody is clever nowadays. You can't go anywhere without meeting clever people. The thing has become an absolute public nuisance. I wish to goodness we had a few fools left.

ALGERNON: We have.

JACK: I should extremely like to meet them. What do they talk about?

ALGERNON: The fools? Oh! about the clever people, of course.

JACK: What fools!

ALGERNON: By the way, did you tell Gwendolen the truth about your being Ernest in town, and Jack in the country?

JACK [in a very patronizing manner]: My dear fellow, the truth isn't quite the sort of thing one tells to a nice, sweet, refined girl. What extraordinary ideas you have about the way to behave to a woman!

ALGERNON: The only way to behave to a woman is to make love to her, if she is pretty, and to someone else if she is plain.

JACK: Oh, that is nonsense.

ALGERNON: What about your brother? What about the profligate Ernest?

JACK: Oh, before the end of the week I shall have got rid of him. I'll say he died in Paris of apoplexy. Lots of people die of apoplexy, quite suddenly, don't they?

ALGERNON: Yes, but it's hereditary, my dear fellow. It's a sort of thing that runs in families. You had much better say a severe chill.

JACK: You are sure a severe chill isn't hereditary, or anything of that kind?

ALGERNON: Of course it isn't!

JACK: Very well, then. My poor brother Ernest is carried off suddenly in Paris, by a severe chill. That gets rid of him.

ALGERNON: But I thought you said that . . . Miss Cardew was a little too much interested in your poor brother Ernest? Won't she feel his loss a good deal?

JACK: Oh, that is all right. Cecily is not a silly romantic girl, I am glad to say. She has got a capital appetite, goes long walks and pays no attention at all to her lessons.

ALGERNON: I would rather like to see Cecily.

JACK: I will take very good care you never do. She is excessively pretty, and she is only just eighteen.[28]

ALGERNON: Have you told Gwendolen yet that you have an excessively pretty ward who is only just eighteen?

JACK: Oh! one doesn't blurt these things out to people. Cecily and Gwendolen are perfectly certain to be extremely great friends. I'll bet you anything you like that half an hour after they have met, they will be calling each other sister.

ALGERNON: Women only do that when they have called each other a lot of other things first.[29] Now, my dear boy, if we want to get a good table at Willis's, we really must go and dress. Do you know it is nearly seven?

JACK [*irritably*]: Oh! it always is nearly seven.

ALGERNON: Well, I'm hungry.

JACK: I never knew you when you weren't . . .

ALGERNON: What shall we do after dinner? Go to a theatre?

JACK: Oh, no! I loathe listening.

ALGERNON: Well, let us go to the Club?

JACK: Oh, no! I hate talking.

ALGERNON: Well, we might trot round to the Empire[30] at ten?

JACK: Oh, no! I can't bear looking at things. It is so silly.

ALGERNON: Well, what shall we do?

JACK: Nothing!

ALGERNON: It is awfully hard work doing nothing. However, I don't mind hard work where there is no definite object of any kind.

[*Enter* LANE.]

LANE: Miss Fairfax.

[*Enter* GWENDOLEN. LANE *goes out.*]

ALGERNON: Gwendolen, upon my word!

GWENDOLEN: Algy, kindly turn your back. I have something very particular to say to Mr Worthing.

ALGERNON: Really, Gwendolen, I don't think I can allow this at all.

GWENDOLEN: Algy, you always adopt a strictly immoral attitude towards life. You are not quite old enough to do that. [ALGERNON *retires to the fireplace.*]

JACK: My own darling!

GWENDOLEN: Ernest, we may never be married. From the expression on mamma's face I fear we never shall. Few parents nowadays pay any regard to what their children say to them. The old-fashioned respect for the young is fast dying out. Whatever influence I ever had over mamma, I lost at the age of three. But although she may prevent us from becoming man and wife, and I may marry someone else, and marry often, nothing that she can possibly do can alter my eternal devotion to you.

JACK: Dear Gwendolen!

GWENDOLEN: The story of your romantic origin, as related to me by mamma, with unpleasing comments, has naturally stirred the deeper fibres of my nature. Your Christian name has an irresistible fascination. The simplicity of your character makes you exquisitely incomprehensible to me. Your town address at the Albany I have. What is your address in the country?

JACK: The Manor House, Woolton, Hertfordshire.

[ALGERNON, *who has been carefully listening, smiles to himself, and writes the address on his shirt-cuff. Then picks up the Railway Guide.*]

GWENDOLEN: There is a good postal service, I suppose? It may be necessary to do something desperate. That of course will require serious consideration. I will communicate with you daily.

JACK: My own one!

GWENDOLEN: How long do you remain in town?

JACK: Till Monday.

GWENDOLEN: Good! Algy, you may turn round now.

ALGERNON: Thanks, I've turned round already.

GWENDOLEN: You may also ring the bell.

JACK: You will let me see you to your carriage, my own darling?

GWENDOLEN: Certainly.

JACK [*to* LANE, *who now enters*]: I will see Miss Fairfax out.

LANE: Yes, sir. [JACK *and* GWENDOLEN *go off.*]

[LANE *presents several letters on a salver to* ALGERNON. *It is to be surmised that they are bills, as* ALGERNON, *after looking at the envelopes, tears them up.*]

ALGERNON: A glass of sherry, Lane.

LANE: Yes, sir.

ALGERNON: Tomorrow, Lane, I'm going Bunburying.

LANE: Yes, sir.

ALGERNON: I shall probably not be back till Monday. You can put up my dress clothes, my smoking jacket,[31] and all the Bunbury suits . . .

LANE: Yes, sir. [*Handing sherry.*]

ALGERNON: I hope tomorrow will be a fine day, Lane.

LANE: It never is, sir.

ALGERNON: Lane, you're a perfect pessimist.

LANE: I do my best to give satisfaction, sir.

[*Enter* JACK. LANE *goes off.*]

JACK: There's a sensible, intellectual girl! the only girl I ever cared for in my life. [ALGERNON *is laughing immoderately.*] What on earth are you so amused at?

ALGERNON: Oh, I'm a little anxious about poor Bunbury, that is all.

JACK: If you don't take care, your friend Bunbury will get you into a serious scrape some day.

ALGERNON: I love scrapes. They are the only things that are never serious.

JACK: Oh, that's nonsense, Algy. You never talk anything but nonsense.

ALGERNON: Nobody ever does.

[JACK *looks indignantly at him, and leaves the room.* ALGERNON *lights a cigarette, reads his shirt-cuff and smiles.*][32]

ACT DROP

SECOND ACT

SCENE

Garden at the Manor House. A flight of grey stone steps leads up to the house. The garden, an old-fashioned one, full of roses. Time of year, July. Basket chairs, and a table covered with books, are set under a large yew-tree.

[MISS PRISM *discovered seated at the table.* CECILY *is at the back, watering flowers.*]

MISS PRISM [*calling*]: Cecily, Cecily! Surely such a utilitarian occupation as the watering of flowers is rather Moulton's duty than yours? Especially at a moment when intellectual pleasures await you. Your German grammar is on the table. Pray open it at page fifteen. We will repeat yesterday's lesson.

CECILY [*coming over very slowly*]: But I don't like German. It isn't at all a becoming language. I know perfectly well that I look quite plain after my German lesson.

MISS PRISM: Child, you know how anxious your guardian is that you should improve yourself in every way. He laid particular stress on your German, as he was leaving for town yesterday. Indeed, he always lays stress on your German when he is leaving for town.[1]

CECILY: Dear Uncle Jack is so very serious! Sometimes he is so serious that I think he cannot be quite well.

MISS PRISM [*drawing herself up*]: Your guardian enjoys the best of health, and his gravity of demeanour is especially to be commended in one so comparatively young as he is. I know no one who has a higher sense of duty and responsibility.

CECILY: I suppose that is why he often looks a little bored when we three are together.

MISS PRISM: Cecily! I am surprised at you. Mr Worthing has many troubles in his life. Idle merriment and triviality would be out of place in his conversation. You must remember his constant anxiety about that unfortunate young man his brother.

CECILY: I wish Uncle Jack would allow that unfortunate young man, his brother, to come down here sometimes. We might have a good influence over him, Miss Prism. I am sure you certainly would. You know German, and geology, and things of that kind influence a man very much. [CECILY *begins to write in her diary.*]

MISS PRISM [*shaking her head*]: I do not think that even I could produce any effect on a character that according to his own brother's admission is irretrievably weak and vacillating. Indeed I am not sure that I would desire to reclaim him. I am not in favour of this modern mania for turning bad people into good people at a moment's notice. As a man sows so let him reap.[2] You must put away your diary, Cecily. I really don't see why you should keep a diary at all.

CECILY: I keep a diary in order to enter the wonderful secrets of my life. If I didn't write them down, I should probably forget all about them.

MISS PRISM: Memory, my dear Cecily, is the diary that we all carry about with us.

CECILY: Yes, but it usually chronicles the things that have never happened, and couldn't possibly have happened. I believe that Memory is responsible for nearly all the three-volume novels that Mudie[3] sends us.

MISS PRISM: Do not speak slightingly of the three-volume novel, Cecily. I wrote one myself in earlier days.

CECILY: Did you really, Miss Prism? How wonderfully clever you are! I hope it did not end happily? I don't like novels that end happily. They depress me so much.

MISS PRISM: The good ended happily, and the bad unhappily. That is what Fiction means.

CECILY: I suppose so. But it seems very unfair. And was your novel ever published?

MISS PRISM: Alas! no. The manuscript unfortunately was abandoned. [CECILY *starts.*] I used the word in the sense of lost or mislaid. To your work, child, these speculations are profitless.

CECILY [*smiling*]: But I see dear Dr Chasuble coming up through the garden.

MISS PRISM [*rising and advancing*]: Dr Chasuble! This is indeed a pleasure.

[*Enter* CANON CHASUBLE.]

CHASUBLE: And how are we this morning? Miss Prism, you are, I trust, well?

CECILY: Miss Prism has just been complaining of a slight headache. I think it would do her so much good to have a short stroll with you in the Park, Dr Chasuble.

MISS PRISM: Cecily, I have not mentioned anything about a headache.

CECILY: No, dear Miss Prism, I know that, but I felt instinctively that you had a headache. Indeed I was thinking about that, and not about my German lesson, when the Rector came in.

CHASUBLE: I hope, Cecily, you are not inattentive.

CECILY: Oh, I am afraid I am.

CHASUBLE: That is strange. Were I fortunate enough to be Miss Prism's pupil, I would hang upon her lips. [MISS PRISM *glares*.] I spoke metaphorically. – My metaphor was drawn from bees. Ahem! Mr Worthing, I suppose, has not returned from town yet?

MISS PRISM: We do not expect him till Monday afternoon.

CHASUBLE: Ah yes, he usually likes to spend his Sunday in London. He is not one of those whose sole aim is enjoyment, as, by all accounts, that unfortunate young man his brother seems to be. But I must not disturb Egeria and her pupil any longer.

MISS PRISM: Egeria? My name is Laetitia,[4] Doctor.

CHASUBLE [*bowing*]: A classical allusion merely, drawn from the Pagan authors. I shall see you both no doubt at Evensong?

MISS PRISM: I think, dear Doctor, I will have a stroll with you. I find I have a headache after all, and a walk might do it good.

CHASUBLE: With pleasure, Miss Prism, with pleasure. We might go as far as the schools and back.

MISS PRISM: That would be delightful. Cecily, you will read your Political Economy in my absence. The chapter on the Fall of the Rupee you may omit. It is somewhat too sensational.[5] Even these metallic problems have their melodramatic side.

[*Goes down the garden with* DR CHASUBLE.]

CECILY [*picks up books and throws them back on table*]: Horrid Political Economy! Horrid Geography! Horrid, horrid German!

[*Enter* MERRIMAN *with a card on a salver.*]

MERRIMAN: Mr Ernest Worthing has just driven over from the station.[6] He has brought his luggage with him.

CECILY [*takes the card and reads it*]: 'Mr Ernest Worthing, B.4, The Albany, W.' Uncle Jack's brother! Did you tell him Mr Worthing was in town?

MERRIMAN: Yes, Miss. He seemed very much disappointed. I mentioned that you and Miss Prism were in the garden. He said he was anxious to speak to you privately for a moment.

CECILY: Ask Mr Ernest Worthing to come here. I suppose you had better talk to the housekeeper about a room for him.

MERRIMAN: Yes, Miss. [MERRIMAN *goes off.*]

CECILY: I have never met any really wicked person before. I feel rather frightened. I am so afraid he will look just like every one else.

[*Enter* ALGERNON, *very gay and debonair.*]

He does![7]

ALGERNON [*raising his hat*]: You are my little cousin Cecily, I'm sure.

CECILY: You are under some strange mistake. I am not little. In fact, I believe I am more than usually tall for my age. [ALGERNON *is rather taken aback.*] But I am your cousin Cecily. You, I see from your card, are Uncle Jack's brother, my cousin Ernest, my wicked cousin Ernest.

ALGERNON: Oh! I am not really wicked at all, cousin Cecily. You mustn't think that I am wicked.

CECILY: If you are not, then you have certainly been deceiving us all in a very inexcusable manner. I hope you have not been leading a double life, pretending to be wicked and being really good all the time. That would be hypocrisy.

ALGERNON [*looks at her in amazement*]: Oh! Of course I have been rather reckless.

CECILY: I am glad to hear it.

ALGERNON: In fact, now you mention the subject, I have been very bad in my own small way.

CECILY: I don't think you should be so proud of that, though I am sure it must have been very pleasant.

ALGERNON: It is much pleasanter being here with you.

CECILY: I can't understand how you are here at all. Uncle Jack won't be back till Monday afternoon.

ALGERNON: That is a great disappointment. I am obliged to go up by the first train on Monday morning. I have a business appointment that I am anxious . . . to miss!

CECILY: Couldn't you miss it anywhere but in London?

ALGERNON: No: the appointment is in London.

CECILY: Well, I know, of course, how important it is not to keep a business engagement, if one wants to retain any sense of the beauty of life, but still I think you had better wait till Uncle Jack arrives. I know he wants to speak to you about your emigrating.[8]

ALGERNON: About my what?

CECILY: Your emigrating. He has gone up to buy your outfit.

ALGERNON: I certainly wouldn't let Jack buy my outfit. He has no taste in neckties at all.

CECILY: I don't think you will require neckties. Uncle Jack is sending you to Australia.

ALGERNON: Australia! I'd sooner die.

CECILY: Well, he said at dinner on Wednesday night, that you would have to choose between this world, the next world and Australia.

ALGERNON: Oh, well! The accounts I have received of Australia and the next world are not particularly encouraging. This world is good enough for me, Cousin Cecily.

CECILY: Yes, but are you good enough for it?

ALGERNON: I'm afraid I'm not that. That is why I want you to reform me. You might make that your mission, if you don't mind, Cousin Cecily.

CECILY: I'm afraid I've no time, this afternoon.

ALGERNON: Well, would you mind my reforming myself this afternoon?

CECILY: It is rather Quixotic[9] of you. But I think you should try.

ALGERNON: I will. I feel better already.

CECILY: You are looking a little worse.

ALGERNON: That is because I am hungry.

CECILY: How thoughtless of me. I should have remembered that when one is going to lead an entirely new life, one requires regular and wholesome meals. Won't you come in?

ALGERNON: Thank you. Might I have a buttonhole first? I have never any appetite unless I have a buttonhole first.

CECILY: A Maréchal Niel?[10] [*Picks up scissors.*]

ALGERNON: No, I'd sooner have a pink rose.

CECILY: Why? [*Cuts a flower.*]

ALGERNON: Because you are like a pink rose, Cousin Cecily.

CECILY: I don't think it can be right for you to talk to me like that. Miss Prism never says such things to me.

ALGERNON: Then Miss Prism is a short-sighted old lady. [CECILY *puts the rose in his buttonhole.*] You are the prettiest girl I ever saw.

CECILY: Miss Prism says that all good looks are a snare.

ALGERNON: They are a snare that every sensible man would like to be caught in.

CECILY: Oh, I don't think I would care to catch a sensible man. I shouldn't know what to talk to him about.

[*They pass into the house.* MISS PRISM *and* DR CHASUBLE *return.*]

MISS PRISM: You are too much alone, dear Dr Chasuble. You should get married. A misanthrope I can understand – a womanthrope, never!

CHASUBLE [*with a scholar's shudder*]: Believe me, I do not deserve so neologistic a phrase. The precept as well as the practice of the Primitive Church was distinctly against matrimony.

MISS PRISM [*sententiously*]: That is obviously the reason why the Primitive Church has not lasted up to the present day. And you do not seem to realize, dear Doctor, that by persistently remaining single, a man converts himself into a permanent public temptation. Men should be more careful; this very celibacy leads weaker vessels astray.

CHASUBLE: But is a man not equally attractive when married?

MISS PRISM: No married man is ever attractive except to his wife.

CHASUBLE: And often, I've been told, not even to her.

MISS PRISM: That depends on the intellectual sympathies of the woman. Maturity can always be depended on. Ripeness can be trusted. Young women are green. [DR CHASUBLE *starts*.] I spoke horti-culturally. My metaphor was drawn from fruits. But where is Cecily?

CHASUBLE: Perhaps she followed us to the schools.

[*Enter* JACK *slowly from the back of the garden. He is dressed in the deepest mourning, with crêpe hatband and black gloves.*][11]

MISS PRISM: Mr Worthing!

CHASUBLE: Mr Worthing?

MISS PRISM: This is indeed a surprise. We did not look for you till Monday afternoon.

JACK [*shakes* MISS PRISM's *hand in a tragic manner*]: I have returned sooner than I expected. Dr Chasuble, I hope you are well?

CHASUBLE: Dear Mr Worthing, I trust this garb of woe does not betoken some terrible calamity?

JACK: My brother.

MISS PRISM: More shameful debts and extravagance?

CHASUBLE: Still leading his life of pleasure?

JACK [*shaking his head*]: Dead!

CHASUBLE: Your brother Ernest dead?

JACK: Quite dead.

MISS PRISM: What a lesson for him! I trust he will profit by it.

CHASUBLE: Mr Worthing, I offer you my sincere condolence. You have at least the consolation of knowing that you were always the most generous and forgiving of brothers.

JACK: Poor Ernest! He had many faults, but it is a sad, sad blow.[12]

CHASUBLE: Very sad indeed. Were you with him at the end?

JACK: No. He died abroad; in Paris, in fact. I had a telegram last night from the manager of the Grand Hotel.

CHASUBLE: Was the cause of death mentioned?

JACK: A severe chill, it seems.

MISS PRISM: As a man sows, so shall he reap.

CHASUBLE [*raising his hand*]: Charity, dear Miss Prism, charity! None of us are perfect. I myself am peculiarly susceptible to draughts. Will the interment take place here?

JACK: No. He seems to have expressed a desire to be buried in Paris.

CHASUBLE: In Paris! [*Shakes his head.*] I fear that hardly points to any very serious state of mind at the last. You would no doubt wish me to make some slight allusion to this tragic domestic affliction next Sunday. [JACK *presses his hand convulsively.*] My sermon on the meaning of the manna in the wilderness[13] can be adapted to almost any occasion, joyful, or, as in the present case, distressing. [*All sigh.*] I have preached it at harvest celebrations, christenings, confirmations, on days of humiliation and festal days. The last time I delivered it was in the Cathedral, as a charity sermon on behalf of the Society for the Prevention of Discontent among the Upper Orders. The Bishop, who was present, was much struck by some of the analogies I drew.

JACK: Ah! that reminds me, you mentioned christenings, I think, Dr Chasuble? I suppose you know how to christen all right? [DR CHASUBLE *looks astounded.*] I mean, of course, you are continually christening, aren't you?

MISS PRISM: It is, I regret to say, one of the Rector's most constant duties in this parish. I have often spoken to the poorer classes on the subject. But they don't seem to know what thrift is.

CHASUBLE: But is there any particular infant in whom you are interested, Mr Worthing? Your brother was, I believe, unmarried, was he not?

JACK: Oh, yes.

MISS PRISM [*bitterly*]: People who live entirely for pleasure usually are.

JACK: But it is not for any child, dear Doctor. I am very fond of children. No! the fact is, I would like to be christened myself, this afternoon, if you have nothing better to do.

CHASUBLE: But surely, Mr Worthing, you have been christened already?

JACK: I don't remember anything about it.

CHASUBLE: But have you any grave doubts on the subject?

JACK: I certainly intend to have. Of course I don't know if the thing would bother you in any way, or if you think I am a little too old now.

CHASUBLE: Not at all. The sprinkling, and indeed, the immersion of adults is a perfectly canonical practice.

JACK: Immersion!

CHASUBLE: You need have no apprehensions. Sprinkling is all that is necessary, or indeed I think advisable. Our weather is so changeable. At what hour would you wish the ceremony performed?

JACK: Oh, I might trot round about five if that would suit you.

CHASUBLE: Perfectly, perfectly! In fact I have two similar ceremonies to perform at that time. A case of twins that occurred recently in one of the outlying cottages on your own estate. Poor Jenkins the carter, a most hard-working man.

JACK: Oh! I don't see much fun in being christened along with other babies. It would be childish. Would half-past five do?

CHASUBLE: Admirably! Admirably! [*Takes out watch.*] And now, dear Mr Worthing, I will not intrude any longer into a house of sorrow. I would merely beg you not to be too much bowed down by grief. What seem to us bitter trials are often blessings in disguise.

MISS PRISM: This seems to me a blessing of an extremely obvious kind.

[*Enter CECILY from the house.*]

CECILY: Uncle Jack! Oh, I am pleased to see you back. But what horrid clothes you have got on. Do go and change them.

MISS PRISM: Cecily!

CHASUBLE: My child! my child. [CECILY *goes towards* JACK; *he kisses her brow in a melancholy manner.*]

CECILY: What is the matter, Uncle Jack? Do look happy! You look as if you had toothache, and I have got such a surprise for you. Who do you think is in the dining-room? Your brother!

JACK: Who?

CECILY: Your brother Ernest. He arrived about half an hour ago.

JACK: What nonsense! I haven't got a brother.

CECILY: Oh, don't say that. However badly he may have behaved to you in the past he is still your brother. You couldn't be so heartless as to disown him. I'll tell him to come out. And you will shake hands with him, won't you, Uncle Jack? [*Runs back into the house.*]

CHASUBLE: These are very joyful tidings.

MISS PRISM: After we had all been resigned to his loss, his sudden return seems to me peculiarly distressing.

JACK: My brother is in the dining-room? I don't know what it all means. I think it is perfectly absurd.

[*Enter* ALGERNON *and* CECILY *hand in hand. They come slowly up to* JACK.][14]

JACK: Good heavens! [*Motions* ALGERNON *away*.]

ALGERNON: Brother John, I have come down from town to tell you that I am very sorry for all the trouble I have given you, and that I intend to lead a better life in the future. [JACK *glares at him and does not take his hand*.]

CECILY: Uncle Jack, you are not going to refuse your own brother's hand?

JACK: Nothing will induce me to take his hand. I think his coming down here disgraceful. He knows perfectly well why.

CECILY: Uncle Jack, do be nice. There is some good in everyone. Ernest has just been telling me about his poor invalid friend Mr Bunbury whom he goes to visit so often. And surely there must be much good in one who is kind to an invalid, and leaves the pleasures of London to sit by a bed of pain.

JACK: Oh! he has been talking about Bunbury, has he?

CECILY: Yes, he has told me all about poor Mr Bunbury, and his terrible state of health.

JACK: Bunbury! Well, I won't have him talk to you about Bunbury or about anything else. It is enough to drive one perfectly frantic.

ALGERNON: Of course I admit that the faults were all on my side. But I must say that I think that Brother John's coldness to me is peculiarly painful. I expected a more enthusiastic welcome, especially considering it is the first time I have come here. .

CECILY: Uncle Jack, if you don't shake hands with Ernest I will never forgive you.

JACK: Never forgive me?

CECILY: Never, never, never!

JACK: Well, this is the last time I shall ever do it. [*Shakes hands with* ALGERNON *and glares*.]

CHASUBLE: It's pleasant, is it not, to see so perfect a reconciliation? I think we might leave the two brothers together.

MISS PRISM: Cecily, you will come with us.

CECILY: Certainly, Miss Prism. My little task of reconciliation is over.

CHASUBLE: You have done a beautiful action today, dear child.

MISS PRISM: We must not be premature in our judgements.

CECILY: I feel very happy. [*They all go off except* JACK *and* ALGERNON.]

JACK: You young scoundrel, Algy, you must get out of this place as soon as possible. I don't allow any Bunburying here.

[*Enter* MERRIMAN.]

MERRIMAN: I have put Mr Ernest's things in the room next to yours, sir. I suppose that is all right?

JACK: What?

MERRIMAN: Mr Ernest's luggage, sir. I have unpacked it and put it in the room next to your own.

JACK: His luggage?

MERRIMAN: Yes, sir. Three portmanteaus, a dressing-case, two hat-boxes and a large luncheon-basket.

ALGERNON: I am afraid I can't stay more than a week this time.

JACK: Merriman, order the dog-cart[15] at once. Mr Ernest has been suddenly called back to town.

MERRIMAN: Yes, sir. [*Goes back into the house.*]

ALGERNON: What a fearful liar you are, Jack. I have not been called back to town at all.

JACK: Yes, you have.

ALGERNON: I haven't heard anyone call me.

JACK: Your duty as a gentleman calls you back.

ALGERNON: My duty as a gentleman has never interfered with my pleasures in the smallest degree.

JACK: I can quite understand that.

ALGERNON: Well, Cecily is a darling.

JACK: You are not to talk of Miss Cardew like that. I don't like it.

ALGERNON: Well, I don't like your clothes. You look perfectly ridiculous in them. Why on earth don't you go up and change? It is perfectly childish to be in deep mourning for a man who is actually staying for a whole week with you in your house as a guest. I call it grotesque.

JACK: You are certainly not staying with me for a whole week as a guest or anything else. You have got to leave . . . by the four-five train.

ALGERNON: I certainly won't leave you so long as you are in mourning. It would be most unfriendly. If I were in mourning you would stay with me, I suppose. I should think it very unkind if you didn't.

JACK: Well, will you go if I change my clothes?

ALGERNON: Yes, if you are not too long. I never saw anybody take so long to dress, and with such little result.

JACK: Well, at any rate, that is better than being always over-dressed as you are.

ALGERNON: If I am occasionally a little over-dressed, I make up for it by being always immensely over-educated.

JACK: Your vanity is ridiculous, your conduct an outrage, and your presence in my garden utterly absurd. However, you have got to catch the four-five, and I hope you will have a pleasant journey back to town. This Bunburying, as you call it, has not been a great success for you.

[*Goes into the house.*]

ALGERNON: I think it has been a great success. I'm in love with Cecily, and that is everything.

[*Enter* CECILY *at the back of the garden. She picks up the can and begins to water the flowers.*]

But I must see her before I go, and make arrangements for another Bunbury. Ah, there she is.

CECILY: Oh, I merely came back to water the roses. I thought you were with Uncle Jack.

ALGERNON: He's gone to order the dog-cart for me.

CECILY: Oh, is he going to take you for a nice drive?

ALGERNON: He's going to send me away.

CECILY: Then have we got to part?

ALGERNON: I am afraid so. It's a very painful parting.

CECILY: It is always painful to part from people whom one has known for a very brief space of time. The absence of old friends one can endure with equanimity. But even a momentary separation from anyone to whom one has just been introduced is almost unbearable.

ALGERNON: Thank you.

[*Enter* MERRIMAN.]

MERRIMAN: The dog-cart is at the door, sir.

[ALGERNON *looks appealingly at* CECILY.]

CECILY: It can wait, Merriman . . . for . . . five minutes.

MERRIMAN: Yes, miss.

[*Exit* MERRIMAN.]

ALGERNON: I hope, Cecily, I shall not offend you if I state quite frankly and openly that you seem to me to be in every way the visible personification of absolute perfection.

CECILY: I think your frankness does you great credit, Ernest. If you will allow me, I will copy your remarks into my diary. [*Goes over to table and begins writing in diary.*]

ALGERNON: Do you really keep a diary? I'd give anything to look at it. May I?

CECILY: Oh no. [*Puts her hand over it.*] You see, it is simply a very young girl's record of her own thoughts and impressions, and consequently meant for publication. When it appears in volume form I hope you will order a copy. But pray, Ernest, don't stop. I delight in taking down from dictation. I have reached 'absolute perfection'. You can go on. I am quite ready for more.

ALGERNON [*somewhat taken aback*]: Ahem! Ahem!

CECILY: Oh, don't cough, Ernest. When one is dictating one should speak fluently and not cough. Besides, I don't know how to spell a cough. [*Writes as* ALGERNON *speaks.*]

ALGERNON [*speaking very rapidly*]: Cecily, ever since I first looked upon your wonderful and incomparable beauty, I have dared to love you wildly, passionately, devotedly, hopelessly.

CECILY: I don't think that you should tell me that you love me wildly, passionately, devotedly, hopelessly. Hopelessly doesn't seem to make much sense, does it?

ALGERNON: Cecily.

[*Enter* MERRIMAN.]

MERRIMAN: The dog-cart is waiting, sir.

ALGERNON: Tell it to come round next week, at the same hour.

MERRIMAN [*looks at* CECILY, *who makes no sign*]: Yes, sir.

[MERRIMAN *retires.*]

CECILY: Uncle Jack would be very much annoyed if he knew you were staying on till next week, at the same hour.

ALGERNON: Oh, I don't care about Jack. I don't care for anybody in the whole world but you. I love you, Cecily. You will marry me, won't you?

CECILY: You silly boy! Of course. Why, we have been engaged for the last three months.

ALGERNON: For the last three months?

CECILY: Yes, it will be exactly three months on Thursday.

ALGERNON: But how did we become engaged?

CECILY: Well, ever since dear Uncle Jack first confessed to us that he had a younger brother who was very wicked and bad, you of course have formed the chief topic of conversation between myself and Miss Prism. And of course a man who is much talked about is always very attractive. One feels there must be something in him, after all. I daresay it was foolish of me, but I fell in love with you, Ernest.

ALGERNON: Darling. And when was the engagement actually settled?

CECILY: On the 14th of February last. Worn out by your entire ignorance of my existence, I determined to end the matter one way or the other, and after a long struggle with myself I accepted you under this dear old tree here. The next day I bought this little ring in your name, and this is the little bangle with the true lover's knot I promised you always to wear.

ALGERNON: Did I give you this? It's very pretty, isn't it?

CECILY: Yes, you've wonderfully good taste, Ernest. It's the excuse

I've always given for your leading such a bad life. And this is the box in which I keep all your dear letters. [*Kneels at table, opens box and produces letters tied up with blue ribbon.*]

ALGERNON: My letters! But, my own sweet Cecily, I have never written you any letters.

CECILY: You need hardly remind me of that, Ernest. I remember only too well that I was forced to write your letters for you. I wrote always three times a week, and sometimes oftener.

ALGERNON: Oh, do let me read them, Cecily?

CECILY: Oh, I couldn't possibly. They would make you far too conceited. [*Replaces box.*] The three you wrote me after I had broken off the engagement are so beautiful, and so badly spelled, that even now I can hardly read them without crying a little.

ALGERNON: But was our engagement ever broken off?

CECILY: Of course it was. On the 22nd of last March. You can see the entry if you like. [*Shows diary.*] 'Today I broke off my engagement with Ernest. I feel it is better to do so. The weather still continues charming.'

ALGERNON: But why on earth did you break it off? What had I done? I had done nothing at all. Cecily, I am very much hurt indeed to hear you broke it off. Particularly when the weather was so charming.

CECILY: It would hardly have been a really serious engagement if it hadn't been broken off at least once. But I forgave you before the week was out.

ALGERNON [*crossing to her, and kneeling*]: What a perfect angel you are, Cecily.

CECILY: You dear romantic boy. [*He kisses her, she puts her fingers through his hair.*] I hope your hair curls naturally, does it?

ALGERNON: Yes, darling, with a little help from others.

CECILY: I am so glad.

ALGERNON: You'll never break off our engagement again, Cecily?

CECILY: I don't think I could break it off now that I have actually met you. Besides, of course, there is the question of your name.

ALGERNON: Yes, of course. [*Nervously.*]

CECILY: You must not laugh at me, darling, but it had always been a girlish dream of mine to love some one whose name was Ernest. [ALGERNON *rises,* CECILY *also.*] There is something in that name that seems to inspire absolute confidence. I pity any poor married woman whose husband is not called Ernest.

ALGERNON: But, my dear child, do you mean to say you could not love me if I had some other name?

CECILY: But what name?

ALGERNON: Oh, any name you like – Algernon – for instance . . .

CECILY: But I don't like the name of Algernon.

ALGERNON: Well, my own dear, sweet, loving little darling, I really can't see why you should object to the name of Algernon. It is not at all a bad name. In fact, it is rather an aristocratic name. Half of the chaps who get into the Bankruptcy Court are called Algernon. But seriously, Cecily . . . [*moving to her*] if my name was Algy, couldn't you love me?

CECILY [*rising*]: I might respect you, Ernest, I might admire your character but I fear that I should not be able to give you my undivided attention.

ALGERNON: Ahem! Cecily! [*Picking up hat.*] Your Rector here is, I suppose, thoroughly experienced in the practice of all the rites and ceremonials of the Church?

CECILY: Oh, yes. Dr Chasuble is a most learned man. He has never written a single book, so you can imagine how much he knows.

ALGERNON: I must see him at once on a most important christening – I mean on most important business.

CECILY: Oh!

ALGERNON: I shan't be away more than half an hour.

CECILY: Considering that we have been engaged since February the 14th, and that I only met you today for the first time, I think it is rather hard that you should leave me for so long a period as half an hour. Couldn't you make it twenty minutes?

ALGERNON: I'll be back in no time. [*Kisses her and rushes down the garden.*]

CECILY: What an impetuous boy he is! I like his hair so much. I must enter his proposal in my diary.

[*Enter* MERRIMAN.]

MERRIMAN: A Miss Fairfax has just called to see Mr Worthing. On very important business, Miss Fairfax states.

CECILY: Isn't Mr Worthing in his library?

MERRIMAN: Mr Worthing went over in the direction of the Rectory some time ago.

CECILY: Pray ask the lady to come out here: Mr Worthing is sure to be back soon. And you can bring tea.

MERRIMAN: Yes, miss.

[*Goes out.*]

CECILY: Miss Fairfax! I suppose one of the many good elderly women who are associated with Uncle Jack in some of his philanthropic work in London. I don't quite like women who are interested in philanthropic work. I think it is so forward of them.

[*Enter* MERRIMAN.]

MERRIMAN: Miss Fairfax.

[*Enter* GWENDOLEN. *Exit* MERRIMAN.]

CECILY [*advancing to meet her*]: Pray let me introduce myself to you. My name is Cecily Cardew.

GWENDOLEN: Cecily Cardew? [*Moving to her and shaking hands.*] What a very sweet name! Something tells me that we are going to be great friends. I like you already more than I can say. My first impressions of people are never wrong.

CECILY: How nice of you to like me so much after we have known each other such a comparatively short time. Pray sit down.

GWENDOLEN [*still standing up*]: I may call you Cecily, may I not?

CECILY: With pleasure!

GWENDOLEN: And you will always call me Gwendolen, won't you?

CECILY: If you wish.

GWENDOLEN: Then that is all quite settled, is it not?

CECILY: I hope so. [*A pause. They both sit down together.*]

GWENDOLEN: Perhaps this might be a favourable opportunity for my mentioning who I am. My father is Lord Bracknell. You have never heard of papa, I suppose?

CECILY: I don't think so.

GWENDOLEN: Outside the family circle, papa, I am glad to say, is entirely unknown. I think that is quite as it should be. The home seems to me to be the proper sphere for the man. And certainly once a man begins to neglect his domestic duties he becomes painfully effeminate, does he not? And I don't like that. It makes men so very attractive.[16] Cecily, mamma, whose views on education are remarkably strict, has brought me up to be extremely short-sighted; it is part of her system; so do you mind my looking at you through my glasses?

CECILY: Oh! not at all, Gwendolen. I am very fond of being looked at.

GWENDOLEN [after examining CECILY carefully through a lorgnette]: You are here on a short visit, I suppose.

CECILY: Oh no! I live here.

GWENDOLEN [severely]: Really? Your mother, no doubt, or some female relative of advanced years, resides here also?

CECILY: Oh no! I have no mother, nor, in fact, any relations.

GWENDOLEN: Indeed?

CECILY: My dear guardian, with the assistance of Miss Prism, has the arduous task of looking after me.

GWENDOLEN: Your guardian?

CECILY: Yes, I am Mr Worthing's ward.[17]

GWENDOLEN: Oh! It is strange he never mentioned to me that he had a ward. How secretive of him! He grows more interesting hourly. I am not sure, however, that the news inspires me with feelings of unmixed delight. [Rising and going to her.] I am very fond of you, Cecily; I have liked you ever since I met you! But I am bound to state that now that I know that you are Mr Worthing's ward, I cannot help expressing a wish you were – well, just a little older than you seem to be – and not quite so very alluring in appearance. In fact, if I may speak candidly –

CECILY: Pray do! I think that whenever one has anything unpleasant to say, one should always be quite candid.

GWENDOLEN: Well, to speak with perfect candour, Cecily, I wish that you were fully forty-two, and more than usually plain for your age.

Ernest has a strong upright nature. He is the very soul of truth and honour. Disloyalty would be as impossible to him as deception. But even men of the noblest possible moral character are extremely susceptible to the influence of the physical charms of others. Modern, no less than Ancient History, supplies us with many most painful examples of what I refer to. If it were not so, indeed, History would be quite unreadable.

CECILY: I beg your pardon, Gwendolen, did you say Ernest?

GWENDOLEN: Yes.

CECILY: Oh, but it is not Mr Ernest Worthing who is my guardian. It is his brother – his elder brother.

GWENDOLEN [*sitting down again*]: Ernest never mentioned to me that he had a brother.

CECILY: I am sorry to say they have not been on good terms for a long time.

GWENDOLEN: Ah! that accounts for it. And now that I think of it I have never heard any man mention his brother. The subject seems distasteful to most men. Cecily, you have lifted a load from my mind. I was growing almost anxious. It would have been terrible if any cloud had come across a friendship like ours, would it not? Of course you are quite, quite sure that it is not Mr Ernest Worthing who is your guardian?

CECILY: Quite sure. [*A pause.*] In fact, I am going to be his.

GWENDOLEN [*inquiringly*]: I beg your pardon?

CECILY [*rather shy and confidingly*]: Dearest Gwendolen, there is no reason why I should make a secret of it to you. Our little county newspaper is sure to chronicle the fact next week. Mr Ernest Worthing and I are engaged to be married.

GWENDOLEN [*quite politely, rising*]: My darling Cecily, I think there must be some slight error. Mr Ernest Worthing is engaged to me. The announcement will appear in the *Morning Post*[18] on Saturday at the latest.

CECILY [*very politely, rising*]: I am afraid you must be under some misconception. Ernest proposed to me exactly ten minutes ago. [*Shows diary.*]

GWENDOLEN [*examines diary through her lorgnette carefully*]: It is very curious, for he asked me to be his wife yesterday afternoon at 5.30. If you would care to verify the incident, pray do so. [*Produces diary of her own.*] I never travel without my diary. One should always have something sensational to read in the train. I am so sorry, dear Cecily, if it is any disappointment to you, but I am afraid I have the prior claim.

CECILY: It would distress me more than I can tell you, dear Gwendolen, if it caused you any mental or physical anguish, but I feel bound to point out that since Ernest proposed to you he clearly has changed his mind.

GWENDOLEN [*meditatively*]: If the poor fellow has been entrapped into any foolish promise I shall consider it my duty to rescue him at once, and with a firm hand.

CECILY [*thoughtfully and sadly*]: Whatever unfortunate entanglement my dear boy may have got into, I will never reproach him with it after we are married.

GWENDOLEN: Do you allude to me, Miss Cardew, as an entanglement? You are presumptuous. On an occasion of this kind it becomes more than a moral duty to speak one's mind. It becomes a pleasure.

CECILY: Do you suggest, Miss Fairfax, that I entrapped Ernest into an engagement? How dare you? This is no time for wearing the shallow mask of manners. When I see a spade I call it a spade.

GWENDOLEN [*satirically*]: I am glad to say that I have never seen a spade. It is obvious that our social spheres have been widely different.

[*Enter* MERRIMAN, *followed by the footman. He carries a salver, table-cloth and plate stand.* CECILY *is about to retort. The presence of the servants exercises a restraining influence, under which both girls chafe.*]

MERRIMAN: Shall I lay tea here as usual, miss?

CECILY [*sternly, in a calm voice*]: Yes, as usual. [MERRIMAN *begins to clear table and lay cloth. A long pause.* CECILY *and* GWENDOLEN *glare at each other.*]

GWENDOLEN: Are there many interesting walks in the vicinity, Miss Cardew?

CECILY: Oh! yes! a great many. From the top of one of the hills quite close one can see five counties.

GWENDOLEN: Five counties! I don't think I should like that; I hate crowds.

CECILY [*sweetly*]: I suppose that is why you live in town? [GWENDOLEN *bites her lip, and beats her foot nervously with her parasol.*]

GWENDOLEN [*looking around*]: Quite a well-kept garden this is, Miss Cardew.

CECILY: So glad you like it, Miss Fairfax.

GWENDOLEN: I had no idea there were any flowers in the country.

CECILY: Oh, flowers are as common here, Miss Fairfax, as people are in London.

GWENDOLEN: Personally I cannot understand how anybody manages to exist in the country, if anybody who is anybody does. The country always bores me to death.

CECILY: Ah! This is what the newspapers call agricultural depression,[19] is it not? I believe the aristocracy are suffering very much from it just at present. It is almost an epidemic amongst them, I have been told. May I offer you some tea, Miss Fairfax?

GWENDOLEN [*with elaborate politeness*]: Thank you. [*Aside.*] Detestable girl! But I require tea!

CECILY [*sweetly*]: Sugar?

GWENDOLEN [*superciliously*]: No, thank you. Sugar is not fashionable any more. [CECILY *looks angrily at her, takes up the tongs and puts four lumps of sugar into the cup.*]

CECILY [*severely*]: Cake or bread and butter?

GWENDOLEN [*in a bored manner*]: Bread and butter, please. Cake is rarely seen at the best houses nowadays.

CECILY [*cuts a very large slice of cake and puts it on the tray*]: Hand that to Miss Fairfax.

[MERRIMAN *does so, and goes out with footman.* GWENDOLEN *drinks the tea and makes a grimace. Puts down cup at once, reaches out her hand to the bread and butter, looks at it and finds it is cake. Rises in indignation.*]

GWENDOLEN: You have filled my tea with lumps of sugar, and though I asked most distinctly for bread and butter, you have given me cake. I am known for the gentleness of my disposition, and the extraordinary sweetness of my nature, but I warn you, Miss Cardew, you may go too far.

CECILY [*rising*]: To save my poor, innocent, trusting boy from the machinations of any other girl there are no lengths to which I would not go.

GWENDOLEN: From the moment I saw you I distrusted you. I felt that you were false and deceitful. I am never deceived in such matters. My first impressions of people are invariably right.

CECILY: It seems to me, Miss Fairfax, that I am trespassing on your valuable time. No doubt you have many other calls of a similar character to make in the neighbourhood.

[*Enter* JACK.]

GWENDOLEN [*catching sight of him*]: Ernest! My own Ernest!

JACK: Gwendolen! Darling! [*Offers to kiss her.*]

GWENDOLEN [*drawing back*]: A moment! May I ask if you are engaged to be married to this young lady? [*Points to* CECILY.]

JACK [*laughing*]: To dear little Cecily! Of course not! What could have put such an idea into your pretty little head?

GWENDOLEN: Thank you. You may! [*Offers her cheek.*]

CECILY [*very sweetly*]: I knew there must be some misunderstanding, Miss Fairfax. The gentleman whose arm is at present round your waist is my guardian, Mr John Worthing.

GWENDOLEN: I beg your pardon?

CECILY: This is Uncle Jack.[20]

GWENDOLEN [*receding*]: Jack! Oh!

[*Enter* ALGERNON.]

CECILY: Here is Ernest.

ALGERNON [*goes straight over to* CECILY *without noticing anyone else*]: My own love! [*Offers to kiss her.*]

CECILY [*drawing back*]: A moment, Ernest! May I ask you – are you engaged to be married to this young lady?

ALGERNON [*looking round*]: To what young lady? Good heavens! Gwendolen!

CECILY: Yes: to good heavens, Gwendolen, I mean to Gwendolen.

ALGERNON [*laughing*]: Of course not! What could have put such an idea into your pretty little head?

CECILY: Thank you. [*Presenting her cheek to be kissed.*] You may. [ALGERNON *kisses her.*]

GWENDOLEN: I felt there was some slight error, Miss Cardew. The gentleman who is now embracing you is my cousin, Mr Algernon Moncrieff.

CECILY [*breaking away from* ALGERNON]: Algernon Moncrieff! Oh!

[*The two girls move towards each other and put their arms round each other's waists as if for protection.*]

CECILY: Are you called Algernon?

ALGERNON: I cannot deny it.

CECILY: Oh!

GWENDOLEN: Is your name really John?

JACK [*standing rather proudly*]: I could deny it if I liked. I could deny anything if I liked. But my name certainly is John. It has been John for years.

CECILY [*to* GWENDOLEN]: A gross deception has been practised on both of us.

GWENDOLEN: My poor wounded Cecily!

CECILY: My sweet wronged Gwendolen!

GWENDOLEN [*slowly and seriously*]: You will call me sister, will you not?[21] [*They embrace.* JACK *and* ALGERNON *groan and walk up and down.*]

CECILY [*rather brightly*]: There is just one question I would like to be allowed to ask my guardian.

GWENDOLEN: An admirable idea! Mr Worthing, there is just one question I would like to be permitted to put to you. Where is your brother Ernest? We are both engaged to be married to your brother Ernest, so it is a matter of some importance to us to know where your brother Ernest is at present.

JACK [*slowly and hesitatingly*]: Gwendolen – Cecily – it is very painful for me to be forced to speak the truth. It is the first time in my life that I have ever been reduced to such a painful position, and I am really quite inexperienced in doing anything of the kind. However,

I will tell you quite frankly that I have no brother Ernest. I have no brother at all. I never had a brother in my life, and I certainly have not the smallest intention of ever having one in the future.

CECILY [*surprised*]: No brother at all?

JACK [*cheerily*]: None!

GWENDOLEN [*severely*]: Had you never a brother of any kind?

JACK [*pleasantly*]: Never. Not even of any kind.

GWENDOLEN: I am afraid it is quite clear, Cecily, that neither of us is engaged to be married to anyone.

CECILY: It is not a very pleasant position for a young girl suddenly to find herself in. Is it?

GWENDOLEN: Let us go into the house. They will hardly venture to come after us there.

CECILY: No, men are so cowardly, aren't they?

[*They retire into the house with scornful looks.*][22]

JACK: This ghastly state of things is what you call Bunburying, I suppose?

ALGERNON: Yes, and a perfectly wonderful Bunbury it is. The most wonderful Bunbury I have ever had in my life.

JACK: Well, you've no right whatsoever to Bunbury here.

ALGERNON: That is absurd. One has a right to Bunbury anywhere one chooses. Every serious Bunburyist knows that.

JACK: Serious Bunburyist? Good heavens!

ALGERNON: Well, one must be serious about something, if one wants to have any amusement in life. I happen to be serious about Bunburying. What on earth you are serious about I haven't got the remotest idea. About everything, I should fancy. You have such an absolutely trivial nature.

JACK: Well, the only small satisfaction I have in the whole of this wretched business is that your friend Bunbury is quite exploded. You won't be able to run down to the country quite so often as you used to do, dear Algy. And a very good thing too.

ALGERNON: Your brother is a little off colour, isn't he, dear Jack? You won't be able to disappear to London quite so frequently as your wicked custom was. And not a bad thing either.

JACK: As for your conduct towards Miss Cardew, I must say that your taking in a sweet, simple, innocent girl like that is quite inexcusable. To say nothing of the fact that she is my ward.

ALGERNON: I can see no possible defence at all for your deceiving a brilliant, clever, thoroughly experienced young lady like Miss Fairfax. To say nothing of the fact that she is my cousin.

JACK: I wanted to be engaged to Gwendolen, that is all. I love her.

ALGERNON: Well, I simply wanted to be engaged to Cecily. I adore her.

JACK: There is certainly no chance of your marrying Miss Cardew.

ALGERNON: I don't think there is much likelihood, Jack, of you and Miss Fairfax being united.

JACK: Well, that is no business of yours.

ALGERNON: If it was my business, I wouldn't talk about it. [*Begins to eat muffins.*] It is very vulgar to talk about one's business. Only people like stockbrokers do that, and then merely at dinner parties.

JACK: How you can sit there, calmly eating muffins when we are in this horrible trouble, I can't make out. You seem to me to be perfectly heartless.

ALGERNON: Well, I can't eat muffins in an agitated manner. The butter would probably get on my cuffs. One should always eat muffins quite calmly. It is the only way to eat them.

JACK: I say it's perfectly heartless your eating muffins at all, under the circumstances.

ALGERNON: When I am in trouble, eating is the only thing that consoles me. Indeed, when I am in really great trouble, as anyone who knows me intimately will tell you, I refuse everything except food and drink. At the present moment I am eating muffins because I am unhappy. Besides, I am particularly fond of muffins. [*Rising.*]

JACK [*rising*]: Well, that is no reason why you should eat them all in that greedy way. [*Takes muffins from Algernon.*]

ALGERNON [*offering tea-cake*]: I wish you would have tea-cake instead. I don't like tea-cake.

JACK: Good heavens! I suppose a man may eat his own muffins in his own garden.

ALGERNON: But you have just said it was perfectly heartless to eat muffins.

JACK: I said it was perfectly heartless of you, under the circumstances. That is a very different thing.

ALGERNON: That may be, but the muffins are the same. [*He seizes the muffin-dish from* JACK.]

JACK: Algy, I wish to goodness you would go.

ALGERNON: You can't possibly ask me to go without having some dinner. It's absurd. I never go without my dinner. No one ever does, except vegetarians and people like that. Besides I have just made arrangements with Dr Chasuble to be christened at a quarter to six under the name of Ernest.

JACK: My dear fellow, the sooner you give up that nonsense the better. I made arrangements this morning with Dr Chasuble to be christened myself at 5.30, and I naturally will take the name of Ernest. Gwendolen would wish it. We can't both be christened Ernest. It's absurd. Besides, I have a perfect right to be christened if I like. There is no evidence at all that I have ever been christened by anybody. I should think it extremely probable I never was, and so does Dr Chasuble. It is entirely different in your case. You have been christened already.

ALGERNON: Yes, but I have not been christened for years.

JACK: Yes, but you have been christened. That is the important thing.

ALGERNON: Quite so. So I know my constitution can stand it. If you are not quite sure about your ever having been christened, I must say I think it rather dangerous your venturing on it now. It might make you very unwell. You can hardly have forgotten that someone very closely connected with you was very nearly carried off this week in Paris by a severe chill.

JACK: Yes, but you said yourself that a severe chill was not hereditary.

ALGERNON: It usen't to be, I know – but I daresay it is now. Science is always making wonderful improvements in things.

JACK [*picking up the muffin-dish*]: Oh, that is nonsense; you are always talking nonsense.

ALGERNON: Jack, you are at the muffins again! I wish you wouldn't.

There are only two left. [*Takes them.*] I told you I was particularly fond of muffins.

JACK: But I hate tea-cake.

ALGERNON: Why on earth then do you allow tea-cake to be served up for your guests? What ideas you have of hospitality!

JACK: Algernon! I have already told you to go. I don't want you here. Why don't you go!

ALGERNON: I haven't quite finished my tea yet! and there is still one muffin left. [JACK *groans, and sinks into a chair.* ALGERNON *continues eating.*][23]

ACT DROP

THIRD ACT

SCENE

Morning-room[1] *at the Manor House.*

[GWENDOLEN *and* CECILY *are at the window, looking out into the garden.*]

GWENDOLEN: The fact that they did not follow us at once into the house, as anyone else would have done, seems to me to show that they have some sense of shame left.

CECILY: They have been eating muffins. That looks like repentance.

GWENDOLEN [*after a pause*]: They don't seem to notice us at all. Couldn't you cough?

CECILY: But I haven't got a cough.

GWENDOLEN: They're looking at us. What effrontery!

CECILY: They're approaching. That's very forward of them.

GWENDOLEN: Let us preserve a dignified silence.

CECILY: Certainly. It's the only thing to do now.

[*Enter* JACK *followed by* ALGERNON. *They whistle some dreadful popular air from a British Opera.*][2]

GWENDOLEN: This dignified silence seems to produce an unpleasant effect.

CECILY: A most distasteful one.

GWENDOLEN: But we will not be the first to speak.

CECILY: Certainly not.

GWENDOLEN: Mr Worthing, I have something very particular to ask you. Much depends on your reply.

CECILY: Gwendolen, your common sense is invaluable. Mr Moncrieff, kindly answer me the following question. Why did you pretend to be my guardian's brother?

ALGERNON: In order that I might have an opportunity of meeting you.

CECILY [*to* GWENDOLEN]: That certainly seems a satisfactory explanation, does it not?

GWENDOLEN: Yes, dear, if you can believe him.

CECILY: I don't. But that does not affect the wonderful beauty of his answer.

GWENDOLEN: True. In matters of grave importance, style, not sincerity, is the vital thing. Mr Worthing, what explanation can you offer to me for pretending to have a brother? Was it in order that you might have an opportunity of coming up to town to see me as often as possible?

JACK: Can you doubt it, Miss Fairfax?[3]

GWENDOLEN: I have the gravest doubts upon the subject. But I intend to crush them. This is not the moment for German scepticism.[4] [*Moving to* CECILY.] Their explanations appear to be quite satisfactory, especially Mr Worthing's. That seems to me to have the stamp of truth upon it.

CECILY: I am more than content with what Mr Moncrieff said. His voice alone inspires one with absolute credulity.

GWENDOLEN: Then you think we should forgive them?

CECILY: Yes. I mean no.

GWENDOLEN: True! I had forgotten. There are principles at stake that one cannot surrender. Which of us should tell them? The task is not a pleasant one.

CECILY: Could we not both speak at the same time?

GWENDOLEN: An excellent idea! I nearly always speak at the same time as other people. Will you take the time from me?

CECILY: Certainly. [GWENDOLEN *beats time with uplifted finger.*]

GWENDOLEN and CECILY [*speaking together*]: Your Christian names are still an insuperable barrier. That is all!

JACK and ALGERNON [*speaking together*]: Our Christian names! Is that all? But we are going to be christened this afternoon.

GWENDOLEN [*to* JACK]: For my sake you are prepared to do this terrible thing?

JACK: I am.

CECILY [*to* ALGERNON]: To please me you are ready to face this fearful ordeal?

ALGERNON: I am!

GWENDOLEN: How absurd to talk of the equality of the sexes! Where questions of self-sacrifice are concerned, men are infinitely beyond us.

JACK: We are. [*Clasps hands with* ALGERNON.]

CECILY: They have moments of physical courage of which we women know absolutely nothing.

GWENDOLEN [*to* JACK]: Darling!

ALGERNON [*to* CECILY]: Darling! [*They fall into each other's arms.*]

[*Enter* MERRIMAN. *When he enters he coughs loudly, seeing the situation.*]

MERRIMAN: Ahem! Ahem! Lady Bracknell.

JACK: Good heavens!

[*Enter* LADY BRACKNELL. *The couples separate in alarm. Exit* MERRIMAN.]

LADY BRACKNELL: Gwendolen! What does this mean?

GWENDOLEN: Merely that I am engaged to be married to Mr Worthing, mamma.

LADY BRACKNELL: Come here. Sit down. Sit down immediately. Hesitation of any kind is a sign of mental decay in the young, of physical weakness in the old. [*Turns to* JACK.] Apprised, sir, of my daughter's sudden flight by her trusty maid, whose confidence I purchased by means of a small coin, I followed her at once by a luggage train. Her unhappy father is, I am glad to say, under the impression that she is attending a more than usually lengthy lecture by the University Extension Scheme[5] on the Influence of a permanent income on Thought. I do not propose to undeceive him. Indeed I have never undeceived him on any question. I would consider it wrong. But of course, you will clearly understand that all communication between yourself and my daughter must cease immediately from this moment. On this point, as indeed on all points, I am firm.

JACK: I am engaged to be married to Gwendolen, Lady Bracknell!

LADY BRACKNELL: You are nothing of the kind, sir. And now as regards Algernon! . . . Algernon!

ALGERNON: Yes, Aunt Augusta.

LADY BRACKNELL: May I ask if it is in this house that your invalid friend Mr Bunbury resides?

ALGERNON [*stammering*]: Oh! No! Bunbury doesn't live here. Bunbury is somewhere else at present. In fact, Bunbury is dead.

LADY BRACKNELL: Dead! When did Mr Bunbury die? His death must have been extremely sudden.

ALGERNON [*airily*]: Oh! I killed Bunbury this afternoon. I mean poor Bunbury died this afternoon.

LADY BRACKNELL: What did he die of?

ALGERNON: Bunbury? Oh, he was quite exploded.

LADY BRACKNELL: Exploded! Was he the victim of a revolutionary outrage?[6] I was not aware that Mr Bunbury was interested in social legislation. If so, he is well punished for his morbidity.

ALGERNON: My dear Aunt Augusta, I mean he was found out! The doctors found out that Bunbury could not live, that is what I mean – so Bunbury died.

LADY BRACKNELL: He seems to have had great confidence in the opinion of his physicians. I am glad, however, that he made up his mind at the last to some definite course of action, and acted under proper medical advice. And now that we have finally got rid of this Mr Bunbury, may I ask, Mr Worthing, who is that young person whose hand my nephew Algernon is now holding in what seems to me a peculiarly unnecessary manner?

JACK: That lady is Miss Cecily Cardew, my ward. [LADY BRACKNELL *bows coldly to* CECILY.]

ALGERNON: I am engaged to be married to Cecily, Aunt Augusta.

LADY BRACKNELL: I beg your pardon?

CECILY: Mr Moncrieff and I are engaged to be married, Lady Bracknell.

LADY BRACKNELL [*with a shiver, crossing to the sofa and sitting down*]: I do not know whether there is anything peculiarly exciting in the air of this particular part of Hertfordshire, but the number of engagements that go on seems to me considerably above the proper average that statistics have laid down for our guidance. I think some preliminary inquiry on my part would not be out of place.

Mr Worthing, is Miss Cardew at all connected with any of the larger railway stations in London? I merely desire information. Until yesterday I had no idea that there were any families or persons whose origin was a Terminus. [JACK *looks perfectly furious, but restrains himself.*]

JACK [*in a cold, clear voice*]: Miss Cardew is the granddaughter of the late Mr Thomas Cardew of 149 Belgrave Square, SW; Gervase Park, Dorking, Surrey; and the Sporran, Fifeshire, NB.⁷

LADY BRACKNELL: That sounds not unsatisfactory. Three addresses always inspire confidence, even in tradesmen. But what proof have I of their authenticity?

JACK: I have carefully preserved the Court Guides of the period. They are open to your inspection, Lady Bracknell.

LADY BRACKNELL [*grimly*]: I have known strange errors in that publication.

JACK: Miss Cardew's family solicitors are Messrs Markby, Markby and Markby.

LADY BRACKNELL: Markby, Markby and Markby? A firm of the very highest position in their profession. Indeed I am told that one of the Mr Markby's is occasionally to be seen at dinner parties. So far I am satisfied.

JACK [*very irritably*]: How extremely kind of you, Lady Bracknell! I have also in my possession, you will be pleased to hear, certificates of Miss Cardew's birth, baptism, whooping cough, registration, vaccination, confirmation and the measles; both the German and the English variety.

LADY BRACKNELL: Ah! A life crowded with incident, I see; though perhaps somewhat too exciting for a young girl. I am not myself in favour of premature experiences.⁸ [*Rises, looks at her watch.*] Gwendolen! the time approaches for our departure. We have not a moment to lose. As a matter of form, Mr Worthing, I had better ask you if Miss Cardew has any little fortune?

JACK: Oh! about a hundred and thirty thousand pounds in the Funds.⁹ That is all. Good-bye, Lady Bracknell. So pleased to have seen you.

LADY BRACKNELL [*sitting down again*]: A moment, Mr Worthing. A hundred and thirty thousand pounds! And in the Funds! Miss

Cardew seems to me a most attractive young lady, now that I look at her. Few girls of the present day have any really solid qualities, any of the qualities that last, and improve with time. We live, I regret to say, in an age of surfaces. [*To* CECILY.] Come over here, dear. [CECILY *goes across.*] Pretty child! your dress is sadly simple, and your hair seems almost as Nature might have left it. But we can soon alter all that. A thoroughly experienced French maid produces a really marvellous result in a very brief space of time. I remember recommending one to young Lady Lancing, and after three months her own husband did not know her.

JACK: And after six months nobody knew her.

LADY BRACKNELL [*glares at Jack for a few moments. Then bends, with a practised smile, to* CECILY]: Kindly turn round, sweet child. [CECILY *turns completely round.*] No, the side view is what I want. [CECILY *presents her profile.*] Yes, quite as I expected. There are distinct social possibilities in your profile.[10] The two weak points in our age are its want of principle and its want of profile. The chin a little higher, dear. Style largely depends on the way the chin is worn. They are worn very high, just at present. Algernon!

ALGERNON: Yes, Aunt Augusta!

LADY BRACKNELL: There are distinct social possibilities in Miss Cardew's profile.

ALGERNON: Cecily is the sweetest, dearest, prettiest girl in the whole world. And I don't care twopence about social possibilities.

LADY BRACKNELL: Never speak disrespectfully of Society, Algernon. Only people who can't get into it do that. [*To* CECILY.] Dear child, of course you know that Algernon has nothing but his debts to depend upon. But I do not approve of mercenary marriages. When I married Lord Bracknell I had no fortune of any kind. But I never dreamed for a moment of allowing that to stand in my way.[11] Well, I suppose I must give my consent.

ALGERNON: Thank you, Aunt Augusta.

LADY BRACKNELL: Cecily, you may kiss me!

CECILY [*kisses her*]: Thank you, Lady Bracknell.

LADY BRACKNELL: You may also address me as Aunt Augusta for the future.

CECILY: Thank you, Aunt Augusta.

LADY BRACKNELL: The marriage, I think, had better take place quite soon.

ALGERNON: Thank you, Aunt Augusta.

CECILY: Thank you, Aunt Augusta.

LADY BRACKNELL: To speak frankly, I am not in favour of long engagements. They give people the opportunity of finding out each other's character before marriage, which I think is never advisable.

JACK: I beg your pardon for interrupting you, Lady Bracknell, but this engagement is quite out of the question. I am Miss Cardew's guardian, and she cannot marry without my consent until she comes of age. That consent I absolutely decline to give.

LADY BRACKNELL: Upon what grounds, may I ask? Algernon is an extremely, I may almost say an ostentatiously, eligible young man. He has nothing, but he looks everything. What more can one desire?

JACK: It pains me very much to have to speak frankly to you, Lady Bracknell, about your nephew, but the fact is that I do not approve at all of his moral character. I suspect him of being untruthful. [ALGERNON *and* CECILY *look at him in indignant amazement.*]

LADY BRACKNELL: Untruthful! My nephew Algernon? Impossible! He is an Oxonian.[12]

JACK: I fear there can be no possible doubt about the matter. This afternoon during my temporary absence in London on an important question of romance, he obtained admission to my house by means of the false pretence of being my brother. Under an assumed name he drank, I've just been informed by my butler, an entire pint bottle of my Perrier-Jouet, Brut, '89; wine I was specially reserving for myself. Continuing his disgraceful deception, he succeeded in the course of the afternoon in alienating the affections of my only ward. He subsequently stayed to tea, and devoured every single muffin. And what makes his conduct all the more heartless is, that he was perfectly well aware from the first that I have no brother, that I never had a brother and that I don't intend to have a brother, not even of any kind. I distinctly told him so myself yesterday afternoon.

LADY BRACKNELL: Ahem! Mr Worthing, after careful consideration

I have decided entirely to overlook my nephew's conduct to you.

JACK: That is very generous of you, Lady Bracknell. My own decision, however, is unalterable. I decline to give my consent.

LADY BRACKNELL [*to* CECILY]: Come here, sweet child. [CECILY *goes over*.] How old are you, dear?

CECILY: Well, I am really only eighteen, but I always admit to twenty when I go to evening parties.

LADY BRACKNELL: You are perfectly right in making some slight alteration. Indeed, no woman should ever be quite accurate about her age. It looks so calculating . . . [*In a meditative manner.*] Eighteen, but admitting to twenty at evening parties. Well, it will not be very long before you are of age and free from the restraints of tutelage. So I don't think your guardian's consent is, after all, a matter of any importance.

JACK: Pray excuse me, Lady Bracknell, for interrupting you again, but it is only fair to tell you that according to the terms of her grandfather's will Miss Cardew does not come legally of age till she is thirty-five.

LADY BRACKNELL: That does not seem to me to be a grave objection. Thirty-five is a very attractive age. London society is full of women of the very highest birth who have, of their own free choice, remained thirty-five for years. Lady Dumbleton is an instance in point. To my own knowledge she has been thirty-five ever since she arrived at the age of forty, which was many years ago now. I see no reason why our dear Cecily should not be even still more attractive at the age you mention than she is at present. There will be a large accumulation of property.

CECILY: Algy, could you wait for me till I was thirty-five?

ALGERNON: Of course I could, Cecily. You know I could.

CECILY: Yes, I felt it instinctively, but I couldn't wait all that time. I hate waiting even five minutes for anybody. It always makes me rather cross. I am not punctual myself, I know, but I do like punctuality in others, and waiting, even to be married, is quite out of the question.

ALGERNON: Then what is to be done, Cecily?

CECILY: I don't know, Mr Moncrieff.[13]

LADY BRACKNELL: My dear Mr Worthing, as Miss Cardew states positively that she cannot wait till she is thirty-five – a remark which I am bound to say seems to me to show a somewhat impatient nature – I would beg of you to reconsider your decision.

JACK: But my dear Lady Bracknell, the matter is entirely in your own hands. The moment you consent to my marriage with Gwendolen, I will most gladly allow your nephew to form an alliance with my ward.

LADY BRACKNELL [*rising and drawing herself up*]: You must be quite aware that what you propose is out of the question.

JACK: Then a passionate celibacy is all that any of us can look forward to.

LADY BRACKNELL: That is not the destiny I propose for Gwendolen. Algernon, of course, can choose for himself. [*Pulls out her watch.*] Come, dear [GWENDOLEN *rises*], we have already missed five, if not six, trains. To miss any more might expose us to comment on the platform.

[*Enter* DR CHASUBLE.]

CHASUBLE: Everything is quite ready for the christenings.

LADY BRACKNELL: The christenings, sir! Is not that somewhat premature?

CHASUBLE [*looking rather puzzled, and pointing to* JACK *and* ALGERNON]: Both these gentlemen have expressed a desire for immediate baptism.

LADY BRACKNELL: At their age? The idea is grotesque and irreligious! Algernon, I forbid you to be baptized. I will not hear of such excesses. Lord Bracknell would be highly displeased if he learned that that was the way in which you wasted your time and money.

CHASUBLE: Am I to understand then that there are to be no christenings at all this afternoon?

JACK: I don't think that, as things are now, it would be of much practical value to either of us, Dr Chasuble.

CHASUBLE: I am grieved to hear such sentiments from you, Mr Worthing. They savour of the heretical views of the Anabaptists,[14] views that I have completely refuted in four of my unpublished sermons. However, as your present mood seems to be one peculiarly secular, I will return to the church at once. Indeed, I have just been informed by the pew-opener that for the last hour and a half Miss Prism has been waiting for me in the vestry.

LADY BRACKNELL [*starting*]: Miss Prism! Did I hear you mention a Miss Prism?

CHASUBLE: Yes, Lady Bracknell. I am on my way to join her.

LADY BRACKNELL: Pray allow me to detain you for a moment. This matter may prove to be one of vital importance to Lord Bracknell and myself. Is this Miss Prism a female of repellent aspect, remotely connected with education?

CHASUBLE [*somewhat indignantly*]: She is the most cultivated of ladies, and the very picture of respectability.

LADY BRACKNELL: It is obviously the same person. May I ask what position she holds in your household?

CHASUBLE [*severely*]: I am a celibate, madam.

JACK [*interposing*]: Miss Prism, Lady Bracknell, has been for the last three years Miss Cardew's esteemed governess and valued companion.

LADY BRACKNELL: In spite of what I hear of her, I must see her at once. Let her be sent for.

CHASUBLE [*looking off*]: She approaches; she is nigh.

[*Enter* MISS PRISM *hurriedly.*]

MISS PRISM: I was told you expected me in the vestry, dear Canon. I have been waiting for you there for an hour and three-quarters.

[*Catches sight of* LADY BRACKNELL, *who has fixed her with a stony glare.* MISS PRISM *grows pale and quails. She looks anxiously round as if desirous to escape.*]

LADY BRACKNELL [*in a severe, judicial voice*]: Prism! [MISS PRISM *bows her head in shame.*] Come here, Prism! [MISS PRISM *approaches in a humble manner.*] Prism! Where is that baby? [*General consternation. The Canon starts back in horror.* ALGERNON *and* JACK *pretend to be anxious to shield* CECILY *and* GWENDOLEN *from hearing the details of a terrible public scandal.*] Twenty-eight years ago, Prism, you left Lord Bracknell's house, Number 104, Upper Grosvenor Square, in charge of a perambulator that contained a baby of the male sex. You never returned. A few weeks later, through the elaborate investigations of the Metropolitan police, the perambulator was discovered at midnight standing by itself in a remote corner of Bayswater. It contained the manuscript of a three-volume novel of more than usually revolting sentimentality. [MISS PRISM *starts in involuntary indignation.*] But the baby was not there. [*Every one looks at* MISS PRISM.] Prism! Where is that baby? [*A pause.*]

MISS PRISM: Lady Bracknell, I admit with shame that I do not know. I only wish I did. The plain facts of the case are these. On the morning of the day you mention, a day that is for ever branded on my memory, I prepared as usual to take the baby out in its perambulator. I had also with me a somewhat old, but capacious hand-bag in which I had intended to place the manuscript of a work of fiction that I had written during my few unoccupied hours. In a moment of mental abstraction, for which I can never forgive myself, I deposited the manuscript in the bassinette and placed the baby in the hand-bag.

JACK [*who had been listening attentively*]: But where did you deposit the hand-bag?

MISS PRISM: Do not ask me, Mr Worthing.

JACK: Miss Prism, this is a matter of no small importance to me. I insist on knowing where you deposited the hand-bag that contained that infant.

MISS PRISM: I left it in the cloak-room of one of the larger railway stations in London.

JACK: What railway station?

MISS PRISM [*quite crushed*]: Victoria. The Brighton line. [*Sinks into a chair.*]

JACK: I must retire to my room for a moment. Gwendolen, wait here for me.

GWENDOLEN: If you are not too long, I will wait here for you all my life. [*Exit* JACK *in great excitement.*]

CHASUBLE: What do you think this means, Lady Bracknell?

LADY BRACKNELL: I dare not even suspect, Dr Chasuble. I need hardly tell you that in families of high position strange coincidences are not supposed to occur. They are hardly considered the thing.

[*Noises heard overhead as if some one was throwing trunks about. Every one looks up.*]

CECILY: Uncle Jack seems strangely agitated.

CHASUBLE: Your guardian has a very emotional nature.

LADY BRACKNELL: This noise is extremely unpleasant. It sounds as if he was having an argument. I dislike arguments of any kind. They are always vulgar, and often convincing.

CHASUBLE [*looking up*]: It has stopped now. [*The noise is redoubled.*]

LADY BRACKNELL: I wish he would arrive at some conclusion.

GWENDOLEN: This suspense is terrible. I hope it will last.

[*Enter* JACK *with a hand-bag of black leather in his hand.*]

JACK [*rushing over to* MISS PRISM]: Is this the hand-bag, Miss Prism? Examine it carefully before you speak. The happiness of more than one life depends on your answer.

MISS PRISM [*calmly*]: It seems to be mine. Yes, here is the injury it received through the upsetting of a Gower Street omnibus[15] in younger and happier days. Here is the stain on the lining caused by the explosion of a temperance beverage, an incident that occurred at Leamington. And here, on the lock, are my initials. I had forgotten that in an extravagant mood I had had them placed there. The bag is undoubtedly mine. I am delighted to have it so unexpectedly restored to me. It has been a great inconvenience being without it all these years.

JACK [*in a pathetic voice*]: Miss Prism, more is restored to you than this hand-bag. I was the baby you placed in it.

MISS PRISM [*amazed*]: You?

JACK [*embracing her*]: Yes . . . mother!

MISS PRISM [*recoiling in indignant astonishment*]: Mr Worthing. I am unmarried!

JACK: Unmarried! I do not deny that is a serious blow. But after all, who has the right to cast a stone against one who has suffered?[16] Cannot repentance wipe out an act of folly? Why should there be one law for men, and another for women? Mother, I forgive you.

[*Tries to embrace her again.*]

MISS PRISM [*still more indignant*]: Mr Worthing, there is some error. [*Pointing to* LADY BRACKNELL.] There is the lady who can tell you who you really are.

JACK [*after a pause*]: Lady Bracknell, I hate to seem inquisitive, but would you kindly inform me who I am?

LADY BRACKNELL: I am afraid that the news I have to give you will not altogether please you. You are the son of my poor sister, Mrs Moncrieff, and consequently Algernon's elder brother.

JACK: Algy's elder brother! Then I have a brother after all. I knew I had a brother! I always said I had a brother! Cecily – how could you have ever doubted that I had a brother? [*Seizes hold of* ALGERNON.] Dr Chasuble, my unfortunate brother. Miss Prism, my unfortunate brother. Gwendolen, my unfortunate brother. Algy, you young scoundrel, you will have to treat me with more respect in the future. You have never behaved to me like a brother in all your life.

ALGERNON: Well, not till today, old boy, I admit. I did my best, however, though I was out of practice.

[*Shakes hands.*]

GWENDOLEN [*to* JACK]: My own! But what own are you? What is your Christian name, now that you have become someone else?

JACK: Good heavens! . . . I had quite forgotten that point. Your decision on the subject of my name is irrevocable, I suppose?

GWENDOLEN: I never change, except in my affections.

CECILY: What a noble nature you have, Gwendolen!

JACK: Then the question had better be cleared up at once. Aunt Augusta, a moment. At the time when Miss Prism left me in the hand-bag, had I been christened already?

LADY BRACKNELL: Every luxury that money could buy, including christening, had been lavished on you by your fond and doting parents.

JACK: Then I was christened! That is settled. Now, what name was I given? Let me know the worst.

LADY BRACKNELL: Being the eldest son you were naturally christened after your father.

JACK [*irritably*]: Yes, but what was my father's Christian name?

LADY BRACKNELL [*meditatively*]: I cannot at the present moment recall what the General's Christian name was. But I have no doubt he had one. He was eccentric, I admit. But only in later years. And that was the result of the Indian climate, and marriage, and indigestion, and other things of that kind.

JACK: Algy! Can't you recollect what our father's Christian name was?

ALGERNON: My dear boy, we were never even on speaking terms. He died before I was a year old.

JACK: His name would appear in the Army Lists of the period, I suppose, Aunt Augusta?

LADY BRACKNELL: The General was essentially a man of peace, except in his domestic life. But I have no doubt his name would appear in any military directory.

JACK: The Army Lists of the last forty years are here. These delightful records should have been my constant study. [*Rushes to bookcase and tears the books out.*] M. Generals ... Mallam, Maxbohm, Magley – what ghastly names they have – Markby, Migsby, Mobbs, Moncrieff! Lieutenant 1840, Captain, Lieutenant-Colonel, Colonel, General 1869, Christian names, Ernest John. [*Puts book very quietly down and speaks quite calmly.*] I always told you, Gwendolen, my name was Ernest, didn't I? Well, it is Ernest after all. I mean it naturally is Ernest.

LADY BRACKNELL: Yes, I remember now that the General was called Ernest. I knew I had some particular reason for disliking the name.

GWENDOLEN: Ernest! My own Ernest! I felt from the first that you could have no other name!

JACK: Gwendolen, it is a terrible thing for a man to find out suddenly that all his life he has been speaking nothing but the truth. Can you forgive me?

GWENDOLEN: I can. For I feel that you are sure to change.

JACK: My own one!

CHASUBLE [*to* MISS PRISM]: Laetitia! [*Embraces her.*]

MISS PRISM [*enthusiastically*]: Frederick! At last!

ALGERNON: Cecily! [*Embraces her.*] At last!

JACK: Gwendolen! [*Embraces her.*] At last!

LADY BRACKNELL: My nephew, you seem to be displaying signs of triviality.

JACK: On the contrary, Aunt Augusta, I've now realized for the first time in my life the vital Importance of Being Earnest.[17]

TABLEAU

CURTAIN

APPENDIX

The excised scene, involving Gribsby, from
The Importance of Being Earnest

[*Enter* MERRIMAN.][1]

MERRIMAN: I have put Mr Ernest's things in the room next to yours, sir. I suppose that is all right!

JACK: What?

MERRIMAN: Mr Ernest's luggage, sir! I have unpacked it and put it in the room next to your own!

ALGY: I am afraid I can't stay more than a week, Jack, this time.

MERRIMAN [*to* ALGY]: I beg your pardon, sir; there is an elderly gentleman wishes to see you! He has just come in a cab from the station. [*Hands card on salver.*]

ALGY: To see me?

MERRIMAN: Yes, sir!

ALGY [*reads card*]: Parker and Gribsby, Solicitors, Chancery Lane. I don't know anything about them. Who are they?

JACK [*takes card*]: Parker and Gribsby. I wonder.[2] [*To* MERRIMAN] Show the gentleman in at once.

MERRIMAN: Yes, sir.

[*Exit.*]

ALGY: What do you think it all means, Jack?

JACK: I expect, Ernest, they have come about some business for your friend Bunbury. Perhaps Bunbury wants to make his will and wishes you to be his executor. From what I know of Bunbury, I think it is extremely likely.

[*Enter* MERRIMAN.]

MERRIMAN: Mr Gribsby.

[*Enter* GRIBSBY.]

GRIBSBY [*to* DR CHASUBLE]: Mr Ernest Worthing?

MISS PRISM: This is Mr Ernest Worthing.

GRIBSBY: Mr Ernest Worthing?

ALGY: Yes, I am Mr Ernest Worthing.

GRIBSBY: Of E.4.[3] The Albany?

ALGY: Yes, that is my address. Charming rooms, too.

GRIBSBY: I am very sorry, sir, but we have a writ of attachment for 20 days against you at the suit of the Savoy Hotel Co. Limited, for £762.14.2.

ALGY: Against me?

GRIBSBY: Yes, sir.

ALGY: What perfect nonsense! I never dine at the Savoy at my own expense. I always dine at Willis's. It is far more expensive. I don't owe a penny to the Savoy!

GRIBSBY: The writ is marked as having been [served] on you personally at The Albany on May the 27th. Judgment was given in default against you on the fifth of June – since then we have written to you no less than thirteen times without receiving any reply. In the interest of our clients we had no option but to obtain an order for committal of your person.[4]

ALGY: Committal! What on earth do you mean by committal? I haven't the smallest intention of going away. I am staying here for a week. I am stopping with my brother. If you imagine I am going up to town the moment I arrive in the country you are extremely mistaken.

GRIBSBY: I am merely a solicitor myself. I do not employ personal violence of any kind. The officer of the Court whose function it is to seize the person of the debtor is waiting in the fly outside. He has considerable experience in these matters.[5] But no doubt you will prefer to pay the bill?

ALGY: Pay it? How on earth am I going to do that? You don't suppose I have got any money? How perfectly silly you are. No gentleman ever has any money.

GRIBSBY: My experience is that it is usually relations who pay!

ALGY: Jack, you really must settle this bill.

JACK: Kindly allow me to see the items, Mr Gribsby. [*Turns over immense folio*] . . . £762.14.2 since last October! I am bound to say I never saw such reckless extravagance in all my life. [*Hands it to* DR CHASUBLE.]

MISS PRISM: £762 for eating! There can be little good in any young man who eats so much and so often.

DR CHASUBLE: We are far away from Wordsworth's plain living and high thinking.[6]

JACK: Now, Dr Chasuble, do you consider that I am in any way called upon to pay this monstrous account for my brother?

DR CHASUBLE: I am bound to say that I do not think so! It would be encouraging his profligacy!

MISS PRISM: As a man sows so let him reap. This proposed incarceration might be most salutary. It is to be regretted that it is only for 20 days!

JACK: I am quite of your opinion!

ALGY: My dear fellow, how ridiculous you are! You know perfectly well that the bill is really yours!

JACK: Mine?

ALGY: Yes, you know it is!

DR CHASUBLE: Mr Worthing, if this is a jest it is out of place!

MISS PRISM: It is gross effrontery. Just what I expected from him!

CECILY: It is ingratitude. I didn't expect that!

JACK: Never mind what he says! This is the way he always goes on. You mean now to say that you are not Ernest Worthing, residing at E.4. The Albany. I wonder, as you are at it, that you don't deny being my brother at all. Why don't you?

ALGY: Oh! I am not going to do that, my dear fellow. It would be absurd. Of course I'm your brother. And that is why you should pay this bill for me.[7]

JACK: I had better tell you quite candidly that I have not the smallest intention of doing anything of the kind. Dr Chasuble, the worthy Rector of this parish, and Miss Prism, in whose admirable and sound judgement I place great reliance, are both of opinion that incarceration would do you a great deal of good, and I think so too!

GRIBSBY [*pulls out watch*]: I am sorry to be forced to break in on this interesting family discussion, but time presses. We have to be at Holloway not later than four o'clock, otherwise it is difficult to obtain admission. The rules are very strict!

ALGY: Holloway?

GRIBSBY: It is at Holloway, sir, that detentions of this character take place always!

ALGY: Well, I really am not going to be imprisoned in the suburbs for having dined in the West End. It is perfectly ridiculous! What nonsensical laws there are in England!

GRIBSBY: The bill is for suppers, not for dinners.

ALGY: I really don't care which it is for! All I say is that I am not going to be imprisoned in the suburbs! For anything!

GRIBSBY: The surroundings of Holloway, I admit, are middle class; I reside myself in the vicinity; but the gaol is fashionable and well-aired – and there are ample opportunities of taking exercise at certain stated hours of the day.[8]

ALGY: Exercise! Good Heavens! No gentleman ever takes exercise. You don't seem to understand what a gentleman is!

GRIBSBY: I have met so many of them, sir, that I am afraid I don't! There are most curious varieties of them. The result of cultivation, no doubt. Will you kindly come now, sir, if it will not be inconvenient to you!

ALGY [appealingly]: Jack! You really can't allow me to be arrested.

MISS PRISM: Pray be firm, Mr Worthing.

DR CHASUBLE: This is an occasion on which any weakness would be out of place! It would be a form of self-deception!

JACK: I am quite firm, and I don't know what weakness or deception of any kind is!

CECILY: Uncle Jack! I think you have a little money of mine, haven't you? Let me pay this bill. I couldn't bear the idea of your own brother being in prison.

JACK: Oh, I couldn't possibly let you pay it, Cecily! It would be absurd!

CECILY: Then you will pay it for him, won't you? I think you would be sorry tomorrow if you thought your own brother was shut up. Of course, I am quite disappointed with Ernest. He is just what I expected.[9]

JACK: You will never speak to him again, Cecily, will you?

CECILY: Certainly not! Unless, of course, he speaks to me first. It would be rude not to answer him!

JACK: Well, I'll take very good care he doesn't speak to you first. I'll take good care he doesn't speak to anybody in *this* house. The man should be cut! Mr Gribsby –

GRIBSBY: Yes, sir!

JACK: I'll pay this bill for my brother. It is the last bill I shall ever pay for him, remember that. How much is the wretched thing?

GRIBSBY: £762.14.2. Ah! The cab will be 5/9 extra – hired for the convenience of the client.

JACK: All right.

MISS PRISM: I must say that I think such generosity misplaced.

DR CHASUBLE [*with a wave of the hand*]: The heart has its wisdom as well as the head, Miss Prism.

JACK: Payable to Gribsby and Parker, I suppose?

GRIBSBY: Yes, sir. An open cheque, please. Thank you![10] [*To* DR CHASUBLE] Good-day! [DR CHASUBLE *bows coldly*] Good-day. [MISS PRISM *bows coldly*] Hope I shall have the pleasure of meeting you again. [*To* ALGY]

ALGY: I sincerely hope not! What ideas you have of the sort of society a gentleman wants to mix in. No gentleman cares much about knowing a solicitor who wants to imprison one in the suburbs.

GRIBSBY: Quite so! Quite so!

ALGY: By the way, Gribsby – Gribsby! You're not to go back to the station in that cab. That is my cab. It was taken for my convenience. You have got to walk to the station. And a very good thing too. Solicitors don't walk nearly enough. I don't know any solicitor who takes sufficient exercise. As a rule they sit in stuffy offices all day long, neglecting their business.

JACK: You can take the cab, Mr Gribsby.

GRIBSBY: Thank you, sir.

[*Exit.*]

NOTES

Lady Windermere's Fan

The play was first staged by George Alexander at St James's Theatre, London, on 20 February 1892, when it ran for 156 performances till mid-July, before being both toured nationally and revived for further performances at St James's prior to Christmas. This was a notable success with a company that catered specifically for upper-class tastes, since their venue was situated in the heart of clubland, close to Mayfair, Belgravia, the court and parliament. Alexander played Windermere and Lily Hanbury his wife; Nutcombe Gould was Darling-ton, while the young Ben Webster was Cecil Graham; Mrs Erlynne was in the capable hands of Marion Terry. Wilde attended rehearsals avidly and, usually through letters to Alexander, but occasionally on his own initiative, gave advice about how he envisaged certain key moments or speeches could best be handled. These letters show that Wilde had a developed interest in the power-relations created either by the positioning of characters within the playing space or by the opposition of still with moving figures on stage.

Six draft-versions of *Lady Windermere's Fan* survive (including the copy sent to the Lord Chamberlain's Office for licensing) and one unauthorized 'acting edition' brought out by French's before the play was published in 1893 by Elkin Mathews and John Lane. The text underwent some notable revisions during rehearsal, since there was some measure of disagreement between Wilde and Alexander about when exactly the audience should become aware of Mrs Erlynne's precise relationship to Lady Windermere. Initially this information had been withheld till the very end of the play, but Alexander appears to have argued that it would be more effectively placed earlier in the action. Though letters show that Wilde at first objected to making this alteration (he argued that the action would be 'too harsh, too horrible' if the audience realized 'that the woman Lady Windermere proposed to strike with her fan was her own mother' (*Selected Letters*, pp. 102–3), he in time came round to this point of view. However, he still devised a means to keep back knowledge of Mrs Erlynne's being Lady Windermere's mother until *after* the incident with the fan. In the revised version, the possibility of such a relationship is intimated by Windermere at the close of Act I; and the fact is confirmed by Mrs Erlynne but only in the concluding moments of Act II, when, on reading Lady Windermere's letter, she realizes that her daughter is about to commit the same mistake that she herself made in the past. After the opening night Wilde wrote to the *St James's Gazette* confirming that he in company with his many friends and with Alexander was convinced that 'the psychological interest of the second act [was] greatly increased by the disclosure of the actual relationship existing between Lady Windermere and Mrs Erlynne'. When Wilde revised the play for publication he chose this later version of the text and incorporated into it numerous descriptive stage directions that draw upon details of Alexander's staging.

DEDICATION

1. *ROBERT EARL OF LYTTON*: Edward Robert Bulwer, Earl of Lytton (1831–91), son of the novelist and politician, Bulwer Lytton; his distinguished diplomatic career took him to many overseas appointments, including Washington, Florence, The Hague, Russia, Vienna and Paris, and as Viceroy to India (1876–80). He disagreed amicably with Wilde over the need for architectural and archaeological accuracy in the designing of stage settings. The two men developed a firm friendship in the last year of Lytton's life when *Lady Windermere's Fan* was being written.

ACT I

1. *Carlton House Terrace*: In the 1890s this was an address favoured by people in high, usually diplomatic, office, which would place the play politically and socially for the contemporary audience.
2. *at home*: The opening line at once establishes the importance of formality and etiquette and a degree of dramatic tension. According to the code of polite behaviour, only the most intimate of friends were expected to call between 5 and 6 o'clock in the afternoon and a man rarely at such a time if he was alone. A butler would normally just announce visitors. Does Parker sense a potential breach in etiquette in the situation, and is he allowing Lady Windermere to determine how matters should proceed? Or has Lord Darlington, waiting below and sensing a possible impropriety in his visit, sent Parker before him as a gesture at decorum? Lady Windermere's hesitation over her reply, her immediate request that Parker admit anyone who should

call and later her reluctance to shake hands with Lord Darlington, should all augment the tone of unease. Lady Windermere is relying on the niceties of good form to keep Lord Darlington at a distance.

3. *of age*: Twenty-one years old.

4. *behind the age*: To be *avant-garde* in some establishment circles in the 1890s where modernity was deemed a challenge to the status quo, implied one was decadent or immoral.

5. *speculation*: I.e. marriage as a financial market, where one's eligibility in large measure depended on the size of one's income and property. Wilde returned to the theme in *The Importance of Being Earnest*, where it underpins much of the comedy of Lady Bracknell's interview with John Worthing and, in the final act, of her sudden interest in Cecily as a likely partner for her nephew, Algernon.

6. *Because the husband . . . vile also*: This aspect of the demand for sexual equality was often talked of in the society drama of the period. Henry Arthur Jones would be the first to construct an entire plot around it in *The Case of Rebellious Susan* (1894). Shaw was to offer a characteristically challenging view on it and the related issue of divorce in *The Philanderer* (written *c.* 1893; staged 1907) and *Getting Married* (1908).

7. *I think life . . . and fast rules*: Ironically this is to become Lady Windermere's viewpoint. It is a sign of Wilde's powers of discrimination that an idea which is first voiced negligently by a practised seducer should, when expressed by his morally awakened heroine, encompass compassion, insight and sound sense.

8. *small and early*: Etiquette varied somewhat over the distinction between a ball and a dance; balls usually involved more than a hundred guests and continued until at least 2.00 a.m. By 'early', Lady Windermere implies her gathering will be a modest affair that ends around midnight.

9. *a game . . . trick*: I.e. the newly fashionable card-game of bridge, involving pairs of partners where each couple seeks to outwit the other by cunning and artful means. The game is won by the couple who gain the majority of the thirteen possible 'tricks'. 'Honours' are the ace, king, queen, knave and ten of the suit that can 'trump' (that is, defeat) the other three suits of cards. This speech is the closest Wilde ever came to imitating the knowing innuendo of Restoration Comedy.

10. *Many a woman . . . all fit*: The 'past' refers to extramarital sexual liaisons that had been the occasion of scandal. For some years such a woman had been a stock figure of melodrama, usually cast in the role of villainess to accord with dramatists' and audiences' horror at her seeming lack of moral probity and self-control. Pinero, perhaps influenced by the success of *Lady*

Windermere's Fan, was the following year to explore the situation with remarkable social and emotional insight as the basis of a tragedy in *The Second Mrs Tanqueray*, while Shaw's radical investigation of such a woman from a financial rather than a conventional moral perspective in *Mrs Warren's Profession* was promptly censored (written in 1893, it was not staged till 1925). Though in Shaw's *Candida* (staged 1900) adultery is finally and firmly resisted by the heroine, much of the action of the play is taken up with a sympathetic portrayal of its attractions and potential in contrast with her marriage.

11. *ponies in the Park*: It was customary for members of high society regularly to drive in Hyde Park during the afternoon to 'take the air'. Married women might drive alone. The inference is that Mrs Erlynne is either being overly bold or acting as a parvenue lacking a proper sense of good form.

12. *Homburg . . . Aix*: Both were fashionable spa towns in the 1890s, where the aristocracy and even royalty went to take the waters, to rest and frequently to gamble in the local casino in the evenings.

13. *And he's only . . . months*: The joke (perhaps to some degree a private one on Wilde's part) is at the Duchess's expense and is designed to expose her as naive. Walter Pater resided and taught in Oxford, which became known in consequence to many as the centre of the Aesthetic Movement and so was frequently accused of fostering decadence and a lack of moral fibre in the students. Unlike the Duchess's overly protected daughter, Agatha, her son has a complete independence. Wilde is making a serious point, highlighting the inequalities of opportunity available to young men and women, which render the likes of Lady Agatha and Lady Windermere peculiarly vulnerable.

14. *without a character*: Used here to mean a letter of reference recommending a former employee as trustworthy, diligent and capable, and so of 'good character'. It was customary to offer such a testimonial when a servant was not dismissed for negligence or misconduct.

15. *a card*: Invitations were conventionally the responsibility of the hostess, who sent an 'at Home' card marked in one corner with the nature of the gathering. The Duchess is trusting to her friendship with Lady Windermere in pressing for an invitation for Mr Hopper; her motive is all too clear. The ease with which Lady Windermere complies is markedly different from her reaction to her husband's similar request. This polite exchange prepares the ground for the later episode, which concludes with the husband breaking the customary pattern by writing an invitation to Mrs Erlynne himself.

16. *I dare not . . . kill her*: See the commentary above for discussion of the important revision that Wilde made here. That revision is wholly at one with the tenor of the play and its preoccupation with façades designed to hide or disguise actualities.

NOTES

ACT II

1. *Drawing-room . . . crowded with guests*: The reception rooms in such a grand
house would be on the first floor and guests would ascend to make their
entrance. In the drafts Wilde specifies white walls for the drawing-room with
red and gold furniture in the Louis Seize style. It is imperative that the formality
of the social ritual involved in arrivals and introductions (the announcing of
the names, the hostess's greeting at the entrance of the suite of rooms)
be observed in production; without it, the rising tension generated by the
expectation of Mrs Erlynne's imminent appearance provoking a 'scene' is
lost.

2. *card*: Traditionally such cards were carried by eligible girls, who wrote down
the names of intended partners for specific dances. (The card carried an
ordered list of the dances.) This allowed mothers and chaperones to exercise
some control over the girls' activities by deciding early which were suitable
partners for their charges and which (such as younger sons who by the laws
of primogeniture stood to inherit little) were not.

3. *beautifully dressed and very dignified*: Mrs Erlynne is an immediately impressive
figure, but not ostentatiously so; she is a woman of taste who calculates the
effect of her appearance to a nicety. Wilde meticulously avoids all suggestion
of the stereotype of 'the woman with a past'. Marion Terry challenged
expectation on her appearance by being clad not in some bold colour, the
like of the heliotrope dress which Wilde specifies for Mrs Cheveley in *An Ideal
Husband*, but in a lustrous white satin ball gown. (Lily Hanbury's ball dress as
Lady Windermere was also white.) The reviewer for the *Echo* (22 February
1892) convinced himself that Mrs Erlynne's dress took on a snake-like sheen
under the stage lighting, but how much did expectation influence his perceptions?

4. *a moment's hesitation*: Good form required that the woman with the higher
rank (Lady Jedburgh) request an introduction. Graham is somewhat perturbed
by this break with etiquette and its possible consequences.

5. *a wicked French novel*: French realist novelists (Flaubert, the Goncourts, Zola,
Maupassant) were allowed far greater freedom of expression especially in the
portrayal of desire and sexuality than the English. Hardy, for example, had
recently been pilloried for his depiction of his heroine in *Tess of the D'Urbervilles*
(1891) as 'a pure woman' (the novel's subtitle) despite her rape and adultery.
French novels were published with distinctive pale yellow paper covers, but
could be rebound to disguise their origins; they were available only to the
educated and upper classes (who could read French) and were readily circulated

among them. However, in the 1880s the publisher Henry Vizetelly began a series of translations, particularly of Zola by, among others, Wilde's compatriot, George Moore; they were produced with fine engraved illustrations and embossed covers. Vizetelly was involved in charges of obscene libel, tried and gaoled.

In this context it is significant that when Wilde was on trial, it was formally noted by the prosecution that he carried a yellow-bound book on one occasion. Also time was devoted to trying to determine the identity and the moral quality of the volume that Lord Henry Wotton gives to Dorian Gray; the supposition on the part of the prosecution was that it was Joris Karl Huysmans's *A Rebours* (1884), which (it was argued) was the ultimate expression of decadence and depravity.

6. *My dear Laura*: This is to be staged as a private exchange; the intimacy of the address establishes an adulterous relationship between them, which serves to emphasize the sheer hypocrisy of Lady Plymdale's comments on Mrs Erlynne.

7. *I am the only person . . . at present*: A characteristic Wildean stab at the upper classes for their want of self-awareness (as distinct from self-possession). Within a jest he succinctly states a major theme of the play.

8. *the cloak to hide his secret*: Just how profoundly ironic this remark is will become apparent only in the final act. Mrs Erlynne is using Lord Windermere to keep the knowledge of her precise relationship with his wife secret; Lady Windermere will in time gratefully use Mrs Erlynne as a means to hide her indiscretion from her husband. Again it is Lord Darlington who alerts the audience to the social actualities behind the games with masks and cloaks, in which he is clearly an accomplished master.

9. *Choose! Oh, my love, choose*: Wilde here cleverly exposes the shallowness of Lord Darlington by the verbal strategies he endows him with: as the man grows ever more passionate, so his language becomes more rhetorical, melodramatic and overtly *theatrical*; he is playing a role.

10. *The music stops*: Melodrama generally accompanied scenes of high passion and crucial moral choice with music to set the tone and augment the audience's emotional response. To some degree that is the tradition that Wilde is drawing on here, except that this music is for the dancing in the ballroom which in its lightness and grace offsets ironically Lord Darlington's intensity and Lady Windermere's bewilderment, anger and fear. It is of course too a reminder of the diplomatic circle, now seen at its ease, from which Lady Windermere will forever be barred, should she take a wrong step. We know from the opening exchange between Lady Agatha and her mother that Lady Windermere has a penchant for waltzes; though now such a dance was considered old-fashioned, it was earlier in the century deemed louche for inciting libidinous ideas in participants on account of their close proximity. It would add greatly to the emotional complexity of this episode for an audience if the dance being played throughout was indeed a waltz. This whole scene and its use of music shows Wilde's ability to create a credible social verisimilitude as background to Lady Windermere's inner torment. By now the symbolic significance of the white dress Lily Hanbury wore in this scene as Lady Windermere would be profoundly ironic: a token no longer of youthful innocence but of sheer naivety.

11. *Except Margaret . . . I assure you*: This remark was omitted from the copy that went to the Lord Chamberlain for licensing but its restoration allows Wilde to establish what Mrs Erlynne later claims, namely that it was not maternal sentiment that brought her back to England but the purely mercenary intention of getting herself back into society by blackmailing her daughter's new husband. It requires a sharp, brittle delivery if Mrs Erlynne's later change of attitude to her daughter is to carry dramatic weight.

12. *her father*: This finally makes all previous intimations about the relationship between Mrs Erlynne and Lady Windermere perfectly clear. Initially Wilde's drafts and the licensed copy had 'my husband', which continued to keep the relationship hidden.

13. *call my carriage, please*: The complex etiquette involved in making a departure allows Wilde to take Lord Windermere out and bring him back into the playing space in a fashion that, while adhering to the demands of realism, continually builds the tension but also allows Mrs Erlynne brief moments of respite alone to examine the situation she has provoked. The sheer rapidity of the sequence helps to establish her character as capable of penetrating intuition, quick-wittedness and cool control. Not for the last time in the play she will be the relatively still centre of the stage action, setting others rapidly in motion around her. That she is invariably the focus of the scene when on stage is being developed by Wilde as a means of defining her will-power, emotional stamina and shameless daring.

ACT III

1. *rooms . . . Lamps lit*: We are now decidedly in bachelor quarters: the furniture is functional and, compared with the brilliant decor of the previous scene, what few properties are included are indicative of the masculine pursuits of drinking and smoking, which Wilde was fond of ridiculing as the only occupations proper to a gentleman. A Tantalus is a kind of wooden frame in which two or more cut-glass decanters are situated and which, by virtue of a cleverly placed wood or metal bar, can only be removed when the bar is unlocked. The device proffers a temptation but denies one the pleasure of drinking till the host chooses to apply the key.

2. *cold as a loveless thing*: Lady Windermere is struggling with the intuition that she has done a rash act of which the consequences are less than gratifying. 'Thing' is a brilliant usage of the word, exactly defining what she will be reduced to socially in the ensuing scandal. Significantly she thinks next by unconscious association of her husband, referring to him intimately by his Christian name as the source till now of the warmth of which she feels deprived (and, after his discovery of her letter, will be denied).

3. *horribly mad*: Recognition of her danger is following rapidly after awareness of how impetuous her gesture in leaving her home has been. Insight is, however, giving way to self-pity; seeing herself as at the mercy of two men's power (Darlington's if she stays; Windermere's if she returns) totally undermines her ability to think through her situation constructively. She capitulates to tragic posturing. That Wilde resorts to melodramatic rhetoric for her long soliloquy critically places the character as feeble in her desperation (as she casts herself in the role of the pathetic victim, so avoiding proper responsibility for her own actions). This is in marked contrast with what we saw of Mrs Erlynne when confronted by a series of difficult situations in the previous act. That Lady Windermere dropped her fan in the presence of the stronger woman (lacking the strength to create a 'scene' and so flout convention) is wholly in keeping with how the role is now being developed. The theatrical tenor of the speech increases to suggest a mind rendered impotent by its own self-questioning; Mrs Erlynne's speech on her arrival by contrast is directly focused on action and intent.

4. *throws off her cloak . . . sofa*: This is a childish and impetuous action; but, as Kaplan and Stowell argue in *Theatre and Fashion*, the moment creates a complex and ironic stage picture. Their research has ascertained that in the original production the actresses wore nearly identical dark cloaks, 'lined with . . . pink bengaline', beneath which both still wore their white ball gowns. Throughout the remainder of the act Mrs Erlynne remains formal in appearance and cloaked in preparation for immediate departure. Lady Windermere in removing her cloak reveals her extreme decolletage: the dress, as sketched in the *Lady* (10 March 1892), exposed most of the arms, while the low-cut bodice had only a modicum of veiling over the breasts. This is a highly compromising display within so distinctively masculine a setting.

5. *how terrible and how unjust*: There has been some critical debate about whether or not the play is improved by Alexander's insistence that Mrs Erlynne's relationship to Lady Windermere be revealed to the audience before the final act and the redrafting which that entailed. Lines such as these would lose their complex levels of irony and pain, if that relationship were not known, and the tone would become merely accusatory.

6. *Nothing*: Again a moment of supreme irony, as Mrs Erlynne refuses the one chance she has of revealing herself to her daughter, which would carry little impact were that relationship not known to the audience. Enlightened, they can appreciate the heroism in this moment of abnegation.

7. *Arthur . . . between you*: A casual slip by Mrs Erlynne almost precipitates the revelation she has just denied herself. For a woman to use a man's Christian name in public was a mark of considerable intimacy.

8. *gesture of pain . . . not dare to touch her*: Continually Wilde devises means of keeping us aware of Mrs Erlynne's courage in suppressing a desire to tell Lady Windermere who she is. The dialogue hovers repeatedly on the verge of a revelation and the audience steadily come to appreciate both the rightness of Mrs Erlynne's instinctive decision not to reveal that she is Lady Windermere's mother and the cost of that decision for her emotionally. The self-righteousness of Lady Windermere by contrast is exposed as profoundly cruel in its unthinking naivety.

9. *for tonight . . . let that pass*: Mrs Erlynne suddenly reveals a crack in her careful composure, a touch of self-awareness that exposes briefly to our view the woman behind the role she has chosen to play. Just as quickly she suppresses this hint of sentiment lest she be tempted into sentimentality. The moral awareness that directs her behaviour is exact and exacting.

10. *your place is with your child*: The insistent rhetoric is the token of Mrs Erlynne's unstated wish that she might redeem her past decision. It is also cleverly apt in psychological terms, since it helps to shift the focus of Lady Windermere's mind away from her own immediate predicament and on to her child's, which might galvanize her into action.

11. *Take me home*: The repetition (incorporated into the first edition from some of the early drafts) exactly captures the implication of the stage direction, '*helplessly, as a child*', and acts as motivation for the '*look of wonderful joy*' in Mrs Erlynne's face at being appealed to as a mother.

12. *Listen . . . voice*: The licensing copy and a surviving actor's typescript both give an offstage line ('I don't think I can come in') to Lord Windermere here.

13. *lots of topics . . . her, Tuppy*: The two women are here in a situation that allows them to eavesdrop on men's conversation; it is proof to Lady Windermere of the accuracy of Mrs Erlynne's description of the 'brains' it costs to get back into society once you have a questionable reputation, as well as a vivid demonstration of how she would be treated were her presence in Lord Darlington's rooms common knowledge. It also shows to Mrs Erlynne the risk she has placed herself in by following Lady Windermere; but it further proves to her the strength of Lord Augustus's affection in that he is prepared to defend her against the younger men's derisory banter (which today would be judged as decidedly sexist). The social realism of this moment is excellently integrated into the dramatic structuring of the whole scene.

14. *This woman has purity and innocence*: Now it is Lady Windermere's turn to hear what is thought of her when the speaker does not know of her presence. Clearly Lord Darlington is a romantic in love with an unattainable ideal of womanhood. Everything he values in Lady Windermere would be compromised and lost the moment she responded to his love.

15. *Takes fan . . . each other*: The intricacies of this sequence need meticulous timing if the audience is to perceive every detail. The group of men allow a director to shift an audience's focus of attention even as they re-direct their own gaze first to Lord Windermere advancing on the figure hidden behind the curtain at the rear of the stage, and then to Mrs Erlynne who enters (stage right) to provide the necessary distraction which allows Lady Windermere to '*glide from the room*' (to stage left). The responses of Lord Windermere and Lord Augustus to Mrs Erlynne's appearance are important to provide tension and dramatic impetus for the final act. Once again she is a focal point, decisive, controlled, perfectly still.

ACT IV

1. *Oh! Life . . . not rule it*: This is a forceful critique of a society that willingly submits to being in the grip of hidebound conventions and codes of behaviour which are honoured in the name of tradition and good breeding, and that rigorously polices its members to ensure that they conform to what is expected of them.

2. *My dear child*: At the moment when Lady Windermere begins to voice a new generosity and a decidedly adult awareness, her husband chooses to assert his patriarchal tone, implying that she is being childish and wilful because she will not accede to his view. He reiterates the word 'child' during the following exchange, whenever Lady Windermere challenges what he clearly sees as his right to dictate how she shall view the world about her. The scene is structured on ironic reversal: where throughout Act I she was inflexible while he appealed for charity and understanding in respect of Mrs Erlynne, now he is utterly inflexible and she insists on behaving unconventionally in refusing to judge others. In effect she is resigning the role she had assumed in the opening act of being a guardian policing public morals, because she has been taught by experience not to trust appearances. This neatly prepares the ground for Wilde's conclusion as shaped by Mrs Erlynne, who rapidly appreciates on joining them that Lord Windermere must never know of his wife's whereabouts the previous evening, if their marriage is to survive.

3. *Moves towards sofa with* MRS ERLYNNE: Wilde wrote to George Alexander during rehearsals for the first production, pointing out how it was essential that this act take place in a space that the audience had come to recognize as Lady Windermere's. He observed: 'This is a very important point.' (There had been talk in the theatre about using the scenery of the opening scene for this final one; Wilde insisted that, if there had to be economies, then the scenery of the second act in Lady Windermere's drawing-room was more appropriate than the very first setting which defined her husband's morning-room.) He then revealed a more important reason for writing: his concern about the precise placing of the sofa for the encounter between mother and daughter and he drew a small diagram to show exactly where this should be. Wilde was anxious that Mrs Erlynne should be 'in full view of the audience. She should not be at the side. The situation is too important.' The sofa was to be centre left and not placed parallel with the footlights but angled so that Mrs Erlynne, on taking her seat at the upper end, would be virtually centre-stage. He concluded: 'Mrs Erlynne should hold the centre of the stage, and be its central figure.' In the following paragraph he discusses the movement of the characters about the stage, opining that, as he is in his own home, Windermere might 'pace up and down – does in fact do so'; Mrs Erlynne, however, should not move about in this fashion: 'She rises from the sofa, as marked in the play, and sits down, but with the possibility of Lady Windermere entering at any moment, for her to walk about, or cross, or the like, would be melodramatic, but not dramatic or artistic.' (See *More Letters*, pp. 109–12.) This gives remarkable insight into how Wilde envisaged the sequence being enacted: his aim was for a punctilious realism that avoided any suggestion of melodrama. Meanwhile, conscious to a remarkable degree of the spatial possibilities of the playing space, he had once again (as at the conclusion to Acts II and III) created a stage picture in which Mrs Erlynne is a still point around whom the other characters move at her command. Though a visitor to the house, it is she who controls when husband and wife leave and enter the room, thus giving herself an opportunity to determine whether her suppositions about them are indeed accurate, because it is only on the basis of this knowledge that she can shape an apt ending to the drama. This simple move here to the sofa becomes, as the scene develops, loaded with symbolic and psychological weight.

4. *serious people*: From the moment of her arrival Mrs Erlynne keeps up a challenging level of banter with Lord Windermere, as if defying him to think the worst of her. While apparently pursuing a line in conversational triviality, she is in fact mounting a serious criticism of him, his values and his social milieu. She sustains this tone with formidable brilliance until her departure. Given our knowledge of her, an audience can by now judge to a nicety when, as here, she is indulging in role-play to advance some privately designed purpose. She knows that she alone possesses the skill to mould the prevailing situation to either an amiable conclusion or a tragic one.

5. *the Club Train*: A luxurious express designed to carry wealthy travellers to Paris with the utmost speed via the Channel Ferry from Dover. Passengers leaving by the daily 4.00 p.m. train could expect to reach Paris shortly before midnight.

6. *manners before morals*: Earlier versions than the first edition give 'Really!' as Mrs Erlynne's response to Windermere's outburst but this sounds like shocked outrage when, as the revision demonstrates, what is wanted is a cool rejoinder that puts him firmly in his place. This is truer to the portrayal of her. And she has caught her host out, since for once he has let his mask slip and impetuously set good form aside in the interest of powerful feeling.

7. *the mother . . . is living*: In the copy submitted for licensing and earlier drafts of the play, this was the moment when Mrs Erlynne's relation to Lady Windermere was finally revealed. Through the revisions the episode has become considerably more complex than the original expression of Windermere's detestation of Mrs Erlynne with its moral and emotional snobbery. Now the dramatic and psychological interest is sustained between the two characters with a fine degree of balance: in him there is the release of all his pent-up anger at having to sustain lies and duplicity in ways that have threatened his marriage; but she knows that the threats are more profound than he appreciates. He wounds her repeatedly with his callous remarks and yet she refrains from telling him details of his wife's movements the previous evening which would silence him immediately. Her purpose in choosing to accept suffering is not yet clear; the uncertainty creates a tension that is not resolved until Mrs Erlynne finally leaves the stage. Wilde's handling of suspense the better to provoke an audience into new moral and social insights is admirably demonstrated in this scene in its revised form. In the draft versions the revelation of carefully delayed information provokes a measure of sensationalism that detracts from the psychological intensity. The earlier versions stayed firmly within the genre of melodrama and its conventions; the revised text moves into more profound and subtle areas of analysis and character-representation.

8. *looking steadily at him*: Despite Windermere's furious attack on her, Mrs Erlynne holds her ground. Her steady gaze he sees doubtlessly as proof of her utter shamelessness and calculated bravado; but with our greater knowledge of her, we can judge it as a token of Mrs Erlynne's moral rectitude and exacting self-awareness. This is another moment where his coarseness seems likely to provoke her into telling him the truth; her restraint shames him.

9. *the fashion then*: Again Mrs Erlynne deflects a mood of growing intensity with an apparently flippant remark. Yet the surface tone belies the emotional complexities that she is experiencing. Wilde has throughout the play created a context in which his audiences can read behind the witty but brittle surface of polite conversation to apprehend the intricacies of feeling such a surface is calculated to keep repressed. Mrs Erlynne needs to resist any resort to emotionalism, if she is to come to the clear-sighted appreciation of her daughter and son-in-law that she needs to resolve their predicament to their (rather than her) satisfaction. In her next speech she is briefly to '*reveal herself*' as her voice takes on a tragic tone; but, sensing the dangers of sentimentality, she quickly recovers herself with '*a trivial laugh*'. That moment allows us fully to comprehend significances which elsewhere in the scene and the play are meticulously implied.

10. *silly modern novels*: This is a shrewd observation of more than immediately contemporary fiction. Fallen women seeking redemption like repentant Magdalens were generally in nineteenth-century literature required to sacrifice themselves (such as Nancy in *Oliver Twist* or Mrs Gaskell's Ruth Hilton in *Ruth*).

11. *in real life . . . any rate*: Early drafts have instead of this line the observation: 'We go to Homburg, or Paris, or Aix, or some place where we can amuse ourselves.' This puts a whole new gloss on the Duchess of Berwick's recommendation to Lady Windermere that she should take her husband to just those very same spa resorts, if she is to recover his affections. The revision, though less comic in its implications, keeps the dramatic focus on Mrs Erlynne's cunning tactic of playing up to Windermere's expectation of her.

12. *If you dare . . . not enter*: Wilde reintroduced this sentence into the first published text of the play which occurred in early drafts but which would appear to have been removed from the text for licensing and from Alexander's performance text; it may have been deemed too shocking in its implications to go before the Lord Chamberlain's office when the future of the whole play might have been jeopardized. It is the darkest utterance in the play and yet it is proof of Mrs Erlynne's astute understanding of Windermere's patriarchal temperament: she has to prevent him using his knowledge of Mrs Erlynne's relationship with his wife at any future time as a means of power over her daughter. Wilde is inviting us to engage with the motive not the threatened deed, but it is characteristic of his mature artistry that an audience is left to interpret that motive from the emotional subtext of the whole act.

13. *If I lost . . . everything*: The ironies are many-layered here. In the context of the scene, the line has a dangerous innocence. But on another level entirely the audience appreciate as she cannot that she does have good reason to honour her mother as an ideal worth emulating, though to judge Mrs Erlynne's recent conduct as ideal requires an audience to embrace an ethical system far distant from what passes for conventional morals. Wilde is establishing the grounds on which he seeks to justify his subtitle.

14. *hesitates . . . leaves the room*: Once again Mrs Erlynne by sheer force of personality controls the movement of the other characters within the stage space. She has used Lady Windermere's absence in quest of the photograph to manipulate Windermere to where she has full control over him; and now she requires his absence, while she sets about determining her daughter's future actions. Her power is inexorable but directed at wholly constructive ends within the parameters that 'good' society allows her.

15. *Shrewsbury and Talbot*: These highly efficient, smooth-riding, noiseless and well-appointed vehicles had been in operation in London for over a decade and were proving an immensely popular means of conveyance.

16. *Enter LORD AUGUSTUS*: Wilde had a precise sense of how spatial relations on stage between actors can create or sustain what has come to be known today as a subtext (dimensions of implied meaning or significance that enrich in performance an audience's appreciation of what is spoken). In this regard his advice to Alexander about staging this sequence, when Lord and Lady Windermere share an intimate exchange together before being disrupted by Lord Augustus's return, is exemplary. Lines such as Windermere's to his wife ('Into your world evil has never entered') and hers later to him ('I will trust you absolutely') show that Mrs Erlynne has succeeded in restoring their marriage to a loving equanimity, although both will be prey to their private consciences, as the ensuing action makes clear. To bring audiences to this insight, he wished the final moments to be staged in a way that sharply distinguished between what they heard to the fore of the stage and what they viewed at the rear:

When Windermere says, on Mrs Erlynne's exit, 'Allow me', he goes to the door. His wife on Mrs Erlynne's exit goes towards him, and I want you both to get to the *back of the stage*. Lord Augustus enters below you, takes you by arm to the front of stage. Lady Windermere watches from the back, till her anxiety becomes unbearable, and then comes down. It is essential that Lady Windermere should not hear one word of Lord Augustus's account of Mrs Erlynne's explanation.

(*More Letters*, pp. 111–12)

The couple's return to marital stability is hard-won and all-too-tenuous; and that is Wilde's final comment on a society that lacks the fundamentals of trust, because it lives by appearances.

17. *a very good woman*: Nineteenth-century playwrights often manipulated the final lines of the dialogue so that the last words spoken voiced the title of the piece. Here with a characteristic flourish Wilde appears to be set to do just this, but then at the last moment substitutes a reference instead to the subtitle of the play so that that challenging reminder is what audiences take away from the theatre at the close of the performance. To the last Wilde's prime focus is on redefining what had become a hackneyed stereotype on the late-Victorian stage (the representation of the woman with a past); and in the process inevitably he has had to refine the crude ethical system which that stereotype was designed to endorse. The final words state his agenda explicitly.

Salomé

Wilde began writing *Salomé* in French late in 1891 (one surviving manuscript is dated as composed in Paris in November, and several friends record Wilde discussing its development as early as 27 October). At least three genuine drafts are extant and two which at various times have been denigrated as forgeries. At some point Wilde submitted his text to the novelist and poet Pierre Louÿs (1870–1925), who suggested corrections to Wilde's French grammar, particularly his use of the subjunctive; Wilde incorporated most into his finished version, but stylistic changes were ignored. There are indications that other friends too were invited to tinker with the grammar. Wilde had been spurred on to complete his drama in French by the hope that the central role would be attempted by Sarah Bernhardt as the final production of her first London season in 1892 at the Palace Theatre. To this end Graham Robertson had set about designing a setting and was discussing with Bernhardt how she might adapt the costumes she wore in *Cléopâtra*, when the Lord Chamberlain intervened and banned the play, ostensibly on the grounds that it was forbidden in England to represent a biblical figure (John the Baptist) on the stage. The ban did not extend to publication, however, and Wilde brought out the French text simultaneously in France (Librairie de l'Art Indépendant) and England (Elkin Mathews and John Lane) in February 1893. French writers the like of Stéphane Mallarmé and Maurice Maeterlinck were full of praise because they could see the extent to which it was a kind of homage paid to French culture, to the novelists Gustave Flaubert and Joris Karl Huysmans and especially the painter Gustave Moreau, who had handled the theme earlier; and they were not troubled by the stylistic linking of such contemporary artists with the rhetoric and imagery of the Song of Solomon. In England, however, the play was greeted by a chorus of ridicule. A year later Mathews and Lane published *Salomé: A Tragedy in One Act: Translated from the French of Oscar Wilde: Pictured by Aubrey Beardsley*. Only the dedication indicates that Bosie had any hand in it, but how much is a matter of dispute: correspondence shows clearly that Wilde was not happy with Douglas's work and virtually took over the job himself. Critics were even less happy with the Englished version than the French: *The Times* (23 February 1893) went so far as to denounce the work as 'offensive in its adaptation of scriptural phraseology to situations the reverse of sacred', especially as the result was a shocking 'arrangement in blood and ferocity'.

It is not surprising, given the differing cultural climates in France and England, that the first staging of the play took place in Paris in 1896 under the direction of Aurelian Lugné-Poë. Next Max Reinhardt mounted productions in Berlin in 1902–3, which in time proved an inspiration to Richard Strauss, whose opera based closely on Wilde's text, as translated for him by Hedwig Lachmann, opened in Dresden in 1905. In England, the play could be performed only under club theatre conditions in private venues. After Wilde's death it was eventually staged first and none too successfully by Florence Farr at the Bijou Theatre in Bayswater in May 1905, and a year later by Charles Ricketts, the painter and stage designer, at the King's Hall, Covent Garden. (Farr acted the role of Herodias for Ricketts, while Herod was a repeat performance by Robert Farquharson who had previously played the role for Farr; the first Salomé was Millicent Murby and in Ricketts's production Letitia Darragh; Ricketts's Jokanaan was the young Lewis Casson.) A pair of productions, one under the direction of Peter Godfrey at the Gate Theatre Studio in London with Margaret Rawlings as the Princess, and the second produced by Terence Gray at the Cambridge Festival Theatre, both in 1929, may have led to the lifting of the ban in 1931 (the two men were in the front-rank of innovative practitioners). Gray immediately responded by staging the play for a full run with Robert Morley as Herod and Beatrix Lehmann as Salomé. The choreography for the climactic dance on all three occasions had been devised by Ninette de Valois (Gray's cousin). Brilliant character-dancer though de Valois was, she made it a matter of principle to refuse to take on any role that required her to speak on stage. Perhaps to compensate her for a decision that robbed her of the chance to attempt a role for which she was otherwise peculiarly gifted, the poet W. B. Yeats in 1934 devised especially for her a dance-play involving masks and mime based on the Salomé story where she could express herself wholly in movement: *The King of the Great Clock Tower*.

For many decades Strauss's opera was performed more frequently than Wilde's play, but it has gained increasing attention from practitioners who work more within the traditions of physical theatre than conventional drama. Lindsay Kemp in 1977 staged an all-male version in the manner of a homoerotic fantasy, in which he played Salomé and Herod was the former dancer Anton Dolin. Steven Berkoff first directed the play in a refined, minimalist, incantatory fashion for the Gate Theatre, Dublin, in 1988 with Olwen Fuere and Alan Stanford as Salomé and the Tetrarch, and then redirected it for the Royal National Theatre at Edinburgh and London in 1989 with himself as Herod and Katherine Schlesinger as the Princess, carrying the stylization to even further extremes. Of all Wilde's plays *Salomé* is the one that has invited the widest range of stylistic invention on the part of cast, director and designer, because it is wholly free of the constraints of nineteenth-century realism.

DEDICATION

1. *My Friend*: Lord Alfred Bruce Douglas (1870–1945) was the third son of the 8th Marquis of Queensberry; he was introduced to Wilde while in his second year at Oxford. Douglas's father objected to their growing relationship and made heated accusations which led Wilde, much influenced in this decision by Douglas, to bring an action for libel against the peer in 1895 with disastrous consequences for himself. Douglas excelled in the sonnet, examples of which he published in two collections, *In Excelsis* (1924) and *Sonnets and Lyrics* (1935). He endeavoured, unsuccessfully, to halt publication of Wilde's *De Profundis*, a long letter written from Reading Gaol which minutely and trenchantly dissects Douglas's character.

SCENE

1. *A great terrace . . . Moonlight*: Wilde sketched a design for a potential staging of the play (which was recently discovered by Professor Joseph Donohue); it shows how he experimented with the spatial relations between the all-important moon, the cistern and the flight of steps:

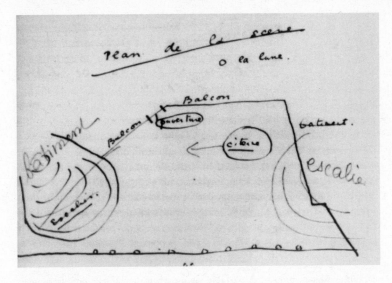

Ricketts recalled discussing a potential production with Wilde, during which he made the following rough drawing that demonstrates how together they elaborated on Wilde's initial thoughts to achieve an effect that was at once exotic, atmospheric and different, yet totally clear of the kind of historicizing clutter that marred much contemporary stage settings for 'period' drama. Ricketts's revision to this design added one further symbolic point of focus not included in Wilde's sketch: the Tetrarch's throne as emblem of his autocratic rule.

This is an ideal setting for obsessive individuals intent on a battle of wills: the play investigates subtly changing power relations between Salomé, Herod and Jokanaan and this is defined for an audience subliminally by the struggle between them for control of the playing space. In his essay 'The Art of Stage Decoration' Ricketts left an account which graphically informs us how to read the image reproduced on the following page:

I proposed a black floor – upon which Salomé's white feet would show; this statement was meant to capture Wilde. The sky was to be a rich turquoise blue, cut across by the perpendicular fall of strips of gilt matting, which should not touch the ground, but form an aerial tent. Did Wilde actually suggest the division of the actors into masses of colour, to-day the idea seems mine! His was the suggestion, however, that the Jews should be in yellow, the Romans were to be in purple, the soldiery in bronze-green, and John in white. Over the dress of Salomé the discussions were endless: should she be black 'like the night'? silver 'like the moon'? or – here the suggestion is Wilde's – 'green like a

curious poisonous lizard'? I desired that the moonlight should fall upon the ground, the source not being seen; Wilde himself hugged the idea of some 'strange dim pattern in the sky'. *(Pages on Art, pp. 243–4)*

Wilde on another occasion recommended that braziers should be placed in the orchestra pit from which clouds of incense would rise throughout the performance so that the actors would be viewed as through a veil or mist as if seen in a dream (an interesting anticipation of the modern theatre's deployment of effects with dry ice). What is apparent from all this is Wilde's desire for an aesthetic simplicity focusing on a schematic use of colour and the meticulous placing of three symbolic spaces: the cistern, the throne and the dance floor, which as the play unfolds would be brought by Salomé's desire into a tragic relation.

2. *Look at the moon*: Like a set of variations on a musical theme, all the main characters in the drama on entering are drawn to gaze at the moon and seek to define its effect on their private perceptions and sensibility. It is a highly poetic device of exposition that introduces the characters' inner selves immediately rather than their social status within the drama. The one exception is the cynical, down-to-earth Herodias ('the moon is like the moon'), who caustically reveals her lack of any imaginative or spiritual potential.

3. *You look at her too much*: The Page's refrain anticipates Herodias's endless complaint about the way Herod constantly gazes at Salomé, even as the Young Syrian's eyes are fixated on her.

4. *Tetrarch*: The title under the Roman Empire given to a subordinate governor within a province. While Antony had granted this title to Herod the Great in 41 BC, he had subsequently been created King of Judaea by the Senate, which was later confirmed by Octavius/Augustus in 31 BC. It was Herod the Great's son, Herod Antipas, who imprisoned John the Baptist. Confusingly in the New Testament, Antipas is referred to as both the Tetrarch by Matthew and Luke, and as King by Mark.

5. *wine*: The three wines are all imported, an indication of Herod's luxurious living.

6. *my country*: Ancient Nubia was situated in southern Egypt and was the land in which the blue and white Nile rivers conjoined.

7. *my country*: Cappadocia was situated in Asia Minor, to the north-west of Syria and Judaea.

8. *latchet*: The fastening or ties (usually leather) for shoes or sandals. The word is copied from Mark 1.7 as translated in the Authorized Version of the Bible (it occurs also in Isaiah 5.27). Much of the verbal artistry and rhetoric used by Wilde to characterize Jokanaan's prophetic speech are derived from these two books of the Bible. Jokanaan (the Hebrew spelling of John) was Christ's cousin and a prophet who foretold the coming of the Messiah. On baptizing Jesus, he claimed that Jesus was the promised one, the saviour. This was politically dangerous, as his subsequent arrest, imprisonment and death proved.

9. *Smyrna*: Important trading centre, then in the province of Lydia and north of Ephesus in what is today Southern Turkey.

10. *They are rough . . . noble lords*: Is this Wilde, the Irish nationalist, cunningly giving voice to a subtle criticism of the English, whose Empire (which had colonized Ireland) was modelled on the Roman prototype?

11. *centaurs . . . sirens*: In classical mythology, a centaur is a horse with human torso, arms and head (sometimes an emblem of wisdom, as they often feature as teachers of the young; sometimes, which seems more relevant to this context, of lechery). 'Sirens' are sweet-voiced temptresses of Greek lore and myth.

12. *Elias*: This is the New Testament form of the name of the Old Testament prophet Elijah. In 2 Kings 2.11, it is recounted that Elijah did not die but was carried up into heaven in a chariot of fire. He is described by Matthew, Mark and John as the precursor of John the Baptist.

13. *basilisk*: Hideous reptile hatched by a snake from a cock's egg; its breath and glance were lethal.

14. *Chaldea*: The southernmost province of Babylonia, reaching almost to the Persian Gulf. Its famed capital city was Ur.

15. *Assyria*: Country to the north of Babylonia and east of Mesopotamia; its capital city was Nineveh.

16. *baldricks*: Low-slung belts to carry a sword or dagger.

17. *the fan ... in his hand*: In accounts of John the Baptist's teaching in the gospels of Matthew (3.12) and Luke (3.17) this phrase occurs as an image of God's wrathful justice. The fan was used to divide the valued wheat from the chaff, which being deemed useless was subsequently burned.

18. *Tyrian*: From Tyre, a rich city and trading centre for the Phoenicians to the immediate north of the province of Galilee.

19. *Babylon*: Capital city of the Empire of Babylonia. Its fall is recalled throughout the Book of Revelation as demonstration of the mutability of earthly power.

20. *Sodom*: Genesis (18–19) records the destruction of this city by divinely sent fire and brimstone for its excess, debauchery and wickedness.

21. *By woman ... into the world*: I.e. the Fall, occasioned by Eve's picking the forbidden fruit of the Tree of Knowledge of Good and Evil, which she encouraged Adam to eat (Genesis 2–3).

22. *Edom*: The land settled by the descendants of Esau, which lay to the southeast of the Dead Sea and to the east of Mount Seir. It is clear from the prophetic books of the Old Testament that the Edomites were traditionally the enemies of the Israelites.

23. *cedars of Lebanon*: Proverbial in the Bible for their great height and luxuriant spreading foliage.

24. *Moab*: Ancient kingdom east of the Dead Sea and immediately north of Edom, peopled by the descendants of Lot, after he and his daughters escaped the destruction of Sodom (see n. 20 above).

25. *Stoics*: School of philosophers deriving from Athens; its founder was Zeno. The focus of their thinking was ethical, and they made a virtue of controlling the passions and being indifferent to pain or death. They were famed in the Roman world particularly for their great self-control, fortitude and the austerity of their life-style. As epicures Herod and Tigellinus would be diametrically opposed to the stoic way of life. Several noted stoics (Cato of Utica and Marcus Junius Brutus) committed suicide when faced with military defeat.

26. *Emperor*: Tiberius. There is no extant writing by the emperor so this diatribe against stoicism is Wilde's invention. Given Tiberius's increasing reliance on astrologers, it is unlikely that he shared stoics' detached attitude to chance.

27. *Alexandria*: The great cosmopolitan cultural centre; the city, founded by Alexander the Great on the north coast of Egypt in 331 BC, fostered one of the chief intellectual communities of the Hellenistic world.

28. *brays*: Pounds or beats small as in a pestle and mortar.

29. *NAZARENE*: A follower of Jesus, who was born in Nazareth.

30. *Messias*: Literally means 'anointed' and was applied to anyone anointed with holy oil, such as in the consecration of the Jewish kings. In time the term, more customarily spelled as Messiah, was extended to refer to the saviour whose coming would redeem Israel, as foretold by the prophets.

31. *a little town . . . into wine*: The miracle at the marriage feast at Cana as recorded in John 2. For the miracles at Capernaum, see Matthew 8 and John 4 (Wilde has treated the accounts with some licence).

32. *daughter of Jairus*: The story of Christ's raising her from the dead is recorded in Matthew 9.18, Mark 5.22 and Luke 8.31.

33. *Samaria*: The northern kingdom of Israel whose inhabitants were of mixed race. Though they upheld most Jewish beliefs and customs, they denied the Jewish priesthood and the authority of the Pharisees. To pious Jews the term 'Samaritan' was intensely pejorative. Jesus's parable of the Good Samaritan (Luke 10.33), which Wilde's text glances at here, tells of the moral superiority of a Samaritan over a Pharisee and a Levite (both high-caste Jews).

34. *Let the people . . . stone her*: The traditional punishment in the Bible for a woman taken in adultery.

35. *I will not dance, Tetrarch*: Given so despotic and whimsical a ruler as this Herod, so daringly blatant a refusal to pander to his every wish or, as here, his command is courting danger; and the moment should be directed as such.

36. *the moon . . . red*: This is a charged symbolic transition, but it also anticipates the kind of technique for creating emotional expressionistic effects which were to be a feature of early twentieth-century theatre.

37. *Bozra*: A city of Moab. Isaiah (63) recounts a vision of a man of mighty stature and muscle, coming from Bozra, clothed in garments stained with blood, who is an emblem of vengeance.

38. *the dance of the seven veils*: Beyond the bared feet and the seven veils, Wilde offers no scenario. Whether the dance is openly seductive and erotic or whether it is merely interpreted as seductive by a besotted Herod is a choice left for actors and director. Much concerning that difficult decision depends on how 'virginal' the actress decides to represent Salomé as being. Lindsay Kemp's performance was a lengthily protracted whirling as if inducing a state of trance, while slaves unravelled endless yards of diaphanous silky material that had been swathed around her body in a manner that seemed relentlessly to increase her spinning until she finally emerged: a near-naked, white-powdered and sequined figure like a fragile butterfly coming from its encompassing cocoon. The device seemed wholly appropriate to the symbolist tendencies of Wilde's conception, metaphorically presenting an enraptured release into a new but frightening sense of freedom in the body by a woman previously trapped in a gawky, adolescent virginity. Berkoff in his production cleverly teased audiences as well as the Tetrarch by having his Salomé *mime* stripping away layers of clothing while remaining fully dressed. You *saw* what you chose to see. This defined in Salomé a kind of knowing chastity, while exposing a debauched lubricity in Herod, played by Berkoff himself, who simulated the character's hovering on the brink of an excited tumescence. He saw 'naked, fulsome young limbs' (Berkoff's words); we saw astute role-play – an actress's *presentation* of a nubile girl in a calculated performance.

39. *chrysolites . . . chalcedony*: These gems were of greater value to Wilde for their exotic, musical names than for their actual worth; most would now be deemed only semi-precious. Chrysolites are varying shades of green tending towards dark olive, while beryls range from paler green to blue and yellow; chrysoprases are akin to beryls but golden-green in colour; sardonyx has alternating layers of white and orange-cornelian; hyacinths are formed from a silicate of zirconium ranging through blue to orange shades; and chalcedony is a form of quartz akin to agate and chrysoprase. All but hyacinths are mentioned in either the Old or New Testament.

40. *Numidia*: African country south of Egypt.

41. *nacre*: Mother of pearl.

42. *Seres*: Ancient people inhabiting the Far East (probably China), who possessed the gift of weaving with silk.

43. *I can throw . . . the air*: In Heinrich Heine's poem, 'Atta Troll' (1841), one potential source of Wilde's inspiration according to Yeats, Herodias (and not Salomé) flings the head of Jokanaan into the air as an expression of triumph and vengeance.

44. *The stage becomes very dark*: If this prescription is carried out precisely, then the audience is left to *imagine* much of the conclusion of the play: the kissing of the head and Salomé's execution, both incidents which are notoriously difficult to realize. Max Beerbohm was convinced after seeing Florence Farr's 1905 staging that the play was best read rather than seen, since the aesthetic awe provoked by the play's long-anticipated but subtly delayed catastrophe was considerably marred by the nausea one experienced at actually seeing the heroine kiss a severed head (a situation oddly made worse for him as the head was clearly a stage-property made of plaster). He thought it impossible to stage a performance that would not destroy the play's predominant, Symbolist-inspired mood of reverie. Ricketts took note of Beerbohm's criticism when mounting the play the following year, and, in addition to dimming the lights, instructed his Salomé (Letitia Darragh) to cover the head with her veil before commencing her final speech. Yeats saw both productions and shared Beerbohm's reservations; when he came to explore the Salomé-subject in his plays, *The King of the Great Clock Tower* and *A Full Moon in March* (1934), he resorted to an extreme of stylization, masked all his players and used a mask for the severed head. Terence Gray decided on this solution too: when Jokanaan emerged from the cistern, all the audience saw was the mask of an emaciated face (the actor did not come fully on to the stage) and so this Salomé played down to a rigid head that was resolutely turned away from her to stare out over the audience. Fixed in this way in the audience's imagination, the mask was plausibly deployed for the decapitated skull. Lindsay Kemp used an ingenious design effect: Salomé at the conclusion of her dance was covered with a gigantic silver cloak that virtually enveloped the stage; the actor playing Jokanaan secreted himself under the cloak and brought his head through a slit in the material at the level of her cradling arm; the conclusion was presented as a haunting duet for the two heads which seemed to float in another dimension of reality on this undulating tide of silver. It was at once intensely sensuous, eerie, timeless and outside any conventional moral code of judgement. Most modern productions have allowed audiences only a dim and fleeting glimpse of the satisfied Salomé in the moonlight, before plunging the stage again into darkness so that the death is realized by sounds alone. This method requires split-second timing, however, if the stages of the conclusion are to be fully registered by an audience.

A Woman of No Importance

The play, which Wilde began in Summer 1892, was staged by Sir Herbert Beerbohm Tree at the Haymarket Theatre on 19 April 1893, where it ran for 113 performances. It was commissioned by Tree as actor–manager, and designed quite clearly as a vehicle for him, echoing in his role of Lord Illingworth many features of the evil but suave aristocrat, the Duke of Guisebury, in Henry Arthur Jones's *The Dancing Girl*, with which he had won a notable personal success in 1891. Like the St James's Theatre, the Haymarket was a decidedly 'smart' venue, where Wilde could assume a cultured and theatrically aware audience who would appreciate his subtle manipulating of dramatic conventions. The cast also included Fred Terry as Gerald and his wife, Julia Neilson, as Hester, Rose Leclercq (later to be the first Lady Bracknell) as Lady Hunstanton, Maud Tree as Mrs Allonby and Mrs Bernard Beere (a noted tragedienne who had assumed several of the roles created initially for Sarah Bernhardt) as Mrs Arbuthnot. The play has been staged twice by Philip Prowse for the Glasgow Citizens' Theatre (1984) and the Royal Shakespeare Company (1991).

Six manuscript or typescript draft versions of the play are extant, including the licensing copy. They show that Wilde had some difficulty in devising apt names for his characters but that the overall scheme of the play underwent little change. Later drafts show him developing certain lines of comedy to enhance his representation of Lady Hunstanton's lapses of memory, Lady Stutfield's insistent use of the word 'very' on every possible occasion and Lady Caroline's snobbish inability to recall Kelvil's name accurately. He began by letting Lord Illingworth hold the stage at length with his irreverent witticisms but increasingly changed this so that Illingworth shared his banter with Mrs Allonby, thereby building up their intimacy with particularly suggestive nuances: they seem in later versions to caress each other with words. The text was generally refined of its borrowings from *The Picture of Dorian Gray* so that conversation would not hold back the development of the dramatic action, once the lax tone and atmosphere of the house party was established. A significant revision late in composition affected the sequence of mime which concludes Act III, which in its second format eschewed melodrama for a more detailed psychological exploration of the consequences of Mrs Arbuthnot informing Gerald that Illingworth is his father. The text of the first edition published by John Lane in 1894 differs substantially from that submitted for licensing by the Lord Chamberlain, showing that Wilde re-incorporated passages of dialogue which had doubtless been cut in rehearsal but which survived in his drafts (this was a procedure he was to adopt again respecting *An Ideal Husband*).

DEDICATION

1. *Gladys*: Wilde numbered Constance Gladys (1859–1917) among his friends from the early 1880s, when she was the wife of the fourth Earl of Lonsdale. After his death in 1882, she married Lord de Grey (subsequently Marquess of Ripon). Wilde generally referred to her as one of his 'two beauties' (the other being Lily Langtry).

ACT I

1. *more than once*: In early drafts Lady Caroline's speech continued with a comment about Lady Stutfield as 'irreproachable . . . but . . . just a little too romantic for a woman who has been married', and that she showed full proof of her devotion to her late elderly husband when on his dying 'her hair turned

quite gold from grief' – a comment which was to be used again by Wilde in other contexts, most notably in Lady Bracknell's account of Lady Harbury.

2. *worked for their living*: Wilde sustains this satirical line of attack on the way Lady Caroline constantly allows a concern for 'good form' to justify all manner of snobbery and prejudice. She anticipates the fuller study of Lady Bracknell.

3. *so sincere*: Wilde originally included the epithet 'upright' in the qualities that Hester admires in Gerald Arbuthnot. Such a word is open to a critical interpretation which would pre-judge the character, and Wilde left it to the audience to discover this less attractive attribute later.

4. *Vienna*: This would be among the highest of diplomatic achievements at this time when the city was not only the capital of the vast Austro-Hungarian empire but the meeting-place of Europe politically and geographically with the Near East. For Wilde it seems to have carried associations of subterfuge, double-dealing and fraud: see *An Ideal Husband*.

5. *unmarried man . . . complications*: This is perhaps a calculatedly veiled reference to the current Foreign Secretary in Gladstone's government, Lord Rosebery (1847–1929), who was a widower (his wife died in 1890). Rosebery's secretary of state was Lord Alfred Douglas's elder brother, Drumlarig. Lord Queensberry, suspecting a homosexual relationship between Drumlarig and Lord Rosebery, first wrote a number of abusive letters about the Foreign Secretary to the Queen, Gladstone and Rosebery himself, and then early in Summer 1893 pursued the Foreign Secretary to Homburg where he threatened to whip him in public; a scandal was only averted by the intervention of the Prince of Wales. (See *De Profundis*.) Earlier in 1893 Drumlarig had been created Baron Kelhead, so it appears more than coincidence that a reference to Lady *Kelso* follows. Douglas was fond of disconcerting the father he hated, and it is conceivable that he encouraged Wilde to frame a private joke here, which only a handful of senior Establishment figures and Douglas's family would be in a position to interpret accurately.

6. *I forget which*: There is rich potential in Lady Hunstanton's lapses of memory for an actress with a strong gift for comic caricature to develop an increasingly hilarious 'running gag'. Barbara Leigh-Hunt in Prowse's production for the Royal Shakespeare Company developed this detail into a defining character-trait, making it the basis of a *tour de force* of comic timing, as her Lady Hunstanton struggled to keep her errant mind under some semblance of control. This in turn made the character's orotund pronouncements all the funnier, since her facts were so insecure.

7. *rises and goes across*: This stage direction implies that on his entry with Mr Kelvil, Sir John sat down with Lady Stutfield and Mrs Allonby, thereby exciting this expression of his wife's possessiveness. An actor has a range of possibilities to select in motivating this and subsequent similar moments in the action. Is he long-suffering and desperate to escape his wife's attentions? Is he with devilish glee provoking her anxieties? Or is he the kind of would-be debonair elderly gentleman who is besotted with younger women?

8. *much good . . . of that kind*: In early drafts this speech was more elaborate: 'And much good may be done by means of a magic lantern that has been nearly eaten by savages or a missionary with slides . . . I mean, you know what I mean?' It is a notable instance where a rather wordy jokiness has been refined to give clarity to a more sharply barbed satirical thrust at the expense of Wilde's upper-class characters.

9. LORD ALFRED: He says virtually nothing, yet consistently is included in the social gatherings of Acts I and III as a silent presence who, as the penniless young man-about-town, steadily and significantly begins to attach himself to the widowed but wealthy Lady Stutfield. It seems a fitting match: both are presented as quite mindless. There is great potential for a director and an actor to build a memorable characterization for Lord Alfred, despite his want of dialogue.

10. *You a married man . . . gratification to Mrs Kettle*: This episode is one of many passages where Lady Caroline appears to be a sketch for Lady Bracknell: here tone and rhythm inevitably recall Worthing's 'interview', which rapidly becomes more like an interrogation.

11. *a beautiful hand*: It is important that Mrs Arbuthnot's handwriting be distinctive so it can be recognized by Lord Illingworth; also, care must be taken over the placing of the letter on the table so that it registers with an audience, even though it is a casual gesture on Lady Hunstanton's part. It is a mark of her respect for Mrs Arbuthnot that, though a social inferior, she has been invited to dine and not just to 'come in the evening', which in high society smacked of favour and patronage. That Mrs Arbuthnot chooses, however, to join the party late can be interpreted as her clear sense of social decorum (she knows her proper place); we have already been informed in the opening dialogue that Lady Hunstanton is 'sometimes a little lax' with her invitations.

12. *want of it in the man*: This was originally the conclusion of Lord Illingworth's preceding speech, but during the stages of composition Wilde divided many of the longer speeches and redistributed the lines. This not only allows a greater dynamism to the dialogue, since Illingworth no longer appears to have all the best lines and to be the last word on every topic, but also builds a sense of complete intellectual rapport between him and Mrs Allonby. They can read each other's minds and moods with a rare precision, gauge each other's subtlest intimations and pursue levels of *double entendre* together to the exclusion of anyone else present. They recall Pierre Laclos' Valmont and Mme de Merteuil in *Les Liaisons dangereuses* (1782), especially in arranging their sinister bet.

13. *Looks steadfastly at MRS ALLONBY*: The male gaze here is not merely sexual (though the couple's shared banter indicates that is present): it shows his appreciation of Mrs Allonby's wit, intelligence, social poise and daring. The gaze invites her to read his mind and wills her to think what his seemingly direct comment about admiring Hester immensely might actually *mean*. Out of that comes her challenge, on which the plotting of the rest of the play is structured.

14. *Sphinxes*: These mythological creatures, half-human and half-feline, were believed to be inscrutable and enigmatic, mysterious and often lethal in their relations with men. 'A Sphinx Without A Secret', a Wilde short story, tells of a woman who lies and indulges in subterfuge to create a degree of mystery which is otherwise wanting in her life; she plays an imaginary role for herself as a romantic heroine.

15. *made love*: At this time would mean simply 'to pay amorous attention to someone', 'to court'.

16. *woman of no importance*: While it is customary for many nineteenth-century plays to end with one of the characters voicing the title, it is most unusual for this to occur at the conclusion of the first act. Wilde is setting up a strategy whereby his own final line will attract immediate attention for its *difference* from typical stage practice. The title would inevitably carry strong resonances for audiences so that its being stated as dismissively as it is here would stress Lord Illingworth's cruel snobbery and indifference.

ACT II

1. *Ladies seated on sofas*: It is important that an audience register the presence of the listening, attentive figure of Hester Worsley well before the dialogue suddenly draws the awareness of the on-stage characters to her presence. We establish a view of these upper-class women (their styles of femininity, the tone of their conversation when they are free of the company of men and therefore more relaxed) before Hester launches into her critique. We are then left to balance her view against our observation and perceptions.

2. *But we don't belong to anyone*: A challenging view that is wittily dismissive of an issue that had been much debated in Parliament over changes in legislation concerning married women's property. Two acts had already addressed the issue and a third was to be passed during 1893.

3. *promissory note*: A signed document containing written promises to pay a stated sum to a specified person at a specified date or on demand; it was a process of indebtedness to another which could be renewed or renegotiated. The joke, a bitterly ironic one, is at the expense of a husband's allowed demands for satisfaction of his marital (usually sexual) rights.

4. *mauvais quart d'heure*: A grim quarter of an hour (French).

5. *absolutely uninteresting*: This passage was considerably revised and is another example where heavy cutting brings greater clarity and bite to the satire. The draft versions have Mrs Allonby giving her involvement in choosing a new wardrobe as her reason for not investigating her husband's past, which dissipates attention away from the psychological point: Mrs Allonby dares to risk admitting that her preference is for a man with a sexually experienced *past*. Her ensuing justification and her prescriptions for the 'Ideal Man' carry resonances of William Congreve's Millamant in *The Way of the World* (1700), particularly in the scene where she sets out her marriage contract with Mirabell.

6. *in our country*: Wilde cut much of his initial invention for this speech, which in early drafts contained implied criticism of both English and American society for setting too much store by money and accident of birth. As revised, the thrust is directed against the English; and the reiterated use of 'good' establishes Hester's sense of her own moral superiority to the women about her by subtle implication.

7. *iron Exhibition . . . curious name*: This is a very up-to-the-minute reference for the first audiences: the World's Fair was to be held at Jackson Park in Chicago from May 1893 (*A Woman of No Importance* opened on 19 April). The building with the 'curious name' was Machinery Hall, which somewhat resembled the Crystal Palace in London and numerous railway stations of the period in being a spectacular engineering design of predominantly glass and iron. There is some evidence to suggest that Wilde hoped his play would be staged there; in which case this reference by a dotty English aristocrat to the very building the American audience were seated within would have raised a good laugh at the expense of English cultural snobbery and Lady Hunstanton's colonialist arrogance.

8. *A man . . . complete without him*: Again Wilde heavily cut his first thoughts here, where Hester listed all the places (the opera, Rotten Row in Hyde Park) where it was thought a positive distinction to be seen in Weston's company. And gave a precise moral indictment of his character: 'A man who, I am told, has brought many women to misery and to shame. A man who has wrecked innocent lives, and poisoned lives that were pure.' The tersely phrased, 'A man with a hideous smile and a hideous past', wonderfully evokes an image of an aging lecher with such exactness that one senses it is rooted in experience.

The implied but deeply felt disgust nicely prepares the ground for Hester's response to Lord Illingworth's flirtatious kiss, which she rightly sees as a physical violation. By confining the signs of Weston's social acceptability to his presence at dinner-parties Wilde further intimates the possibility of her having directly encountered him. This one example carries particular moral force, which much strengthens the contrast with the socially unacceptable women who have suffered at Weston's hands.

9. *Set a mark . . . go free*: The image conjured up is of God's branding of Cain after his murder of Abel (Genesis 4.16). This and Hester's references to the pillars of fire and of cloud (which draw on Exodus 13.21 where God sends such signals to guide Moses and the Israelites in their flight from Egypt through the deserts towards the Promised Land) suggest a kind of evangelical fervour, which she will transcend as the action develops. The pillars, which in the Bible are offered as compassionate symbols of God's promise of ultimate security, are reduced by Hester to emblems of stark moral categories, binary oppositions that intimate systems of punitive judgement.

10. *Might I . . . Thank you*: Ian Small, in his edition (1983), observes from his study of the manuscripts that this brilliant undermining of Hester's moral posturing was actually an afterthought of Wilde's, a handwritten addition to the fullest of the surviving draft versions. The comedy of the moment, which generally raises one of the loudest laughs in a performance, is expertly placed to warn audiences not wholly to endorse Hester's standpoint.

11. *When I knew . . . with his father*: This was precisely Lord Alfred Douglas's case: he too was an impoverished man-about-town, supported by his mother, Sybil, Marchioness of Queensberry, who had divorced her husband, John Sholto Douglas, in 1887 when her third son (Lord Alfred) was seventeen.

12. *All Americans lecture*: Wilde had made a profitable lecture tour of the States in 1882 where he lectured chiefly about 'The English Renaissance' and on 'House Decoration'.

13. *to know my mother*: 'Know' is used by Gerald in the sense of 'getting acquainted with', but the word is horribly applicable to the situation in the biblical sense of 'having sexual experience with another'.

14. *All women . . . That is his*: Originally in the drafts this witticism was given wholly to Mrs Allonby. Divided between her and Lord Illingworth, the effect is once again to evoke an intensely intimate rapport between the two, which is yet another kind of *knowing*.

15. *Eton or Oxford*: This was the traditional route into a diplomatic career, ensuring that admission to the highest ranks of public service was like gaining membership of an exclusive club.

16. *the lady in black velvet*: Wilde revised the conspicuously shabby image that

he initially considered Mrs Arbuthnot should present; and, in consequence, though in the first production Mrs Bernard Beere in the role wore black throughout, her two dresses were decidedly smart. Mrs Arbuthnot is a needle-woman and has brought Gerald up to a degree that admits him to polite rural society, which she also frequents; and so appropriately Mrs Beere's dresses were well-cut and figure-defining. This begins to intimate from her arrival that there is more to this character than circumstances and appearances would suggest. Mrs Arbuthnot may elect to wear black to be in keeping with her penitential state of mind; but her origin is upper class and this fact was reflected in the choice of materials and of design for her clothes. She should present an enigma. Mrs Beere's attire immediately set her off from the other women on stage who were sumptuously dressed in lighter colours decorated with jewels or spangled tulle.

17. *violin heard from music-room*: As in *Lady Windermere's Fan*, Wilde contrives here to observe the tenets of realism (the country-house party with its evening recital by one or more of the guests: a staple Victorian convention) while providing a musical accompaniment to what becomes a scene of steadily mounting passions and anguish. While polite entertainment is the pursuit of most of the guests, Mrs Arbuthnot finds herself increasingly trapped psychologically by Lord Illingworth and wounded by the need to disappoint the son she adores.

18. *Rachel*: Till now forenames have been deployed only as a mark of possessive intimacy: by Lady Caroline when addressing her husband and by Lady Hunstanton when giving instructions to her servants. For the original audiences Lord Illingworth's breach of etiquette in addressing her by her first name would be surprising, if not shocking, and, together with the identifying of Gerald as '*our* son' and the complex signification (referred to in n. 16) of Mrs Arbuthnot's appearance, at once presents audiences with the full story of the past. In the context of Victorian dramatic practice, this is a daring stroke of invention. Wilde comes out with the facts in a totally off-hand manner, focusing audience interest on the psychological competition that will now ensue for possession of Gerald and control of his future. It is of course wholly in line with Wilde's characterization of Lord Illingworth that he should be the one who calmly and decisively frustrates convention, insisting on a new perspective to the otherwise hackneyed topic of the woman with a past. Lord Illingworth was utterly unscrupulous in his previous relations with Mrs Arbuthnot; and he is to use all the energy of his remarkable mind to trap her into acquiescing in his plans for Gerald.

19. *began in your father's garden*: An ironic observation, given Lord Illingworth's remark to Mrs Allonby in Act I: 'The Book of Life begins with a man and a woman in a garden.' The idea of the garden begins to feature increasingly throughout the play in Wilde's structures of symbolism.

20. *six hundred a year*: This was a most generous allowance in the period.

21. *duty to marry me*: Wilde not only captures the different moral qualities of the parents, but also the opposed codes of values revealed by the way Mrs Arbuthnot and Lord Illingworth each recalls them and their influence. This is exemplary exposition, where one set of details illuminates both the past situation and the present one.

22. *Leave me . . . leave me that*: The biblical references here shift and elide: initially the passage recalls the tale of King Ahab who in spite of his wealth and power coveted Naboth's vineyard (1 Kings 21) and this is an apt parallel; but with the image of Gerald as the 'ewe-lamb', Mrs Arbuthnot's emotionalism loses all pretence of self-control. It is an absurdly sentimental conception. Throughout the play Wilde tends to deploy biblical references and imitations of its more incantatory rhetorical rhythms as a judgement against the characters whom he requires to voice them: Illingworth's reference to the Garden of Eden (see n. 19 above) exposes his cynicism; Hester's misapplication of biblical imagery earlier in this act reveals her want of charity; and here imagery and rhetoric define Mrs Arbuthnot's fear and excessive self-pity, which patently cannot *touch* a man like Lord Illingworth. In fact her tactic plays directly into his hands, as his curt reply demonstrates: he questions the very basis of her parental authority over Gerald by dismissing her emotional hold over her son as *unnecessary*.

23. *why . . . accept this post*: This is a cunning trap, inviting Mrs Arbuthnot to risk losing her son's esteem by admitting her past and his illegitimacy. Lord Illingworth calculates this move out of his awareness of her deep-rooted sense of shame. The energy of mind that underlies his cruelty and (in Beerbohm Tree's performance in the role) a genuine pride in his newly discovered paternity make him a far more intricate creation than the stereotypical wicked and wanton aristocrats of earlier melodramas.

ACT III

1. *lolling on a sofa . . . in a chair*: The stage picture conveys a great deal through the body language of the two characters: Lord Illingworth, loose-limbed and relaxed; Gerald, unsure of his position, upright (in both senses of the word), tentative and on edge. The father is the epitome of the gentleman he is himself about to define, while the son has little to recommend him socially beyond his youth, and is all too aware of the fact.

2. *The future . . . his clothes*: The gulf between the two men in terms of experience and thought is captured by this exchange. Gerald fails to appreciate that there is a conscious ideology underpinning his father's cultivation of the pose of dandy, which makes it more than a matter of wearing 'nice things'. Lord Illingworth, keen to develop an understanding with his son, does not however put him down smartly, but makes Gerald appreciate that there is a philosophy behind his manner, of which the knotting of a necktie is but an outward detail.

3. *the plain and the coloured*: Toy theatre sheets at this time were either printed plain for colouring by children and cost one penny, or were printed in colours and cost two-pence. The metaphor expresses a sexist disdain for women as either tedious or emotional.

4. *Peerage*: Two published lists of peers were available in the 1890s: Burke's and Cokayne's.

5. *Dorcas . . . tambour frame*: In Acts 9. 36–40, Peter raises from the dead a widowed seamstress named Tabitha (or in the Greek Dorcas) who made clothes for the sect during their meetings. A Dorcas by the nineteenth century had come to mean a gathering of charitably disposed ladies who met to make clothing for the poor. The frame is two circles of thin wood that could be placed one inside the other to keep material draped over the inner ring firmly in position while it is being embroidered.

6. *Humane Society*: For the rescuing of drowning persons. It had been in existence since 1774.

7. *Bimetallism*: System of economics involving the use of both gold and silver as legal currency or tender to any amount at a fixed ratio to each other.

8. *admirable homes . . . reformed*: Societies for the rescue, reformation, rehabilitation and often assisted emigration of 'fallen' women were legion by this date; many ran homes in major cities which were refuges but with a strongly evangelical bias.

9. *the sins . . . God's terrible laws*: Once again in her unthinking zeal Hester is misquoting the Bible and *The Book of Common Prayer*; her words draw on the second commandment of the Old Testament where to strengthen the prohibition against worshipping graven images and false gods, there is threat of punishment which extends beyond the perpetrators of idolatry to their offspring: 'for I the Lord thy God am a jealous God, and visit the sins of the fathers upon the children unto the third and fourth generation'. That Mrs Arbuthnot finds this a *terrible* law emphasizes her despair at the thought that her beloved Gerald should suffer. Early drafts extended Hester's speech to encompass the confidence that she felt instinctively on their meeting that she and Mrs Arbuthnot would share the same moral standards, which set them apart from the other women staying with Lady Hunstanton. Mrs Arbuthnot tries to shift the focus of the conversation by remarking that these other women are at least happy, and Hester counters with the belief that neither of them would wish to experience that kind of happiness. In its revised form the ironies are more searching and less overt: Mrs Arbuthnot recognizes Hester's moral stance as indeed akin to her own, but the experience that has led her to that creed sets her woefully apart from the young woman who is endeavouring to create a friendship between them. Wilde is very daring in using the Bible in this way to demonstrate in his characters a want of understanding and sympathy, qualities into which they need to grow.

10. *sits down . . . strokes his hands*: There is a sinister edge as Mrs Arbuthnot endeavours to recreate the emotional ambience when her son was a child. It is a high point in Wilde's dramatic artistry that he can simultaneously invite both sympathy and criticism for Mrs Arbuthnot as she struggles to influence Gerald's thinking without having the honesty and trust necessary to tell him the truth. She expresses a wealth of love but that feeling is being manipulated to achieve a precise objective and so lacks integrity.

11. *poppies*: *Papaver somniferum*, the species which is the source of opium.

12. *No nice girl would*: Earlier drafts had Gerald supposing that in all probability 'the young girl in question was no better than she should have been'. By cutting this sentence, Wilde throws the whole force of Gerald's speech on to the word *nice* (his favourite epithet), which fully intimates what the first version coarsely stated. The revisions show Wilde growing confident of an intelligent audience's ability to respond to intimations and to perceive and apprehend subtextual implication.

13. GERALD *clutches . . . from the room*: Wilde completely revised this final sequence of mimed action during composition and in the process wholly changed its significance. In the early version this stage direction reads:

MRS ARBUTHNOT *sinks on her knees and bows her head.* HESTER *with a look of pain glides from the room.* LORD ILLINGWORTH *bites his lip, hesitates for a moment and then goes off.* GERALD *forces his mother back, and with a look of horror and amazement, gazes into her face.*

Here the final tableau with Gerald and his mother endorses Lord Illingworth's view that Mrs Arbuthnot has brought up her son to be her worst judge, that she knows this and that this continually influences all her actions and decisions. The crisis when it comes proves him right, or so the body language suggests. The morality underpinning this sequence is conventional and the resulting tone is sensational. The revised version begins with Gerald's initial response to his mother's outburst, but significantly the quality of his gaze into her face is not defined but left for the actor to judge in relation to how the action develops. His mother reads his face as overwhelmingly judgemental and sinks to the floor in shame. Hester leaves silently (again the motivation is left open). Lord Illingworth continues to bite his lip through the episode as in the early drafts but this gesture is accompanied by a marked frown. Has he interpreted Gerald's gaze differently, especially since he continues to support his mother and not abandon her to side with his father or to go off alone? But this is all seen ultimately as framing for what is a momentous decision on Gerald's part as to what his own conduct should be. This should be the focus of the scene in performance. What he decides is his proper duty is implicit in his lifting his mother to her feet, supporting her with his arm and taking her from the room. Where the previous act ended with Mrs Arbuthnot seemingly abandoned and at her most vulnerable, now it is Lord Illingworth who is alone and defeated.

ACT IV

1. *Sitting-room . . . L. C.*: The stage direction noticeably offers no prescriptions for the appearance of Mrs Arbuthnot's sitting-room but it does specify a large window opening out on to a vista of a cottage garden, which begins to intimate a potential resolution. We have moved over the previous three acts from one open-air setting, situated on a lawn beneath the terrace of a grand house with formal gardens, through two shrouded, artificially lit interiors to another room from which at least there is the prospect of a sun-filled garden. Wilde used settings as more than pictorial backgrounds for his dramatic action, and here the created playing space will steadily take on precise symbolic connotations.
2. *I should like . . . English home*: In early drafts this speech continued: 'It would be such a new experience for him.' Wilde was right to cut this, since it would rob the initial remark of much of its irony: for once Mrs Allonby is not fully apprised of the situation or of Lord Illingworth's role in it, and this gives the observation ramifications of which she is completely unaware. The laugh is partly against her. What she does not know is that Illingworth has in the past refused to share such a space with Mrs Arbuthnot; has the previous evening refused to do so again; but is even now contemplating the degree to which he might conform to propriety and find a way of sharing some common ground. There is the further irony that, by drawing attention in this way to the tone and style of the room, Mrs Allonby's remark proves how impossible it is to conceive of any kind of union between Lord Illingworth, who is so at home in the grander spaces of Lady Hunstanton's mansion, and Mrs Arbuthnot, whose moral character is everywhere defined by the room she has created as her private space.

3. *blushing*: Considered a becoming sign of a modest, virginal and so easily shockable nature. But it is also an early sign of sexual arousal. Both connotations are toyed with in this exchange.

4. *the ordinary ending*: Wilde uses 'ending' here clearly to alert the audience to a number of ways in which he might resolve the action of the play, so that they come to appreciate the better the particular originality of his chosen resolution. 'Ordinary' here implies the stereotypical, the required, *closed* ending where in Mrs Arbuthnot's eyes a hard-won happiness in the fact of marriage quickly sours.

5. *Women are hard on each other*: This is one central aspect of Wilde's theme: prevailing moral conventions required women to police each other's conduct and bar from their company any who transgressed permitted patterns of behaviour. Cf. *Lady Windermere's Fan*. But his explorations in this play go far deeper, to investigate how this policing can be internalized by women of a sensitive and scrupulous nature the like of Mrs Arbuthnot. Guilt suffuses every aspect of her being, influences her every action, since she continually sits in judgement upon herself (so deeply has conventional morality been ingrained in her psyche). Marriage with Lord Illingworth would not free her from this inner prison of despair, for which she alone possesses the key.

6. *Enter HESTER behind*: She is again required by much of Wilde's plotting to be a hidden presence, of whom the audience (but not the other characters) are aware. Normally within melodramas, such a concealed, listening figure would lurk with evil intent. That Wilde repeats the strategy here reminds the audience of the scenes in Act II the better to appreciate the extent to which she has grown in sympathy and moral insight.

7. *the pearl of price*: Cf. Matthew (13.45–6) where Jesus likens the kingdom of heaven to a pearl of great price which a merchant sells everything he owns to acquire.

8. *when you were naked . . . gave you food*: Again Mrs Arbuthnot is echoing words from Matthew (25.35–6): 'For I was hungry, and you gave me to eat: I was thirsty, and you gave me to drink: I was a stranger, and you took me in: naked, and you covered me; sick, and you visited me: I was in prison, and you came to me.'

9. *Hannah*: The mother of the biblical prophet Samuel (1 Samuel 1–2), who became an emblem of piety and maternal devotion.

10. *embracing Mrs Arbuthnot*: With this embrace the movement of Wilde's plot towards its daringly unconventional conclusion begins. The role of Hester throughout the play requires a capacity for subtle mime from the actress, since on two notable occasions the motivation for her sudden entry into the dialogue has to be indicated to an audience through changing body language as this relates to her acutely attentive listening to the speakers on stage from whom she is concealed. A director must find ways of drawing an audience's awareness to Hester's figure without distracting attention from the characters concurrently sustaining the dialogue.

11. *enters*: This is a further breach of etiquette on Lord Illingworth's part. Given that the stage has been defined as Mrs Arbuthnot's domain, this is a characteristically brutish invasion of her privacy, indicative of his increasing chauvinism.

12. *According . . . entailed*: In early drafts Lord Illingworth was given a rejoinder to Mrs Arbuthnot's rejection of any proposition he might offer in which he accused her of being 'a very bad mother' and continued by insisting she should listen as what he has to say might interest her. Cutting this preamble makes for more incisive characterization of Illingworth, who now rides roughshod over Mrs Arbuthnot's attempt to halt his progress and end their exchange. An 'entailed' property is one where the succession is settled on specific individuals (usually the eldest son of an eldest son or the possessor of a particular title) so that it cannot be bequeathed at will to whomever the current owner chooses.

13. *goes towards window*: By a superb creative irony on Wilde's part, what Lord Illingworth sees from the window is the realization of an image he had casually played with in the opening act. There it defined his elegant cynicism; later (see Act II, n. 19) the image was repeated by Mrs Arbuthnot to define her tragic perception of the role played in her life by illusion and betrayal when she recounts how her passion for George Harford began in her father's garden; now in its physical portrayal it epitomizes the promise of a future and the potential for change and growth (but a future and a change from which Lord Illingworth himself is decidedly barred).

14. *Bring us together, Rachel . . . choose*: Lord Illingworth finally admits defeat and is decidedly humbled in having to plead with Mrs Arbuthnot. This moment of pathos, which excites a degree of pity for the character, is cleverly calculated by Wilde to precede one final and damning demonstration of Illingworth's cruelty and the subtle psychological sadism of a snob like him when frustrated in what he wants and sees as his absolute right.

15. *Children begin . . . forgive them*: Wilde gives no indication about the tone in which these words should be spoken. They could be treated (and have been in performance) as a moment of vindictive triumph for Mrs Arbuthnot, but this risks melodramatic histrionics which do not seem in keeping with her, however much she speaks of her hatred for Lord Illingworth. A quieter, controlled delivery of the words allows the full irony of their repetition to resonate as a judgement upon him for his own earlier callousness.

16. *fin-de-siècle*: Literally this means 'end-of-the-century' or 'end-of-an-era'; but by the early 1890s it had begun to be consistently applied to *avant-garde* artists and their works, where it tended to connote antinomianism, decadence or moral nonconformity (that is, everything in the way of social behaviour or artistic expression that defied preferred norms, conventions, tastes, social and sexual practices).

17. *leaves the room*: In performance it is extremely difficult to time this episode accurately. The striking with the glove has to appear an impulsive response to Lord Illingworth's final insult, and yet there is but a split second between a perception of what precisely the word is that is to conclude his sentence and the enacting of the blow to his manly pride. To be hit by a woman would be demeaning enough for a man such as Illingworth has come to be represented as being; but the nature of the blow and the means to effect it are a parody of the traditional laws of chivalry and of duelling, where the challenge to fight in defence of insulted honour required either the throwing down of a glove or its use in striking an opponent about the face. Mrs Arbuthnot's gesture, therefore, condemns Lord Illingworth both as man and as gentleman. If too rushed in the enacting, then the full implications of what she has instinctively done are not given time to impress an audience. If too slow, then the episode looks contrived and an audience will not give due thought to its symbolic intent.

18. *A man of no importance*: See Act I, n. 14. By working a variation on the title that changes the gender of the individual who is casually dismissed, Wilde invites his audience to look beyond mere plotting and its resolution and consider the nature of the social and ethical journey on which he has guided them. The shift in wording highlights how his theme has centred on investigations into issues of gender and particularly into male chauvinism. Lord Illingworth may appear the debonair representative of polite society; but the woman he attempts to marginalize continually as 'other' ultimately renders him ignominious and displaces him from both the stage and the focus of audience interest which he has consistently dominated throughout the preceding three acts.

An Ideal Husband

Wilde began this play under contract to John Hare, the actor–manager, in Autumn 1893; by the early spring Hare had turned it down on the grounds that he found the conclusion unsatisfactory (Hare was notoriously quixotic: he turned down *The Second Mrs Tanqueray*, which he had commissioned from

Arthur Wing Pinero, because he found much of the action too daring). Fortunately the young Lewis Waller, who was making a name for himself for a line in manly romanticism (he was dashingly handsome), had begun to express an interest in staging provincial touring productions of *Lady Windermere's Fan* and *A Woman of No Importance* to launch himself as an actor–manager; he had also approached Wilde for a one-act play that he could add to a mixed bill he was planning to showcase the range of his talents and technique. Then Waller was offered the Haymarket Theatre for a season while Beerbohm Tree's company was touring and responded to Wilde's offer of *An Ideal Husband* for his opening production. The play, rehearsed over Christmas, opened on 3 January 1895 with Waller as Chiltern. Charles Hawtrey, who possessed a dapper way with light comedy, played Goring; Julia Neilson, a distinguished Hester Worsley for Tree in 1893, was Lady Chiltern; and Maud Millet as Mabel Chiltern and Florence West as Mrs Cheveley completed the cast. Some sense of Waller's production can be gleaned from the detailed stage directions, which Wilde added extensively on publishing the text. Sir Robert was a perfect vehicle for Waller, since he generally did not excel in comedy; the comedy never touches his character, which abounds in details requiring earnestness, anguish and self-delusion, which Waller clearly could carry off while retaining the audience's engagement on account of his charisma as an actor and matinee idol. The most notable of recent revivals was Sir Peter Hall's in 1992: it was several times extensively recast, toured the country and America, and returned for a further extended run to London. Its popularity reflected national unease at the Tory government's public vaunting of the desirability of a return to Victorian (or 'family') values while repeatedly getting themselves caught out by the press in a variety of scandalous exposés of their private lives. The hypocrisies of today's political world (as reviewers noted) neatly paralleled the moral compromises and clever cover-up operations being negotiated by Wilde's political animals.

Seven or eight manuscript or typescript drafts survive for each act of *An Ideal Husband*; they demonstrate how Wilde took time to find an appropriate tone to develop for the scenes between Mabel Chiltern and Lord Goring. The fond, teasing intimacy of their exchanges, drawing not a little on the Beatrice and Benedick episodes in Shakespeare's *Much Ado about Nothing*, is beautifully calculated to offset the passionless rigours of the Chilterns' marriage. The revisions show Wilde having some difficulty in devising a convincing means of thwarting Mrs Cheveley's schemes; the idea of the bracelet came quite late. Wilde extensively revised the play in 1898–9, for publication by Leonard Smithers in 1899: the changes and additions particularly sharpened the complexities of Goring.

DEDICATION

1. *Frank Harris*: (1856–1931), a long-standing and staunch friend to Wilde through all his troubles, was a fellow-Irishman with a carefree and cavalier attitude to the truth, whose autobiography was banned for its explicit handling of sex. It was as editor successively of the *Saturday Review*, *Fortnightly Review*, *Vanity Fair* and *Evening News* that he made his reputation; while with the last of these, he popularized the provocative or sensationalized headline. In 1920 he published a biography of Wilde. The play's dedication was in part an expression of gratitude to Harris for his kindness in settling Wilde's debts in Paris and sustaining most of the expenses of a winter spent together at Napoule near Cannes on the French Riviera (1898–9). Privately Wilde confessed that he found Harris exhausting, since he expected Wilde to be continually at a high intellectual pressure.

ACT I

1. *Grosvenor Square*: A house in the centre of Belgravia would signify considerable wealth and in all likelihood a high diplomatic office for the owner. That Wilde calculates on audiences recognizing François Boucher's *Triumph of Love* (since it conveys so many ironic resonances), indicates the extent to which delight in his work (and the paintings of Antoine Watteau) was a prevailing fashion among the wealthier patrons of the Haymarket Theatre. Much discussion, especially of the refined eroticism of this school of eighteenth-century French art, was the vogue in artistic circles, as is reflected in a novel, *Evelyn Innes* by George Moore, which was to be published in 1898; the heroine is taken to view the extensive collection by these artists which is housed in the Dulwich Art Gallery by a man who subtly uses such a discussion in his attempt to seduce her. Louis Seize furniture was particularly opulent in style and finish, and by this date pieces were collectors' items of great value. The whole setting is an ostentatious display of the owner's moneyed taste and influential position in society.

2. *a portrait by Lawrence*: Sir Thomas Lawrence (1769–1830), the most favoured portraitist of his age, had an immense European practice. He was limner to George III and after 1820 president of the Royal Academy.

3. *Tanagra statuette*: Clearly Wilde's favourite style of beauty in young women, since Sybil Vane in *Dorian Gray* and Sybil Merton in *Lord Arthur Savile's Crime* are also likened to these much prized miniature terracotta statues that were found in tombs dating from the fourth and third centuries BC at Tanagra in Greece.

4. *Row*: Rotten Row in Hyde Park was a favourite place for the upper classes to take exercise.

5. *star*: The insignia of the Order of the Garter. The remark draws attention to Lord Caversham's political standing, which prepares for his role as emissary from the Prime Minister in the final act.

6. *à la marquise*: Literally 'in the style of the marquise', from a fashion current in the age of Louis XV, and denotes a favourite style of dressing the hair among mature women of some standing at this time. Again it reflects a concern with French taste.

7. *heliotrope, with diamonds*: In the first production Florence West wore not brilliant purple but a dress of 'dark emerald-green satin', which was decorated with festoons of roses and (which excited much adverse comment) stuffed swallows at neck, waist and on the extensive train. She certainly sported Venetian red hair, since William Archer described her as 'tawny-haired' in his review. It seems to have been when revising the text for publication that Wilde included these elaborate, literary stage directions, as if intended for readers, since at that date Wilde could foresee no prospect of further productions. The directions are more in the style of Shaw.

8. *Vienna*: See *A Woman of No Importance*, Act I, n. 4.

9. *Vandyck*: Sir Anthony Van Dyck (1599–1641), portraitist, was born in Antwerp, and studied under Rubens. On a visit to England in 1620, he established himself with a portrait of Lady Arundel and subsequently on a visit in 1632 was knighted by Charles I. His work is best known for the fine psychological detail with which he represented his sitters.

10. *Pessimism . . . spectacles*: 'Blue' to distinguish them, presumably, from the rosy spectacles associated with the vision of optimists and idealists. The joke touches on the prevailing fashions in philosophy of the time and the rivalry between Kant and Schelling's 'transcendental' idealism and the dark, brooding pessimism associated with Schopenhauer and Nietzsche.

11. *Corots*: Camille Corot (1796–1875) worked chiefly in landscape painting, centred on Barbizon, near Fontainebleau; Wilde and George Moore both wrote appreciatively of his delicate twilight effects and of his guiding principle of sacrificing accurate detailing for unity of impression.

12. *old Greek . . . Penelope*: Odysseus, who was compelled by the gods to roam the Mediterranean seas after the sacking of Troy, while his wife, Penelope, waited patiently for his return, despite the attentions of numerous suitors. In praising the single life Mrs Cheveley may be covertly opening her attack on Gertrude Chiltern. Her flippant treatment of the subject of marriage would define her as 'fast'.

13. *Boodle's Club*: Founded in 1763, among the oldest of London clubs, though it was originally known as the Savoir Faire. Edward Gibbon, author of *The Decline and Fall of the Roman Empire* (1776–88), was an early member. The elegant frontage on St James's Street was built in 1765.

14. *The music is in German . . . understand it*: Cf. Lady Bracknell's strictures and anxieties about the nationalism of music, voiced when she is devising a programme of entertainment for an evening party. French songs she considers improper and so cannot be allowed; but 'German sounds a thoroughly respectable language.'

15. *morbid*: Generally meaning 'unwholesome, sickly, decadent'; or, less severely, 'contrary or against the agreed norm'. It would appear that Lord Goring uses the term in the final sense, but that Mrs Marchmont takes him to mean decadent, the most fashionable meaning.

16. *supper*: At fashionable evening parties, it was the polite practice for men at the close of a dance to offer some form of refreshment to their partners, whom they then accompanied back to their chaperones when the overture to the next dance was played.

17. *Suez Canal shares*: In 1875 Disraeli had made Britain half-owner of the Suez Canal: travelling to India became a less hazardous journey via the Canal, and Britain gained controlling influence in Near Eastern politics.

18. *a second Panama*: Designed to link the Atlantic and Pacific Oceans, and largely initiated by Vicomte Ferdinand de Lesseps who had played a major role in the Suez venture; but the scheme came to grief in 1889 through wide-ranging corruption on the part of both the backers and French officialdom. The canal was eventually completed in 1914, but as an American enterprise.

19. *a good platitude . . . whole world kin*: A thinly veiled intertextual reference to Shakespeare's *Troilus and Cressida*: 'One touch of nature makes the whole world kin' (III.iii.169). The context there is Ulysses' speech to Achilles explaining why Ajax is the newly honoured hero rather than Achilles, who, not having of late displayed his heroism, is now quite forgotten. The 'touch' refers to a common tendency in Ulysses' opinion to overpraise whatever is new simply for fashion's sake. It is significant that Wilde turns attention to a play that measures private integrity in terms of a loving relationship in the balance with public need and necessity, that questions the value of reputation and the grounds on which it is constructed and that interrogates the divide that separates professed values from motivation.

20. *You thought . . . possession*: In early drafts Wilde had included details about Mrs Cheveley's relations with Baron Arnheim: how she inherited a Hungarian villa of his where in an inlaid escritoire she found the compromising letter, on which Arnheim had written the sum he had given Chiltern, which established his fortune and reputation. This would slow the action in perform-ance and, more importantly, draw an audience's attention away from the impact on Sir Robert of hearing that the letter is extant and available for general publication.

21. *sitting down on the sofa*: Throughout this episode Mrs Cheveley's position is a correlative of the power relations between herself and Sir Robert: she stands when she needs to assert her superior force of will and sits only when she is sure of success.

22. *Ladies' Gallery*: Situated in the House of Commons immediately above the Press Gallery.

23. *I will arrange . . . subject*: Traditional practice in the House still is for a member of one's own party to raise a question, which creates a context requiring one to make a statement. This is a procedure whereby issues can be brought up for discussion which have not been timetabled for debate.

24. *the Park*: Hyde Park.

25. *Claridge's*: Fashionable hotel situated in Brook Street, Mayfair.

26. *en règle*: Literally 'in accordance with the rule' where *rule* refers to polite etiquette (French).

27. *Catches sight of something . . . cushion*: The way that this means of resolving the plot of the play is introduced is exemplary. Rather than stressing its importance, Wilde has the discovery of the brooch/bracelet be the means of provoking a light-hearted confession from Mabel Chiltern of how she covets it. The conversation with Lord Goring focuses interest on the object as simply beautiful rather than significant. That Lord Goring has seen it before and knows the intricacies of its construction is established quietly and without comment or explanation. Any hint of the melodramatic is upstaged by the comedy of Mabel Chiltern's frustrated expectation that she is about to be proposed to by Lord Goring and her petulant departure when he states he gave it formerly to someone else, which implies the possibility of an earlier engagement.

28. *Besides . . . different lines*: How quickly Mrs Cheveley's advice about resorting to platitudes has been seized by Chiltern! We have experienced enough of his manner, rhetorical style and verbal register when he felt wholly secure in his position to perceive the shocking decline now, as he resorts to evasions and uneasy or brittle generalizations about conduct in political life. These last are the worst, since he previously took such pride in being a man apart, and his wife honoured and endorsed that pride.

29. *That great inheritance . . . do not destroy*: In moments of emotional stress in the two earlier plays, Wilde had characters such as Mrs Arbuthnot and Lady Windermere resort to a biblical style of utterance that hovers on the edge of parody. Invariably these are states of mind which the characters in question will ultimately transcend, and the suggestion of mannerism causes one to take a detached response to the emotionalism as excessive, self-pitying and, in some as yet undefined and unanalysed way, morally questionable. Similarly here Lady Chiltern's words, because they seem second-hand, convey neither the ring of integrity nor truth to complexities of feeling.

30. *We needs must love . . . see it*: Another bold intertextual reference; words given by Tennyson in his *Idylls of the King* (1842–85) to Queen Guinevere when, admitting to her adultery with Launcelot, she realizes her fall from grace (King Arthur is 'the highest'). Again, as with the quotation from *Troilus and Cressida*, the preoccupation is with value and estimation, what creates it and how it may be destroyed. But Lady Chiltern is quoting the words of a woman who has only learned the true value of the man she once loved in the moment when he is lost to her for ever. The words convey one meaning, but the context creates much profounder levels of significance. Does Lady Chiltern too sense that her husband is lost to her, and in that loss is she beginning to perceive that he held a meaning in her life for more than his sense of public duty? Is this indeed to be the triumph of love over duty as the final image of Sir Robert's silhouette against the brightly illuminated tapestry implies?

31. *Put out the lights . . . lights*: Another intertextual reference, recalling Othello's words on entering Desdemona's chamber with the intention of murdering her: 'Put out the light, and then put out the light' (*Othello*, V.ii.7). Again Wilde focuses on the consequences of a lost reputation; and hovering behind the words Sir Robert utters lies Othello's realization that in murdering his wife he has lost a pearl 'richer than all his tribe'. It is possible to play both this line and the one from Tennyson to convey to audiences that shock and self-pity are making Sir Robert and his wife act roles that are alien to their best natures and best interests, though appropriate to their immediate emotional states.

ACT II

1. *height of fashion . . . armchair*: Lord Goring is the epitome of aristocratic nonchalance: magnificently dressed, he nonetheless carries it off with superb negligence. Despite the relaxed body language, he possesses an acutely alert mind and precise sense of moral scruple. The quality that Wilde is representing here is a late nineteenth-century embodiment of what in Renaissance times was the *sprezzatura* cultivated by noblemen: a total ease of accomplishment in all they undertook. There is a distinct contrast here between Lord Goring and the restlessly pacing Sir Robert.

2. *pillory*: A particularly vicious form of public humiliation and punishment in which an offender was locked upright into a wooden framework that sported holes for head and hands and left as an object of ridicule, abuse and on occasions disfigurement or even death.

3. *The god . . . wealth*: Sir Peter Hall's production in 1992 stressed this particular idea by confronting the audience on their arrival and between the acts with a frontcloth which was dominated by an enlarged image of a Victorian gold sovereign with its central embossed head of the Queen: the visual pun on 'sovereign' as coin and monarch gave an exact social context.

4. *A thoroughly shallow creed*: It is the mark of Lord Goring's supreme command of himself and the situation that he can sustain his friendship with Sir Robert while so emphatically distancing himself from his friend's philosophy and code of ethics.

5. *some strange book*: Such tomes that have a deep influence on individuals' lives recur throughout Wilde's works, most notably in *Dorian Gray*; Wilde told Yeats that Pater's *Studies in the History of the Renaissance* (1873) was such for him.

6. *I never knew . . . empty hollow*: Kerry Powell in *Oscar Wilde and the Theatre of the 1890s* (1990) has written in detail of Wilde's extensive knowledge of the plays of Henrik Ibsen. This passage anticipates a situation and sustained imagery from Ibsen's *John Gabriel Borkman*, which was not completed until 1896. Borkman is obsessed with a vision of releasing unparalleled wealth from the ore which he believes could be mined from the local mountain range; as the director of a bank he is in a position to use and squander the savings of numerous people in pursuit of this chimera; he is gaoled, released into a kind of exile within his own house but dies when he escapes into a snowstorm, still questing for his vision, when he senses a hand of ice close about his heart. When Wilde was about to be released from Reading Gaol, he asked Robert Ross to bring him two books that might afford him mental companionship and security in facing the world: one was *John Gabriel Borkman*.

7. *Factory Acts . . . Franchise*: These were in fact all issues that the Liberal party were promoting after they were returned to power under Gladstone in the election of 1892.

8. *Bachelors' Ball*: During the season the parents of marriageable girls gave private parties and dances, but there were also a number of more official gatherings, such as the Bachelors' Ball, once debutantes had been presented at court.

9. *If you ever . . . at once to me*: The sudden urgent tone of this, which surprises Lady Chiltern, indicates how well Lord Goring knows the inner characters of his friends and how astutely he has judged their likely independent reactions to the present crisis.

10. *ravishing frock*: The dress for the first production was described by 'Florence' in the *Sketch* (9 January 1895) as of 'eau de Nil satin, patterned with a tiny spot and an equally diminutive conventional leaf'. There were decorations involving orange velvet bows, black ostrich feathers, a black satin waistband, an orange velvet collar, 'epaulettes of black satin covered with lace' and a 'picture hat' of black velvet trimmed with yet more ostrich feathers.

11. *The Morning Post*: The leading London newspaper for retailing information about the activities of West End society. Members of the upper classes frequently paid to have paragraphs printed listing the persons attending their private functions.

12. *moue*: An enigmatic pursing of the lips which hovers wittily between being expressive of a kiss and of annoyance.

13. *bimetallist*: See *A Woman of No Importance*, Act III, n. 7.

14. *tableaux*: It was a popular way of raising money for charities at this time for beautiful young women in elaborate costuming to be grouped in representations of famous paintings or scenes from history or mythology. These were rehearsed and then displayed at society parties as part of the evening's entertainment. The still poses were sustained while appropriate accompanying music was played.

15. *Undeserving*: Victorian charitable institutions struggled to determine between the needs of the deserving as distinct from the undeserving poor. Charles Booth had researched and written the key text attempting such a discrimination in *Labour and Life of the People* (1889). Wilde continually joked about how much the denizens of high society were in need of assistance: see, for example, Canon Chasuble's reference in *The Importance of Being Earnest* to the 'Society for the Prevention of Discontent among the Upper Orders'.

16. *Drawing Room*: Debutantes were formally presented to the Queen and her court as a sign of their coming out into society at what was officially known as a 'Drawing Room'.

17. *assisted emigration*: This was a radical project for reforming the criminal classes or for giving what was deemed a start in life for the healthy but impoverished. It was also a way of increasing an English presence in colonial territories to oversee a native labour force and so, it was deemed, increase agricultural yield or industrial production. The philosophy of Empire produced some questionable ventures which, under the guise of philanthropy, were really furthering material interests.

18. *Bath . . . Pump Room*: The spa town was more likely to have been visited at this date for social entertainment than for reasons of health.

19. *Higher Education of Women*: This was still a subject of debate, despite the founding of several women's colleges at Oxford, Cambridge and London universities, and would remain so until women received the franchise.

20. *Welsh Church*: Gladstone had proposed to disestablish the Anglican Church in Wales, which had provoked much controversy. The Liberals had also contemplated instituting measures to abolish the House of Lords where the Home Rule Bill and a number of other attempts at radical legislation had been blocked. Given this last point, Lady Markby's thoughtless chatter about how sensible the House of Lords is as an institution is comically insensitive.

21. *Blue Book . . . yellow covers*: The 'blue books' were rather arid, statistic-ridden reports of Parliamentary committees; the 'yellow covers' were the format in which modern French novels were published. *The Yellow Book*, a bound and illustrated quarterly journal containing contemporary literature and art-work by English writers and designers, had been in circulation since April 1894, and was considered by many to be the epitome of French-inspired decadence.

22. *so broken-hearted . . . took up*: The convent was to be the fate of George Moore's heroine Evelyn Innes, who in the first of two novels takes to the stage as a Wagnerian soprano but then suffers a religious crisis and in the sequel, *Sister Teresa* (1901), takes the veil. Decorative art needlework was fostered by William Morris, championed by Wilde, and the source of a successful business by W. B. Yeats's sister Lily who had been apprenticed to Morris's daughter, May, in her embroidery workshop at Kelmscott.

23. *wonderful new genius*: Discovering geniuses to lionize at their social gatherings was a regular hobby of society hostesses with pretensions to establishing a salon in the continental manner. Wilde damningly described the attempt of the Russian émigré Andre Raffalovich to start such a gathering as scarcely rising above a 'saloon'.

24. *If by then . . . Robert Chiltern*: This is a dangerously melodramatic exit line. Anna Carteret playing Mrs Cheveley in Hall's production downplayed the moment by teasingly enunciating the word 'origin' as if quoting herself from the previous act in order to remind Sir Robert of what Baron Arnheim had written as a gloss on the incriminating letter.

25. *A horrible . . . for money*: The unstated image is that of the common stereotype of the prostitute with her overly painted face.

26. *You were to me . . . the ideal of my life*: Wilde has cleverly reversed the gender stereotyping that underpins the writing of much conventional melodrama: here we have a man with a past being berated by a woman because she can no longer place him on the elevated pedestal where she feels he and his gender are best situated as objects for adoration.

27. *The sin of my youth . . . prevented me*: The violence evoked by Sir Robert's rhetorical imagery is profoundly disturbing (one recalls Dorian Gray's murder of Basil Hallward, who painted the portrait which is a record of his guilt and his savage attack on the painting itself) for what it implies about his obsession with preserving his reputation at any cost. Immediately after this, he shifts his ground from self-pity and guilt before his accusing wife and begins to blame her for his total ruin. It is a shocking ending to the act because of the sinister and menacing qualities that rage is bringing to the surface in Chiltern's character when the dictates of 'good form' lose their control over him. He is wild and dangerous and his wife is left speechless by his tirade. Her desolate figure, abandoned and vulnerable, is recalled in the ensuing act, and gives an audience precise understanding of the motivation that led to the writing of her remarkably impassioned letter to Lord Goring. Wilde's control of plot-structuring is deft in its handling of visual effects as frequently as verbal statement to further developments in the action.

ACT III

1. *Adam room*: Though the reference to the architect and interior designer Robert Adam (1728–92) intimates that the overall effect of this room is decidedly grand and in the neo-classical style, what is most conspicuous in the stage direction (given the prominence of its placing) is the prescription for three sets of doors, all essential to the ensuing action. Hall was inspired by this to handle the act as if it were farce: Lord Goring is forever being intruded upon by the one person he at that moment least wishes to see, which is indeed a staple premise for good farce. Four grand persons were trying to act in a grand private tragedy whose pretensions to a high seriousness were continually undermined by the bizarre coincidences of the situation as it evolved. This sufficed to admit to the melodramatic nature of the action, while keeping the potential excesses firmly under control: the complex tone encouraged audiences to remain remarkably detached – concerned, but at the same time amused and bemused by all these aristocrats playing so intensely with one man's reputation. Tone and playing style *placed* the characters as objects for critical and satirical scrutiny: it was as if Wilde the fervent socialist were controlling the action. It was greatly aided by the totally impassive presence of Phipps: meticulously obeying orders, yet himself wholly detached from the lives of the famous, who seemed far inferior to his magisterial poise. This Phipps was indeed the inscrutable Sphinx referred to in the stage-directions.
2. *looks at him*: Lord Goring cannot be sure whether or not a witticism was intended.

3. *breezes*: Period slang for a display of temper or irritability akin to that Lord Caversham consistently adopts in Lord Goring's presence.

4. *Lamia-like*: From Keats's poem 'Lamia' (1819): a serpent-woman of 'dazzling hue', coloured vermilion, golden, green and blue, and covered with silver scales like chain-mail. The dress that Florence West wore in the original production was, however, yellow satin with rubies and red decorations surmounted by a cloak of black satin lined with red, 'the cape being cut in battlements over a deep frill of lace' (*Sketch*, 9 January 1895).

5. *I shall have to alter all this*: To the astute listener, this is a clear indication of what Mrs Cheveley is about to propose to Lord Goring. The way the remark slips out unchecked shows her confidence of success.

6. *built up my life upon sands of shame*: The veiled reference is to Christ's parable contrasting the two men who built houses: the one who built on rock was secure against tempests and floods; but the other who built on sand suffered its collapse with the coming of the storms (see Luke 6.48–9).

7. *hock and seltzer*: Lord Byron created a fashion for this mixture of white German wine and soda water, which was taken as a restorative; it was one of Wilde's favourite drinks.

8. *Laura*: A wickedly ironic choice of name by Wilde: Laura was the name of the woman who inspired the poet Petrarch with a passion that became proverbial for its constancy and purity, out of which he created a cycle of highly innovatory love poems. The intimacy implied by this invitation to use each other's Christian names would be appropriate only between a husband and wife or an engaged couple.

9. *my lawyer . . . dictated by yourself*: Lord Goring is implying that, though Mrs Cheveley was the one guilty of misconduct, he chivalrously arranged matters so that it appeared as if he were the guilty party, allowing her to sue him for breach of promise to wed.

10. *Yes . . . think that*: Wilde takes care to represent his dandy as neither hypocritical nor amoral.

11. *The Book of Numbers*: Behind the witty rejoinder is a more serious barb. This Old Testament book not only lists all the lines of descent through honourable marriage of all the various tribes under Moses' care, it is also preoccupied with the wanderings of the Israelites in the deserts of Sinai and Moab as they journey still out of sight of the Promised Land.

12. *It is so demoralizing . . . to the bad*: Wilde with a characteristic attention to the need to prepare for effects is developing the immediate situation while also sketching in the basis of the stand that Lord Goring will take in the final act when he argues this theme in an extended form as he persuades Lady Chiltern not to allow her husband to resign.

13. *Voilà tout*: Literally, That's that, or, That is all. The callousness is defined by the offhand flippancy of the French idiom.

14. *glance is like a swift arrow*: The play analyses ways in which people succumb to an obsession with power as a means of controlling others: it has been Sir Robert's greatest ambition and the motivating force behind his political career, and he reveals little in himself that may support an alternative identity; Lady Chiltern uses her idealizing of her husband to keep him in thrall to her emotionally, since he lives in dread of failing to live up to her expectations. Mrs Cheveley as represented in this act is the most frightening example of someone totally possessed by the need for power, which is developed through a series of alarming visual metaphors: on arriving she is to appear Lamia-like, playing the sexual predator; frustrated of her intent, she seems to wither, to become 'dreadful to look at' as her mask falls (even as the Lamia, when ultimately challenged about her real identity under a critical male gaze which refuses to accept her enacted illusions, degenerates till 'all is blight'); getting the upper hand again by the theft of the letter seems to revivify her, as if like a vampire feeds on blood she feeds on power.

ACT IV

1. *Canning*: George Canning (1770–1827) was a remarkable statesman who entered Parliament in 1794 and was under-secretary of state by the age of twenty-six. His eloquence was renowned, particularly when his oratory was directed against slavery, or in support of Catholic Emancipation or the repeal of the Corn Laws.

2. *the unemployed*: The unemployed were a troubling issue for Whigs and Tories: both parties feared their growing numbers at this date and their potential for united political action such as the Trafalgar Square riots of 1886.

3. *I am sure ... opportunities*: This pert response, which can be calculated to raise a burst of laughter in performance, intimates an openness and warmth in the relationship between Mabel Chiltern and Lord Goring which is markedly absent by contrast in the marriage of Sir Robert and Lady Chiltern.

4. *I am delighted to hear it*: This is another instance of judicious cutting on Wilde's part. Mabel in earlier versions went on: 'I certainly don't want to marry a man of genius. I'd be very unhappy with him. I like you. You have no past: and no future. You are a perfect darling. Just the sort of man every girl should marry.' The elaboration robs the initial joke of its punch; and delays and so somewhat minimizes the impact of the ensuing comic touch concerning 'temptations'.

5. *Second palm tree*: There is a small textual crux here. The 'second palm tree' is Mabel Chiltern's instruction to Lord Goring earlier in the act, but the published text has '*Third* palm tree' at this point in Lord Goring's speech. It is not clear whether this was an oversight on Wilde's part, or intended as a joke (that Lord Goring cannot remember specific instructions). It is possible that an actor might make some comic mileage out of this, but it is not in keeping with the way Wilde has characterized the role elsewhere in the play. Editors generally emend the line to conform with Mabel's direction and that precedent has been followed here.

6. *or should want of them*: This speech continued in the draft versions with Lord Goring hypothesizing about his own future marriage and how he would hope for 'pity, gentleness, kindness, forgiveness' from his wife, should he do 'some weak or wrong thing'. This caused Lady Chiltern to question him whether his perception of her was of a 'hard and unwomanly' individual, which elicited the reply: 'I think you hard but not unwomanly.' This is rendering explicit what in the final text is the unstated objective of Lord Goring's address to Lady Chiltern; she now senses the implications of his words without seeking clarification; and Wilde trusts the audience to perceive this too. The whole speech has posed problems for some of Wilde's critics because Lord Goring, whose words have until now sparkled with originality of thought and expression, seems to be offering a decidedly conventional view of woman's place within marriage (and one that even in its expression draws heavily on the writings of John Ruskin). But elsewhere in the play Lord Goring has shown himself to be an acute judge of character, and a good actor here can convey the impression that Goring knows his listener so thoroughly as a woman of politically advanced opinions but limited emotional awareness and understanding that he has calculated his words to a nicety, asking her, if not to be, then at least to *play* the forgiving angel in the Chiltern household. Lady Chiltern believes strongly in social duty and so Lord Goring, in asking her to be the dutiful wife, is inviting her to be true to her own principles for the greater benefit of society.

7. *A man's life . . . a useless sacrifice*: Feminist and socialist critics alike have taken exception to this speech which represents Lady Chiltern as a kind of puppet programmed by Lord Goring. But this is to miss the careful structuring of the change that Lady Chiltern's character undergoes during this act: she is entering into a state of awareness that is new, strange and frightening for her, precisely because it is a mind-set that has been constructed for her by Lord Goring; the subtle repetitions in the dialogue show the extent to which she is at present distanced emotionally from what she is bringing herself to say. The moment is shocking, because it represents a woman's experience of losing all sense of a secure identity. Lady Chiltern ceases to *act* a part and comes totally to inhabit her new self only when she has the courage to admit to her husband to being the woman that Lord Goring was expecting. She believes that she is setting her relationship with Chiltern at risk but is impelled to tell the truth to save Lord Goring from an apparently compromising situation. She finds that her husband's love and trust are constant, and her courage is rewarded with a new-found joy in their marriage.

8. *For both of us . . . beginning*: The ending is worth comparing with that of *Lady Windermere's Fan*: there the characters are all left with their masks and illusions intact, each wholly unaware (except for Mrs Erlynne) of the true situation and how close that situation came to tragedy; here husband and wife have discovered much about each other, have grown immeasurably through facing hazards together and are hesitantly now finding new ways of relating to each other through their emotions rather than through abstract, intellectualized concepts of duty (marital and social).

A Florentine Tragedy

This remarkable play was begun by Wilde in 1894 and may have been a response to Lewis Waller's idea of staging an evening of one-act plays with at least one contribution by Wilde. It was written in tandem with *La Sainte Courtisane*, which like *A Florentine Tragedy* concludes with an unexpected emotional and psychological reversal: an anchorite succeeds in converting a pagan courtesan to Christianity, but in the process is himself converted to paganism, only to be spurned by his newly devout student. The fact that Wilde frequently spoke of continuing work on *A Florentine Tragedy* has led to the supposition by some critics that it is incomplete; Robert Ross in first editing the play described it as a 'fragment' and commissioned an opening scene from the poet Sturge Moore which explained the situation and developed the characters of Bianca and Guido. And yet it is perfectly self-sufficient as it stands; indeed Moore's addition overly clarifies the adulterous relationship, which robs Wilde's play of its crucial element of suspense. Dramatically the play is far more powerful if the audience are as uncertain as Simone and like him are trying to come at the truth: Simone plays a meticulously timed game of cat-and-mouse with Bianca and Guido. He waits to be absolutely sure before he acts; and, when he does so, it is wholly unexpected and then as the dark undertow to an apparently innocent fencing spat. The play as it stands is a study in suppressed emotion: Simone must guard against any display of jealousy until Guido incriminates himself. A fastidious attention to value is what characterizes

Simone the merchant and is the quality that Bianca despises in her husband; but he understands the varying motives that inspire others to purchase from his stock; and he reads Guido's refusal to haggle as proof of his guilt. Throughout feelings are continually defined by other areas of experience: buying and selling, and later the display of swordsmanship. It is a grimly humorous tragedy, edged with bitter satire at men's relentless commodification of women; but its length is perfectly conceived in respect of the dramatic action.

A Florentine Tragedy was first performed after Wilde's death in 1906 by the Literary Theatre Society directed by Ricketts and incorporating Moore's additions; it played in a double-bill with *Salomé*. Max Beerbohm considered *A Florentine Tragedy* the more accomplished piece of dramatic craftsmanship and praised George Ingleton's sardonic detachment in the role of Simone. His one cavil was with the point at which the play ends: that the unexpected reversal is not 'led up to' nor in any way explored before the curtain falls. He opines elsewhere in his review that the actress playing Bianca was somewhat incapable of realizing the demands of the role, and this may be the cause of his discomfort with the character's reawakened passion for Simone. Wilde leaves the motivation enigmatic, so that good performers have a range of possibilities to explore to bring credibility to those final two lines. There have been few attempts subsequently to stage the play, which deserves a better reputation than it currently possesses. Zemlinsky based an opera on it, which was staged at Covent Garden in October 1985.

A Florentine Tragedy is one of the few plays Wilde attempted in blank verse. His first such experiment, *The Duchess of Padua*, resorts to so close an imitation of the Shakespearean mode that at times the dialogue risks pastiche. However, the verse in *A Florentine Tragedy* is spare and sinewy, close to the vernacular rather than to the archly poetic, except where Simone needs to expatiate on the magnificence of the articles he is trying to sell to Guido; or Guido launches into praise of Bianca. The whole movement of the dramatic rhythm inexorably works towards those two forceful questions with which the action ends, where the placing of the word 'why' as the last syllable of a line gives it a strange and poignant power. If Wilde shows an influence in this work, it is Browning's 'My Last Duchess' (1855), with its similar shrewd-eyed, seemingly dispassionate observation of adultery and subtly calculated revenge. The text printed here follows that in Robert Ross's *Collected Edition* of Wilde's works of 1908, including the gap in the text marked by a line of asterisks (see n. 12).

1. *most honest friend*: The passage does not echo a Shakespearean rhythm, but does repeat a Shakespearean device of reiterating a word till it takes on the quality of a threat, or comes to seem in time the antithesis of what the word usually conveys. The obvious Shakespearean example is Antony's continual

reiteration of the words 'And Brutus is an honourable man' in his oration over Caesar's corpse, which steadily turns the mob against the man that they had just acclaimed for being 'honourable', as the word itself comes subtly through its repetition to be imbued with connotations of viciousness. It is important that the actor playing Simone respect the equivalent of one whole line's worth of silence before taking up the conversation again with 'And yet . . .' Has he been waiting for a response that is not forthcoming? Or is he leaving a pause so that the insistence on that word 'honest' be fully registered?

2. *damask*: Like the more modern brocade, a luxurious fabric woven with two threads of contrasting colours so that designs in one shade, often as here of flowers, appear to stand out against a background of a different hue. When the weaving is of silk (as is likely in material coming from Lucca, a town northwest of Florence), the ground tends to have a silvery sheen while the main design is coloured but less shiny.

3. *Bellosguardo . . . Fiesole*: Two small picturesque towns on hillsides overlooking Florence.

4. *Medea*: In classical myth, an enchantress who killed her children when their father, Jason, threatened to abandon her and marry the princess Creusa, while they were living in exile in Corinth, having fled Medea's father's kingdom of Colchis after she had assisted the hero and his companions, the Argonauts, in stealing the famed Golden Fleece.

5. *ell*: Measure of length, equivalent to 45 inches.

6. *cut-velvet*: Another luxurious fabric, generally woven from silk but designed to leave a thick, short pile on one side, that was then trimmed away (cut) to leave patterns which were raised against a flattened background. The raised designs in Renaissance times were often embroidered with jewels.

7. *male ruby*: Correct terminology to describe a valuable precious stone of great depth and clarity in its colour (here a deep crimson or purple, rather than a shade nearer pink).

8. *Cellini . . . Lorenzo*: Benvenuto Cellini (1500–71) was an Italian goldsmith, sculptor and engraver of rare skill. He was also a notorious fighter, an activity that frequently resulted in his imprisonment. After working for some years at the papal court for both Clement VII and Paul III, he turned first to France and the patronage of Francis I and later to his hometown of Florence, where his patron was Cosimo I de Medici (1519–74) and not, as is implied here, Lorenzo 'the Magnificent', who had died in 1492.

9. *wear horns*: Emblem signifying that a man has been cuckolded.

10. *distaff*: Cleft stick on which wool or flax was wound ready for spinning. It was the traditional emblem of good housewifery.

11. *Lucretia . . . Tarquin*: In Roman legend, Lucretia, the wife of Collatinus, was raped by Sextus Tarquinius, son of the king of Rome, while her husband was away fighting with the army. Having revealed her condition to her husband, she committed suicide. An insurrection ensued in which the Tarquins were expelled from the city and a republic founded.

12. *their wool*: Ross's edition records a break in the text at this point and this has been respected here. In psychological terms, however, there is no break in the flow of ideas: Bianca, following Guido's lead, chides Simone for talking of tiresome national politics. He subtly takes up her thread of thought and asks whether there is nothing worth talking about but the room in which they are situated, which means discussing the emotions and relations that are currently trapped there.

13. *chapman*: Pedlar.

14. *And makes the reeling earth . . . round her beauty*: Was Wilde, in an attempt to contextualize his play with a degree of Renaissance reference, reflecting here the period's fascination with cosmology? In 1543 Copernicus published his proofs that the sun (and not, as previously thought in the Ptolemaic System, the earth) was the centre of the universe.

15. *Hyblean bees*: Famed from classical times as yielders of the sweetest honey.

16. *Duomo's bell*: The cathedral of Florence dominates the city's skyline with its vast dome and independent bell-tower and baptistery.

17. *Ahab . . . Naboth's goodly field*: In 1 Kings 21 is told the story of Naboth whose one family possession, a vineyard, was situated near the palace of King Ahab, who coveted it for a garden. But his offers of recompense were refused by Naboth. Queen Jezebel arranged a scheme whereby Naboth during a celebratory feast was accused of cursing God and the king by two suborned witnesses. Naboth was dragged from the banquet and stoned to death. Ahab took possession of the vineyard. But Elijah, the prophet, came and cursed him in the name of God, threatening his line with extinction.

18. *Ferrara's*: In Italy, a great centre for the crafting of swords, rapiers and daggers in Renaissance times.

19. *most shamefully*: The repeated use of 'shame' here precisely balances 'honest' at the start of the play.

20. *looks at BIANCA*: The short stage direction recording the moment when Guido dies is placed by Ross at the start of this long direction which goes on to record Simone's and Bianca's responses to that death. It has been moved in this edition to the point where Guido logically dies so that the motivation behind Simone's words, 'Now for the other', becomes evident. Having assured himself that the aristocrat is dead, he turns his murderous attentions on Bianca till her approach forestalls his intention. Beerbohm makes the psychological patterning of the conclusion clear, when in reviewing Ricketts's production he describes this moment as follows: 'The wife shrinks against the wall. She sees in her husband's eyes that she, too, is doomed. And now comes the ending for the sake of which, I take it, the play was written – the germ of psychological paradox from which the story developed itself backwards. The wife falls to her knees, and, with real love in her voice, cries, "Why did you not tell me you were so strong?" The husband pauses, stares at her, lets drop his dagger, saying "Why did you not tell me you were so beautiful?"' (*Last Theatres*, p. 250).

The Importance of Being Earnest

How one of the great comedies in the English language came to be staged is an intricate piece of stage history: Wilde had contracted himself to George Alexander for the play for an advance of £150 in Summer 1894, after submitting a detailed outline of the plot in four acts. A finished draft was sent to Alexander late in the autumn; but in the covering letter Wilde frankly opined that in his view his farcical comedy as now realized was ill-suited to Alexander's romantic style; he admitted that 'the people it wants are actors like Wyndham and Hawtrey' (*Letters*, p. 126). Alexander presumably agreed, since he turned the play down, whereas Charles Wyndham immediately seized the chance of staging *The Importance of Being Earnest*, for production at his Criterion Theatre (another very stylish haunt of the upper and middle classes). Meanwhile Alexander's luck faltered when his staging of Henry James's *Guy Domville* met with a very poor critical reception, leaving him with no choice but to take it off the boards. (*An Ideal Husband* was playing to packed houses to the profound chagrin of James.) Alexander was now suddenly bereft of a production, and Wyndham generously released *The Importance of Being Earnest* to him with the proviso that he should have first refusal of Wilde's next venture.

The comedy went instantly into rehearsal at the St James's, ready for an opening night on 14 February (St Valentine's Day); but by now it had been trimmed down to a sprightly three acts, as in the version submitted to the Lord Chamberlain for licensing. Alexander played Jack Worthing and Allen Aynesworth, Algernon; Rose Leclercq, the original Lady Hunstanton in *A Woman of No Importance*, now essayed Lady Bracknell, while the role of Gwendolen was entrusted to a relative newcomer, Irene Vanbrugh, who was soon to establish her name with delicate innovative interpretations in comedies by Pinero and Sir James Barrie. It was a triumphant success and the play looked set for a lengthy run; but Wilde's trials, sentencing and bankruptcy intervened, and, though Alexander endeavoured to sustain the play by removing Wilde's name from the theatre posters and hoardings, he was soon forced by pressure of opinion to close after only 83 performances. He bought the exclusive performing rights for *Lady Windermere's Fan* and *The Importance of Being Earnest* at the enforced sale of Wilde's effects (but bequeathed them to Wilde's son).

Alexander revived *Importance* after Wilde's death and chose to celebrate his twentieth year of management at the St James's on 1 February 1910 with both a further restaging and a souvenir edition, published by Methuen. Revivals have been legion, though over the twentieth century critical attention and audience enthusiasm have increasingly focused on the performance of the actress playing Lady Bracknell, as if this affords the benchmark by which the whole production, its style and tone, are to be judged (Edith Evans, Judi Dench and Maggie Smith have each given notable and decidedly different readings of the role). So much a part of contemporary English culture has the play become that a number of dramatists have recently exploited audiences' familiarity with its every detail to create witty subversions of its word play and comedic conventions in order to interrogate its iconic status as a 'classic' and the cultural tastes which have determined that situation: Edward Bond's *The Sea* (1973), Tom Stoppard's *Travesties* (1974) and Mark Ravenhill's *Handbag* (1998) all draw inspiration from it, even as Wilde in composing *The Importance of Being Earnest* drew heavily on the work of his contemporary, W. S. Gilbert, particularly his 'heartless' black comedy, *Engaged* (1877), and a forgotten work by William Lestocq and E. M. Robson, *The Foundling* (1894).

Draft versions of the play survive in both the four-act and three-act formats. The text that Wilde revised for publication was a typescript owned by Alexander, which is itself extant; he added many after-thoughts or re-pointed certain lines to heighten the satiric edge. *The Importance of Being Earnest* was first published by Leonard Smithers in February 1899; but Robert Ross brought out a revised version in 1908–9 as part of his collected edition of Wilde's writings, which he claimed contained many of Wilde's last thoughts on certain lines. Subsequent editions tend to be based on Smithers's text with collations drawn from Ross's. (See the commentary and notes to the Appendix for composition and publication details of the four-act version.)

DEDICATION

1. *Robert Baldwin Ross*: (1869–1918), Wilde's literary executor, friend and champion, was Canadian by birth, though much of his life was spent in England. He was a literary journalist and art historian, who supported Wilde emotionally throughout his term in prison and financially in the period

following his release; Ross worked tirelessly to pay off the bankruptcy on the Wilde estate, enabling him to edit and publish a collected edition of the works. His publishing of *De Profundis* (1905) led to vilification and persecution by Lord Alfred Douglas. Wilde, writing in Ross's copy of *Importance*, described him as 'the Mirror of Perfect Friendship'.

ACT I

1. *Half-Moon Street*: A most fashionable Mayfair address situated off Piccadilly.

2. *Is marriage . . . as that*: While sustaining the comic mode, Wilde starts the play by sounding a rather ominous note: three pairs of characters are desperate for marriage, despite the grim remarks on the subject by Lane and Lady Bracknell, whose own relationship with her husband sounds from her and Gwendolen's account of it anything but ideal or fulfilling.

3. *That will do . . . thank you*: In earlier drafts Lane announced as he was leaving that there were two creditors waiting for Algernon, and this introduced what became throughout the action a developed line of comedy concerning his debts and the troubles he lands everyone in by trying to evade all responsibility for them. Much of this material was cut by Wilde, particularly after the decision to reduce the play from four acts to three, although enough remains so that Lady Bracknell's description of her nephew as being a most eligible bachelor even though he has 'nothing but his debts to depend upon' may elicit laughter. See also Appendix.

4. *take some slight . . . five o'clock*: As dining grew ever later in the evening, it became fashionable to offer refreshments to callers during the latter part of the afternoon: tea, elegant sandwiches, rolled bread and butter, tea-cake and muffins created the impression of a substantial repast, though it was polite to eat but little of what was displayed.

5. *I call that business*: With a seemingly flippant remark Wilde introduces a staple theme: the struggle of the various couples in love to bring passionate instinct, high ideals, compatible interests and more mercenary considerations to do with income, social status and future security into an acceptable state of balance.

6. *Scotland Yard*: The Metropolitan Police operated from this address after 1891.

7. *More than half . . . shouldn't read*: Various forms of policing and censorship of a rather subtle kind occurred in late-Victorian society: Mudie's library and the railway bookstalls of W. H. Smith controlled fashions in reading by simply refusing to take books they deemed indecent; theatrical censorship still prevailed through the interventions of the Lord Chamberlain's office (though, as in the case of George Bernard Shaw's early plays, much of what was banned for performance could subsequently be read in published form, over which the Lord Chamberlain had no authority). French fiction and drama were considered most improper reading, but since these were accessible only to the educated there was no active censorship against them except in the form of public opinion.

8. *Tunbridge Wells*: Genteel and consequently expensive town in Kent, formerly a spa resort, which was a popular place of retirement for the middle classes.

9. *The Albany*: This institution, situated near Burlington House in Piccadilly, still rents sets of rooms or chambers for bachelor gentlemen, which are grouped around a central courtyard after the style of Oxford and Cambridge colleges and the Inns of Court.

10. *the whole truth . . . never simple*: This play abounds in a technique of verbal comedy which plays games with hackneyed clichés such that the original concept is exposed as naive, bogus or absurd while the re-phrasing confidently asserts a more accurate insight. It is a style of comic writing and speech which later Irish writers, notably Samuel Beckett and Flann O'Brien, were to develop with considerable ingenuity.

11. *Willis's*: This restaurant in King's Street, St James's (its full name was Willis's Rooms) was a favourite haunt of Wilde and Bosie, being the most celebrated restaurant of the 1890s. It was a short walk from Alexander's theatre.

12. *sent down . . . or two*: As guests descended from the drawing-room, each man was required to accompany a particular lady and attend to her for the duration of the meal. It was the duty of the hostess to assign these partners, and if the gathering was especially large a seating plan would reveal to the men to which of the women they should present themselves.

13. *I am going to kill my brother*: The comedy abounds in instances where a chance remark or joke suddenly rebounds on the speaker to his or her confusion when it unexpectedly materializes later. Jack in Act II will indeed attempt to kill off his brother but in circumstances that rapidly develop out of his control. All the characters feel they can shape the plot to their private satisfaction but continually find chance interfering; that chance eventually fulfils everyone's desires requires a *tour de force* of clever structuring by Wilde.

14. *the corrupt French drama*: Plays by Eugène Scribe (1791–1861), Alexandre Dumas *fils* (1824–95) or Guillaume Augier (1820–89) generally required considerable bowdlerization before they were sufficiently acceptable to the Lord Chamberlain to be granted a licence.

15. *Wagnerian manner*: The popular joke at the expense of Richard Wagner

(1813–83) was that his operas were excessively loud. Wilde described his son Cyril when a baby as having 'a superb voice' which he 'freely exercises' in a style 'essentially Wagnerian' (*Letters*, p. 63).

16. *icy coldness*: In early drafts Lady Bracknell greeted Jack with a formal 'Good afternoon, Mr Worthing'; substituting what amounts to a mimed snub immediately establishes the frosty nature of their relations, which advances the plot with remarkable succinctness and comic irony.

17. *Lady Harbury*: In Alexander's production Lane returned on stage at this point bearing a teapot from which he proceeded to pour Lady Bracknell a cup, which, being ever-resourceful and anticipating his superiors' every need, he delivered exactly on cue to her request. With Lane thus occupied, Algernon as attentive host would therefore have to be the one to respond to her further request for cucumber sandwiches.

18. *my table completely out*: It was considered very bad form to have an odd number of guests sit down together to dine; there should be an equal number of male and female diners.

19. *Mamma . . . to her about*: An instance of a joke-line that actually prepares for the conclusion of this episode and provides the occasion for the next.

20. *Gwendolen*: Wilde meticulously observes the protocol about when it was permitted to use a forename. In any scene one can gauge how close the characters suppose they are to marrying and when they feel distanced from each other by their manner of address. Jack supposes from Gwendolen's admission of her love for him that a proposal will be accepted and so promptly addresses her with her forename, as was customarily allowed after a couple became engaged. When later Jack talks of their marrying without actually having yet proposed, Gwendolen rapidly reverts to calling him Mr Worthing to prompt him to the necessary action.

21. *restrains him*: Alexander had Irene Vanbrugh place her hand on his shoulders (he was playing Jack) and push him back down on his knees, an action which she repeated as she observed: 'Mr Worthing has not quite *finished* yet.' When Wilde's stage direction later requires the pair to *rise together* as Gwendolen announces to her mother that they are engaged, Alexander again made it clear that it was Gwendolen who was completely in control by having her lift him to his feet by placing her hands under his elbows.

22. *in Grosvenor Square*: It is Wilde's socialist sympathies which frame this joke at Lady Bracknell's expense. Behind her argument lies an ill-concealed fear that by educating the masses the aristocracy might be in danger of losing their privileges; and behind that fear lies the conviction that, as education might encourage the lower orders to question their status in society, an ignorant populace is the one way of ensuring the continuing stability of the *status quo*.

The reference to Grosvenor Square was a late addition to the text when the play was in proof, but it is what gives the joke, and the social satire which underpins it, its barbed precision.

23. *Between seven . . . a year*: This was a sizeable fortune at that date.

24. *Liberal Unionist*: A number of Liberal MPs voted against their own party at the time of Gladstone's bill advocating Home Rule in Ireland (1886); they preferred that the existing union between Ireland and England should be maintained. Wilde is implying that Jack has no political interests whatever by aligning himself with such a minority.

25. *Both . . . carelessness*: This, one of the funniest lines in the play, exists in two versions and is the only serious crux in the text. The line as given here would appear to be what was uttered at the first performance; and was how Wilde himself emended it in the typescript prepared for Smithers's edition (previously in the draft versions the line appears as 'Both? – that seems like carelessness.') Ross, however, insisted that his memorial reconstruction was Wilde's final thought on the phrasing: 'To lose one parent, Mr Worthing, may be regarded as a misfortune; to lose both looks like carelessness.' This has tended to be the version printed and preferred by some actresses playing Lady Bracknell. (To complicate matters, on 1 February 1910 Alexander published the play as a souvenir to celebrate twenty years of his management of the St James's Theatre; and that text contains Ross's version.)

26. *the Wedding March*: Directors are faced with a choice, since Wilde does not specify whether he intended the march from Wagner's *Lohengrin* or that from Mendelssohn's *Incidental Music to 'A Midsummer Night's Dream'*. They were equally well known. Traditionally, Wagner's music accompanies the arrival of the bride's procession at the chancel, and Mendelssohn's march is played as the married couple and their entourage process from the vestry out of the church. Either would be appropriate here. The Mendelssohn became a firm favourite in Victorian society, after it had been played at the wedding of the Princess Royal at Windsor in 1848.

27. *Gorgon*: Mythological monster in the form of a snake-haired woman who turned all she gazed upon to stone.

28. *only just eighteen*: This was the age at which women 'came out' in society and were deemed to be marriageable.

29. *I'll bet you . . . other things first*: This is precisely the pattern of the womens' encounter at the conclusion of Act II.

30. *the Empire*: Music-hall in Leicester Square, the Empire Theatre of Varieties, which at this date was under the management of George Edwardes. The theatre was famous for its ballets and notorious for its promenade, which was densely populated with prostitutes.

31. *smoking jacket*: Casual garment, usually flamboyantly decorated with frogging and quilting, worn indoors as informal evening wear by men when they were not at home to any but their closest friends.

32. *and smiles*: This is Wilde's final version of the tableau on which the curtain should fall. Originally, once Jack was out of earshot, Algernon had the riposte: 'And besides, I *love* nonsense.' Max Beerbohm recalled how Alexander raised his glass of sherry while uttering the line. Alexander's typescript copy records that in addition to glancing at his cuffs, he repeated the address out loud. The version published would seem by far the subtlest, since it wittily advances the action by intimating to alert spectators future developments in the plotting while simultaneously leaving them with the image of Algernon's unshakeable self-possession and his insatiable appetite for refreshment.

ACT II

1. *he always . . . leaving for town*: This is an instance of the way jokes blossom and multiply in this play: comic lines create a context which enables amplification and enrichment when variations on them are played later. Remembering Lady Bracknell's strictures about the 'respectability' of the German language endows the reiteration here with subtle nuances. When Jack leaves for town to play at being Ernest, then he is at his most vulnerable since he is about to indulge in behaviour that is anything but respectable. That he should endeavour to disguise his own peccadillos by taking a high moral tone with his ward places his hypocrisy with a rare comic precision. This is comedy which is both psychological and social; it is adult comedy in that it requires an audience to engage imaginatively with implications by carrying experiences over from one part of the play to another. The fact that the jokes expose the speakers to criticism ensures that they resist any intimation of xenophobia.

2. *As a man sows . . . reap*: Galatians 6.7.

3. *Mudie*: Lending library established by the bibliophile Charles Edward Mudie (1816–90) in 1842, which in large measure catered for the upper classes, and maintained a nation-wide business chiefly focused on the circulation of fiction, especially bound in a three-volume format. Subscribers would arrange to have a box of current publications sent to them at monthly intervals.

4. *Egeria . . . Laetitia*: Egeria was the nymph who instructed Numa Pompilius, king of Rome, in the arts of judicial responsibility, government and self-discipline; her teachings were later the basis of the city's laws. Laetitia, another Latin name, means 'joy' and 'delight'.

5. *you will read . . . sensational*: Early drafts had a discussion about Capital and

Labour, socialism and rational dress codes for the New Woman. This was cut because it delayed Algernon's arrival, which is more central to the plot. The rupee had fallen sensationally since 1873; by the 1890s its value had been reduced to half what it had previously fetched in sterling.

6. *Mr Ernest Worthing . . . the station*: Franklin Dyall, who originally played Merriman in Alexander's production, got a huge laugh and a round of applause with this line, which delighted Wilde: 'It shows they [the audience] have followed the plot' (Hesketh Pearson, *The Life of Oscar Wilde* (Harmondsworth: Penguin, 1985), p. 257).

7. *He does*: This is the first of the grand entrances in this act which are promptly subverted by laughter. Algernon clearly intends to make an effect both in appearance and manner; he endlessly talks of himself as unique and dresses accordingly; but his dashing arrival is undermined by Cecily's disappointment at finding he looks like everyone else. The timing is not easy: an overly flamboyant Algernon will excite the laugh, when it is imperative that it is delayed till provoked by Cecily's comment; but it cannot be delayed too long, as that risks an audience's missing the connection between it and what Cecily was ruminating immediately before Algernon's entrance, in which case her comment will fall flat.

8. *emigrating*: Common means at that time for reforming errant offspring: sending them to learn a sense of duty and responsibility by working in the colonies.

9. *Quixotic*: Coined from the name of Cervantes's hero in *Don Quixote* (1605) and was applied to anyone who pursued lofty, chivalrous but utterly impractical ideals, often with disastrous consequences for his material or physical well-being.

10. *Maréchal Niel*: A yellow rose, popular with Victorian gardeners since the 1860s.

11. *deepest mourning . . . black gloves*: The second grand entrance. Alexander's commentary on his script makes it clear he prolonged the laughter as much as possible by directing the actors playing Chasuble and Prism to separate in quest of Cecily and come downstage to either side before turning at the front to see and greet Jack. This ensured that the dialogue would not cut short the laughter before it had time to run its course. Such being the pieties of the time, it was daring of Wilde to offer the image of a man in full mourning and invite an audience to find it a subject for ridicule.

12. *sad, sad blow*: At this point Alexander produced a vast black-bordered handkerchief and proceeded to dab at his eyes.

13. *manna in the wilderness*: When the Israelites after escaping from Egypt began to starve in the desert, God answered their appeals for food by sending this bread-like substance to be gathered every morning once the dew had evaporated (Exodus 16).

14. *Enter to JACK*: This is the third grand entrance, this time carefully staged by Cecily.

15. *dog-cart*: Light, speedy vehicle, generally designed for sporting use and including a box intended for carrying gun dogs (hence the name).

16. *effeminate . . . attractive*: Gibe by Wilde at the expense of the Victorian cult of manliness. As the critics Alan Sinfield and Joseph Bristow have shown, robust, stalwart, 'manly' men feared sensitive, intellectual men (whom they chose to label effeminate) at this time because of the greater appeal they appeared to hold for women, whose company they were happy to frequent. Shaw explored the contrast, for example, in Marchbanks with his poetic sensibility and the Reverend Morell of the Church Militant in *Candida*.

17. *ward*: It was not unknown for an older man to pass off his mistress in public as his ward; and it was not uncommon for genuine wards to be wedded in time to their guardians. Both themes occur in nineteenth-century fiction, drama and opera. Gwendolen's imagination begins to alert her to possibilities of a not too pleasing kind.

18. *Morning Post*: See *An Ideal Husband*, Act II, n. 11.

19. *agricultural depression*: By the final decades of the century, relatively cheap imported foodstuffs from the colonies led to a fall in prices against which British farmers had difficulty competing, given an increased *laissez-faire* policy by governments over the market economy. A consequence of this was the large-scale movement of workers from the land into the cities where job prospects were generally better.

20. *This is Uncle Jack*: Again this is a sequence that makes great comic play with the central entrance: first Jack and then Algernon enter briskly and confidently only to have their cover blown as their games with double identities get exposed. Alexander as Worthing moved rapidly across the stage in the initial production at this point to try to prevent Cecily saying the line; failing in this, he then moved as rapidly over to Gwendolen to try to explain himself. This cleared the central entrance for Allen Aynesworth as Algernon, who entered in a suitably debonair fashion, throwing his hat nonchalantly on to a seat, as he moved downstage to join Cecily. There he was promptly discomfited by Gwendolen's announcement of his precise identity. This grouped the pairs of lovers to either side of the stage and from this point onwards, Alexander blocked the couples' moves in exactly symmetrical patterns to emphasize the increasing artificiality of the situation.

21. *call me sister, will you not*: Jack's prophecy from Act I has come about, but not before Algernon's more cynical prediction, that before calling each other sister the women will call each other 'a lot of other things first', has also occurred.

22. *retire . . . with scornful looks*: Wilde's early drafts and Alexander's copy indicate that they both considered some rather violent response on the part of the men should accompany the women's departure. Alexander required the retreating actresses to snort, after which Jack with an exact replica of the snort elbowed Algernon in the chest.

23. *continues eating*: Expecting that this conclusion would raise a burst of laughter and much applause if it were well-timed, Alexander planned for the curtain to rise again and devised further business to prolong the audience's amusement: Jack was to seize the plate of tea-cakes, only to have it grabbed by Algernon; and, when next he tried to cut cake for himself, Algernon was to take that as well. The second curtain was to fall on Jack slinking over to Algernon's seat in an attempt to 'filch' some food for himself.

ACT III

1. *Morning-room*: Large, usually quite airy room for informal and relaxed family use, to which outsiders were not customarily admitted. Visitors would be met formally in the drawing-room. The fact that later Lady Bracknell is present in such a room adds to her sense of discomfort: it is not the done thing.

2. *dreadful popular air from a British Opera*: In the copy belonging to the American impresario Charles Frohman, an annotation reveals this to be 'Home, Sweet Home' from Henry Bishop's *Clari or The Maid of Milan* (1823).

3. *Can you doubt . . . Fairfax*: Wilde's drafts show that originally he had envisaged the two men behaving like a pair of Siamese twins, exactly replicating each other's movements at this moment as very stylishly they first sat, adjusted their trousers, then reclined on a sofa beside each other.

4. *German scepticism*: Wilde may be referring here to current German philosophy or, more likely, to developments in biblical exegesis which had begun to question elements of the miraculous in a spirit of scientific enquiry.

5. *University Extension Scheme*: Such a scheme of public lectures and classes existed as a recent initiative within the University of London, which pioneered extra mural teaching.

6. *revolutionary outrage*: In the early drafts Wilde had Lady Bracknell express surprise that Bunbury was so eminent a figure as to be the focus of a political assassination. Outrages of the kind mentioned here by implication had occurred in political life: Fenian (IRB) activities since the 1870s had included bombings in England at Manchester and Clerkenwell, the Phoenix

Park murders took place in Dublin in 1882, while the Walsall anarchists had come to wide public attention during their trial in 1892.

7. *NB*: North Britain.

8. *premature experiences*: Wilde began severely cutting his initial sketches for the dialogue as this act moved towards its close, and particularly in the speeches of Lady Bracknell, who at first tended to expatiate at some length on any point.

9. *the Funds*: Cecily's vast fortune yields a dependable income from government stocks. The full title would be 'the Consolidated Funds', but was often abbreviated to either 'the Funds' or to 'consols'.

10. *profile*: The term was taken from the French and so pronounced and accentuated as 'pro*feel*'.

11. *When I married . . . in my way*: To make sure audiences did not miss the social point, Wilde initially had Lady Bracknell describe her husband as 'one of the wealthiest *commoners* in England'. In other words she and he are *parvenus*, though clearly it is she who has subsequently done the social climbing for them both.

12. *He is an Oxonian*: That is, he was educated at Oxford. This line appears to have been added during rehearsals, since it occurs as a manuscript insertion in Alexander's copy and was included by Wilde only when checking the proofs of the published text.

13. *Mr Moncrieff*: Actors who take care to point up the social niceties can make witty comedy out of the shifts between formal and informal modes of address in this scene as earlier in the exchanges between Jack and Gwendolen in Act I.

14. *Anabaptists*: This fervent religious sect was the butt of much Renaissance comedy, such as Ben Jonson's *The Alchemist* (1610). Though the term was now historical and antiquated, it was revived by Victorian Tory churchmen as a snide term of abuse for the more evangelical wing of the Baptists.

15. *Gower Street omnibus*: Horse-drawn public conveyances had the names of their destinations painted on the side at this time.

16. *who has the right . . . has suffered*: The reference is to Christ's defence of the woman taken in adultery, whom he saved from a public stoning by asking if there was anyone present among her accusers so totally guiltless that he could act with god-like impunity (John 8). Jack's assumption is a brilliantly funny subversion of the trope of the woman with a past that Wilde had been interrogating since *Lady Windermere's Fan*.

17. *On the contrary . . . Being Earnest*: Wilde ends with the play's title in the traditional Victorian manner. Alexander's blocking of the concluding tableau with the couples grouped symmetrically around the stalwart figure of Lady

Bracknell emphasized this firm sense of closure. The title, however, also calls to mind Wilde's motto for the play: much of the comedy has sprung from people behaving with such obsessive earnestness of purpose that they have lost all sense of proportion. This is Lady Bracknell's besetting sin and by insisting that she is a pinnacle of convention, good form and normality and that others must in consequence behave according to her dictate, she instils that absurdity in others. If the play has reached its sure haven of happiness, it is only after pursuing that conclusion through extremes of artifice. The characters' determination to achieve the promise of matrimony at whatever cost has constantly reduced them to the level of ridicule; and Alexander's blocking of his production in ways that were almost choreographic (making the actors seem at times like dancing automata) clearly emphasized this.

Appendix: The excised scene, involving Gribsby, from The Importance of Being Earnest

Wilde originally designed *The Importance of Being Earnest* as a four-act play, but later with George Alexander condensed the action. One particular theme was pared away almost completely, concerning Algernon's attempts to avoid giving his accumulating debts any serious attention, and the major cut was an episode from Act II: see pp. 359–63. It is taken from what is believed to be Wilde's final draft of the four-act version, called 'Lady Lancing', which his American agent, Elisabeth Marbury, submitted to Charles Frohman in November 1894 with a view to his mounting a production in New York. (When Frohman's production opened finally in April 1895, it was of the three-act version.) His copy of the four-act script was eventually acquired by the New York Public Library in 1953; it was discovered by Ruth Berggren and published by the Vanguard Press in 1987. Two other editions of the four-act version have been published: one, edited by Sarah Augusta Dickson in 1956, is transcribed from early manuscript drafts that had independently come into the possession of the New York Public Library; the other, published in 1957, is a reconstruction by Vyvyan Holland, Wilde's son, based on a German translation printed in Leipzig in 1903. The notes below record significant differences between the early draft edited by Dickson and the Frohman text, which is printed here from Berggren's edition. The text has been standardized to conform with the editorial principles and layout of the rest of the volume.

It would seem appropriate to include this scene, since it was one that Wilde fought over with Alexander. Alexander wished to eliminate it on the grounds that it was superfluous to the main action, even though Wilde himself thought it one of the funniest scenes. It is to be noted, however, that overall Alexander's redactions of the text substantially reduced the role of Algernon in ways which ensured that Jack Worthing (Alexander's own role) was clearly to be seen as the leading part; since the Gribsby episode has Algernon decidedly as its central focus, with Jack being very much the supporting player for a time, it is hardly surprising that Alexander decided to cut it.

1. *Enter MERRIMAN*: Jack, Algernon, Miss Prism, Cecily and Canon Chasuble are already on stage.

2. *I wonder*: In Dickson's transcript the following dialogue reads:

JACK: Parker and Gribsby: I wonder who they can be? I expect Ernest they have come about some business for your friend Bunbury. Perhaps Bunbury wants to make his will, and wishes you to be executor. [*To* MERRIMAN] Show Messrs Parker and Gribsby in at once.

MERRIMAN: There is only one gentleman in the hall, sir.

JACK: Show either Mr Parker or Mr Gribsby in.

MERRIMAN: Yes, sir. [*Exit*]

JACK: I hope Ernest, that I may rely on the statement you made to me last week when I finally settled all your bills for you. I hope you have no outstanding accounts of any kind.

ALGY: I haven't any debts at all, dear Jack. Thanks to your generosity, I don't owe a penny, except for a few neckties I believe.

JACK: I am sincerely glad to hear it.

Presumably the material about paying debts was excised as overly anticipating the content of the ensuing scene with Gribsby and so robbing it of surprise. The material about Bunbury was then redeployed after Merriman's exit to cover the time he might be supposed to take in bringing Gribsby into the garden.

3. *E.4.*: This address was changed to B.4 when it was pointed out that there was a set of occupied rooms with this number.

4. *committal of your person*: In Dickson's transcript this speech is extended: 'But, no doubt, Mr Worthing, you will be able to settle the account, without any further unpleasantness. Seven and six should be added to the bill of costs for the expense of the cab which was hired for your convenience in case of any necessity of removal, but that I am sure is a contingency that is not likely to occur.' Algy's next speech began with an indignant repetition of 'Removal!'; and his speech was interrupted after mention of his brother with a polite 'Pleased to meet you, sir' addressed from Gribsby to Jack.

5. *in these matters*: Again, in Dickson's transcript this speech is extended: 'In the point of fact he has arrested in the course of his duties nearly all the

younger sons of the aristocracy, as well as several eldest sons, besides of course a good many members of the House of Lords. His style and manner are considered extremely good. Indeed, he looks more like a betting man than a court-official. That is why we always employ him.'

6. *Wordsworth's . . . and high thinking*: This sentence was preceded in Dickson's transcript by an observation about how Algy's debts are 'a painful proof of the disgraceful luxury of the age'. The Wordsworth reference is to the sonnet 'O Friend! I know not which way I must look' (1802).

7. *this bill for me*: In Dickson's edition this speech continues: 'What is the use of having a brother, if he doesn't pay one's bills for one?' In consequence, Jack's speech then began: 'Personally, if you ask me, I don't see *any* use in having a brother.'

8. *hours of the day*: Dickson's edition concludes this speech: 'In the case of a medical certificate, which is always easy to obtain, the hours can be extended.'

9. *He is just what I expected*: When the play was condensed into three acts, Cecily's remark was moved to immediately after Algy's first entrance in this act so that it deflates him completely.

10. *Thank you*: Dickson's edition continues, before Gribsby's departure:

JACK: You are Gribsby, aren't you? What is Parker like?

GRIBSBY: I am both, sir. Gribsby when I am on unpleasant business, Parker on occasions of a less severe kind.

JACK: The next time I see you I hope you will be Parker.

GRIBSBY: I hope so, sir.

THE STORY OF PENGUIN CLASSICS

Before 1946 ...'Classics' are mainly the domain of academics and students, without readable editions for everyone else. This all changes when a little-known classicist, E. V. Rieu, presents Penguin founder Allen Lane with the translation of Homer's *Odyssey* that he has been working on and reading to his wife Nelly in his spare time.

1946 *The Odyssey* becomes the first Penguin Classic published, and promptly sells three million copies. Suddenly, classic books are no longer for the privileged few.

1950s Rieu, now series editor, turns to professional writers for the best modern, readable translations, including Dorothy L. Sayers's *Inferno* and Robert Graves's *The Twelve Caesars*, which revives the salacious original.

1960s The Classics are given the distinctive black jackets that have remained a constant throughout the series's various looks. Rieu retires in 1964, hailing the Penguin Classics list as 'the greatest educative force of the 20th century'.

1970s A new generation of translators arrives to swell the Penguin Classics ranks, and the list grows to encompass more philosophy, religion, science, history and politics.

1980s The Penguin American Library joins the Classics stable, with titles such as *The Last of the Mohicans* safeguarded. Penguin Classics now offers the most comprehensive library of world literature available.

1990s The launch of Penguin Audiobooks brings the classics to a listening audience for the first time, and in 1999 the launch of the Penguin Classics website takes them online to a larger global readership than ever before.

The 21st Century Penguin Classics are rejacketed for the first time in nearly twenty years. This world famous series now consists of more than 1300 titles, making the widest range of the best books ever written available to millions – and constantly redefining the meaning of what makes a 'classic'.

The Odyssey continues ...

The best books ever written

PENGUIN 🐧 CLASSICS

SINCE 1946